Turbulence Before Takeoff

The Life & Times of Aviation Pioneer
Marlon DeWitt Green

Best Wishes!

Flint Whitlock

Flint Whitlock has written the deeply moving personal story of Marlon D. Green and his struggle to become an airline pilot. To read Turbulence Before Takeoff *is to revisit the difficult and sometimes dangerous times of the Civil Rights Movement, when Martin Luther King, Jr. inspired a generation of young African Americans, including Marlon, to achieve their dreams.*

— John Seigenthaler, Special Assistant to Attorney General
Robert F. Kennedy, 1961-62

———•—•—

In Turbulence Before Takeoff, *Flint Whitlock offers an insightful biography of Marlon Green, a compelling figure in modern aviation history, and the on-going saga of civil rights in the American experience. Whitlock reconstructs in this highly readable biography the gripping and prolonged struggle of Green to overcome the obstacle of racial exclusion, a quest that ultimately took him to the U.S. Supreme Court. Marlon Green's case became a milestone event in aviation history.*

— Von Hardesty, Curator,
Smithsonian National Air and Space Museum

———•—•—

Turbulence Before Takeoff *offers great insight into what one man—and his family—endured when all he wanted to do was "his life's work" as an airline pilot. It also recounts the tensions permeating through the 1950s and '60s in the fight for civil rights. The story is tremendous, provocative, and well written and is a testament to courage, perseverance, and faith.*

— Xavier Samuels, Southwest Regional Vice President
Organization of Black Airline Pilots

Turbulence Before Takeoff is the brilliantly written story of Marlon Green, a man who dared to dream of a better life for himself and his family, and his struggle to make his dream of flying as a commercial airline pilot come true. The civil rights news items winding through the story brought me back to those troubling times in our history and greatly added to the emotional tone of the story. This is a must-read for everyone interested in aviation, civil rights, or fascinating biographies of historical pioneers.

— Di Freeze
Author of *Icons of Aviation*

—··◆··—

This latest contribution to the broad panoply of aviation history literature is a peculiarly American story. Although challenged by the lightning rod of race issues of his youth, and the turbulent changes that the nation experienced during the decades of the 1940s through the 1960s, the central figure in this poignant story could easily be substituted for any number of young Americans during the same period. Nearly every aspiring aviator can identify with some element of this story. The author has done an outstanding presentation of in-depth research that artfully merges the tenor of the times, the intimate details of youthful optimism, and the realities of career growth in aviation – while at the same time recording a social revolution. This book should be read and made a part of the library of every aviation enthusiast.

— Dan Hagedorn
Senior Curator at The Museum of Flight, Seattle

The importance of Marlon Green's pioneering efforts cannot be overestimated. The challenges he faced alone were unimaginable. The fact that he was successful requires us to respect and cherish the opportunities we enjoy. His legacy lives on in the diverse workforce that makes up our aviation industry today. Our challenge is to never forget his sacrifices and continue to provide opportunities for future generations.

— Calvin Allen, Captain, Delta Airlines
Organization of Black Airline Pilots

Turbulence Before Takeoff

The Life & Times of Aviation Pioneer
Marlon DeWitt Green

by Flint Whitlock

CABLE PUBLISHING

Brule, Wisconsin

TURBULENCE BEFORE TAKEOFF:
The Life & Times of Aviation Pioneer Marlon Dewitt Green

First Edition

Published by:
Cable Publishing
14090 E. Keinenen Rd
Brule, WI 54820

Website: cablepublishing.com
E-mail: nan@cablepublishing.com

Hardcover: ISBN 13: 978-1-934980-66-8
             ISBN 10: 1-934980-66-8

Soft cover: ISBN 13: 978-1-934980-67-5
             ISBN 10: 1-934980-67-6

Library of Congress Control Number: 2008938036

Printed in the United States of America

Dedicated to the memory of
Peter Vincent Green, Ph.D.
Artist, Writer, Musician, Scientist
1955 - 2003

CONTENTS

TRIBUTE

AS WE TURN THE PAGE in our nation's history, having elected our first African American President, it is important that we acknowledge the tremendous possibilities that were solidified by Marlon D. Green's place in American history.

The adversities he faced, and conquered, during the late 1950s and early 1960s to gain employment as an airline pilot should always be a beacon of hope for those choosing the field of commercial aviation. His determination to be treated equally to "just get a job" provided commercial airlines a platform to seek out qualified minority candidates and gain valuable talent from many others with comparable talent.

This tribute is written with a profound humility for our African American history and the many he- (she-) roes who have directly and indirectly paved the way, knowing that Captain Green is among them. His selfless contribution was and is the encouragement often overlooked as we seek to assure young people that they can be and will be the thread that runs through our quilted history, never to be forgotten.

— Cheryl Chew, Executive Director
The Organization of Black Airline Pilots

PROLOGUE

HIS EYES EXPERTLY scanned the complex array of familiar dials, gauges, and switches before him. Off to his right, muffled by his headset, the grumbling roar of the two four-blade turboprop engines on the starboard wing was a comforting sound, the slight vibration he felt rumbling through the cockpit a reassuring reminder that this was what he had just spent the last nine years of his life fighting for.

As he finished the pre-flight checklist with the captain in the left seat, thirty-six-year-old Marlon DeWitt Green felt the growing tingle of excitement that this moment was about to bring. It had been so long in coming, so wrenching an experience, and so expensive, that he could hardly believe it was here.

After the aircraft received clearance by the tower to taxi to the end of runway, First Officer Green looked ahead out of the cockpit windshield and saw a long, smooth strip of concrete in front of him, the bright blue Colorado sky and the warming ball of the sun high above.

The captain released the brakes of the Vickers Viscount 800 that was straining to move, and the sixty-five-seat passenger plane crawled forward, slowly at first, then with a quickening pace, until take-off speed was reached and the 60,000-pound aluminum bird lifted off the runway.

As Marlon continued to scan the gauges and listen for any abnormal sound coming from the engines, he heard the landing gear retract into their wells below the wings and felt his heart soaring into the sky. The exhilaration of flight he had first experienced as an Air Force enlisted man in Hawaii back in 1947, eighteen years earlier, came rushing back to him, a familiar yet ever-new sensation.

He had done it. Despite all the obstacles, road blocks, and dead ends thrown in his path, he had actually done it. As his strong brown hands encircled the steering yoke he reflected on his struggle—his and Eleanor's, and the kids', too—to become a pilot for a regularly scheduled U.S. airline. There was a swirl of emotions coursing through him at this moment, emotions that needed to be held in check if he were to perform his job to his and Continental Airlines' expectations. If, perhaps, a tear formed in the corners of his eyes, his sunglasses would prevent the captain from seeing them.

And, as he always did when taking off, he said his short, silent prayer to St. Thérèse of Lisieux, France, the patron saint of aviators: "St. Thérèse of the child Jesus, protect us on our flight."

As the Viscount gained altitude and all the gauges registered normal readings, it is possible that Marlon allowed the memory of how it all began to intrude into his thoughts.

———·•·—

CHRISTMAS, 1935. FRANKLIN Delano Roosevelt is in the third year of his first term as president of the United States. The Great Depression is in the fifth year of its dismal reign.

It is a time difficult for nearly everyone, but most especially for those who cling precariously to the bottom rung of the economic ladder—the African-Americans or, as they were called until the late 1960s, the Negroes.

Persons of color have never had an easy time in America. A caste system as pernicious and institutionalized as that in India or South Africa takes hold, and a set of pro-white, anti-Negro rules, known as "Jim Crow"* laws, proliferates throughout the South.

Whites and Negroes are kept separated—in public bathrooms, swimming pools, phone booths, on trains, buses, schools, sports teams, at drinking fountains, lunch counters, in restaurants, theaters, hotels, and hospitals. Negro doctors do not care for white patients, nor can the blood of black donors be injected into the veins of white people needing a transfusion. Negro preachers do not preach to white congregations. Negro teachers do not instruct white pupils. Negro lawyers do not represent white clients, nor do Negro judges and jurors decide the fate of white defendants. Negro football and baseball players do not play on white teams. Negro pilots do not fly white passengers.

---

* The origin of the term "Jim Crow" is shrouded in the dim past but, according to one source, it originated with Thomas Dartmouth "Daddy" Rice, a struggling white actor who, in 1828, performed in blackface as an exaggerated, highly stereotyped Negro character he called "Jim Crow." Within a decade the term "Jim Crow" was being used as a racial slur—not as offensive as "nigger," but on a par with "coon" or "darkie." The popularity of minstrel shows aided the spread of Jim Crow as a demeaning racial slur. By the end of the nineteenth century, however, the meaning shifted and the phrase "Jim Crow" was used to describe laws and customs that oppressed Negroes. (www.jimcrowhistory.org)

Negro actors and actresses in films are consigned to minor roles, usually as servants and slaves or as parodies of their own race. With few exceptions, Negro soldiers cannot serve in combat units. Those Negroes who work in offices are employed, more likely than not, to sweep the floors and take out the trash. And just the mere act of a Negro male glancing too long at a white woman in some towns of the South is enough to get him tortured and lynched.

It is a life of general discrimination, segregation, demeaning jobs, low pay, and anti-miscegenation laws that are designed to keep Negroes "in their place," i.e., at the bottom of the heap. Even in communities where Negroes are in the majority, they are, for the most part, powerless. As a result, Negroes, whether in the North or South, quickly learn where their "place" is, and rarely attempt to cross the line or challenge The System.

In front of their small home in El Dorado (pronounced do-RAY-do), Arkansas, six-year-old Marlon DeWitt Green* and his older brother Rudolph know almost nothing of this larger world. They have no concept of race or color, no idea that they are regarded as "inferior" or "second class" by many whites simply because of the pigmentation of their skin, or because their ancestors were from Africa instead of from Europe. Marlon and Rudolph haven't yet grasped the idea that they reside in the black section of El Dorado, or even that there are two sections in El Dorado—one black, one white—separate and unequal. But they will soon learn.

In the fading twilight of the soft, southern Christmas evening, they dart about the front yard of the modest home on South Smith Avenue, both with large, tin replicas of the Pan American "China Clipper" amphibious airliner in their small hands, gifts given to them by their hard-working parents, McKinley ("Daddy Kinney") and Lucy ("Mama Lucy"). They swoop and spin across the patchy lawn, around and around the bare-branched catalpa tree, swinging their arms to and fro to mimic the movements of real aircraft (even flying upside-down and backwards), making roaring noises as if to simulate the sound of four mighty, piston-driven engines, although neither has ever ridden in a real plane or seen one up close.

---

* Marlon's father picked the name "Marlon" for its resemblance to "Mahlon" of the Protestant Bible, and "DeWitt" from DeWitt Clinton, the New York governor (1817-1823) who was the driving force behind the building of the Erie Canal.

Mama Lucy calls the boys to dinner, and the two dash for the front porch, each trying to out-race the other, each urging his toy airplane to carry him faster—Marlon knows a spanking awaits him if he is late. As they reach the porch, Marlon takes one last glance up into the sky—a sky full of color—and can only see pink clouds and an unlimited future.

He and his tin plane zoom up the wooden stairs and into the house where his parents, Rudolph, and younger sister Jean are sitting down to dinner. He is right on schedule.

INTRODUCTION

IT IS SATURDAY, March 20, 2004, and I am waiting for Marlon Green.

I am sitting in the cavernous lobby of the Mandarin Oriental Hotel on an island in Miami's Biscayne Bay. The huge, modern lobby is sparsely, yet tastefully, furnished in retro *Jetsons*-style furniture. An odd combination to be sure.

I look at my watch. I'm early, but then I'm always early when meeting someone for the first time. The night before, Marlon had described himself to me, so I scan each visitor to the lobby, hoping I can pick him out.

I'm a little nervous because, for one thing, I am meeting an historical figure, someone who was a pioneer in his profession, someone who is mentioned in the Smithsonian book and exhibit, *Black Wings: African-American Pioneer Aviators*, was once a tough answer on *Jeopardy*, and whose name also appears in an edition of the board game, *Trivial Pursuit*. I'm also nervous because, secondly, although I have interviewed scores of military veterans for my previous books, I have never, ever, except for one time in Vietnam, had an extended, in-depth, race-centered conversation with an African-American.

I grew up in Calumet City, at that time an all-white southern suburb of Chicago, hugging the Illinois-Indiana state line. I was an only child in a family of Democrats, but my father had been from central Illinois, not exactly a bastion of liberal mind-set. My father, who in all other respects, was a nice guy, seemed to harbor, as did most of the other white adults I knew at that time, an unstated uneasiness around blacks. He was never overt about it, but there was a certain desire for avoidance that I, a sensitive young person, detected.

Then there was the summer in the early fifties that I spent at my aunt's and uncle's house in Mount Vernon, Illinois. One hot and muggy day, I requested that I be allowed to go swimming at the municipal pool. I clearly remember my aunt stating that the pool was not open. When I inquired as to the reason (I assumed there must have been some problem with the plumbing, or perhaps polio, which was known to haunt public swimming pools at that time), I was informed, with regret, that some of the local "coloreds" had tried to use the pool for which their tax dollars had paid and that the city fathers, realizing that they could no longer restrict who could and couldn't use the pool, decided to close it to everyone. I did not then know the meaning of the word "draconian," but it seemed to me a pretty harsh thing to do. Plus it seemed terribly unfair—not only to me but also to the "coloreds"* who just wanted a relief from the sticky, sweltering central Illinois summer.

Many of us Northerners, too, were getting our first hint that life for Negroes was beginning to change, for, like an early spring crocus, the emergence of racial equality began nudging its way upward into white America's consciousness in the mid-1950s. A series of events at that time—some good, some terrible—emblazoned themselves into our psyches in quick order.

The first major civil-rights event of which we were aware, in our own teen-aged oblivion, was the May 17, 1954, unanimous decision of the Supreme Court, under Chief Justice Earl Warren, in the *Brown v. the Topeka Board of Education* case.**

This was swiftly followed in the summer of 1955 by an incident so horrific that it shocks the world to this day and focused a hard, pitiless spotlight on the South. That August, fourteen-year-old Emmett Till from Chicago was visiting relatives in Money, Mississippi, for a few weeks. Apparently no one had instructed the brash teenager as to how Negroes were "supposed" to behave in the South. One day, young Till made the fatal mistake of wolf-whistling at the attractive wife of a white store-keeper. Enraged by the youngster's innocent impertinence, husband/

---

* The *Columbia Guide to Standard American English* (2003) points out the changing nature of what to call Americans of African heritage. Until the 1960s, the terms "Negro" and "Colored" were the most commonly used both within and outside the African-American community. With the advent of the "Black Power" movement (and the popularity of such empowering slogans as "Black is Beautiful") in the 1960s, the previously pejorative term "black" became acceptable. In recent years the terms "Afro-American," "African-American," and "people of color" have come to the fore. As the editors of the *Columbia Guide* caution, "As long as racial matters continue to be sensitive, terminology may suddenly change as events give sanction or take it away."

** On May 17, 1954, the United States Supreme Court, under Chief Justice Earl Warren, in the *Brown v. the Topeka Board of Education* case, ruled unanimously to strike down the widespread practice of school segregation. This provoked outrage in southern states and smugness in the North. Protests were organized against the ruling, the Ku Klux Klan stepped up its campaigns of intimidation, and segregationists dug in their heels, determined not to allow the "Yankee" Supreme Court to upset the status quo and tell them with whom their children must go to school.

storekeeper Roy Bryant and a few friends set out to teach him a lesson. Snatched from his bed at his great-uncle's shack in the middle of the night, Emmett Till was taken away, tortured, shot, and horribly abused. His body was then weighted down and thrown into the Tallahatchie River. Dredged up a few days later, Emmett's mangled and decomposing corpse was shipped back to his mother in Chicago who, remarkably, insisted upon an open-casket funeral as a way of shocking the world. Ten thousand people turned out to view Emmett's body—if one can even call it that. Gruesome photos of the boy's mangled, unrecognizable face were splashed throughout Negro newspapers and magazines; it is a wonder that the incident did not spark a nationwide race riot, an insurrection, a revolution.

A few months later, on December 1, 1955, a seamstress from Montgomery, Alabama, named Rosa Parks was arrested for violating a municipal ordinance that required Negro passengers on city buses to sit in the back and leave the front seats for white folks. Still fuming over the Emmett Till murder, and fed up with Jim Crow laws that denied them equal opportunity and basic human dignity, the Negro community of Montgomery rose up in Mrs. Parks' defense. A young (twenty-four-year-old), local pastor by the name of Dr. Martin Luther King, Jr., organized the Montgomery Improvement Association and called for all of the city's Negroes to boycott the bus system. It was a roaring success. The boycott went on for 382 days and gained worldwide attention. The Warren Court, as the United States Supreme Court under Chief Justice Earl Warren came to be known, ruled in June 1956 that the racial segregation of public transportation facilities was illegal. The nationwide campaign for civil rights had won its second battle.

The third event that broke through America's carapace of self-deception about racial matters was the case of Autherine Lucy. She was a grade-school teacher from Alabama who had graduated from the all-Negro Miles College in Fairfield, Alabama, and decided to study for her master's degree at the all-white University of Alabama. The university refused to admit her, but a court order forced the school to relent. On the third day of classes, in September 1956, the campus was swarming with mobs out to do her harm. She was pelted with eggs, epithets, and death threats on her way to class, even though accompanied by a police escort. The school then suspended her, saying that it was for her own safety. But the National Association for the Advancement of Colored

People (NAACP) lawyers, who had done much to get her into the school to begin with, filed a contempt of court lawsuit against the university. Discouraged by her experience and fearful for her safety, she gave up, moved to Texas, and got married.

Freshest in my and my classmates' consciousness at the time was the potential civil war brewing in Little Rock, Arkansas. There, the first big test of the 1954 *Brown v. Board of Education* decision was about to face the fire. In September 1957, nine Negro students were admitted, by court order, to Little Rock's previously segregated Central High School. Again, death threats, racial epithets, and an escort by American soldiers became a regular part of the curriculum for the Negro students just trying to get an education. Since the students were our contemporaries, I believe we—*some* of us, at least—had more than a modicum of empathy for them.

In September of my sophomore year, 1957, a new student suddenly appeared in my high school. His name was Ray Stuckey, and he was very quiet—probably nervous about being the only Negro student in our all-white high school in our all-white community.

White kids in the late 1950s were, like kids everywhere and in every generation, absorbed in their own world. We danced to Elvis at our school sock hops. We took our girlfriends to see the movie *Gigi*, or went with our buddies to see the World War II epic, *The Bridge on the River Kwai*. Now that the U.S. had launched *Explorer I*, our own answer to Russia's *Sputnik*, we were feeling better about ourselves and the Eisenhower administration in the global scheme of things. We were also proud that the world's first nuclear-powered submarine, the U.S.S. *Nautilus*, was also American, and had successfully traveled to the North Pole under the ice.

Anyway, with my desire to be fair to all persons, no matter their color, as a sophomore in 1957 I approached Ray Stuckey in the school library where he was sitting at a table by himself (I don't think the other students were necessarily discriminatory—although I could be wrong on that point—but no one to my knowledge had as yet welcomed him). I introduced myself, shook his hand, and in perhaps what would be viewed nowadays as being overly friendly and paternalistic, like an obsequious church deacon pouncing on a new parishioner, welcomed him grandly to our school. He was very quiet, maybe trying to figure out what this overly friendly white boy wanted. We chatted briefly; I found out he played basketball, and so invited him to go talk with Coach Jepsen and try out for the team, even though I, the sports editor of the school newspaper, had no clout or connection with either Coach Jepsen or the team.

As far as I can recall, that was the first and last time Ray Stuckey and I ever had a conversation, although we would nod to each other in recognition in the hallways between classes. Ray Stuckey was with us for less than a year, and then he disappeared, to where I have no idea. With the singular exception of his photo as a member of the 1957-1958 Spanish Club, the class photos in the four yearbooks that chronicled my high-school career were a blizzard of white faces.

And now, as I scan the Mandarin Oriental hotel lobby and look for a black man I have never met, and glance down at my long list of questions I want to ask him, I am slightly nervous, for I know we are going to delve into, at least for me, uncharted racial waters. Do I really want to poke around in the dusty attic of the life of Marlon Green? Do I really want to ask probing questions about race with a semi-famous black man? Aren't I out of my element? After all, I am mainly comfortable probing combat veterans about their battlefield experiences; do I have any business plunging into the touchy minefield of race?

About the time the butterflies inside me are at their most active, I see a person matching the description Marlon had given me over the phone the night before: tall, dark, and handsome. He is wearing blue jeans, a blue denim workshirt, and walks with that erect, brisk gait of someone who had once been in the military. He waves at me, smiles, and strides over to where I am sitting. Extending my hand, I say, "Marlon Green, I presume?" He catches the reference—the historic meeting between Stanley and Livingston in deepest Africa—and immediately grins. His hair and beard are salt-and-pepper, and his eyes have a twinkle to them. I like him straight away.

Like many black persons in America, Marlon carries wounds and ravages of racism and discrimination. They are many and they are deep, but they are not visible. The scars are psychological but no less real than if they were the lash marks administered by a slavemaster or a hooded Ku Klux Klan member.

After our preliminary pleasantries are over, I haul out my tape recorder, pop in a blank cassette, and begin asking questions. Marlon is as open and forthcoming as I think he is capable of being, but some blockage exists. It could be due to the fact that I'm a white stranger he doesn't know and doesn't yet quite trust, or it could be the result of his many years of conditioning as a pilot, a profession that does not encourage the free expression of emotion. I have known several pilots in my lifetime and, while all are outwardly genial and good-natured, most have not been given to emotionality—and with good reason. Pilots are supposed to be cool, calm, collected, confident, and in control in the face of a crisis. The airlines would frown on a pilot who came on over the intercom and announced, "This is your captain speaking. We have a serious problem AND WE'RE ALL GONNA DIE!"

I find the story Marlon tells of his life fascinating, complex, maddening, infuriating, inspirational, and deeply saddening—all at the same time. But it is, as I soon discover, only *half* the story.

CHAPTER 1:
SOUTHERN LIVING

THE STORY OF Marlon Green and his quest to fly begins in the central Arkansas city of El Dorado.

It is 1940. Approximately 20,000 people live in El Dorado, with slightly more than half of them white. It is a time of racial segregation across much of America, but particularly in the South.

The town square more resembles a motion-picture studio's back lot than an actual town. Taking up the center of the square is the impressive, multi-columned Union County Courthouse, with its "White Only" and "Colored Only" drinking fountains and restrooms. A sparkling white-marble Confederate monument in front of the courthouse reminds passersby, both white and Negro, on whose side this town and this state fought during the Civil War (AKA, the War Between The States, the War of Secession, the War of States' Rights, or, as some hard-line Southerners are wont to call it, The War of Northern Aggression). An inscription on the monument reads, "Truth crushed to earth shall rise again."

A profusion of locally owned businesses ring the courthouse square—shoe stores, drug stores, clothing stores, jewelry stores, and barbershops (one for white customers, another for colored). A four-story office building, the site of millionaire Dr. J. Shelton Rushing's dental practice, stands at the corner of Main and Washington. Nearby is the Sterling Department Store. Down the street stands an eight-story building, called by locals "the Eight-Story Building," El Dorado's tallest structure and home to the administrative offices of Lion Oil Refinery.[1]

On this square, at 4:30 P.M. on October 9, 1902, a shoot-out took place. A long-simmering feud between the four Parnell brothers (Jim, Tom, Mat, and Walter) and Marshal Guy B. Tucker erupted into gunplay on that autumn day, leaving two of the brothers (Tom and Walter) and Constable Harrison Dearing dead, and three others, including Marshal

Downtown El Dorado, Arkansas
The statue to the Confederacy is visible left of center.
(Author photo 2005)

Tucker, wounded. Although the shoot-out became part of El Dorado lore, it was not the town's only claim to fame.

To understand just how far Marlon D. Green has come, it is necessary to go back to the beginning or, in this case, before the beginning—all the way back to 1803. In that year, one of the great real-estate deals of all time took place. Under the direction of President Thomas Jefferson, the United States government bought 827,987 square miles from Napoleon Bonaparte, the emperor of France, for the then-staggering sum of $15 million. The deal was known as the Louisiana Purchase.

Soon thereafter, white settlers began moving into the area, and it wasn't long before the vast, unspoiled tract of land—stretching from the Gulf of Mexico to Canada and from the Mississippi River to the Rocky Mountains—was divided up into territories. Statehood soon followed for many of the territories: Louisiana became the eighteenth state in 1812, and Arkansas, abutting Louisiana on the north, followed in 1836, becoming the twenty-fifth star in the American flag.

Bordered on the east by the mighty Mississippi, and bisected by the Arkansas River, the rich soil and heavily timbered hills of Arkansas represented a lush and lovely paradise, amenable to most varieties of farming and ranching. In 1851, about 115 miles south of the Arkansas state capital at Little Rock, and a few miles north of the Louisiana border, in Union County, a sleepy little town named El Dorado was incorporated on 160 acres donated by a wealthy merchant named Matthew F. Rainey. The Ouachita River that ran through the county was seen as a flowing highway by farmers wishing to send their crops to market in New Orleans, and soon cotton growers began clearing the land for their plantations.

In the 1800s, cotton was king, and plantations sprouted like the cotton plants themselves. To work the vast fields, Arkansas plantation owners needed large numbers of workers. Most white folks weren't interested in the back-breaking labor performed under a blazing sun, so the plantation owners bought their workers from slave traders who had brought Africans against their will to America. For decades, slavery remained the status quo until 1861 when eleven Southern states, rebelling against the notion that the government in Washington, D.C., could tell them how to run their lives and businesses and economies, seceded from the Union and took up arms to win their independence.

El Dorado managed to avoid most of the ravages of the Civil War and the upheavals that followed; no major battles were fought in Union County.

The war ended badly for the South in 1865. Freed slaves felt the anger of the defeated whites when, during the Reconstruction Period under President Andrew Johnson, many Negroes were placed in positions of authority over their former white masters. Schools and land were also provided to the disadvantaged ex-slaves by the North as a way of helping them become educated and economically able to get on their feet.

But Johnson was not strongly committed to civil rights, and Reconstruction became a disaster for the Negro population for whom it was to have been a boon. Mobs of resentful whites soon tossed the novice Negro politicians out of office, reclaimed land that had been given to ex-slaves as compensation for past injustices, and went on a racial rampage that had not previously been seen.

One of the malefactors of the Negroes was the Ku Klux Klan, a bed-sheet-draped, secret society formed in 1865 in Tennessee.

According to a study by the Southern Poverty Law Center, the Klan's beginnings were prosaic and peaceful—almost comical. Six young former Confederate soldiers in Pulaski, Tennessee, bored with peace, decided to form a secret social club that was more to relieve their small-town *ennui* than as a way to terrorize anyone. Grandiose-sounding titles and elaborately hokey initiation rituals were dreamed up, and the founders searched for an amusing, alliterative name for their club, finally coming up with "Ku Klux Klan" (later abbreviated simply to "KKK"). Dressing up in white sheets with tall pointed hats, the club members spent their evenings galloping through the quiet streets of their town, whooping and hollering like fraternity boys, and generally raising Cain but doing no one any harm.

Soon neighboring communities learned of the existence of this club and additional "chapters" or "klavens" were born. It didn't take long for the members to discover the frightening effect the night rides by hooded figures had on the recently freed Negro population, and some Klan members began using their scary anonymity to intimidate the former slaves. Soon the Klan had transformed itself from a harmless social group to a malevolent society that delighted in terrorizing Southern Negroes and their few white supporters with murder, mayhem, arson, torture, and other acts to "remind" Negroes where their "place" was.[2]

An uneasy *detente*—those "Jim Crow" laws again—came into existence to keep Negroes and whites from intermingling. The situation in El Dorado was probably no better and no worse for Negroes during Reconstruction than any other place in Arkansas, and the two races learned how to co-exist without actually mixing—and without the Negroes challenging the existing social order. Whites ran the city government, the police department, owned most of the businesses, and made most of the money; Negroes did the manual labor, attended inferior schools, earned a pittance, and deferred to the whites. But that was the way of the South, and few had the courage (or suicidal tendency) to challenge the system or upset the status quo.

In 1890, 455 people were living in El Dorado. In the next three decades, the population swelled to 4,000—the result of the area's wealth of timber. The local Chamber of Commerce is fond of billing El Dorado as "Arkansas' Original Boomtown," and with good reason, for it wasn't just timber that caused an inrush of fortune seekers but gushers of "black gold"—oil. Oil had been discovered in Arkansas at least as early as 1887 but, before the advent of the internal combustion engine, it was considered more of an annoyance than a treasured commodity. However, gasoline-powered engines soon came along and changed the face of society, industry, and commerce forever.

El Dorado grew fat and rich on oil, but the slippery substance was a cursed blessing. It was not until June 13, 1920, when a tremendous explosion at a test well in El Dorado killed five people, that the city fathers became convinced that they were, as the town's name suggests, sitting on a gold mine.

On January 10, 1921, a well owned by the Bussey Oil Company blew, spewing the shiny black liquid all over the landscape. Within the span of a month, the population of El Dorado jumped to 20,000 as wildcatters, speculators, and people looking for work moved in. Less than a year later, the wooden obelisks of 460 producing wells sprouted everywhere—parks, backyards, school yards, former cotton plantations—and ten million barrels of oil were quickly sucked out of the smelly, saturated ground. Naturally, with a boom of this magnitude, the local authorities were unable to maintain control and, on New Year's Day, 1922, some drunken revelers began firing pistols in the streets, the bullets plunking off street signs, street lamps, church bells, and people; fourteen persons lay dead by the time the last bullet was fired.

In an age before the Environmental Protection Agency had even been imagined, the unregulated oil fields of El Dorado soon became Arkansas' version of Love Canal.* Oil was everywhere. It seeped through the soil and into the groundwater supply. It killed trees, lawns, vegetables, birds, squirrels, rabbits, deer, dogs, and cats. Its overwhelming stench blotted out the fragrance of flowers. It blackened cars and houses. Housewives could not hang their washing out to dry, or allow their children or pets to play outside. It was not uncommon for citizens to come home from church or work drenched in the black stuff that misted like rain through the air. It was also common for oil to be stored in open ponds, where lightning or a carelessly discarded match would set the oil ponds aflame.

In 1924, Arkansas ranked fourth in the U.S. in terms of oil production but, two years later, output began to fall and the price of the commodity took a nosedive during the Great Depression. The boom had turned to bust. People couldn't move out of El Dorado fast enough, and the town, wearing its black oil shroud, settled into a kind of half-life existence.[3]

---

* A neighborhood of Niagara Falls, New York, which had been used as a toxic-waste dump for decades. In the late 1970s, the extent of the contamination was discovered and the EPA forced most of the entire city to be evacuated.

There were two sections of town—the primarily white northern half, and the predominantly Negro southern half, literally on the other side of the tracks. The Negroes, when they crossed the tracks into the northern part, did so to work for white families and white-owned businesses. In the late 1920s, a young Negro named McKinley Green and his wife Lucy, whom he married on April 10, 1921, in Vicksburg, Mississippi, moved into a small home on South Smith Avenue, a block south of the tracks in a neighborhood known as "Fairview." The house had been built by McKinley's parents at some unknown point in the late 1800s and consisted of a living room, kitchen, bathroom, and one bedroom— probably no more than 500 square feet total. In the back yard were a couple of twenty-five gallon galvanized steel wash tubs and a black, cast-iron pot set on bricks so that a wood fire could be lighted beneath it to heat water for bathing and washing clothes. A clothesline was strung between two trees.

McKinley's mother, Mary Ellen (known simply as "Ellen") later moved next door. Across the street from McKinley and Lucy's house was the New Bethel Missionary Baptist Church from which lustily voiced spirituals and hymns poured every Sunday.

McKinley Green was a proud and hard-working man. Born in 1900 in El Dorado, he had labored in a brickyard, and was skilled at carpentry and masonry (he was forever building additions onto his small home). He and Lucy wanted children, but there were major complications. Lucy had given birth to seven

Marlon's parents, McKinley and Lucy Green, El Dorado, Arkansas (date unknown)
(Courtesy Green family archives)

The heavily remodeled Green family home on South Smith Avenue, El Dorado. The Greens' church, New Bethel Missionary Baptist Church, is in background. (Author photo 2005)

babies, but none had lived more than a year. Then, in 1928, Rudolph Valentino Green was born and survived. And then, as if to make up for all the infant deaths, there came a profusion of babies: Marlon (June 6, 1929); Jean Evelyn (1933); James Zell (1936); and Allen David (1941)—all born in the bedroom of the Smith Avenue house.

Both parents were better-than-average cooks; McKinley enjoyed canning pears, and Lucy was known for her meatloaf but, for some unknown reason, she was unable to get biscuits to rise. When he got a little older, son James recalled that "the kitchen was pretty much Lucy's domain. If 'Daddy Kinney' ever questioned 'Mama Lucy's' cooking ('Don't you think the flame's a little high on that burner?'), she would turn on him and he would take his iced tea and retreat. 'C'mon kids—let's leave your mama alone and go sit on the porch,' he'd say. He spent a lot of time on the porch."

Just as the kitchen at home was Lucy's lair, corporal punishment was also her prerogative, and she was not shy about administering discipline with a switch, hairbrush, or bare hand.

Marlon recalled that, if his father didn't approve of something, he would never spank the children but rather respond with a quiet, "You ain't gonna be a fool all your life, are you?"[4]

"Daddy was a very encouraging person," reported James Green. "He didn't believe in corporal punishment. Mama made up for whatever he didn't dispense in that category. Mother was a strict disciplinarian."[5]

During the Depression, life in El Dorado was difficult for the Green family, as well as for most of the other Negro families in the neighborhood. In 1936 or 1937, McKinley made the hard decision to seek work up north, and set off for Lansing, Michigan, where he found a job at the Drop Forge Company. For seven months, he sent as much of his meager paycheck home as he could, and then returned. Job opportunties hadn't improved much in his absence, so he went to work for a wealthy white dentist in town, Dr. J. Shelton Rushing. It was a position McKinley kept for the next forty years. He worked long hours—from seven a.m. to seven p.m.—and, because he had no car, walked from South Smith Avenue to Dr. Rushing's fancier home at 2224 North Madison, over a mile to the north.

Marlon recalled that his father was "in charge of Dr. Rushing's household staff that included a handyman around the property; one

The home of Dr. J. Shelton Rushing at 2224 North Madison, El Dorado, where McKinley Green was employed (Author photo 2005)

McKinley Green in the kitchen of the Rushing home (Courtesy Green family archives)

woman who would be classified as a maid and when they had parties, they'd hire help as necessary."

Dr. Rushing also owned vacation properties in Hollywood, Florida; Mason, Texas; Aspen, Colorado; and a houseboat on the Arkansas River. McKinley Green supervised the help in all the houses.

Marlon said, "My dad was in charge of the cooking at Dr. Rushing's home. There were times when he didn't do all the cooking himself, but he was in charge of the people who did. He was the *major domo*—I like that word. He had many skills. He was pretty outstanding as a cook, and he could tell you the name of almost every flower or plant that grew in southern Arkansas. There was one time when he won a prize for crocheting or knitting at the county fair."[6]

Brother James recalled that Dr. Rushing was one of the wealthiest men in El Dorado. "Dr. Rushing was a dentist, but he rarely practiced because he was too busy managing his millions of dollars in oil investments; he had several other dentists who worked for him."

James Green also remembered being very unhappy every November because his father would go down to Texas with the doctor's entourage—

a trip that always seemed to fall on his birthday. "I was the only one in the family whose birthday would take place when Daddy wasn't there," he said. "They'd come back with all the venison from the deer hunt. We got fed up with venison—so Daddy would give it to other people in the community. He was a very generous man."

———•-•••••———

L IFE FOR THE Green kids in El Dorado was slow-paced, langorous, *Southern*. During summers that seemed weighted with heat and humidity, when they could scrounge up enough coins, Marlon and his siblings would go to one of the movie theaters in town that would admit "colored" patrons (although they were required to sit in segregated areas, usually the balcony).

James Green recalled that the price of admission was twelve cents. "We'd get to see a double feature, a cartoon, a newsreel, and a serial all for twelve cents. The theaters were segregated; at the Ritz, we were up in the balcony, what we called the 'Buzzard's Roost.'"[7]

"El Dorado had four movie houses," Marlon remembered. "The Ritz, the Star, the Rialto, and the Majestic.* The Majestic was 'white only.' I often fantasized that someday I would buy them and admit all equally. In those days, however, I had no plan to acquire the loot that this fantasy would require."

In 1939, after being mesmerized by Clark Gable's performance in *Gone With The Wind*, Marlon began to dream that he would become the first black movie superstar. He even had picked out a screen name for himself: Dark Fable.[8]

So caught up with Hollywood was Marlon that one day, after viewing a Western, he came home, grabbed his BB gun, and decided to reenact a scene for his younger brother, James, who recalled, "I think Marlon O.D.'d on the movie. He came back and said, very dramatically, 'You're playing a crucial role; stand there.' Then he proceeded to shoot me in the butt with the BB gun! I told him it hurt, but he said we had to keep the scene going. I must have been about six or seven at that time and Marlon was probably thirteen or fourteen. But I had such

---

* Except for the Rialto, which has been restored to its 1930s glory, the other theaters are long gone.

admiration for my older brother—he had such an outstanding mind that anything he wanted me to do was all right with me."

James Green also recalled that the boys liked to play and joke around with each other but that Marlon was the most intellectually gifted. "He was well-read as a young man. He used to quote Socrates and all the Greek philosophers. In talking with some of his classmates, I learned that Marlon was the one the teachers always admired because of his depth of knowledge, his intelligence. Our parents really stressed with us the value of education."

This was evidently true, for Rudolph, James, Allen, and their sister Jean went on to earn bachelor's degrees; Rudolph earned his doctorate. All four brothers also served in the Air Force.[9]

———

To OTHERWISE AMUSE himself, Marlon basically did what every other normal American kid of any color growing up in the thirties did: He played sand-lot baseball and football with the neighborhood boys; rolled old automobile tires down the street; became an expert marksman with a slingshot; played marbles; went fishing; and climbed trees.

Sometimes, on halcyon summer days, when the humidity hung heavily in the air and the cicadas thrummed their mating calls from the trees, Marlon would take off with his friends and siblings to attend the games of the local, all-white minor-league baseball team, the El Dorado Oilers, against clubs from Greenville and Jackson, Mississippi, and Memphis, Tennessee. Naturally, the seating arrangements at the ball park were segregated. To save the money their parents had given them for admission to the ball park, the boys—the "knot-hole gang," as they called themselves—would station themselves in the branches of a large tree just beyond the center-field fence.[10]

Although Rudolph, Marlon, James, and Allen Green were keenly interested in sports and desired to play on organized teams, their father would not permit it. "We dearly wanted to," said James, "but he would not let us play sports in high school because the black high school we attended did not have an insurance program. They had insurance in the local white schools but not in the black schools. So if you got hurt playing for dear old Booker T. Washington High, the parents would have to pay the doctor and hospital bills. Daddy was so very practical; he knew he couldn't afford it if we got hurt. So we played baseball in the fields and we attended sporting events—he encouraged that."[11]

———·•·———

IN DECEMBER 1941, when Marlon was twelve, the United States was suddenly thrust into World War II. Recruiting stations were overwhelmed with young men wanting to get into the war and fight against the dastardly Nazis and Japanese, who both considered themselves racially superior to most other cultures.

Ironically, such was the tenor of the times that many American whites, even in the midst of a war that had as one of its goals the overthrow of a regime that espoused injustice, inequality, and racial

> **NEWS ITEM:**
> (Washington, D.C., June 25, 1941) President Franklin D. Roosevelt today signed into law Executive Order 8802, which ends racial discrimination in American defense industries.
>
> The momentum for the ground-breaking order was provided by labor organizer A. Philip Randolph, founder of the Brotherhood of Sleeping Car Porters, a union of railroad employees. After successfully negotiating a contract between the union and the Pullman Company in 1937, Randolph applied continuous pressure on President Roosevelt to bring about an end to discrimination in the employment of Negroes in the federal government. He was planning to organize a massive protest march on Washington in 1941 when Roosevelt signed the order. [12]

hatred, continued to spew their own home-grown prejudice onto the oppressed American Negro population.

In September 1942, for example, after *LIFE* magazine ran a photo-illustrated article about Paul Robeson starring in Shakespeare's *Othello* at the Cambridge Summer Stock Theater, the publication received a small avalanche of letters complaining about the mixing of the races as depicted in the article. W. Ira Lane, of Houston, Texas, wrote to say, "The article...where the Negro and whites act in the same play, is more than I can stomach. What in the hell is the country coming to?"

Another upset reader, R. J. Divine of Covington, Kentucky, aimed his criticism squarely at *LIFE's* editors: "I was not interested in the merits of this production but in the horrible, indelible, undeniable and terrifying fact that there are white men with so little respect for themselves that they would cause to be printed the picture of a Negro man with his arm around a white woman in a love scene."

A third letter writer made a feeble attempt at fairness. "There is a large group of people in this country, including myself," wrote B.D. Tomlinson of Georgetown, South Carolina, "who believe that a better deal is due the Negro, but we also believe that the time is not ripe, if ever, for the actual social mingling of the two races. Such pictures, in my humble opinion, have a tendency to create in some Negroes a longing for something that cannot be theirs and can only lead to a feeling of frustration."[13]

These were sentiments that would not have seemed out of place in the magazines and newspapers of Hitler's Third Reich.

—·•·—

THE EL DORADO Police Department, like most police departments across the South at that time, was viewed by members of the local Negro community as a malevolent, rather than a protective, force. One policeman for whom Marlon Green has few fond memories was an officer named Barney Southall, a cop not known for his sensitive dealings with minorities.

"He was a police officer who had a disposition, an M.O., of being brutal and intimidating to blacks," Marlon noted. "I don't know if this extended to other races. I personally never had any confrontations with him, but I had acquaintances who had been his victims. He became known as 'Southall the Brutal,' or something like that. This characteristic became attached to his name and his service on the police force. 'Racial intimidation' is how I would put it."[14]

Officer Southall was still on patrol when James Green became a teenager, and the younger Green noticed the policeman had not mellowed in the intervening years. "He was like the local Gestapo," James said. "He was a menace to the black community. He used to come into the black community and would indiscriminately choose someone to insult. However much he insulted you, you were not to react. A lot of people sometimes lost their composure—some of the people were inebriated—and he would take advantage of that situation. If you said something back to him, he'd say, 'You don't talk to me like that, boy,' and then he'd get out his nightstick and beat you over the head with it. Our parents were quick to warn us about exhibiting certain behaviors that might not necessarily be in our best interests if Southall was around."[15]

Southall had a partner who was almost as intimidating, a cop named Ambrose. "He seemed to be almost a cartoon character," Marlon recalled, "trying to fit in with his tough boss as his sidekick. On his own shift he imitated some of the characteristics he picked up from Southall."

A block south of the Green home was a rough street called, curiously, "E and B Street." Marlon shudders when he thinks of the neighborhood. "In the section of my town on Saturday night, on E and B Street, there were shootings, knifings, cutting with broken bottles—not every Saturday night, but much too frequently for my liking. Barney Southall had a field day on Saturday nights. And then, across town, in the other black section of El Dorado, there was Liberty Street, in what was called the 'St. Louis' section of El Dorado. They had similar characteristics. These were not expressions of my life. Liberty Street and E and B Street in Fairview just didn't appeal to me as places where I wanted to be."[16]

Life for the Negro residents of El Dorado in the 1940s involved a series of small, daily humiliations. Even mundane activities that whites take for granted, such as visiting a doctor, often resulted in Negroes being placed in demeaning circumstances. In El Dorado at the time, there was only one Negro physcian. White doctors would see Negro patients, but the laws and customs dictated that the two races be separated even in the waiting room. James Green recalled, "Some of the doctors didn't have waiting rooms, so they would convert a closet where they kept the mops and brooms into a partial waiting room for black patients. And we had to wait there until all the white patients were seen before the doctor would see us. It was terrible the way we were treated back in those days."

Despite the injustices that Negroes were forced to endure at the hands of their fellow white citizens, James Green still has some fond memories of growing up black in El Dorado. "Our teachers were very skilled and dedicated. They were part of the community and were concerned about us beyond just the dissemination of education. They were interested in us as total persons. They were friends of our parents. You would see them at church, in the markets, and in the community. More than anything, our teachers exerted influence on us because we had so much respect for them. It was a continuation of the education process, even outside the classroom. Our teachers were role models for us, and those of us who made something of our lives later on owe a great deal to those teachers. I worry that, in the black community today, we're de-emphasizing the value of education."[17]

Although the Negro schools in El Dorado and throughout the South suffered from inadequate funding, they made up for it in many cases with their cadre of outstanding, influential teachers. Marlon remembers with special fondness his fifth-grade teacher, Edith Dunning, who lived across the street from the school with her husband, the only Negro physician in town: "Mrs. Dunning was probably in her early forties, about five feet six inches tall, and a little on the heavy side."

He most remembers her for teaching him something he has never forgotten: "Mrs. Dunning said if you want to learn to speak English, listen to [actors] Claudette Colbert and Ronald Colman—people who speak the English language in a style you might want to emulate.

"Now I have to digress here to clarify that there was a time in my life, and it's still operable, that I wanted to be 'an American.' At the time this formulation first came to me—it didn't originate with me, it isn't new—there was a standard of speech for the English language that was not characteristic of 'Steppin Fetchit' or 'Amos and Andy.'* They weren't, to me, representative of a black man, an Afro-American, a Negro—whatever racial appellation went along with it. Black or white, you should speak 'American English.' I'm trying to synthesize this idea of wanting to be 'standard' or 'average'—not for personal goals, necessarily. This becomes apropos to a lot of personal expressions about race later on, with the groups in the sixties and seventies. There are some expressions of black power or racial identity that I don't want to adopt.

---

* Stepin Fetchit, whose real name was Lincoln Perry, was the first African-American movie "superstar." He made millions during the 1920s and 1930s while playing to the worst stereotypes whites had of blacks—lazy, dim-witted, inarticulate, and subservient. In reality, Lincoln Perry was an immensely talented, literate, and intelligent man who once wrote for the black newspaper, *The Chicago Defender*. (www.imbd.com)

"Amos and Andy" was a popular syndicated radio program of the 1920s and 1930s in which two white actors (Freeman Gosden and Charles Correll) exaggerated Negro dialects and pretended to be southern black farm hands who moved from Georgia to Chicago and tried to adjust to urban life. Although the shows were well-written and had both fans and detractors, and did not necessarily depict Negroes in a demeaning light, they nevertheless remain controversial to this day. (www.midcoast.com)

"My father was the one who had made it concrete to me first, but Mrs. Dunning made it appealing, this aspiration to avoid regionality of speech: 'Don't speak with a Southern dialect; don't speak with a Northern dialect.' Somebody said there is a segment of speech called 'The Ohio Standard.' People in Ohio seem to be the least regionally identifiable. This is part of my upbringing: to try to speak 'standard' English.

"I must also say this—I don't have a hatred of Africa, but I want to pursue the idea of me as one who is obviously related to the continent of Africa but one who is not culturally related to it.* Those were aspirations and items of confusion about identity that were part of my upbringing. Michael Jackson is not the answer—you don't get whiter. I never contemplated any change from my chocolate-brown complexion. I wanted to be educated and identified with the culture of the United States. But there was a time—Frank Sinatra had a song during the Second World War, 'The House I Live In'—that expressed this idea of equality for all of us. There were some other performers and some other songs that had the same idea, that we are 'a brotherhood of man,' as the expression of that idea. Mrs. Dunning got me on the footing that I felt comfortable with for pursuing the patterns of speech—not ostentatiously or falsely. I can't remember ever consciously trying to diverge from that. Whatever the difference is, it did occur. There are so many expressions of choice regarding cultural habits."

Marlon became the valedictorian of his class at Fairview Elementary and even sixty years later remembered the valedictory address he gave at graduation in 1943: "We who stand tonight at the meeting between a happy past and an unknown future have reached, not the end, but the commencement of our lives. And what those lives are to be depends in great measure upon the foundations we have been building for them during these past eight years at Fairview Elementary School."[18]

—•·•—

IN 1943, WHILE Marlon was standing between his happy past and unknown future, rioters, fueled by racial animosities, were tearing Detroit apart. With the Motor City a haven for persons of all colors

---

* In 2004 Marlon used DNA testing to trace his ancestry back to the Mbenzele people of Cameroon and the Tuareg people of Niger.

seeking high-paying jobs in the automobile factories that were now churning out trucks, tanks, jeeps, aircraft, and other tools of war, some 50,000 Negroes had streamed into the city. Overcrowding and competition for jobs and promotions, along with unusually hot weather for June, had set tempers boiling. What began as a minor fist fight between a few whites and Negroes on the bridge leading to the amusement park on Belle Isle in the Detroit River escalated quickly into a full-scale riot. Soon hundreds of youths were battling each other with fists, clubs, bats, knives and guns. The civil war went into its second, then third, then fourth day, and President Roosevelt called out 6,000 troops to quell the unrest.

When it was finally over, twenty-five Negroes and nine whites were dead, and at least 700 persons were injured. Property damage was in the hundreds of thousands of dollars. It was another victory for intolerance, and Nazi Propaganda Minister Josef Goebbels probably had a field day exploiting America's societal divisions.[19]

—·—·—●—·—·—

THERE WERE NO major disturbances in placid El Dorado in 1943, racial or otherwise. About the most raucous thing that was heard on South Smith Avenue was the sound of the Greens' spinet piano. James recalled that their father never took a piano lesson in his life. "I'll never understand how he learned the keys and chords and all that," said James, "but he did." McKinley could play by ear (mostly hymns) and Marlon's brother Rudolph soon picked it up, prefering boogie-woogie to hymns. Sister Jean also took lessons for a while, but Marlon did not. He did possess an especially fine tenor-baritone singing voice, however, and sang spirituals and hymns while Daddy Kinney accompanied him on the piano.[20]

—·—·—●—·—·—

BECAUSE THE GREENS' financial situation did not allow them the luxury of buying a car, about 1944 or 1945 Dr. Rushing gave McKinley one of his old Ford sedans; the family now had its own mode of transport. The car also enabled the family to take modest summer vacations to visit relatives in Vicksburg, where Mama Lucy was born. "What

Martha's Vineyard is to Northerners, Vicksburg was to the Greens of El Dorado," observed Marlon. "One of my fondest childhood memories is petting a colt in the backyard of a relative's home there."[21]

The car was also a source of frustration to the Green kids. "We were never allowed to drive the family car," recalled James. "Daddy couldn't afford the insurance to cover us kids."

Marlon's awareness that his family was somehow different from the whites of El Dorado came at an early age. To earn a bit of money, Marlon's younger brother James began shining shoes at Dixie Barber Shop on El Dorado's main square. One day, while applying polish and rag to a man's shoes, James was aware that the man's five- or six-year-old son was watching his every move. He then turned to his father, pointed at James, and asked, "Daddy, is that a nigger?"

James recalled, "It was very insulting and it was rather tense there in the barber shop for a moment, because it came during a time in the South that you had no recourse to an insult directed at you."[22]

Still later, in a prudent act of self-preservation, older brother Rudolph left town after it became common knowledge that he was dating, or was at least "friendly" with, a white girl. At the time, Rudolph was working as a "utility man" at Morris & Company, a women's apparel store on the north side of the town square; when Rudolph departed, Marlon was hired to take his brother's place.

One day, while he was folding boxes in the back room, Robert Rochmill, the store manager, approached Marlon with a new task: "A dog has 'cut loose' on the sidewalk out front; I want you to clean it up."

It was then that Marlon realized that if he didn't leave El Dorado and find a way to better himself, it was the type of work Marlon could look forward to for the rest of his life.

From 1943 to 1946, Marlon attended El Dorado's all-Negro Booker T. Washington High School, where he was an excellent student and participated in a variety of activities, including the glee club, choral group, debating team, and theater. As of yet, however, he had no idea what he wanted to do with his life beyond high school. What he *did* know was that the opportunities for a young Negro male were extremely limited in El Dorado.

He had just finished his junior year of high school when an unexpected opportunity suddenly dropped out of the sky. It was his ticket to the future.[23]

CHAPTER 2:
MARCHING TOWARD EQUALITY

IN 1944, AT the age of fifteen, Marlon committed a very unusual act for a black person who had grown up in the Southern Baptist faith: He converted to Roman Catholicism.

Eventually, all the Green siblings, with the exception of James, converted. A new priest, Father Raymond Marmon, had come to town and began proselytizing in El Dorado's Negro neighborhoods, subsequently winning a number of converts for his church, the Holy Martyrs of Uganda Roman Catholic Church.

James Green recalled that the priest was a young, progressive, charismatic fellow. "At the church's annual summer carnival," James explained, "the priest would walk around in his vestments, chatting with folks, and carrying a *beer*! That was something that would *not* have been allowed in the Baptist church! The Catholics said, 'Everything is acceptable in moderation,' and it made a powerful and positive impression on the young people of El Dorado. As a consequence, a lot of black people crossed over and joined the Catholic church."[1]

Marlon noted that his conversion had "upset the social equilibrium of my Baptist family. My good father objected to this wild radicalism because of prejudices and ignorance on this subject which have since been corrected."[2]

But Daddy Kinney finally accepted his son's choice. "If you're going to be a Catholic," he told Marlon, "be a good one."[3]

The conversion to Catholicism was one of the most influential events in Marlon's life. Just prior to beginning his senior year of high school, he received a scholarship to the all-Catholic, all-Negro Xavier Preparatory High School, which was affiliated with Xavier University in New Orleans. He jumped at the chance.[4]

XAVIER PREP SCHOOL stood on Magazine Street at what was formerly the site of the original Southern University, the first publicly funded
college for Negro students. Xavier was the only all-Negro Catholic university in the country, with an emphasis on pharmacy and social work.[5]

The university was founded in 1915 by Mother M. Katharine Drexel
of the Sisters of the Blessed Sacrament for the purpose of educating
blacks and Native Americans. A wealthy heiress before becoming a
nun, she used her $20 million fortune (her father was a business part-
ner of J.P. Morgan; the family firm eventually became the Wall Street
brokerage of Drexel Burnham Lambert) to establish the Order of the
Sisters of the Blessed Sacrament and then build schools for "Indians
and Colored People." She also founded the first mission school for
Indians, in Santa Fe, New Mexico.* Scores more around the country
soon followed.[6]

As at Washington High, Marlon continued to demonstrate his
scholastic prowess and looked forward to graduating from Xavier Prep
at or near the top of his class and going on to the seminary. He had
already selected the one he wanted to attend: Epiphany Apostolic
College in Newburgh-on-the-Hudson, New York, operated by the
Josephite Order, which was dedicated to serving Negro communities.

On Saturdays at Xavier Prep, Marlon made a little extra money by
cleaning the cafeteria for Sister Ancilla, the nun who ran it. He noted,
"Sister Ancilla hired me, yes; at a living wage, no."

While doing his cafeteria chores one Saturday, Marlon was introduced to one of the physical education instructors at the university—a
petite young woman known as Miss Gallagher—Eleanor Gallagher—
from Boston. At the time, Eleanor and another instructor, Emma Joan
(pronounced Jo-Anne) Stanley, were roommates in a residence attached
to the cafeteria building. Marlon recalled, "Eleanor was teaching physical education and biology or anatomy—some subject related to physical education. She also taught dance classes. Joan was a biology
teacher. Anyway, Sister Ancilla introduced me to Eleanor—Miss
Gallagher."

---

* At the time of the nun's death in 1955, there were more than 500 sisters of the Order
teaching in sixty-three schools throughout the country. Mother Drexel was canonized
by Pope John Paul II on October 1, 2003. (Cohen, 58)

A few weeks later, with the Senior Prom fast approaching, Marlon was in something of a panic; he had a date for the prom with a lovely Negress named Lois Deslonde but didn't know how to dance. "I was in the gym at the university," he said, "putting up crepe-paper streamers in preparation for the dance, and I asked Miss Gallagher, whom I knew from this previous introduction by Sister Ancilla, if she would teach me how to dance. I think she had a dance group out on the gym floor at the time, so she said she would show me the two-step. It was fundamental and would get me through the evening without breaking anybody's toes or stepping on their dresses."

The brief dance lesson was apparently successful, for Marlon and Lois continued to see each other and, after his graduation, continued to write to one another. Marlon was beginning to think that they might have a future together until it struck him that Catholic priests were prohibited from marrying.[7]

NEWS ITEM:

(Monroe, Ga., July 25, 1946) Four Negroes were ambushed and killed today along a road in this rural area. Police found the four persons, Roger and Dorothy Malcom and George and Mae Murray Dorsey, tied up and shot scores of times by rifles, pistols, shotguns, and a machine gun.

The gruesome slaying seems connected to a dispute between twenty-four-year-old black sharecropper Roger Malcom, a World War II veteran, and Barnette Hester, the white farmer for whom he worked. Malcom was convinced Hester was having an affair with his pregnant wife, confronted Hester, and injured him with a knife. He was jailed for his assault.

A group of Hester's friends wanted retribution for the stabbing and arranged for a white farmer, Loy Harrison, to bail Malcom out of jail so they could kill him.

As the car carrying the Malcoms and the Murray Dorseys was traveling to Harrison's farm on the pretext of working his land, the mob ambushed the car at the Moore's Ford Bridge over the Appalachee River, dragged the two Negro couples from the vehicle, bound them with rope, and murdered them.

The FBI is investigating.[8]

MARLON GREEN GRADUATED as co-valedictorian from Xavier Prep in May 1947. That summer he returned to El Dorado, hung out with his friends, tried to stay out of officer Barney Southall's way, and then, as September rolled around, packed a couple of suitcases with his belongings and headed off to New York to begin his new life at Epiphany Apostolic College on the Hudson River.

His first few weeks and months at the seminary were enjoyable. The cool tinges of autumn painted the foliage on campus in a fiery palette, and he enjoyed Epiphany's intellectually and spiritually stimulating atmosphere. The hours devoted to prayer and quiet contemplation were deeply comforting, and in the library he was surrounded by a glittering universe of writings by and about some of Catholicism's most influential scholars, theologians, and philosophers—men such as Erasmus; Hugh of St. Victor; St. Francis of Assisi; St. Athanasius; and St. Thomas More. Here he could delve into St. Augustine's *Confessions*; St. Thomas Aquinas and his *Summa Theologica*; the twelfth-century theologian Peter Lombard's *Libri Quatuor Sententiarum*; *Summa Universae Theologiae* by Alexander of Hales; the voluminous epistemological discourses of St. Bonaventure; and so much more that Marlon knew he could not read even half of the books in a lifetime.

Here, too, he was first introduced to the writings of Thomas Merton, an American Trappist monk whose essays, books, and faith-inspired poetry were just beginning to influence a whole generation of Christians and Buddhists. Eighteen-year-old seminarian Marlon Green, seeing that everyone at the school, both black and white, was treated equally, was at peace with his decision to become a priest.

But he soon became aware that there was something physically wrong with him. He came down with a mysterious ailment that the school's clinic misdiagnosed as gonorrhea. Thinking Marlon had been sexually active despite his protests to the contrary, the administrators expelled him from the school.

"I knew I hadn't been guilty of any sexual activity with any other person, so I was very much hurt by their decision to interpret whatever this infection was as gonorrhea and remove me from the seminary. We appealed through the pastor of my church, Father Marmon. He said he wished they would reconsider, but they didn't. Being in the seminary and becoming a priest was my hope at that time, but my hope was dashed."

Crushed, he returned home to El Dorado in December 1947 to ponder his future. For a month, he tried to determine another course for his life. Perhaps he could go on to a secular college; his grades were certainly good enough. Although his family had little money to spend on a college education, he was sure he could earn a scholarship.

Then the idea of joining the military struck him. Although the armed forces were segregated, Marlon thought there might be some opportunities in uniform.* In the military he could learn a trade and earn more than the menial jobs in El Dorado paid Negro youngsters. He talked with an armed forces recruiter and began exploring his options.[9]

Marlon noted, "This interest centered around the chance of spending three years in the as-yet undesegregated Air Force, during which I hoped to learn something—possibly aircraft mechanics—which would be of value in earning a livelihood in civilian life. There was also a desire to gain some knowledge of the world by travel at government expense." Yes, the military began to look like a good choice.[10]

——————

THROUGHOUT THE NATION'S history—and even before the United States became an independent nation—black Americans have served with honor in the armed forces. Their service, however, was not always honored, nor free from the same injustices and prejudices Negroes received from the general civilian populace.

In pre-Revolutionary Colonial America, the various militias called upon every man, whether white or black, free or slave, to assist in maintaining the peace against marauding Indians. However, the slave revolts of the 1660s soon caused many colonial leaders, especially in the South, to think twice about the wisdom of arming the slaves. As a result, Negroes were excluded from service in the ad hoc regiments; their only place in the ranks of colonial militias was as drummers, fifers, and laborers. However, in some communities, when the number of whites available for military duty was insufficient, Negroes were reluctantly recruited to bear arms, and some slaves were even promised freedom if they performed well in battle.

---

* Through a presidential order, President Harry S. Truman desegregated the military on July 26, 1948.

To avoid the draft, colonials were allowed to find substitutes for themselves. As a result, a number of northern whites who had been drafted paid Negroes to take their places in the ranks or aboard naval vessels.

In the Revolutionary War battles of Lexington, Concord, Ticonderoga, and Breed's (Bunker) Hill, musket-carrying Negroes fought side-by-side with their white counterparts and made significant contributions to the ultimate American victory. But anti-Negro elements continued to worry about an insurrection of slaves and freedmen and, in 1775, persuaded General George Washington to issue an order that prohibited any new recruitment of Negroes. However, while facing manpower shortages, and learning that a number of Negroes in the South had joined British forces to fight against the white colonists in hopes of winning their emancipation, the Continental Congress reversed the order. More Negroes were actively recruited, and Rhode Island even formed an all-Negro battalion.

It is estimated that approximately 5,000 Negroes served in military units during the Revolutionary War. Their honorable service and the promises of the white governors, however, did not translate into new respect or benefits for Negroes as a group, and they were quickly returned to their subservient status when the war ended.

Barely had the new nation won its independence when another conflict with Great Britain broke out. Although some Negroes did serve in the War of 1812, they were officially excluded from military service during this conflict.

The situation changed dramatically during the Civil War (1861-1865). Fearing that the border states would side with the Confederacy if the North employed Negro soldiers, President Abraham Lincoln barred enlistment to Negroes. As early as 1862, however, with Union casualties rising and recruiters having difficulty meeting their quotas, some generals went against the official policy and actively recruited Negroes. Once Lincoln issued his Emancipation Proclamation on January 1, 1863, the recruiting of Negroes by the North was stepped up. The 54th Regiment of Massachusetts, made famous to modern audiences by the 1989 movie *Glory*, is perhaps the best-known of the 166 all-black regiments.[11]

The New York Draft Riot in July 1863 was one of a number of violent disturbances that broke out in northern cities in reaction to a federal conscription order. A mob of working-class Irish in New York City were angered by the Conscription Act that exempted persons from being drafted into the military if they paid a fee of $300. To show their displeasure toward the Act, as well as their anger toward Negroes for whose benefit they felt the war was being waged, the mob for three days swept through the streets, attacked police, burned buildings (including the Colored Children's Asylum), beat and shot Negroes, and lynched them from lamp posts. By the time order was restored, 1,200 people, most of them Negro, had died.[12]

The authors of *Blacks and the Military* noted, "Yet it was the participation of Negroes in the Civil War, according to President Lincoln, that ensured a Northern victory and the preservation of the Union." During the conflict, the Bureau of Colored Troops recruited and organized nearly 180,000 Negro soldiers into regiments and battalions; another 111,000 Negroes volunteered for duty in state and independent units. Battle deaths among Negro soldiers were extrememly heavy: over 38,000 were killed during the four years of the conflict.

After the war, most Negro regiments were disbanded, but two infantry and two cavalry regiments—which received the nickname "Buffalo Soldiers" because their "nappy" hair reminded the Native Americans of buffalo fur—were retained for duty on the far western frontier to protect white settlements from Indian raiding parties. Here the Negro soldiers, many of whom were former slaves, performed with exemplary courage. During the Spanish-American War of 1898, and again in General John J. Pershing's 1916 Punitive Expedition against Pancho Villa along the U.S.-Mexico border, Negro units conducted operations with professionalism.

Upon America's entry into World War I in 1917, thousands of Negroes were drafted into the armed services. Most were assigned to menial, non-combat jobs, primarily as laborers in the Services of Supply (later the Army's Quartermaster branch). Of the 200,000 Negro American soldiers sent to France, only a small fraction saw combat, and some of those who did were judged by white officers to be less than effective. Other Negro units, such as the 369th Regiment, which served under French command, won praise from their superiors for their aggressive fighting spirit on the battlefield.

Life in the U.S. Navy was no pleasure cruise for Negroes, either. Most of those who joined were assigned to work as stewards, mess boys, and coalmen in the engine rooms. The Marines accepted no Negroes, nor did the fledgling Air Corps. As the authors of *Blacks and the Military* state, "The Army remained segregated, and it adopted a policy of black quotas that would keep the number of blacks in the Army roughly proportionate to the number of blacks in the national population. The number in the Army never even approached the quota during this period—on the eve of World War II, the Army's own mobilization plan allowed for only about six percent of blacks in the total enlisted force.... And the Army's continuing commitment to a white officer corps was evidenced by the fact that there were only five black regular Army officers on duty, three of whom were chaplains."

Shortly before World War II, pressure by Negro leaders, Negro-run newspapers and organizations, as well as liberal politicians, prompted the Roosevelt administration to relax or abolish the strict racial barriers and establish greater opportunities for Negroes wishing to enlist. The War Department was reluctant to accede to these desires, for it feared that integration would be detrimental to unit morale and cohesion. While more Negroes were permitted to join the military, and all-colored units were formed, the War Department's policy of racially separated units was strictly enforced. After all, segregation was the accepted practice in civilian life and the military saw no need to go against the status quo. At Army posts across the country, separate facilities were constructed and maintained for both whites and Negroes; there were white barracks and Negro barracks, white service clubs and Negro service clubs, white snack bars and Negro snack bars, white drinking fountains and Negro drinking fountains, etc.[13]

———•••◆•••———

ON DECEMBER 7, 1941, one of the first American heroes of what would become World War II was a Negro sailor on board the U.S.S. *West Virginia*, anchored at Pearl Harbor. Unable to reach his battle station in the anti-aircraft battery ammunition magazine during the Japanese assault, Ship's Cook Third Class Doris "Dorie" Miller, the ship's heavyweight boxing champion, distinguished himself by carrying injured sailors to safety. An officer then ordered him to the bridge to assist the ship's commanding officer, who lay mortally wounded. With hundreds of enemy planes attacking the Pacific Fleet, Miller rushed to a .50-caliber anti-aircraft machine gun and blazed away until ordered to abandon the sinking ship. For his courage, he received the Navy Cross, the Navy's highest award.*

Once America was in the war and began to suffer heavy battle casualties, the rules regarding minority recruitment were slightly relaxed. In 1942, the Navy and Marines began to accept Negro enlistees, but their combat contributions were limited; virtually all were assigned to non-combat units to perform menial chores, such as stevedore duty—the loading and unloading of ships.[14]

General Dwight D. Eisenhower, the Supreme Allied Commander in Europe, wrote frankly about the difficulty of race relations within his own army: "Prior to my arrival in England censorship had been established by American headquarters on stories involving minor difficulties between Negro troops and other soldiers, or civilians. These incidents frequently involved social contacts between our Negro soldiers and British girls. The British population, except in large cities and among wealthy classes, lacks the racial consciousness which is so strong in the United States. The small-town British girl would go to a movie or dance with a Negro quite as readily as she would with anyone else, a practice that our white soldiers could not understand. Brawls often resulted and our white soldiers were further bewildered when they found that the British press took a firm stand on the side of the Negro."[15]

After American forces landed in Normandy in June 1944 and began their long march across France toward the heart of Germany, the Allied supply lines became badly extended. A plan to provide a constant stream of supply trucks from the ports to the front lines was instituted. This remarkable supply chain was called "The Red Ball Express," and the vast majority of drivers were Negroes. Without this unbroken, rolling chain of food, ammunition, and other vital supplies, the American combat units would have been unable to maintain the pressure on the Nazi foe, and the whole offensive would have ground to a halt. In the heavy fighting around Aachen and the Hürtgen Forest in the

---

* On November 24, 1943, while serving aboard the escort carrier U.S.S. *Liscome Bay* during the battles for Makin and Tarawa Atolls in the Gilbert Islands, Miller was among 646 sailors who lost their lives when their ship was torpedoed and sunk by a Japanese submarine. In 1973, the U.S.S. *Miller*, a *Knox*-class frigate, was commissioned and named in his honor. (www.history.navy.mil/faqs/faq57-4)

fall of 1944, several all-Negro platoons were assigned as replacements for the hard-hit, formerly all-white 1st and 104th Infantry Divisions. Reports indicate that the Negro troops performed with distinction.

Although several all-Negro divisions had been formed, all but one of them were broken up and their members reassigned to non-combat units. The sole exception was the 92nd ("Buffalo") Infantry Division, which was engaged in heavy fighting against Germans entrenched in the "Gothic Line" defenses of the northern Italy's Apennine Mountains in the fall of 1944. Led by all-white officers, the 92nd sometimes performed less than satisfactorily. Studies showed that white officers regarded being assigned to a Negro division as a professional slap in the face, for there was evidence that the Army "dumped" inferior and incompetent officers into black divisions because they were not "good enough" to lead white troops. It is quite possible, therefore, that the 92nd's sometimes sub-standard performances had as much to do with sub-standard leadership as it did with sub-standard followership.[16]

In 1945, the Army's chief historian, Walter L. Wright, Jr., observed:

> American Negro troops are, as you know, ill-educated on the average and often illiterate; they lack self-respect, self-confidence, and initiative; they tend to be very conscious of their low standing in the eyes of the white population and consequently feel very little motivation for aggressive fighting.
>
> In fact, their survival as individuals and as a people has often depended on their ability to subdue completely even the appearance of aggressiveness. After all, when a man knows that the color of his skin will automatically disqualify him for reaping the fruits of attainment, it is no wonder that he sees little point in trying very hard to excel.... We cannot expect to make first-class soldiers out of second- or third- or fourth-class citizens. The man who is lowest down in civilian life is practically certain to be lowest down as a soldier. Accordingly, we must expect depressed minorities to perform much less effectively than the average of other groups in the population.[17]

This broad generalization, of course, excludes the many Negro soldiers who *were* aggressive, who *did* take the initiative, and who *did* fight bravely, even at the cost of their own lives. And, of course, it completely ignores the sterling record of one of the most remarkable groups of African-American warriors: the all-Negro 332nd Fighter Group, famously known as the "Tuskegee Airmen."

———•–•◆•••—

CHARLES ALFRED "CHIEF" Anderson, born in Bridgeport, Pennsylvania, in 1907, became one of the most important persons in the history of black aviation. Anderson had fallen in love with flying as a youngster and, at twenty, tried to sign up for flying lessons, but no flight school would take a Negro student. Undiscouraged, he sought out individual pilots willing to give him private lessons. In August 1929 he soloed and received his license.

Shortly thereafter, Anderson made the acquaintance of Ernst Bühl, a German Air Force pilot in World War I, who had come to America and operated an airport near Philadelphia. Seeing Anderson's prowess in the cockpit, Bühl gave him further instructions and helped him earn his Commercial and Air Transport pilot license in 1932—the first Negro to receive such a license.

In 1933 and 1934, to promote the idea of flight to the Negro population, Anderson made several long-distance flights around the country and, with Dr. Albert Forsythe (a Negro physician from Atlantic City, New Jersey, whom he had taught to fly), made a transcontinental flight in 1934. The two also set many other firsts, such as piloting the first plane to land on the island of Nassau, Bahamas, and the first Negro pilots to make an international flight (Atlantic City, New Jersey, to Montreal, Canada).

In 1939, the federal government began setting up flying schools at colleges around the country in the event that the United States might be drawn into the growing world conflict. Thousands of young men flocked to the program. However, as none of these flight schools was established at a Negro college, a student at Howard University in Washington, D.C., sued the government. As a result, a flight-training program was set up at Howard and at Tuskegee Institute, a Negro college in Tuskegee, Alabama.

That same year, Charles "Chief" Anderson organized Howard's civilian pilot training program and then, in 1940, was given the opportunity to train civilian pilots at Tuskegee Institute.

In April 1941, Eleanor Roosevelt, the wife of the president, visited Tuskegee. Impressed with the array of planes lining nearby Moton Field, she asked Anderson if Negroes were really capable of flying such machines. He answered in the affirmative and invited Mrs. Roosevelt to go for a ride with him in a Piper Cub. Horrified, the Secret Service agents tried to talk her out of it, but to no avail. When the Secret Service called the president in a panic to inform him of her impending venture, he simply shrugged and replied, "If she wants to do it, there's nothing we can do to stop her."

The ride went off without a hitch and, shortly after Mrs. Roosevelt's return to Washington, D.C., the decision was made to form the first Negro Air Corps at Tuskegee in September 1941. The Army Air Corps also established technical training for Negroes at Chanute Field, in central Illinois.[18]

Eleanor Roosevelt, wife of the president, takes a ride with Charles "Chief" Anderson at Tuskegee, April 1941. (Courtesy Smithsonian National Air & Space Museum)

Captain Benjamin O. Davis, a 1936 graduate of the U.S. Military Academy at West Point, New York, and the first Negro Army Air Corps officer to solo, was one of the original thirteen cadets in the Tuskegee program and earned his pilot's wings in March 1942. Davis would soon command the 99th Pursuit Squadron, the first all-black combat aviation unit.

On March 7, 1942, the first graduating class of Tuskegee Airmen, as the pilots of the 99th would be known, began their career as one of the most storied units in U.S. military history. The 99th was deployed to North Africa in April 1943, where its P-40 "Warhawk" aircraft supported the Allies in the Mediterranean Theater of Operations. The squadron compiled an outstanding record in just four months, and Davis was promoted to colonel and assigned to the all-black 332nd Fighter Group, flying P-47 "Thunderbolts" and, later, P-51 "Mustangs" in escort of American bombers hitting Nazi targets from Italy to Berlin. Under the 332nd's umbrella were the 99th, 100th, 301st, and 302nd Fighter Squadrons.

Benjamin O. Davis, shown as a colonel during World War II while in command of the 332nd Fighter Group (Courtesy Smithsonian National Air & Space Museum, Ref. No. 86-12761)

The group took part in the invasions of Sicily and Italy, and the 332nd flew 15,533 sorties and shot down 111 enemy aircraft, including three of the super-fast German ME-262 jet fighters. The 332nd also accounted for destroying 150 German aircraft on the ground, 950 rail-cars, trucks, and other motor vehicles, and one German Navy destroyer.[19]

Members of the group earned 150 Distinguished Flying Crosses along with 744 Air Medals, fourteen Bronze Stars, and eight Purple Hearts. Sixty-six Tuskegee Airmen lost their lives during the war, and another thirty-two were downed and taken prisoner.[20]

It was the Tuskegee Airmen, with pilots such as Davis and Daniel "Chappie" James, who proved to the world that black warriors could be just as good—if not better—as any white fighters, including those of Hitler's "Master Race." And, while it is impossible to say that the Tuskegee Airmen were directly responsible for desegregating America's armed forces, their magnificent contributions to the war effort certainly aided the cause of integration.

However, few incidents of racial discrimination within the armed forces were more outrageous than the one heaped upon the 477th Bomber Group, designated to be an all-Negro outfit flying B-25 medium bombers. Activated on January 15, 1944, at Selfridge Army Air Field, forty miles from Detroit, the 477th was made up of a number of Tuskegee Airmen who had completed their combat tours in the Mediterranean, as well as newly recruited flight and ground crews. With its Tuskegee heritage, the 477th had the makings of greatness and no doubt would have given a good account of itself against the enemy.

Unfortunately, the 477th was under the thumb of two bigoted white officers, Colonel Robert E. Selway, Jr., its commanding officer, and General Frank O'Driscoll Hunter, a Georgian and commander of the U.S. First Air Force, under which the 477th was subordinate.

General Hunter spoke bluntly to the group:

The War Department is not ready to recognize blacks on the level of social equal to white men. This is not the time for blacks to fight for equal rights or personal advantages. They should prove themselves in combat first. There will be no race problem here, for I will not tolerate any mixing of the races. Anyone who protests will be classed as an agitator, sought out, and dealt with accordingly. This is my base and, as long as I am in command, there will be no social mixing of the white and colored officers. The single Officers Club on base will be used solely by white officers. You colored officers will have to wait until an Officers Club is built for your use. Are there any questions? If there are, I will deal with them personally.[21]

For his part, Colonel Selway incurred the wrath of the Negro officers and enlisted men of the 477th by placing in positions of authority only white officers, and by personally snubbing and refusing to socialize with Negro officers. Despite the fact that many of the Negro officers had more combat flying time than the whites assigned to the unit, Selway made sure that only whites commanded the Group's four squadrons.

Trouble was brewing. There was a rumor that Negro agitators in Detroit were going to cause trouble on behalf of the 477th. On May 5, 1944, without explanation, the 477th was suddenly loaded onto troop trains and taken south to Godman Army Air Field, a tiny base near Fort Knox, Kentucky—a base wholly inadequate for a unit the size of a bomber group. Many of the Negro soldiers felt the move was being done strictly for racial reasons; as far as they were concerned, it was obvious that General Hunter was not interested in preparing the Group for combat and preferred to see it fail and be dissolved. With a chronic shortage of personnel, the 477th was incapable of maintaining its training schedule, and no combat assignment for which the men hungered seemed on the horizon. Morale sank.

The towns near Godman were none too pleased to have several thousand Negroes suddenly descend upon them. White merchants refused to sell goods to the black airmen, white restaurant operators refused to serve them, and white hotel and boarding house operators declined to rent to the wives of the airmen.

Despite the fact that a 1940 Army regulation (AR 210-10) required officers' clubs be open for the use of both Negro and white officers, Selway, operating on orders from Hunter, illegally established two clubs—one for each race. Furthermore, Negroes were barred from the officers' club at Fort Knox. A general wave of hostility and resentment began to rise up.

In April 1945, matters came to a head after the 477th moved again, this time from Godman to the ironically named Freeman Field near Camp Atterbury, Indiana. Freeman Field had two separate officers' clubs—one for whites and one for Negroes. On April 3, 1945, in a concerted effort to test the segregation status quo, a group of sixty Negro officers attempted to enter the whites-only club, but were stopped by the provost marshal and subjected to house arrest.

In addition, having heard about the treatment accorded their fellow officers at Freeman Field, a similar mutiny broke out back at Godman Field. There, a group of over 100 Negro officers (led by the future mayor of Detroit, Second Lieutenant Coleman A. Young) refused to obey the illegal segregated-facilities rules any longer and were themselves arrested to face court-martial. The War Department stepped in and freed all but a small handful of mutineers. The revolt, for the most part, had been successful, but showed what a sorry state existed between races in the Army.[22]

Another mutiny involving Negro troops occurred in 1944, this one following a terrible tragedy.

On the evening of July 17, 1944, at the Naval Magazine facility at Port Chicago, California, northeast of San Francisco, the merchant ship S.S. *Quinalt Victory* was being loaded with 4,600 tons of high explosive and incendiary bombs, depth charges, and ammunition. Another ammunition ship, the *E.A. Bryan*, packed with 5,000 tons of munitions, was moored at the same pier. On the pier's tracks, waiting to be off-loaded, stood sixteen rail cars filled with 429 more tons of high explosives. Loading this dangerous cargo were 320 cargo handlers, crewmen, and sailors—202 of them Negro.

The dangerous work on the piers at Port Chicago and other Navy facilities was done by the men of the Navy's ordnance battalions, which were primarily staffed by Negro enlisted men. Like their white officers, these men had received very little training in cargo handling, let alone working with high explosives.

Shortly after ten P.M., an enormous explosion rocked the port facility as both cargo ships and the freight cars detonated, sending a blazing mushroom cloud thousands of feet into the sky, leveling or damaging virtually every structure at the facility, and causing seismic shockwaves that were felt as far away as Boulder City, Nevada. The blasts also destroyed the nearby town of Port Chicago and caused damage nearly fifty miles away in San Francisco, leaving a crater in the Sacramento River bottom sixty-six feet deep, 300 feet wide, and 700 feet long.

All 320 workers involved in the loading at Port Chicago were killed instantly, and another 390 were injured, many horribly. It was the worst home-front disaster of World War II, and accounted for fifteen percent of all African-American casualties of World War II.

Within a month, repairs at Port Chicago had been made and the facility was back in operation. Many of those who survived the devastating blasts were ordered to return to their jobs loading munitions—an order 258 shaken Negro sailors refused to obey.

Of this number, 208 were locked into a barge, faced summary courts-martial, and were sentenced to bad conduct discharges and the forfeiture of three months' pay for disobeying orders. The remaining fifty were singled out for general courts-martial on a charge of mutiny. The sentences could have been death, but the accused received between eight and fifteen years at hard labor after a trial which a 1994 review said had strong racial overtones. In January 1946, all of the men were given clemency.*[23]

Congress introduced a bill to grant $5,000 to the family of each dead sailor, but Mississippi Democratic representative John Rankin objected to the amount once he discovered that most of the beneficiaries were Negro. Under pressure by Rankin, Congress reduced the amount to $3,000 per family.

(The exact cause of the explosion at the Port Chicago Naval Magazine was never determined, although some sources attribute it to a mistake in the loading of torpedoes and other ordnance into the S.S. *Quinalt Victory*.)[24]

----•--•-•-----

IT TOOK PRESIDENT Harry S. Truman's Executive Order Number 9981, on July 26, 1948, to officially (if not factually) desegregate the military years earlier than most other segments of American society.** Even then, the Army continued to drag its feet; it was only the Air Force and Navy which showed a marked willingness to open their ranks to Negroes.

---

* On December 23, 1999, President Bill Clinton pardoned Freddie Meeks of Los Angeles, one of the few still-living members of the original fifty.

** A. Philip Randolph, the guiding force behind Roosevelt's 1941 order to end discrimination in defense-industry hiring, was also the prime mover behind Truman's directive. (afroamhistory.about.com)

By the late 1940s, then, Negroes began to see the military as a stepping stone to a better education, better pay, and better chances for an improved life, free of many of the racial barriers that had been erected since the 1600s to hold them back.[25]

———·•·↓·••———

MARLON GREEN STUDIED the recruiting literature from the various branches of service to see which might suit him best but was still suspicious of the Navy, given its long history of racial discrimination.

"The Navy at that time had a record of considerable racism and limitations," he said. "Being a ship's cook was almost all you would ever be able to be in the Navy then. The black hero at Pearl Harbor, Dorrie Miller, had been limited so much. I don't know what skills he had, but he was the one black serviceman in the Navy I knew of because of his spectacular commitment at Pearl Harbor. The Army had done some experimenting with separate units, but the Air Force had come along with something more hopeful than what little history I knew of the other two branches. Even though the Air Force was still segregated, it had an appeal to me—in relation to race and to progress—that the other services didn't have."

Marlon visited the local Air Force recruiting office, signed up, and took a physical. A few weeks passed before he was notified that he had been accepted. He entered the Air Force on February 5, 1948, and was ordered to report to Lackland Air Force Base in San Antonio, Texas, for basic training.

"When I was finishing basic training in May 1948," he said, "I had to decide what I wanted as training for my MOS—Military Occupation Specialty. My choice was aviation mechanic. It just so happened that when my class of recruits graduated from basic training, there was no room at Keesler Air Force Base [in Biloxi, Mississippi]—no slot for blacks available for six weeks. The Air Force had to do *something* with me, so on June 5, 1948, they sent me to Wheeler Air Force Base in Hawaii. Wheeler is adjacent to Schofield Barracks and Pearl Harbor. That's where I began my actual duty as an enlisted man in the Air Force."[26]

Marlon didn't realize it, of course, but the transfer to Hawaii was about to change his life forever.

CHAPTER 3:
THE KNACK

ALTHOUGH HAWAII WAS beautiful, Marlon's assignment there was no paradise. "My initial desire to become an aircraft mechanic was stifled by the fact that applications for such training by Negroes were not favorably considered at that time."[1]

Instead, in January 1949, Marlon was assigned to an aviation engineer squadron, consisting of about thirty airmen. He recalled, "We had white commanders—a captain and a lieutenant—who were in charge of our squadron, but all the enlisted personnel, with the exception of the first sergeant, McCaffrey, were black. Our job was to do whatever maintenance was required to keep the air force base in line. 'Digging ditches,' is how I described it."

Besides the exhausting, unfulfilling work, Marlon was also lonely. He had been writing letters to his high-school prom date, Lois Deslonde, but the long-distance relationship didn't seem to be going anywhere.

Shortly after arriving in Hawaii, a Christmas card sent by Eleanor Gallagher, the pretty little gym teacher who had taught him the two-step back at Xavier Prep, caught up to him, and he wrote back. "We liked each other," he said of her. "We corresponded about the things that were happening with us in our lives. Perhaps it was the romantic setting of Hawaii—a twenty-year-old with lots of time on his hands, listening to a lot of recordings, reading a lot of books, full of a lot of imaginings and longings. We were open enough to communicate these feelings to each other so that our liking became more than a liking. There was a distance, physically, and the racial considerations were daunting. But somehow we got interested in each other and communicated a love for each other. It got kind of convoluted—on again, off again."[2] (For her part, Eleanor recalled, "I would say that at that point, it was 'sharing and caring.'")[3]

Marlon Green in Hawaii,
Christmas Day, 1949
(Courtesy Green family archives)

During the day, Marlon had other things on which to concentrate. "The work I and the unit did was menial," he recalled, "but the captain and the lieutenant and the first sergeant weren't the ones who had made the decision to assign me to that unit. They didn't seem involved in any racial animosity that I could detect."

Nevertheless, Marlon hated the hard, demeaning manual labor to which he and the other black enlisted men in his unit were subjected. Manning a broom or shovel was not why he had joined the Air Force. Except for their uniforms, they could have been slaves on a plantation a hundred years earlier, toiling away beneath the broiling sun. But the time he spent in proximity to the airfield gave him hope.

As he sweated beneath the hot Hawaiian sun and rested during breaks, he would see the shiny military aircraft wheeled out to the flight line and prepped. Then the pilots would emerge from the hangers like matadors entering the bull ring and go through their pre-flight inspections. The propellers would be turned to distribute oil to the cylinders, then the pilots would switch on their engines and, with a great, ear-busting roar, a cloud of white-blue smoke would belch from the exhaust

Marlon Green (kneeling) with two Air Force buddies, Frank Fleming (left) and Rudolph Moton, at Wheeler Air Base, Hawaii, 1948 (Courtesy Green family archives)

tubes. The pilots would then taxi their aircraft to the far end of the runway, rev up the engines and roll forward, gaining speed until they were going fast enough to overcome gravity. Marlon would watch them take off, as weightless as birds, and the thought struck him: *That's what I want to do.*

He went to his superiors and told them he wanted to apply for pilot training. "At that time, you had to have had two years of college or the equivalent," Marlon recalled. "I didn't have two years of college, but there was a provision that if you passed a two-year college-equivalency test, you could apply for the training." He studied in preparation for the test, passed it, and was provisionally accepted into the Air Force pilot-training program.

On March 3, 1949, the officers who were aware of his upcoming assignment transferred him to another facility that would give him greater exposure to aircraft—nearby Hickam Air Force Base. "For the remainder of my time, before going back to the States for pilot training, I was assigned to the flight line of the 1500th Maintenance Squadron," Marlon said, "and given whatever jobs were available for a guy who didn't have any skills but who had desire and ambition to learn to fly." [4]

Officially, Marlon was assigned to the position of squadron supply clerk and, according to his January 1950 efficiency report, written by his supervisors—Major William J. Campbell and Major John T. Cavanaugh—had an "attention to duty and ability to learn and absorb new ideas" that was "outstanding." Major Cavanaugh added, "The airman is outstanding in his devotion to duty. His desire for self improvement as evidenced by his taking courses at U of H [University of Hawaii], application for Cadets, etc., are commendable. He is very neat and courteous. Highly recommended [for promotion]." [5]

Campbell and Cavanaugh made provisions for Marlon to be exposed to the atmosphere of flying. Whenever possible, Marlon would head to the flight line in the evening and catch a hop on a flight. At that time pilots, in addition to being medically qualified, had to have at least four hours a month of flying time to maintain their flying status and earn their flight pay.

Marlon said, "I would go out to the flight line in the evening just for the chance to meet the pilots, get into a plane, and spend a few hours observing them while they were getting their four hours in."

In March 1950, Marlon's dream of becoming a pilot began to take shape when he was promoted to sergeant and transferred from Hawaii to the 3510th Basic Pilot Training Wing at Randolph Field, near San Antonio, Texas. There he began the first seven of a total of thirteen months of the pilot training he needed to successfully complete in order to earn his wings.

"Randolph was the only basic-training school for pilots at that time," Marlon said.* "After you spent seven months at Randolph, you had to make a choice—assuming that you completed all your training satisfactorily—whether you wanted to pursue fighter pilot training or multi-engine pilot training. My decision was for multi-engine."

Marlon loved Randolph Field from the very first moment he entered its gates. The handsome, mission-style buildings were nothing like the utilitarian structures at most military installations, and the atmosphere seemed more akin to a college campus than a military base. The instructors and fellow cadets were accepting of him, one of the few Negroes attending the school.

Just as Xavier Prep (and, for a few months, Epiphany Apostolic College) had helped Marlon expand intellectually and culturally, so too did the the Air Force. He recalled, "There were efforts to achieve a *cultural* standard in the Air Force; how you sat at the table to take your meals, for example, or the conversations and exchanges that go on between Air Force upper classmen and lower classmen that are similar to that between college freshmen and upper classmen. The training at Randolph was Air Force pilot training *and* officer training. They wanted to try to find in the officer corps an approximation of the West Point or Annapolis ideals."

In June 1950, a few months after Marlon reported for training at Randolph, North Korea invaded its neighbor to the south, and the Korean War, or "police action," as it was called, began. Fortunately for Marlon, cadets in flight school were not subject to being sent to Korea and were allowed to finish their training.

Sergeant Green was enrolled in Class 51-B at Randolph, and it was there that he acquired the nickname "Doc." In the military, when roll call is being taken, it is customary for the sergeant taking the roll to call out the soldier's, sailor's, or airman's last name, followed by his first

---

* The U.S. Air Force Academy in Colorado Springs, Colorado, where most U.S. Air Force pilots are today trained to fly, was not established until 1954.

Cadet Marlon Green photographed in front of the Randolph Field administration building (dubbed the "Taj Mahal" by the cadets), March 1950 (Courtesy Green family achives)

two initials. Thus, John Paul Jones becomes "Jones, J.P." At roll call, then, Marlon D. Green became "Green, M.D.," the "M.D.," of course, being the abbrevation for medical doctor. Shortening "Doctor" turns it into "Doc." Marlon D. Green became known thereafter to his friends and associates as "Doc."

"At Randolph, we had two- or three-story buildings built around the quadrangle or parade ground—four buildings, A, B, C, D," said Marlon. "Mine was the 'Mighty Fourth'—D building. These were all Class A military accommodations. It was a pleasure to be assigned to Randolph for this course of training, marching to the flight line and marching back from the flight line after night flying to have special chow. We had the finest of facilities. That was really impressive and inspiring. We also had an Olympic-size pool. One of the requirements for completing pilot training was to be able to swim the length of the pool; swimming was never a high feature in my life. But you had to do that to get through the course; I made it. The work was demanding, but it was all in a setting where you really enjoyed the outcome."

Marlon was assigned to a dormitory-style room with three other cadets—all white. "I generally had the impression that everybody was trying to do 'the right thing,' to coin a phrase. I was really impressed with my roommates. Hal Watson was from California, Bill Ferguson was from Wisconsin, and Danny "The Weatherman" Lewallen was from Indiana. I never noticed any struggle on their parts to be especially nice

Posed Air Force photo of Marlon "Doc" Green (left) and roommate Harold "Hal" Watson standing at a "brace" for Upperclassman Robert Scott in front of "D" Barracks, Randolph Field, Texas. The caption reads, "We can lick gravity, sir, but sometimes the paperwork is overwhelming" — a quote borrowed from rocket scientist Wernher von Braun. Photo appeared in *The Crisis* magazine, November 1950.
(Courtesy Green family archives)

Marlon in flight gear,
Randolph Field, 1950
(Courtesy Green family archives)

The four cadet pilot roommates at Randolph Field. Left to right: Bill Ferguson, Danny Lewallen, Marlon Green, Harold Watson, circa April 1950 (Courtesy Green family archives)

to me or generous to me or deferential to me in any way. Nobody among these three gentlemen blinked an eye at my being there with them while going through this course. They carried on with good grace."

One of Marlon's classmates in 51-B at Randolph was a cadet by the name of Virgil Ivan "Gus" Grissom who, in the next decade, would be one of the original seven Project Mercury astronauts. "Grissom had a degree from Purdue University in Indiana; I believe it was in Mechanical Engineering. He was not my close buddy, but we had sing-alongs, so I knew him." Marlon laughed. "I remember reading some-where—maybe in Tom Wolfe's book, *The Right Stuff*—about him being a particularly rowdy member of the astronaut crew, as opposed to, let's say, John Glenn. When I heard about his supposedly blowing the hatch of the 'Liberty Bell Seven' space capsule in 1961, I wasn't particularly surprised. But I don't remember him from our cadet days as being espe-cially rowdy or particularly bad in any sense at all."[6]

Gus Grissom, a classmate of Marlon Green, and later a Mercury 7 astronaut
(Courtesy National Archives)

AFTER LEARNING ABOUT the theory of flight and taking classroom courses in the operation of aircraft, the students were introduced to the aircraft they would actually fly: the T-6 "Texan" trainer—a two-seat, propeller-driven aircraft. The T-6 was the perfect plane in which to learn to fly. First built in 1935, the T-6 continued to be built until 1945, with more than 15,000 coming off the North American Aviation Company's assembly line in California. With its forty-two-foot wingspan and 600- horsepower Pratt and Whitney engine, the T-6 was a powerful, responsive, forgiving aircraft that was a joy to fly.[7]

Marlon has vivid memories of his flight instructors. "I had one instructor who seemed to be expressing an attitude that might be motivated by racial sentiment," he noted, "but he was the only one. Personality clash or whatever, there was nothing overt about it. He did not call me anything offensive, but maybe there was a smidgeon of condescension. I was removed from being assigned to him and assigned to a different instructor, who was much more to my liking. I don't remember praying about it, but it was almost like the answer to a prayer. I think each instructor had two students. Our instruction was a morning and afternoon type thing—we flew in the morning and had ground school in the afternoon."

Flight training went on day after day. The cadets learned every part of their T-6 from propeller to rudder. They learned how to perform a detailed pre-flight check, start the engine, taxi, take off, climb, turn, roll, dive, fly on instruments, and land. They practiced "touch-and-go" landings for hours on end. Cadets who were slow learners or otherwise failed to demonstrate a "knack" for flying were "washed out" of the program. Marlon Green was one of those who demonstrated the knack.

Marlon poses by a T-6 trainer at Randolph Air Base, April 1950
(Courtesy Green family archives)

One thing that wasn't part of flight training, however, was making any actual parachute jumps. Marlon noted, "Our training was mostly theoretical—how the parachute should be used in case you had to bail out. They had a tower structure there so you could dangle and have all your weight suspended in a harness and see what your disposition was to this encroachment on your 'family jewels.' There was never any occasion when I had to jump out of an airplane. My mother was amazed when I told her that I had never jumped out of an airplane. She said, 'Suppose you have to do it one day? How're you gonna know how to do it?'"

The answer to her question was nearly discovered by accident one day after he had soloed. Marlon was practicing spin-recovery maneuvers in his T-6—a fairly simple maneuver, but one which required a lot of nerve. He would send the plane at a sharp upward angle until it stalled, keeled over, and began spinning downward like a falling leaf. He would then give the engine some power, push the control stick forward, kick the rudder in the opposite direction of the spin, and the aircraft would then stop spinning. Pulling back gently on the stick would cause the plane to level out. But on one of these practice maneuvers the T-6 refused to respond to his attempts to bring it back under control. He gave it power, pushed the stick forward, and kicked the rudder to the left. Nothing happened. He tried pulling the stick back, then moving it left and right. Still nothing. He waggled the rudder, the elevators, the ailerons. He might have been waggling his ears for all the effect his actions were having on his plunging, spinning, out-of-control airplane.

He was at about 8,000 feet above Texas and falling like a concrete block going several hundred miles an hour, the altimeter needle spinning backwards like a clock filmed in time-lapse. Rather than call the tower and declare an emergency, Doc decided the best course of action was to abandon ship—and fast. But there was no ejection seat on the T-6, nothing to blow himself out of the canopy, like jet fighters have. He would have to manually unlock the canopy, reach up and slide it back out of the way, unbuckle his seat belt, and then, while struggling to overcome the tremendous G-forces, stand up and leap from the cockpit into space, all the while hoping to avoid being slammed or cut in half by the wildly rotating, blade-like tail surfaces.

"I had taken my hands off the control stick and was busy trying to retract the canopy so I could bail out," he recalled. "Essentially, the airplane was on its own. At the time I reached back for the canopy control, there was an intervening grace that made things smooth again, but the concern was real for a moment. Concentrating on opening the canopy seemed to be the thing to do, because it was enough to distract me from what I had been doing—trying to control the plane. The airplane had taken care of itself. I credit myself for the good instinct to say, 'I won't be reaching back for the canopy anymore because the airplane has brought itself under control. Now fly it home and land it.' That's what I did. Needless to say, I did not report the incident to the people on the ground." He would later admit that the incident with the T-6 was the scariest moment of his life. "It gave me the most heartbeats per minute."

Marlon remembered that his class at Randolph was lucky: There were no fatal flying accidents, although some of his classmates later died in mishaps. "Dan Wakefield, in my class, was quite a character. I think he was killed after we left Randolph while he was in training at Luke or Williams, one of those two bases. A black guy from Jackson, Mississippi, named Arthur Babbington Keating, was also a classmate of mine. He had finished Randolph and went to one of the fighter pilot training bases in Arizona for training; while there he was killed in an automobile accident around Thanksgiving or Christmas at the end of 1950. As far as I know, it was a single-driver, one-car accident. Wakefield is the only one I can remember who was killed in an airplane accident, but not at Randolph."

After his basic pilot training course was completed, Marlon was assigned to Reese Air Force Base in Lubbock, Texas, for multi-engine instruction. There he trained on the B-25 twin-engine bomber. The B-25 "Mitchell" was obsolescent by this time but was still in use by the Air Force as a training aircraft and for other duties. He loved piloting the bomber and scored well in all his examinations. Graduation from multi-engine school was set for March 24, 1951; on that day he would receive his pilot's wings and be commissioned a second lieutenant in the Air Force.

Deciding it would be unwise to continue pursuing Eleanor, he turned his attentions to Lois Deslonde, his Xavier Prep prom date, and invited her to attend his graduation from Reese. Lois was living in New Orleans and, during the past few weeks, the two of them had become serious by letter. No longer bound by a vow of celibacy, Marlon was contemplating marriage; Lois had different ideas.

"I don't know if I formally proposed," he said, "but in our discussions of the prospect of marriage, she revealed that she wanted to pay her mother back for some of the expenses her mother had incurred from the prep school in '47. Lois went on to Xavier University, and I assume it was her mother's hard work that made it possible for her to continue with her studies there. She graduated and later became, not a nun, but a member of some charitable religious organization."

---

* Later renamed Chennault Air Base.

After receiving his pilot's wings and second lieutenant's gold bars, Marlon received orders assigning him to the Lake Charles Air Base* in Louisiana, to learn how to fly the B-29 Superfortress—the same type of plane that dropped two atomic bombs on Japan and ended World War II.

With Lois Deslonde no longer in his future, Marlon's romantic interests turned back to Eleanor Gallagher. "She was a person whom I knew and liked, but I wasn't too sure of as a prospective mate." To test the waters, he wrote her a letter, informing her that he was going to be stationed near New Orleans, and wondered if perhaps the two of them might get together while he was there.

This being 1951, and the proscriptions against interracial dating and marriage being as strong as ever, especially in the South, Marlon's decision to even approach Eleanor Gallagher as a possible romantic partner was as risky as trying to escape from a plunging, out-of-control aircraft.[8]

CHAPTER 4:
ELEANOR

———•—•—◆—•—•———

ELEANOR GALLAGHER WAS the first of five children born to William and Anna Gallagher, an intellectual and politically active Boston Catholic couple.

Following Eleanor were four siblings: Anne, William, Jr., Donald, and Paula. The Gallaghers lived in a two-story duplex in South Boston that had once belonged to Eleanor's father's parents. "It was on a hill just below Dorchester Heights, where there is a monument memorializing the Revolutionary War," Eleanor said. "George Washington's engineers built fortifications and artillery positions that forced the British army and fleet to retreat from Boston in March 1776.* South Boston High School is also located on the hill, below the monument."

She said that her father was always interested in law and politics. He was a graduate of a teachers' college—Wentworth Institute, now Wentworth Institute of Technology. After graduation, he was offered a job teaching in the Boston Public School system but, instead, accepted a position in the printing department of the Boston Public Library at Copley Square. "He loved his job and eventually became head of the department," she said. "He was an inveterate book lover and highly literate; we always had a library of books in our home. I scarcely ever recall his coming home without at least one book in hand. One of my faculty friends from Xavier University, who had an opportunity to meet him, said that, in his speech, he reminded her of a university professor."

But William Gallagher was not a well man. As a member of the 26th ("Yankee") Division, he had been wounded in World War I and had shrapnel embedded in his body, as well as respiratory problems due to having inhaled poison gas in the trenches of France. He was also a heavy smoker, which only aggravated his condition.

---

*March 17 became a Massachusetts state holiday to commemorate "Evacuation Day"—the day in 1776 when British forces ended their siege and abandoned the town.

Eleanor's mother, Anna Woelfel
Gallagher, circa 1930s
(Courtesy Green family archives)

Eleanor's mother, Anna Woelfel Gallagher, had had only an elementary school education, but she was, according to Eleanor, "very, very smart. At some point, when the five of us children were still quite young, she became president of a women's insurance organization in our area—a branch of the Ladies Catholic Benevolent Association—which she headed for more than twenty years. The main office of the L.C.B.A. was in Erie, Pennsylvania, and at that time the branches of the organization were mostly centered in the northeastern

Gallagher family at Christmas, circa 1950. Back row (left to right): Donald J., Anne M., Eleanor M., William B., Jr. Front row: Paula V., William B., Sr., Anna M.
(Courtesy Green family archives)

part of the U.S. It was an all-women's organization, long before the word 'feminist' came into common usage. The organization still exists and is currently called the Loyal Christian Benefit Association; men are now involved in its leadership. It is still headquartered in Erie."

Anna Gallagher was also active in a variety of other pursuits. She took classes in the evening in sundry topics, and took part in other community and social affairs for women at their local parish, the Gate of Heaven Catholic Church.* "My mother played the piano, loved both music and dance, and I remember her dancing and performing on the stage at church programs. Besides being busy with five children, she had a full community events calendar. Both my parents were on-going community activists."

The Gallaghers' home was within walking distance of Carson Beach. "We all swam," said Eleanor. "From a bedroom window I could see Boston Harbor and I loved watching ships coming into port. Every morning in the summer we would check the table of tides in the newspaper to know when the swimming would be best. That would determine our beach schedule and the tenor of our summer lives for the day. My mother would later cook the delicious clams that we dug when the tides were low."

Eleanor was reading at an early age and was promoted from kindergarten to first grade after a week in school. "I had just had my fifth birthday. I think that starting school young was, in many ways, a handicap. Since we grow at different levels emotionally and intellectually, I was almost always the youngest in every grade, even in college. I've often looked back on that time and have observed a certain degree of naïveté that persisted through much of my schooling—even in college."

Somehow, though, Eleanor acquired a highly developed sense of inclusion during her childhood, when she played with neighborhood children whose parents or grandparents were Italian, Polish, Lithuanian, and German immigrants. Relating to others whose languages and family lifestyles were different from hers and forming strong bonds with them was just a natural part of her growing up.

---

* The church was closed as part of the financial reorganization of the Boston Catholic Archdiocese in the late 1990s due to the widespread sexual abuse complaints filed in the court system, but later reopened because of pressure from the parishioners.

Eleanor and her mother share a laugh at Carson Beach, South Boston, circa 1948. (Courtesy Green family archives)

When she was in the third grade at the Gate of Heaven parish school, an incident occurred which forever etched itself into Eleanor's mind and eventually became a shaping influence in her life. "I was seven years old, and we had just returned from our spring Easter break. Our teacher, a nun, asked us to relate what we had done during our Easter vacation. "One pupil—her name was Peggy O'Connor—said, 'I went to Virginia to visit my grandparents, and I noticed that, if you were a colored person, you had to step off the sidewalk and into the street if someone white was walking on the sidewalk.' I thought: 'How stupid!' And I never forgot Peggy's name or the incident."

Somewhere around the age of eight or nine, Eleanor began going to daily Mass by herself. "I am naturally a morning person, so walking the four blocks to church in the early morning hours was an easy habit to cultivate. The rest of our household would still be asleep. And the times were such that safety was never an issue. My parents had no objections to these early morning excursions, and I was not deterred by the changes of the seasons—trudging through snow in the winter, astonished by nature's rebirth in the spring, luxuriating in the cool, clear mornings of summer, and the golden glory of New England in the autumn. What wonderful mornings alone—nurtured by a natural inclination to be reflective and savor the silence!"

As she progressed through grade school, Eleanor's parents determined that, instead of her attending the parish Catholic high school, she should apply to Boston's Girls' Latin School (her father had aspirations of her becoming a lawyer, and thus required that she have the best schooling).

At the time, Boston had what many considered one of the finest public school systems in the country. The Girls' Latin School was established in 1877 to provide an equally good classical education as that offered at the all-boys Boston Latin School, America's oldest public school, founded in 1635.*

The five Gallagher children each went to a different high school—selected by their parents to conform to what they thought their particular aptitudes and interests were.

Although younger than her classmates, Eleanor enrolled at Girls' Latin School as a high-school freshman. Even though it was nearly two decades before *Brown v. Board of Education*, Eleanor recalls that Girls' Latin School was racially integrated—something she accepted as normal. "Any girl, from anywhere in the city, was eligible for admission if she had an interest in attending and was in the top academic percentile of her current school," she said.

When she was sixteen, Eleanor remembered thinking that her life's work might be to join a religious order, specifically the Carmelites, an order of nuns separated from direct contact with society. "My thoughts proved to be more romantic than serious," she said, "because each time the idea occurred that this might be my calling, I had a simultaneous thought: *I would have to give up riding horses!* We had a riding club at school and every Wednesday that activity was the highlight of my life. So much for a vocation to the religious life!"

In addition to her intellectual interests, Eleanor also demonstrated athletic ability in sports, particularly swimming; the school had an exceptional physical education program. She felt that Doris Armstrong, her pioneering physical education teacher, was an early and important influence in her life. There were several Negro girls in her class who played sports and Eleanor became good friends with them.

---

* The school is now called Boston Latin Academy, and is co-educational.

"After field hockey or softball or whatever, we would go to the ice-cream parlor at Howard Johnson's and have a Coke," she said. "It all seemed really natural. Differences in race, religion, languages, and economic status were irrelevant as we participated in sports, as well as in the classroom.

"We were able to participate in multiple sports in season—usually extra-curricular—and in dance and gymnastics as regular classes. Because of the excellence of that program, at least four in our graduating class went on to major in health and physical education in college. One of them was E. Doris McKinney, who became a lifelong friend.

"Doris was African-American, although the term then was 'colored.' She lived in Roxbury, which was then somewhat integrated. We were never in the same academic classes but developed our friendship through similar interests in various sports: field hockey, basketball, volleyball, softball and, during our lunch periods, table tennis. We were part of the large number of sports' devotees at Girls' Latin. She was the first person of color whom I knew. Though the neighborhood I grew up in was diverse in terms of languages and religion and educational backgrounds, it was all-white." (Due to Doris's race, Eleanor's mother forbade Doris from visiting the Gallagher home. Eleanor, however, was welcome in the McKinney home—a welcome she used frequently.)

Doris McKinney, Eleanor's good friend from Boston, photographed in 1943
(Courtesy Green family archives)

Another wonderful memory from her school days was a chance meeting with the poet Robert Frost. One day, while commuting to school on public transportation, an older man boarded and Eleanor stood up to offer him her seat. "To thank me, he handed me a small piece of paper he pulled from his pocket. It was a poem he said he had just written, though it was not signed. Several stops before mine he exited; I noted it was in front of Boston University, where he was probably then teaching. It was not until later, after reflecting on the incident, that I realized who he was. Whenever I read his poetry, I flash on a recollection of that day, and, especially, have often recalled his familiar, frequently quoted lines: 'Two roads diverged in a woods, and I...I took the one less traveled by, and that has made all the difference.'"

———•———

WILLIAM GALLAGHER WAS especially interested and active in Boston politics and veterans' affairs, and Eleanor has vivid memories of the many adult conversations in her home that centered around political issues. "I also have a picture of my father in 1943 when he was the Chief Marshal of Boston's annual St. Patrick's Day Parade, earlier called 'Evacuation Day,' and led the parade on horseback," said Eleanor.

During the First World War, William Gallagher had served in the same unit as a brother of John McCormack, a Democratic member of Congress (and for whom the House of Representatives building in Washington, D.C., is named). The Gallagher and McCormack families grew up in the same neighborhood and maintained a friendship over the years.

On occasion, prominent people were guests in the Gallagher household. "On March 17, 1943," said Eleanor, "when my father was the Chief Marshal of the parade, Hamilton Fish III came to lunch at our home. Fish was a member of a family prominent in New York politics and served in the U.S. Congress for more than twenty-five years. In World War I he became commander of the 'Harlem Hellfighters,' the highly decorated all-black 369th Infantry Regiment."*

---

* Fish served in the U.S. House of Representatives from 1920 to 1945, was an isolationist, anti-Semitic, staunchly anti-Roosevelt, and was believed by some to be pro-Nazi.

William B. Gallagher as Chief Marshal of the 1943 Boston St. Patrick's Day
Parade, then known as Evacuation Day (Courtesy Green family archives)

William Gallagher was a confirmed Democrat, but later became
vehemently anti-Roosevelt, preferring the heated rhetoric of the weekly
radio broadcasts by arch-conservative Father Charles E. Coughlin,
which ran from 1926 to 1939.

"Father Coughlin was known as the 'Radio Priest,'" Eleanor recalled,
"and my father imposed a curfew on noise and distractions from the
Gallagher children whenever the program was on. We also probably
had every issue of Father Coughlin's newspaper, *Social Justice*, stacked
in our living room. When, in the 1930s, Father Coughlin's message took
on a more anti-Semitic tone, he was 'silenced' by his superior, Archbishop

Edward Mooney. I recall all this because of the anti-Semitic expressions I heard from my father, and with which I disagreed."

In stark contrast to her father's anti-Semitic attitudes, Eleanor began to develop a sense of inclusiveness and justice, and a strong desire to see that everyone, whatever their color, religion, or national origin, be treated fairly.

Another of Eleanor's favorite school friends was Deborah Tepper, a Jewish girl. Eleanor said, "Our math teacher, Harold Meserve, was a Harvard graduate and an extraordinary teacher whom I still remember with much gratitude. He wanted to challenge our abilities, so Deborah and I resolved that we would arrive at school early on certain days and put our math problems on the blackboard to compare solutions. It was fun, and we shared an unusual bond as a result. One day she asked if I would like to stop by her house on the way home from school. It was then I learned her father was an artist and her family lived in or near the well-known neighborhood of Beacon Hill—an historic area of Boston. The special invitation was to enable her to share the treats of a Jewish holiday with me. In an instant, whatever I had heard at home regarding conversations relating to Father Coughlin and anti-Semitism went up in smoke. It was another 'Peggy O'Connor moment' of learning."*

———•••••———

IN ADDITION TO her intellectual interests, Eleanor Gallagher loved sports and excelled at them. "We had an incredible physical education program at [Girls' Latin] school where just about every sport was available to us. If we didn't have the facilities at the school, the school found the facilities for us elsewhere. For example, we didn't have an area where we could play field-hockey, but there was a college about a mile from the school that had a playing field; our teacher, Doris Armstrong, made arrangements for us to use it. The same was true for swimming and horseback riding; we could go to the YWCA to swim, or to a school-selected stable to ride horses. The people from the riding facility would come and pick us up at school. In my senior year I rode every week."

---

* Deborah Tepper went on to graduate from Radcliffe College, later obtained a doctorate at Harvard, and became a university professor.

When she graduated from Girls' Latin School, Eleanor received a full college scholarship that could be used at Radcliffe College (now incorporated into Harvard), Simmons College, or Boston University. "My parents and I selected Radcliffe as the first choice and my father scheduled an interview at the college. My recollection is that the appointment was with the college president, Ada Comstock. The interview was very short, and when we left, my father took my hand—and I still remember the feeling of sadness that was conveyed to me. There were no words exchanged, for we both knew that discrimination had taken place. We were an Irish-Catholic family from South Boston. He had grown up seeing the signs: 'Irish Need Not Apply.' The choice for college became Boston University, Sargent College. Harvard and Radcliffe still echo the so-called 'Brahmin' tradition of Boston."*[1]

DESPITE ITS CURRENT perceived reputation as being a highly diverse and liberal city, Boston was not always so. There was a period of time, beginning in the 1840s and 1850s, when the Irish, escaping the Potato Famine, poverty, and disease in their home country, were despised on these shores because those who had come earlier from England, Scotland, and northern Europe had a natural resentment and fear of those who came later—a situation that exists to this day. Jews, Slavs, Italians, Negroes, and Latinos all suffered the same sort of discrimination when their turn came.

It is said that no group in the America of the 1840s-1850s was of lower socio-economic class than the Irish—lower, even, than the blacks. A common expression of the period was, "Let Negroes be servants, and if not Negroes, let Irishmen fill their place."[2]

Yet, no group of immigrants loved America more, nor fought harder for her, than the Irish. During the Civil War, all-Irish units were formed,

---

* Doris McKinney and Eleanor both attended Sargent College at Boston University. Doris went on to receive her doctorate at BU and was on the faculty at Bennett College, and then later at the University of North Carolina, Greensboro, from which she retired. Ironically, both Eleanor and her daughter Monica had occasions in more recent years, when attending separate programs at Harvard and Radcliffe to live and/or study in a building named Comstock Hall.

and Irishmen—whether soldiers or prize-fighters—were grudgingly respected for their bravery and their aggressive nature. It is not by chance that many of America's toughest police officers and firemen have been Irish.

When William Gallagher, the son of Irish immigrants, was growing up in Boston, he experienced the same residual prejudice but was determined to overcome it through education, courage, and industriousness. Radcliffe's unspoken discrimination against his daughter dredged up hurtful memories of the past.

———•———

AT BOSTON UNIVERSITY'S Sargent College, Eleanor majored in health and physical education. She recalled, "Some faculty members at BU weren't as liberal in their racial attitudes as Girls' Latin faculty had been." Although her friend Doris McKinney was the senior class president, Eleanor remembered that a school administrator requested Doris not attend the Senior Prom; she ignored the advice, but was deeply hurt by this overt display of racism. "We were shocked that she was told not to attend," Eleanor said. "Doris told us that they couldn't stop her and that she was going. A group of us arranged our 'dance cards' in advance to exchange partners and the evening went smoothly."*

Upon receiving her diploma from Boston University in the spring of 1943, Eleanor received a number of offers from colleges to become a physical education instructor; she chose the offer from Mercyhurst College in Erie, Pennsylvania. "It's a Catholic college run by the Sisters of Mercy," Eleanor explained.

"At that point, women's colleges were becoming aware of the need to have strong physical education programs. I can't remember now exactly why I chose Mercyhurst—probably because it was closer to home than the other schools where I had job offers—and it was a Catholic college. I never had any interest in teaching in the Boston school system."

Eleanor, along with a handful of lay faculty, lived at the college. Most of the faculty members were nuns and they, too, lived on campus,

---

* Dance cards were small folders where partners for each of the evening's dances would be determined and listed beforehand.

Eleanor Gallagher with her parents on graduation day from
Sargent College, Boston University, 1943
(Courtesy Green family archives)

which is located on a hill overlooking the city of Erie. "It was quite beautiful and elegant," said Eleanor.

But Eleanor began to experience a growing disenchantment with the administration at Mercyhurst. She noted, "We had a wonderful gym that on the weekends wasn't being used. One day, I visited a community recreation center in downtown Erie and noted that all the children were black—and that their facilities were inadequate. All they had was a small building with no gym. I spoke to the director to find out if they had access to a gym and he said, 'No.' When I returned to the college, I spoke to our dean and asked if the children from the community center

A view of the Mercyhurst campus, 1943 (Courtesy Green family archives)

Eleanor (third from left) and other faculty members at Mercyhurst, 1943
(Courtesy Green family archives)

could use our gym on weekends; I would take responsibility and super-
vise them. She said she would have to discuss it with the Board of
Trustees. The answer was negative, and no reason was given. I was
very disappointed and perplexed that an opportunity to reach out to a
disadvantaged community had been refused. It caused me to question
the gap between values and practice in a religious community."

For some weeks, the injustice of the refusal continued to eat away at
Eleanor. "I was out refereeing a field hockey game one day, and it

seemed as if I heard a voice saying, 'Eleanor, you can't do this any longer.'" She listened to the voice—and submitted her resignation.

She quit Mercyhurst and enrolled in graduate school at New York's Fordham University. Her contract at Mercyhurst had included room, board, and salary so, for two years, she was able to save much of her pay for the possibility of graduate school. After a year of study at Fordham, Eleanor received her master's degree in psychology. "I had a caring mentor there, Reverend Joseph Donceel, S.J., for whom I have had lifelong appreciation; a great model of scholarship and commitment. I remember that for one of his classes I wrote a paper on the 1943 Detroit race riots and, in doing research for the paper, discovered the work of Swedish economist Gunnar Myrdal. In 1944, he had published an enormous book of nearly 1,500 pages entitled *An American Dilemma: The Negro Problem and Modern America*. His conclusion was that the 'Negro problem' was 'a white man's problem,' and that whites as a collective were responsible for the disadvantageous situation in which blacks were trapped. The exhaustive and influential Myrdal study was later cited in *Brown v. Board of Education*.

"Fordham offered me a doctoral fellowship to stay—I hadn't applied for it, so it was a wonderful and unexpected opportunity. But my father had had a heart attack that year, and there were four in my family to go to college after me and, what with the cost of living in New York City, I knew that I would probably have needed some additional financial support to accept the fellowship; I knew I could not ask my parents for that. So I decided to look for another job teaching. My aunt, who was a nun on the faculty at Regis College in Massachusetts, gave me a list of all the Catholic colleges in the United States as possibilities. I applied to three of them and received offers from all three. One was in Indiana, another in Illinois, and the third was Xavier University in New Orleans."

That summer Eleanor bicycled through New England with her friend Doris McKinney, who at that time was teaching at Bennett College, a college for Negro women in Greensboro, North Carolina. "I told her that I had received an offer from Xavier, and she said, 'I hear it's a great school, but it's too bad you won't consider it.' I thought, I haven't even made any decision about where I would like to go and here's my friend Doris assuming that I'm not going to consider it because it would mean going to the South and because the school was for Negroes and Indians! It was a challenge, so I decided to take the offer from Xavier."

Eleanor's parents were terribly upset by her decision. "My mother cried, and my father said, 'All your education, Eleanor—you're throwing it away to teach at a Negro college.' They went to the airport with me when I left—it was the first time I had flown—but they were very pained. However, it was *my* decision and what *I* wanted to do. I believed it was a good decision and was sorry that *they* didn't see it in the same positive light."

⸺ ·•·↓·•· ⸺

ELEANOR QUICKLY DISCOVERED that New Orleans was a far cry from Boston. In many ways it was like stepping back into an antebellum past, with magnificent mansions whose gabled porches were held up by massive columns; magnolias and azaleas blooming everywhere; trees heavy with moss-dripping limbs; and an oppressively humid climate that not even winter could abate.

At Xavier University, Eleanor was given a heavy teaching load, but she loved it. "I taught dance; I taught swimming and tennis; I taught and refereed basketball; the school had a football team, so I coached the cheerleaders." The college also had an opera program, and Eleanor was the choreographer when the operas included dances. In addition, she taught anatomy and physiology to physical-education majors, plus a course in statistics—"Tests and Measurements"—and taught a course in clinical psychology in the graduate school. "I never thought much about the amount of work. I was young and those were my growing-up years. They were just rich with opportunities and experiences. I would have to say they were the richest years of my early life; I felt very blessed."

Not everyone in her family shared her joy. Eleanor recalled the time that her mother came down to visit at the school. "After she returned to Boston, she told her friends that I was doing 'missionary work' in the South."

Eleanor roomed with another new arrival at Xavier, Emma Joan Stanley, from Indiana. "Joan Stanley was a brilliant person," Eleanor said. "She had graduated from college at eighteen and had been teaching at Berea College in Kentucky before coming to Xavier, but in a lot of ways she was even more immature than I was. She looked like Ingrid Bergmann, the Swedish-born movie star in the 1940s. Her father was a professor who taught Greek and Latin, and her mother had been a concert pianist but became mentally ill when Joan was about fifteen. Joan didn't feel that she had had a happy childhood, what with her mother's concertizing and mental illness, and her father's classic interests."

Joan taught botany at Xavier. "Joan knew absolutely every plant by its botanical name and she felt impelled to teach me, but I had no interest," Eleanor said, chuckling. "She was very distressed with me because we would go for a walk and she would point at a flower or a leaf and say, 'Eleanor, what is that?' And I would say, 'I don't remember,' and she'd get very annoyed. But I think she was probably an exciting teacher in the classroom because of her incredibly deep interest in botany."

Joan was not fond of living in the campus apartment, however. "She wanted to live in the French Quarter," Eleanor said, "but I didn't, so she moved out and went to live there." Eleanor received a new roommate, Marie Salvucci, from Newton, Massachusetts, who joined Eleanor in Xavier's Physical Education Department.

Joan Stanley
(Courtesy Green family archives)

Marie Salvucci
(Courtesy Green family archives)

One day a nun at Xavier came to Eleanor and said she was interested in staging a major May Day festival that would be racially integrated, complete with music and hundreds of school children dancing. Eleanor said, "She asked if I would teach folk dances to my student dance group and then have the dancers go around to the various schools and teach the children."

The festival was a *huge* success, Eleanor said, with some 200 children, plus their parents, taking part. "We held it on the grounds of Notre Dame, the seminary for Diocesan priests in New Orleans. It was amazing to see all these squares of children dancing. Because the groups of children were organized by schools, which were segregated, there was no 'mixing' of races, but there was a *semblance* of integration."

—··◆··—

NO MATTER HOW fulfilling her teaching and social life were, however, Eleanor's experiences in New Orleans were tempered by the signs of Jim Crow segregation that were everywhere. There were "Whites Only" and "Colored Only" notices applied to restrooms, drinking fountains, and swimming pools. Eleanor would go into restaurants and see only white faces—except for those who were waiting on the customers or bussing the dirty dishes or mopping the floors or working in the kitchen. She would ride a bus or streetcar and notice the Negro riders confined to the rear of the conveyance. She would see black men step off the sidewalk and into the street in deference at her approach. The pervasiveness of American apartheid overwhelmed and dismayed her.

It also made her angry and inspired her to do something about it.

She learned that Negro faculty members who had been at the school far longer than she were being paid less than she was, and she did a little investigating, in hopes of somehow correcting the disparity. After her inquiring into faculty salaries was discovered, she was "called on the carpet" by the administration for poking her nose into matters that shouldn't concern her. "I was informed that the cost of living for Negroes in New Orleans was less than that for whites," she said, "which supposedly 'explained' the difference."

One day while downtown, she visited a Catholic church to attend confession and was shocked to see a sign on the pews in the rear of the church that said "For Colored Only." She had already seen similar signs at other public facilities around town, but this was too much.* She decided to speak to one of the parish priests and express her dismay about the sign and what it represented. His response was, "This is the South—that's just the way it is. I am not responsible."[3]

Later, Eleanor heard about another priest, Father Joseph Fichter, a Jesuit originally from New Jersey, who had been assigned to the Deep South in 1947. As the chair of Loyola University's Sociology Department, Fichter was a controversial champion of social justice at a time when it was dangerous to speak out on matters of race, even if one wore the vestments of priesthood.

In *Black, White, and Catholic*, R. Bentley Anderson's epic study of the New Orleans Catholic Church's internal struggle to confront racism and segregation, he points out, "In the 1940s, the Roman Catholic Church had not yet come to terms in its complicity in maintaining racial segregation in the southern United States, and, it is fair to say, had not yet adequately challenged race policy within or without the church."

The Archbishop of St. Louis, Missouri, however, had, in 1947, courageously desegregated his parishes; the archbishop of Washington, D.C., would do the same the following year. But, as Anderson writes, "In the postwar period, a majority of the Roman Catholic clergy and laity did not challenge social morés concerning race relations. For most Catholics, segregation, if it was a problem at all, was a social, political, and/or legal problem but not necessarily a moral one." Joseph Fichter, Society of Jesus, however, would soon make it one.[4]

Fichter was following in the path of Marist Father James H. Blenk, who became the archbishop of New Orleans in 1906. Blenk was not blind to the segregation in the Southern churches and did what he could to institute changes without upsetting the entire Southern societal applecart. Using the Society of St. Joseph of the Sacred Heart, whose priests ministered solely to Negroes and Negro Catholics, Blenk began creating and staffing a number of schools—from elementary to colleges—that would serve as an educational foundation upon which he hoped to build bridges into the Negro community. Assisting in this

---

* Cleo Moran, a Xavier roommate who became one of Eleanor's life-long friends, said that Eleanor, in an early act of civil disobedience, swiped "Colored Patrons Only" signs from New Orleans buses, hid them under her coat, and used them to "decorate" her apartment. (Cleo Moran, letter to Eleanor Green, March 2005)

Father Joseph H. Fichter, S.J., spearheaded efforts to desegregate New Orleans Catholic churches in the 1940s and 1950s.
(Courtesy Special Collections and Archives, Monroe Library, Loyola University, New Orleans)

effort were the Holy Ghost Fathers, the Sisters of the Blessed Sacrament, and the Sisters of the Holy Family, the latter a group of Negro women. At no time, however, was it ever suggested that Negroes and whites should attend the same churches together.

After Blenk's successor, Archbishop John W. Shaw, died, the post was assumed in 1935 by Joseph Francis Rummel, a German immigrant. Neither Shaw nor Rummel did much to change the racial status quo of New Orleans's ecclesiastical segregation. Father Fichter, on the other hand, had no such compunctions and, in February 1949, launched a crusade to end segregation, at least within New Orleans' Catholic churches. From the pulpit, he gave sermons on the evils of segregation—sermons that were not well received by the majority of his white parishoners—and was subjected to a backlash; calls for his dismissal were received by Rummel and other church superiors. But Fichter refused to be diverted from his path.

Change, however, did not happen swiftly. In 1949, Father Fichter founded the Commission on Human Rights of the Catholic Committee of the South (which Eleanor joined) in hopes of being able to do something to rectify the segregation situation. As a result of Father Fichter's dogged persistence, the pressure coming from CHR's members, and his own soul-searching, Archbishop Rummel in 1955 ordered the desegregation of the city's parochial schools, beginning with the start of the 1956-1957 school year. Many white parents, citing the belief that "God must not have wanted the mixing of the races, for he created different races," were outraged and demanded that Rummel delay the implementation of the plan.*

But, despite the hopes and dreams of Eleanor and other members of CHR, there was no popular uprising of white Catholics demanding that the pillars of segregation be toppled. Indeed, most white Catholics in New Orleans refused to interject themselves into the controversy and break with long-standing Southern traditions of discrimination, bigotry, and the separation of the races. Furthermore, believing that Father Fichter and his CHR organization were Communist-inspired, J. Edgar Hoover had the FBI secretly investigate the priest and the membership.[5]

Using students largely from Loyola University, Father Fichter developed sociological projects and distributed questionnaires about race and segregation in white churches to white congregations. As Cleo Moran, a later Xavier roommate of Eleanor's, noted, "He was a very holy man who endured with patience the hostilities society heaped upon him because of the stands he took."[6]

FOR EVERY SMALL step forward in terms of ending segregation in the South, however, it seemed that two giant steps were taken backward.

To cite but one example, Eleanor learned that the world-famous Martha Graham Dance Company was going to put on a recital at Newcomb College, the women's college at nearby Tulane University, and she wanted to take her all-Negro modern dance class to see the performance. But, because Tulane was until 1964 an all-white institution, Eleanor knew that certain conventions needed to be observed. She called Tulane's Sophie Newcomb College to see if her students could attend but was told no. She then asked Xavier's president, Mother M. Agatha Ryan, to contact Tulane and use her influence to get permission. Again, the answer was no Negroes would be allowed to attend. Mother

---

* Many of Fichter's thoughts and experiences in Louisiana were captured in his stunning 1951 book, *Southern Parish: Dynamics of a City Church*. At the time, *Southern Parish* was an underground classic, sold only from under the counter at the Catholic Book Store, literally in a plain brown wrapper. To do otherwise would, it was feared, provoke a backlash against the Church for "meddling" in the affairs and traditions of the Old South. (Eleanor Green interview by author, May 17, 2004)

Agatha then asked her administrative assistant—a white man—to negotiate with Newcomb; still the white college refused.

Eleanor was crushed, but she and roommate Marie Salvucci, also a member of the Xavier faculty, decided to go by themselves. "I thought that by attending I could at least share a report of the program with my class," she said. "By the end of the program, though, I just felt like crying. I couldn't even get up out of my seat. Marie suggested I go backstage and talk with Martha Graham, and that she'd wait outside for me."

Eleanor did go backstage and met with Martha Graham and told her that the request for her students to attend the concert was denied because of race. The dancer was visibly dismayed at the news. "Taking my hands in hers, she said, 'Oh, my dear—if you had only come to me before the performance, I would not have performed.'"*

———•••———

ONE DAY WHILE visiting the Xavier Prep School cafeteria that adjoined her on-campus apartment, Eleanor met a tall, good-looking Negro high-school student by the name of Marlon Green. Her memory of their first meeting is rather hazy, and at odds with Marlon's. "My first memory is meeting him in the cafeteria where he was working," she said. "But I don't recall that meeting really well."

Her initial impression was of an engaging young man with a great smile, but nothing else of significance. There were no bells or fireworks that went off, no sense that she was chatting with her future husband.

She also does not share Marlon's recollection of her teaching him to dance in time for the prom. "I remember he was there when I was teaching some of the students to dance in the university gym. And I don't know why he would have been over in the college gym, unless he had come with some of his classmates to...well, I really don't know. Because I wouldn't have been doing anything with dance at the prep school; I was never even *in* the prep school."

———•••———

---

* When asked if Martha Graham had offered to put on a special performance just for her students at Xavier, Eleanor said, "No."

THE 1947 SCHOOL year ended and Marlon Green graduated from Xavier Prep; Eleanor was not invited to his graduation, nor did she attend. She had, for all intents and purposes, completely forgotten about him.[7]

It was not until late in the fall of 1947 that she heard from him again— a letter from Epiphany. "I felt guilty about not seeing him when he graduated," she said, "in not acknowledging anything, so I sent him a Christmas card. My first feelings for Marlon were simply friendly. It was not until probably a year after he graduated from Xavier Prep that I found out he had entered a Catholic seminary. A friend of his mentioned it to me and I decided to send him a Christmas card at the seminary and to wish him well. A couple of months passed, as I recall, before my card caught up to him and he responded. He was then in the Air Force and I guess was lonely and decided I might be an interesting correspondent."[8]

Unknown to her, in the interim, Marlon had been expelled from the seminary and had enlisted in the Air Force; he didn't receive her card until he was in Hawaii. Then the correspondence began to pick up speed. But he was a long way from New Orleans, and there were eligible young men much closer—both in geographic proximity and to her age—whom she dated. The letters she sent to Marlon remained chatty, platonic, and non-committal. Somewhere on a Hawaiian island, however, a young Air Force enlisted man was getting different ideas.

A year passed, and the letters from Sergeant Marlon Green continued to arrive regularly in her mailbox. Then he informed her that he had been accepted to pilot-training school in San Antonio. After graduation from training at Randolph, Marlon, in another letter, said that he was going to be assigned to the Lake Charles Air Base in Louisiana, not far from New Orleans, and would there be a chance that the two of them might get together? She agreed to visit him. If she had any trepidation about the taboos concerning interracial dating in the South at that time, she dismissed it with her belief that, "People are people, and we are all equal," she said.[9]

In late 1949, well before the friendship between Marlon and Eleanor blossomed into a romance—at least in Eleanor's mind—she attended a teachers' conference in Arkansas, not too far from El Dorado. At Marlon's urging, she stopped by to visit his family. "I don't think she described herself as being in a romance with their son," Marlon recalled, "but she went and visited them and they liked her."[10]

———•••••———

THE TWO BEGAN dating surreptitiously in 1950. Marlon's and Eleanor's relationship brought new meaning to the word "discreet," for a third person always accompanied them on their dates: Jim Crow. His was a shadowy, malevolent presence that lurked in doorways and behind bushes, a heavy-breathing chaperone and red-necked enforcer of the laws of Louisiana and the die-hard traditions of the Old South.* The legal penalties against "mixed-race" dating, cohabitation, or marriage were severe, and included jail time.

The social penalties were even worse, for if any white segregationists should happen upon the scene and see a Negro and a white woman holding hands, kissing, dining together, sitting together on a bus seat, or acting like their being in close proximity to one another was anything more than coincidental and momentary, a terrible fate could befall the Negro. Threats, kidnappings, beatings, torture, and lynchings were common occurrences for black males who dared cross the color line— even in the 1950s, nearly a century after slavery had been abolished.

Once, after Marlon had ridden the bus from Lake Charles Air Base to spend a weekend visiting Eleanor in New Orleans, and was waiting outside the Greyhound terminal on Canal Street to return, Marlon and Eleanor were saying their fond farewells in the privacy of roommate Marie Salvucci's Ford station wagon, parked at the curb. In an era before tinted windows, Marie, who knew and liked Marlon, stood guard over the trysting spot, hoping to keep the eyes of passersby away from the two occupants.[11]

The scheduled hour came for the bus to depart. Marlon remembered that they "were able to separate and leave each other pleasantly, whereas we had some tension there for a few minutes."[12]

Eleanor recalls the incident with greater trepidation than does Marlon. "Marlon seems to have dismissed or forgotten it," she said, "but the police and/or security followed him into the men's room after

---

* Title 14, Chapter 1, of the State of Louisiana's Criminal Code (revised 1950) stated that "Miscegenation is the marriage or habitual cohabitation with knowledge of their difference in race between a person of the Caucasian or white race and a person of the colored or negro race. Whoever commits the crime of miscegenation shall be imprisoned, with or without hard labor, for not more than five years."

Marlon and Eleanor with Marie Salvucci's car during their clandestine courtship
period in New Orleans, February 27, 1950 (Courtesy Green family archives)

his sudden departure from the car. In the men's room, Marlon changed
into his Air Force officer's uniform and the men following him were
non-plussed to see the man they thought they were looking for emerge
in different clothing. We did not know he had changed clothing in the
bus station and suspected the worst. Marie and I anxiously waited to
hear from him after his return to the air base."[13]

IN 1950, MARIE Salvucci temporarily left Xavier to finish her master's
degree, and a new physical-education instructor, Cleo Moran, arrived
from Detroit to take her place. She and Eleanor became roommates and
close friends. Cleo said about her decision to teach at Xavier, "I was
young and wanted a career that would help people. I wanted to do
something worthwhile. New Orleans was such an attractive venue for

Cleo Moran, one of Eleanor's roommates in New Orleans, 1950
(Courtesy Green family archives)

that; I couldn't imagine being able to help people and live in such an interesting place at the same time."

"Eleanor was an excellent teacher," she recalled, "absolutely top-notch." She also learned that Eleanor was dating Marlon and approved. "I was very impressed with him. He was really something—extremely handsome and charming—unbelievably charming, as lots of the men in New Orleans at the time were. I used to think they held contests among themselves to see who could be the most charming. He really was a master at it."

On occasion, Cleo and Eleanor visited the flight line at the air base to watch Marlon fly. "He was so good," Cleo said. "I would see him land these military planes at the field and he would set those things down so smoothly. Just unbelievable. He was just very skilled."[14]

Soon Marlon would need all the skills and charm he could muster.

CHAPTER 5:
REFUSING TO CONFORM

SOMEHOW, IN THE spring of 1951, and despite the myriad social and legal obstacles and barriers erected between them, Marlon asked Eleanor to marry him; she accepted.

Knowing they could not marry in Louisiana—or anywhere else in the South, for that matter, due to the anti-miscegenation laws—they decided to get married in California, where a wedding between a black person and a white person had been decriminalized only in 1948. Marlon and Eleanor set the date for December 29, 1951.

Now came the hard part: telling their respective families. "I knew my parents would have a negative reaction," Eleanor said. "I had no doubt about that." She was right. While her mother was "disappointed" at the announcement, her father was livid; it was bad enough she had "thrown away her education" to go down South and teach at a Negro college; now she was throwing her *life* away by marrying a Negro!

"My aunt, who was a nun on the faculty of Regis College, a Catholic college in Massachusetts, also did not approve," said Eleanor. "She wrote to me, saying something like, 'How could you do this to your parents?'"*[1]

Marlon said his own family raised no fuss over the planned interracial marriage. "There was no *Guess Who's Coming to Dinner*** type of family argument," he related. "They were willing to accept that their son had made this decision."[2]

Eleanor does not recall that the Green family took the news with such gracious equanimity. In fact, her memory is that Marlon's family reacted with some alarm, and that his brother Rudolph made a special

---

* Eleanor indicated that, about a year later, her aunt wrote again and said she had been wrong to oppose the marriage. "I don't know what caused her change of heart," Eleanor said.

** A reference to the 1967 Academy Award-winning Hollywood film (directed by Stanley Kramer and starring Sidney Poitier, Spencer Tracy, Katherine Hepburn, and Katherine Houghton) which explored the then-explosive topic of interracial dating and marriage.

Marlon's older brother
Rudolph and his wife
Virginia, with their daughter
Marcia, circa 1953
(Courtesy Green family archives)

Marlon's sister Jean,
photographed in
the mid-1950s
(Courtesy Green family archives)

trip to New Orleans in an unsuccessful effort to dissuade them from going through with the marriage. Marlon's sister Jean, too, was vocally opposed to the union.

James Green, during his service with the
U.S. Air Force, 1956
(Courtesy Green family archives)

Allen Green, photographed in the 1970s
(Courtesy Green family archives)

Marlon's parents took the news better than did some of his siblings and other members of the community. Marlon's younger brother James distinctly remembers a conversation that centered around the upcoming wedding: "Rumors were swirling in the black community of El Dorado that Lucy and Kinney Green's son Marlon was going to marry a Caucasian lady. I heard my mother answer one of the neighbors who asked indignantly, 'What do you think of that, Sister Green?' She said, 'If he likes it, I *love* it!' And that was the end of *that* discussion!"[3]

Gradually, Eleanor's parents softened somewhat their opposition. She noted, "Later they kind of accepted it—as long as we never went to Boston and had their friends find out. I'm sure the response of my brothers and sisters was negative, too, but they never laid it on me. I can't recall feeling any worries about a bi-racial marriage, probably because Marlon was then an officer in a newly integrated Air Force."[4]

Every upcoming wedding generates stress and anxiety, but Marlon and Eleanor were under the added pressure of dealing with the disapproval of their families. Dismayed by the reactions of both families, and unable to abide the segregation of the South any longer, Eleanor quit her job at Xavier and moved to Los Angeles, where Esther Clark, an understanding aunt-by-marriage, was the assistant to the fashion editor at the *Los Angeles Herald Examiner.* Esther Clark had some surgery scheduled and arranged for Eleanor to take her place at the paper while she recuperated. For his part, Marlon concentrated on his duties at Lake Charles Air Base, and filled his free time with a few night courses at the local McNeese State College.[5]

Eleanor told Father Fichter about her parents' hardened attitudes and he offered to write a letter that was part emollient, part sermon, in an effort to win their hearts:

Dear Mr. and Mrs. Gallagher,

Eleanor's decision to marry comes as a great surprise to you, and you are undoubtedly very much concerned about it. It's a decision which involves a lot of problems, not only for herself and her future husband, but also for their families. These difficulties should not be minimized, nor at the same time should they be exaggerated. At first thought, you are probably convinced that Eleanor is making a terrible mistake which will ruin her life and eventually bring utter unhappiness to herself, Marlon, and the families and friends of both.

While people surely should be realistic about their plans for the future, I do not think that dire forebodings about Eleanor's proposed marriage are realistic.

If Eleanor told me she wanted to marry a non-Catholic, I would be completely opposed to the marriage, and I believe she would be making a terrible mistake. Religious differences create spiritual problems in marriage and jeopardize one's eternal salvation. For the life of me, I cannot understand why Catholics, even priests, accept quietly and complacently religious inter-marriage, but are horrified at the thought of racial inter-marriage of two Catholics.

It ought to be the other way around - and it is - for people whose main aim is to serve God on earth. Racial differences bring difficulties, whether in marriage or in any other human relations, only in so far as we fail to look at people the way God looks at them. Prejudices are man-made and sinful. They are widespread, and they make trouble because we are so far removed from God's plan of life. We are living in a stupid, sinful society where human beings have forgotten the divine law of universal love.

Eleanor's decision in this case is a kind of proof that you have brought her up properly. You have every reason to be proud of her strength of character, her clearsightedness, her ability to direct her life according to fundamental principles. She is not letting you down in any way. On the contrary, she is reflecting your own good home training by refusing to conform to worldly standards and values....

I think that when a girl is preparing for marriage she needs the love and understanding and prayers of her mother and father. I ask you to fulfill this need in your own gracious way. Eleanor's decision to marry is a weighty and responsible one, and she deserves not only your support but your enthusiasm.[6]

Marlon recalled that Father Fichter's letter did little good. Eleanor's mother was relatively understanding, but her father, himself the victim of anti-Irish discrimination, remained vehemently opposed. According to Marlon, "Eleanor's father said something like, he never wanted to hear Eleanor's name mentioned again."[7]

A MONTH BEFORE the wedding, Father Fichter wrote again to Eleanor:

I want to wish you every grace and blessing for your wedding. The words are stilted but you know what I mean. I think that you are both close to God; you've weighed all angles; your intentions are supernatural; now it remains for your faith in God and love in each other to sustain you. May God bless you ever. [8]

The week before the wedding, Father Fichter wrote once more, expressing his regrets that, due to prior commitments in Washington, D.C., he would be unable to attend. He said,

May the Child Jesus and His Mother accompany you and

Marlon throughout your married life.... The announcement of your marriage is the most beautiful thing of its kind I have ever seen.... My very cordial wishes for a Christmas full of grace and joy, and for a lifetime of married happiness.[9]

Marlon was granted leave from the Air Force for his wedding ceremony and a brief honeymoon. The church he and Eleanor chose for the nuptials was St. Brendan's Catholic Church at 310 South Van Ness Avenue in Los Angeles (featured, incidentally, at the end of the 1953 science-fiction film, *The War of the Worlds*). It was a very small wedding held in a very large space. Attending was Eleanor's lone family member, Aunt Esther, and the friends from her Los Angeles rooming house. Eleanor's former Xavier roommate, Joan Stanley, was the maid of honor. No one from Marlon's family was present.

NEWS ITEM:

(Mims, Fla., Dec. 25, 1951) Harry T. Moore, the 46-year-old head of the Florida branch of the National Association for the Advancement of Colored People, was killed when a bomb exploded under the bedroom of his central Florida house; his wife Harriett, badly wounded in the attack, died nine days later.

Besides being Christmas Day, December 25 was also the couple's twenty-fifth wedding anniversary.

Speculation for a motive in the deadly bombing centered around Lake Country Sheriff Willis McCall. In 1949, Moore had organized an NAACP campaign in protest of a wrongful conviction of four Negroes who were framed and found guilty for raping a white woman in Groveland, Florida. In 1951, the U.S. Supreme Court ordered a new trial.*[10]

"A trip from Arkansas to California would have involved an expense that was not contemplated," Marlon explained. Charles Terry, an Air Force captain and doctor who had been stationed with Marlon at Lake Charles and was now assigned to Long Beach Air Force Base, was the best man. Terry's wife Ruby was also present.[11] According to the couple, the priest, Father Thomas F. Fogarty, was less than overjoyed to

---

* Before this trial could be held, McCall shot two of the "Groveland Four" who were in his custody and handcuffed, killing one and wounding the other. A third man was shot and killed by a Klan posse. After the shootings, Moore urged Governor Fuller Warren to suspend the sheriff; three weeks later Moore and his wife were killed. (www.fmuiv.edu/urbanaffairs/jem)

St. Brendan's Catholic Church, Los Angeles, California
(Courtesy Green family archives)

preside at the integrated wedding but, as Marlon said, "He performed the ceremony and, consequently, a good time was had by all. But I think his own preference would have been to the contrary."

The Greens faced another dilemma: Marlon was assigned to the 68th Strategic Reconnaissance Wing which had been activated in October 1951 at Lake Charles Air Base, Louisiana. Marlon and Eleanor knew they couldn't return to Louisiana as husband and wife because they would be violating that state's anti-miscegenation laws. Because of this, Marlon applied to the Air Force for a "compassionate transfer" to some state that would be more accepting of their mixed marriage. Acceding to his request, the Air Force came through with a transfer to the 91st Air Refueling Squadron at Lockbourne Air Force Base* in Ohio.[12]

---

* Lockbourne, named after a nearby town, was activated in June 1942. Lockbourne was renamed Rickenbacker Air National Guard Base in 1974.

The wedding of Eleanor Gallagher and Marlon Green at St. Brendan's in Los Angeles, December 29, 1951. The maid of honor is Joan Stanley and the best man is Captain Charles Terry, M.D., U.S. Air Force.
(Courtesy Green family archives)

Well-wishers greet Marlon and Eleanor after the wedding ceremony
(Courtesy Green family archives)

Eleanor moved to Columbus ahead of Marlon and began house hunting. She found a two-bedroom unit at the newly constructed Beverly Manor Apartments at 342 North Virginia Lee Road, adjacent to the upscale Bexley neighborhood, east of downtown Columbus; in May, Marlon arrived and the Greens were reunited. Eleanor related that the apartment manager was "less than pleased" to discover that her husband was a Negro.

To supplement Marlon's second-lieutenant's salary, Eleanor took a job as a social worker with Catholic Social Services. She said, "I think Marlon did not like the idea of my working. I made good friends there, but the job had its downside, in terms of many of the clients, and it was quite stressful." In the summer of 1952, Eleanor learned that she was pregnant.

Eleanor gave birth to Joseph Benedict Green on a March day in 1953, after thirty-one hours of labor at the Lockbourne Base Hospital. "Before the pregnancy I had had a medical procedure to remove a cyst," she related, "and the doctor told me on my return check-up that it was unlikely I would ever be able to have children because I had a 'structural problem.' Within three months I was pregnant with Joseph! So much for medical expertise!"

The Beverly Manor Apartments complex in which Marlon and Eleanor lived while he was stationed at Lockbourne Air Force Base, near Columbus, Ohio. The complex has since been torn down. (Courtesy Mary Ann Watson, 2005)

Eleanor (right) having lunch in the Greens' Columbus apartment with Helen McDaniel (left) her supervisor at Catholic Social Services, and co-worker Jane Gavin (center), 1953 (Courtesy Green family archives)

But Joseph was not a well baby. After he was born, he was diagnosed as having asthma and required a special diet and supplements in order to survive.[13]

* * *

SHORTY AFTER REPORTING for duty at Lockbourne, "Doc" Green was assigned to attend a six-week squadron officers' course at Maxwell Air Force Base in Montgomery, Alabama. Air Force pilots are required to log a certain number of flight hours each month in order to maintain proficiency and receive their flight pay. On weekends, to maintain his flight status, Marlon got in his monthly "hours" by signing out a plane and flying up to Lockbourne to spend two days with Eleanor. On Sunday nights he flew back to Maxwell.

At Maxwell, a subtle but no less pernicious form of racism reared its ugly head—the issue of white barbers cutting the hair of Negro customers. Marlon said, "We were required to get haircuts every two weeks, but the barber on the base refused to cut the hair of black customers." In a letter to Eleanor dated October 29, 1952, Marlon informed her that one day his section leader "approached me in a secretive but very sincere manner and informed me that they wouldn't cut my hair at the base barber shop.... The policy (by whose order I do not know) is not to cut the hair of Negroes in this barber shop and I was refused services when I went in."[14]

After making a verbal report of the incident to the base commander's office, he put the report in writing to the Air Training Command Inspector General. Marlon said, "The I. G. lacked the guts to do anything. Apparently, the problem was bigger than he could deal with. I had to go off base to get my hair cut."[15]

IN 1952, THE Cold War was a fact of life in America and around the world. Atomic-bomb testing was being carried out in desolate sections of the American Southwest and on remote Pacific islands, and school students regularly prac-

> **NEWS ITEM:**
>
> (Yanceyville, N.C., Nov. 11, 1952) Negro sharecropper Mack Ingram, 45, was convicted today by an all-white jury of assault by "leering" at a shapely, 19-year-old white girl at a distance of 60 feet. The incident occurred in this rural area on June 4, 1951.
>
> The girl, Mrs. Edward Webster, told the court that Ingram's leering so frightened her that she ran across a freshly plowed corn field to get away from him. Ingram faces a possible sentence of up to two years in prison. His lawyers said they would appeal the conviction.[16]

ticed "duck and cover" drills to be prepared in case of a nuclear attack. In order to be ready to retaliate at a moment's notice should the Soviet Union assault the United States, bombers from the Strategic Air Command (SAC), armed with atomic bombs and under the command of General Curtis E. LeMay, were continually in the sky and stationed at key sites around the world. Lockbourne Air Force Base was one of those SAC bases, and Marlon was one of the pilots who refueled the Boeing B-47 Stratojet bombers in mid-air.

The maneuver—using a converted, propeller-driven B-29 bomber as a flying gas station for the jet-powered B-47s and fighters—was not a job for the careless or faint-at-heart. Air Force history is replete with mid-air refueling disasters; performing the operation took a pilot with steady nerves and a steady hand—at both ends of the fuel pipeline. "Doc" Green performed the job with the skill of a surgeon.

It was life on the ground, however, that was becoming intolerable for Marlon. According to him, serving in SAC under LeMay was "oppressive. There were transfers on short notice with long absences. Many

Class photo of the C-97 training class in Palm Springs, Florida, 1952. The only Negro pilot in the class was Marlon Green (back row, second from right). (Courtesy Green family archives)

An aerial tanker of the type flown by Marlon Green performs the delicate and dangerous mission of refueling fighter jets in mid-air.
(Courtesy Green family archives)

people felt LeMay was a racist, egomaniac, and warmonger."[17]

Born in Columbus, Ohio, in 1906, Curtis Emerson LeMay was also considered by many to be one of the most powerful and controversial Air Force officers of all time. In 1942, as commanding general of the 3rd Bombardment Division, he had led bombing runs over Germany from England. In 1944, LeMay was transferred to the Pacific, where he headed the 20th Bomber Command in the China-Burma-India (CBI) theater. From there his bombers could—and did—decimate Japan; later in the war he became Chief of Staff of the Strategic Air Forces in the Pacific. After the war, he served in high positions at the Pentagon and was head of U.S. Air Forces in Europe. In 1948, he was selected to command SAC, headquartered at Offutt Air Force Base, near Omaha, Nebraska; Lockbourne was under the aegis of SAC.

LeMay's unflattering nickname—behind his back, of course—was "Iron Ass," due to his demanding, hard-driving, highly critical style. A story that circulated through the SAC ranks was that one day as he puffed on his ever-present cigar while approaching a fully fueled B-52 bomber on the flightline, a brave guard requested that he put out the stogie. "The plane might catch fire and blow up, sir," the guard warned. "It wouldn't dare," growled LeMay in reply.*[18]

General Curtis E. LeMay, commanding general of the Strategic Air Command (SAC) (Courtesy National Archives)

---

* In 1968, LeMay became the running mate for American Independent Party presidential candidate (and former segregationist Alabama governor) George Wallace. Many are convinced that LeMay's belligerent, warmongering stance led to his and Wallace's resounding defeat.

Marlon had the misfortune to cross paths with LeMay, who had come to Lockbourne for a visit on a day Marlon was on duty as the Airdrome Officer. "Every day at a flying facility, there's an officer—a pilot—who is assigned to be the Airdrome Officer," explained Marlon. "You wear an armband that says 'A.O.' You check a lot of things: the lighting along the runway to see if all is in working order; the fire station, to see if sufficient staff are on duty; and you greet any VIPs who may arrive at your base during your twenty-four hours on duty as the Airdrome Officer.

"I was a second lieutenant at the time, and was the last man in the greeting line for LeMay; I think there were seven people in the line. LeMay went down the line and shook six hands; the seventh hand—mine—he didn't shake. It was hurtful to me, this experience. I felt slighted because of the color of my skin and his disdain for that color, as I later heard rumors that he was a racist."

Curtis LeMay wasn't the only officer who rubbed Marlon the wrong way. He also had a run-in with another general at Lockbourne—the base commander, Brigadier General Clifford S. Hovik. "He was number two on my list of Curtis LeMay-type personalities," Marlon said, "with initials to fit: C. S. Hovik. Clifford 'Chicken-Shit' Hovik."

Marlon's antipathy toward Hovik centered around an incident involving mittens. Instead of wearing regulation gray wool gloves during an inspection one day, Marlon had on a pair of non-regulation, gray wool mittens with black leather palms. Hovik saw this breach of military discipline and gave Marlon forty demerits, known as "stripes." As a result, Marlon believes his promotion from second to first lieutenant was delayed for six months. Marlon noted, "You had to be a grand foul-up not to be promoted from second lieutenant to first after you completed eighteen months. I think it was nothing more than the mittens incident that held up my promotion for six months beyond. It was exactly two years from my commission date to my being promoted from second to first lieutenant." Following on the heels of the racial slights and outright discrimination he had had already received in Hawaii and elsewhere, Marlon added the "mittens incident," LeMay's snub, the barber shop, and the delayed promotion to his growing list of resentments against the "desegregated" Air Force.[19]

TO GET AWAY from the "chicken-shit" atmosphere of Lockbourne, in June 1953 Marlon volunteered for combat duty in Korea, where the war was winding down. Eleanor said she couldn't recall specifically if Marlon had "volunteered," but remembers vividly that he was "not happy" with his assignment at Lockbourne. "A couple of incidents were very hurtful to him," she recalled, "and he may have 'volunteered' without giving me an explanation of why he did so."

The Air Force temporarily assigned him to Vance Air Force Base at Enid, Oklahoma, for additional training; as it was only a temporary change of duty stations, Eleanor stayed behind in Columbus to care for Joseph. Eleanor's mother came to Columbus briefly to see the new baby and make sure Joseph and Eleanor were doing all right.[20]

In June 1953, Marlon had been in Oklahoma for less than a month when a cease fire was agreed to by the North Koreans and the United Nations' forces; the Korean War went on permanent hold. Marlon joked, "When the North Koreans heard I was coming, they copped a truce!"

With his services not required in Korea, Marlon was transferred to Mitchel Air Force Base in Hempstead, Long Island, New York. But before reporting to Mitchel, Marlon was sent to Wilmington, Delaware, to qualify in the Douglas B-26 "Invader" bomber, which he would be flying in his next assignment.

In November 1953 Marlon, Eleanor, and baby Joseph moved into a rented home at 306 Mitchel Avenue, East Meadow, Long Island. In June 1954, the Greens' second child, Maria Theresa, came into the world.[21]

The Hempstead Plains, an area where the air base was located, has a long and storied military history. During the Revolutionary War, the British troops were encamped there; during the War of 1812, it was an American post. It was also a military base during the war with Mexico (1846-1848), and was known as Camp Winfield Scott during the Civil War. During the Spanish-American War (1898-1899), the name was changed to Camp Black. After being used as a supply depot and training camp for the 42nd ("Rainbow") Infantry Division during World War I, its name was changed to Mitchel Field, in honor of Major John P. Mitchel, a former mayor of New York, who died in a training-flight accident in 1918.*[22]

---

* The base was permanently closed in 1961.

A Martin B-26 bomber similar to the type flown by Marlon Green while assigned to the 2nd Tow Target Squadron (Courtesy National Archives)

At the base, Doc was assigned to the 2nd Tow Target Squadron, where he flew B-26 aircraft that, as the name of his unit implies, towed aerial targets for gunnery practice—and prayed that no one would mistake his plane for the target! (The targets were long, red sleeves made of cloth and towed via a cable a half-mile long. Most missions were flown far out to sea off Montauk Point, Long Island.)[23]

With Marlon a "rag-drag" pilot, Air Force life at Mitchel settled into a predictable routine. He had never given the idea of space flight much thought until 1955, when he heard that the Air Force was looking for volunteers for experimental test-pilot training.* Although the American space program was still many years in the future, the top test pilots

---

* In 1947, the U.S. Air Force's Flight Performance School moved from Dayton, Ohio, to Muroc Air Base in Southern California's dry Mojave Desert and was renamed the Experimental Flight Test Pilot School. Although many astronauts were later graduates of the school, perhaps its most illustrious alumnus was Chuck Yeager who, on October 14, 1947, flew the Bell X-1, America's first research rocket aircraft. Shortly thereafter, in the XS-1, Yeager became the first pilot to break the sound barrier. (www.edwards.af.mil)

became eligible for a new program that would eventually be known as Project Mercury—America's effort to put a man into outer space and return him safely to Earth.

Marlon threw his name into the hat. On March 16, 1955, he applied for the training and his application began moving up the chain of command. He didn't really expect to be selected, but his life had been marked by shooting for the impossible and getting it, so what was there to lose? After all, hadn't he become an Air Force pilot without having graduated from—or even attended, except for a brief stint at a seminary—college? If he could do that, who was to say that becoming an experimental test pilot or an astronaut was impossible? After all, he had the requisite thousand hours of flying time, even though none of them were in jets.

Surprisingly, approval was recommended by his squadron commander, Lieutenant Colonel Ralph L. Knapp:

> Lt. Green possesses a very high degree of piloting skill.... In addition to his skill Lt. Green's greatest asset is his eager attitude and willingness to fly. While other squadron duty pilots average 30 hours per month he will average 50 or 60 hours. He has indicated a very great interest in experimental and test flight, and should prove very effective in this type of assignment.
>
> After completing the training requested, Lt. Green could be trusted with making wise decisions concerning flying qualities and suitability of future Air Force aircraft.[24]

The application was forwarded to the Ninth Air Force and the Tactical Air Command, which also gave its approval. Marlon's application, however, turned out to be a waste of ink and paper; the government was looking for pilots with an overwhelming resumé: thousands of hours in high-performance jets, plus considerable time as test pilots, an advanced degree in a highly technical field and, if possible, combat experience—everything that author Tom Wolfe called "The Right Stuff."

Not surprisingly, Marlon's quest to become a test pilot ended on a desk at the headquarters of the U.S. Air Force Experimental Flight Test Center at Edwards Air Force Base, California, on June 28, 1955. Here the Center's Selection Board rejected his application "for lack of educational prerequisites."[25]

Marlon kept towing those targets and gradually forgot his brief dreams of becoming a test pilot.*

———•┼•••———

IN JULY 1955, the Greens' third child, Peter Vincent, was born. With Marlon away much of the time, towing targets over the Atlantic, Eleanor had her hands full with three children.[26]

———•┼•••———

IN 1955 RACIAL attitudes in some quarters began to undergo a sea change. That year, a young Negro Broadway actor burst upon American movie screens in a convention-challenging film titled *Blackboard Jungle.* With Sidney Poitier's intense portrayal of a conflicted high-school student, black actors were suddenly seen as more than just mammies and porters and doormen and jungle inhabitants and slaves—background extras who could comfortably blend in with the wallpaper. Here was a brilliant star in black skin. Sidney Poitier, perhaps unlike any other black celebrity before him, did not

NEWS ITEM:
(New York, Jan. 7, 1955) Marian Anderson, the 57-year-old contralto who was barred because of her color from singing in 1939 at Washington, D.C.'s Constitution Hall by the Daughters of the American Revolution, became the first Negro singer to perform with New York's Metropolitan Opera, performing the role of Ulrica in Verdi's *Masked Ball.*

The orchestra was forced to temporarily halt several times during the performance due to the thunderous and sustained applause Miss Anderson received.[27]

---

* In 1963, Air Force Captain Edward J. Dwight, Jr. was nominated to be the first African-American astronaut but did not make the final selection. The first black pilot accepted into NASA's astronaut program was Robert H. Lawrence, Jr. (1967). Tragically, Lawrence was killed in an aviation accident before his space launch was scheduled. The first African-American to fly in space was Air Force Colonel Guion S. Bluford, Jr. (1983) aboard the space shuttle *Challenger;* he made three additional flights. The first black female astronaut was Mae C. Jemison, M.D. (1992); Bernard A. Harris, Jr. was the first African-American to walk in space (1995). (Hardesty, 76-77)

just cross the color line—he threw a six-span cantilevered bridge over it.*

Then, in August 1955, news of the gruesome murder of Emmett Till tore across the country like a tsunami, extinguishing the flicker of hope that race relations in America were slowly getting better; that the *Brown v. Board of Education* decision meant that schools would finally desegregate; that whites and Negroes would learn to live in harmony. The murder of young Emmett Till, so savage and violent and hateful, proved otherwise. A great many people felt that all of the small-but-important civil-rights gains that had recently been made had been thrown into the Tallahatchie River, along with the teenager's brutalized body. Paul Hendrickson, author of *Sons of Mississippi*, wrote,

> *Jet* magazine, in showing the photographs of the battered corpse a little while after the killing, reported to its readers that when Till was pulled from the sludge-green river, a piece of skull three inches square fell loose from his head. Those pictures in *Jet* helped awaken a generation of future black activists to what would soon, in the next decade, be called "the movement." That's the true legacy of the lynching of Emmett Till—it put so many eyes on the eventual prize.[28]

DESPITE THE FACT that Marlon declared B-26 duty at Mitchel his "most enjoyable assignment," the Air Force had different plans for him. "I put in a preference for the B-66 "Destroyer" bomber, which was newly in service at that time. It was a twin-jet, light bomber designed by the same designer of the B-26, which I flew and loved. I wanted the next assignment to be as a pilot of the B-66. It turned out that the Air Force didn't grant that assignment but, instead, assigned me to amphibian rescue service with the Grumman SA-16 'Albatross' aircraft."

The SA-16 Albatross was a twin engine, high-wing aircraft—the

---

* Over the next decade, Poitier went on to play a variety of roles in critically acclaimed and high grossing interracial dramas such as *Something of Value* (1957); *Raisin in the Sun* (1961); *Lilies of the Field* (1963); *A Patch of Blue* (1965); *The Defiant Ones* (1966); *To Sir, With Love* (1967); *In the Heat of the Night* (1967); and *Guess Who's Coming to Dinner* (1968), among others, that rocketed him the type of Hollywood stardom formerly reserved only for white actors. (Katz, 918)

Lieutenant Marlon Green and white classmates at the SA-16 ("Albatross")
training class, West Palm Beach Air Force Base, Florida, 1956
(Courtesy Green family archives)

biggest amphibian Grumman ever built. It was an air-rescue vehicle and
had a crew of five: pilot, co-pilot, navigator, radio operator, and mechanic. It could land on the water and had retractable landing gear, enabling
it to also land on hard surfaces, and it had pontoons out on each wing
for flotation and stability. At one time, the Navy and Coast Guard both
employed it. Marlon noted, "In the fifties and sixties, wherever a flier was
down, there was an SA-16 somewhere in the area. So my next assignment
after Mitchel was training in the SA-16 in West Palm Beach, Florida."

MILITARY PERSONNEL AND their families never stay in one place for
very long, and soon Marlon received orders transferring him to Johnson
Air Base at Irumagawa, Japan. It was an "accompanied" tour, which
meant the entire Green family would be moving overseas. Marlon was
anticipating a three-year tour of duty with the 36th Air Rescue Squadron
whose mission, as the name says, was to rescue downed fliers.[29]

Eleanor's father, meanwhile, maintained his hardened attitude
toward her marriage to a Negro, and she was distraught over his

SA-16 "Albatross" amphibious rescue plane of the type flown by Marlon Green
(Courtesy National Archives)

recalcitrance, especially since she and Marlon had three children her father had never seen. Eleanor also knew that her father was not well; a heavy smoker all his life, he had developed a serious heart condition, and she was not sure how much longer he had to live; she feared he would die before seeing his grandchildren and meeting her husband.

Fate suddenly intervened to rectify the situation.

On a Sunday in the summer of 1956, about a month before the Greens were due to depart for Japan, they attended Mass at the Mitchel Air Force Base chapel and were returning to their housing on the base. At it happened, Eleanor's sister Anne lived in Westbury, New York, almost next door to the base; Anne told Eleanor that their parents would be visiting her over the weekend. Anne didn't invite Marlon and Eleanor over because she was afraid her father would not be open for a meeting after so many years of distance and hard feelings.

"There was also a time when Anne would not have been open to such a meeting, either," said Eleanor, "but she had since had a change of heart." On the way home from Mass, Eleanor, realizing that she and Marlon and the three children were only about a block from Anne's house, screwed up her courage and proposed to Marlon that the five of

Eleanor's parents, Anna and William, with Marlon, holding Peter, Maria, and Joseph, in Westbury, New York, shortly before the Greens departed for Japan.
(Courtesy Green family archives)

them drop in uninvited and unannounced; Marlon agreed. Not knowing what kind of reception they would receive, Eleanor suggested that Marlon and the kids wait in the car while she went in to test the familial waters.

"It was summer and it was warm," she said. "The front door was open and through the screen door I could see my father alone in the living room. I opened the door and went in and said, 'Hi, Dad.' He put his arms around me and we embraced. I can't recall if my mother and sister then came into the room, but I said to him, 'Marlon and the children are out in the car.' Somebody said, 'Well, everybody, come in.'

"The meeting between Marlon and my father was polite and warm at the same time, because it was unexpected and there were no anxieties built up—it just happened. I can't recall how long we stayed. All I recall is that it was a *gift* that this happened. There was a reconciliation. About a month later, when we were ready to pack up and leave New York, Anne organized a family picnic. My mother and father came back for it. For my father to see the children and meet Marlon face to face was good, very good."[30]

CHAPTER 6:
ESCAPADE IN JAPAN

MOVING A FAMILY overseas is a big job but, fortunately for military families, the government picks up the expenses. Moving Eleanor was harder; she was pregnant again—this time with her fourth child, Monica—but having complications. Ordered to bed by her doctor, Eleanor was hospitalized at the Presidio in San Francisco and prohibited from traveling to Japan until her condition stabilized; Marlon flew on ahead. While she was in the hospital, a family friend, Patty Ruegg, took care of Joseph, Maria, and Peter.

Eleanor and the three children then spent a couple of months at an apartment in San Mateo, California. She finally got clearance to make the trip, and Monica Helen Green was born in Japan in August 1956.[1]

MARLON INITIALLY FOUND his assignment at Johnson Air Base in Japan interesting and rewarding. Because the war next door in Korea had evolved into a tense truce, there were no shot-down pilots needing to be rescued. Most of his and the squadron's time was spent in rescue training.[*2]

---

* Shortly after Japan's capitulation in September 1945, the Japanese Army Air Base at Irumagawa was renamed Johnson Air Base. During World War II, Irumagawa Field was home to the Toyo-oka Flying School, which trained thousands of Japanese pilots for their war against the Americans and other Western allies in the Pacific. Here trained many of the aviators who attacked Pearl Harbor on December 7, 1941, which propelled the United States into the conflict. Near the end of the war, Irumagawa Field was also a prime training facility for *kamikaze* suicide pilots.

During the Korean conflict, Johnson was a key base for many strategic units that carried out missions against the North Koreans and Red Chinese. Besides hosting Marlon's 36th Air Rescue Squadron, Johnson Air Base also was home to the U.S. Fifth Air Force headquarters, 41st Air Division, 3rd Bombardment Wing, 35th Fighter Group, and 8th Photo Recon Squadron, among other units. (users.evl.net)

Japan was fascinating—a far cry from anything the Greens had known before—with its strange language, beautiful scenery, and different customs. The family lived off the base in a housing development built for American military families in Irumagawa. A helper, Akiko Nakamura, was hired by the Greens to prepare lunch for the children and keep the small house tidy.

Eleanor enjoyed living in Irumagawa. "The house we lived in was built by the Japanese in the Japanese view of what an American house would be. The homes had little porches on the front, and they had kitchens that approximated their idea of what an American kitchen would be. But the bathroom looked like a Japanese bathroom and it was wonderful. We also had acres and acres of tea fields adjacent to our home and an incredible view of Mount Fuji, which was about fifty or sixty miles away."[3]

Marlon (left) and his brother James, who was also in the Air Force at the same time, join a small group of tourists at the Imperial Palace in downtown Tokyo, 1956.
(Courtesy Green family archives)

Eleanor, Marlon, and kids with Akiko Nakamura in Japan, 1957
(Courtesy Green family archives)

Eleanor enjoyed taking advantage of the many cross-cultural opportunities that the area offered. Irumagawa, located on the Kanto Plain in
Saitama Prefecture (the equivalent of an American state), is approximately thirty miles northwest of the heart of Tokyo. It is perhaps most
famous for its Tanabata Festival on the first weekend in August, which
includes hundreds of small vendor stalls, colorful parades, spectacular
fireworks shows, and elaborate decorations all over town. Tanabata is
one of the biggest festivals in Saitama and is visited by some 200,000
people over the two-day period.[4]

While Marlon was on duty, Eleanor occupied her time by taking
courses in Japanese flower arranging and helping four-year-old Joseph
learn to speak Japanese. With Marlon, the family sometimes went to
the Ginza—Tokyo's main shopping district. It being only eleven years
since the end of World War II, there were still visible scars throughout
the area: buildings and whole blocks that had yet to be repaired following the countless bombing raids and devastating fires. The Japanese
people, however, were invariably polite to their American occupiers.
And the Japanese seemed to be entirely "race neutral;" neither Marlon

nor Eleanor recalled any incidents of discrimination or non-acceptance of their mixed marriage.[5]

Surrounded by water, Japan has a very humid climate—on a par with New Orleans—which caused Joseph's asthmatic condition to worsen. Marlon felt perhaps the best thing for Joseph was for the family to be transferred to some less-humid place back in the States. Eleanor related that after Marlon took Joseph for one of his regular check-ups at the medical center on base, he requested a transfer back to the United States because of his son's health, but his request was refused. "I personally didn't think it was necessary to leave Japan," she said. "I thought that, with medication, Joseph's asthma could be controlled." But Marlon was determined to be transferred.

In November 1956, Eleanor received a telegram from the States informing her that her father had passed away on Armistice Day, November 11. "Because of our previous meeting at my sister Anne's house," Eleanor said, "I felt we had made our reconciliation and that there was no real need for me to fly back for the funeral." Besides, trying to get a seat back to Boston in time on an Air Force plane would have been very complicated.

In lieu of her going back, Navy Chaplain Father John Carr, a former elementary schoolmate of Eleanor, paid a personal visit to the Greens in Irumagawa. "He knew my whole family," she said. "He told my mother that he was going to Japan and would look me up, which he did. He came by and talked about my father's death. The visit helped to bring closure."[6]

—‒ • • ╷ • • ‒—

THE CONSTANT RESCUE training was beginning to bore Marlon. A few days before Christmas 1956, though, a call for a real rescue finally came in. "Five airmen at a radar station on a mountaintop were stranded by a snowstorm," Marlon recalled, "so we were sent out to make an emergency air drop of supplies."[7]

The mission was fraught with difficulties; indeed, an attempted air drop the previous day by another crew was called off due to hazardous flying conditions. But First Lieutenant Green and five crewmen, knowing that other men's lives depended on their accomplishing the mission, climbed into their SA-16 Albatross on the morning of December

23 and headed for the radar outpost atop a snow-shrouded, 1,800-foot-high peak 100 miles north of Nagoya—a two-hour flight from Johnson.

Snow flurries, poor visibility, and high winds made finding the radar station "interesting," according to Marlon, but his navigator was able to pinpoint the location. From an altitude of less than 100 feet, six bundles of food and clothing were expertly dropped into a fifty-foot-square area; due to the high winds, no parachutes were used. The grateful men atop the peak reported the free-fall drop as "perfect."[8]

———•·•·•·———

IN EARLY 1957, while Marlon was serving as duty officer at his Johnson Air Base desk, veteran RKO Studios movie producer/director Arthur Lubin (perhaps best known for his *Francis, the Talking Mule* comedies) breezed into the office, looking for a location and some extras for a scene in a movie he was shooting, *Escapade in Japan*.

The thin plot involved a young boy who is saved from a plane crash at sea by a Japanese fishing-boat family and makes friends with their son. Thinking they have broken the law, the two boys set out on an adventurous trip to Tokyo while being pursued by the authorities who only want to reunite them with their parents.*

Seeing the handsome First Lieutenant Green at the desk, Lubin asked Marlon if he'd like to have a bit part in the film, adding that he would "win Brownie points with the NAACP" if there were blacks visible on screen. Being a natural ham, Marlon agreed.

Marlon's big scene: The phone on his desk rings, he picks it up, says, "Thirty-sixth Air Rescue Squadron, Lieutenant Green." He is informed that there is a "distressed plane in your area." Marlon turns and presses a button on the wall, sounding an alarm that scrambled the crews. Elapsed screen time: less than ten seconds. It wasn't exactly the starring role he had envisioned for himself as the handsome actor "Dark Fable" back in 1939 in El Dorado, but the half day it took to film the scene was a pleasant diversion nonetheless.

———•·•·•·———

---

* The film starred Cameron Mitchell (best known for his stage and screen appearances as "Happy" in *Death of A Salesman*), Teresa Wright (who won the Best Supporting Actress Oscar for her role in *Mrs. Miniver*), and an up-and-coming actor by the name of Clint Eastwood; Academy-Award winner Max Steiner (*Gone With The Wind*) wrote the musical score. (Katz, passim)

An assistant cameraman uses a clap board to begin
Marlon's big scene in the 1956 Hollywood film, *Escapade in Japan.*
(Courtesy Green family archives)

ONCE THE FILMING was complete and the artificial excitement of
movie production gone, Air Force routine returned to Johnson. With
few actual downed aircraft in the vicinity of Japan or Korea requiring
rescue, the job at the 36th Air Rescue Squadron grew dull and unrewarding again for Marlon. It was all training, maintenance, training,
inspections, training.

Marlon began to get restless. Perhaps the cause was the Air Force's
stultifying bureaucracy, or the often-senseless rules, or the low pay. Or
it might have been hearing about some of the other pilots at Johnson
who were resigning their commissions to take high-paying jobs with the
rapidly expanding civilian airline industry back in the States. Airline
pay was good—better than good—outstanding. An airline pilot could
make in two or three months what an Air Force pilot earned in a year.

Marlon ruminated over the possibility of submitting his application,
too, but heard that the airlines wouldn't even consider hiring any pilot
who was still on active military duty. The prospects did not seem too
bright, but he had never before backed down from a challenge.

Then came a news story that really whetted his desire to leave the service and fly for a commercial carrier. "I read about it in the *Air Force Times*," Marlon said. The gist of the article was that the commercial airlines were "re-thinking" their policies of racial segregation toward flight-crew members and would soon make a dramatic change to that policy. Even though the news was several months old—the *New York Times* and *Time* magazine had reported the information back in October 1956—it was brand new to Marlon, and he was intrigued.[9]

In the fall of 1956, Averill Harriman was running for re-election as governor of New York, and he had used the New York State Fair Employment Practices Commission to bolster his campaign effort by coercing a statement from the air carriers serving New York state, reiterating their 'policy of non-discrimination.'"

The original article, published in the *New York Times* on October 2, 1956, reported on an agreement that was reached between the New York State Commission Against Discrimination and Allegheny, American, Braniff, Capital, Delta, Eastern, Flying Tigers, Mohawk, National, New York, Northeast, Northwest, Pan American, Riddle, Seaboard and Western, Slick, TransWorld, and United Airlines. The story said that the airlines agreed to a "policy statement" that would open the way for the hiring of minorities for cockpit and cabin positions. Only Seaboard and Western, the reporter noted, had a Negro pilot, but that airline flew only cargo, not passengers.

The article also said that the airlines previously had been hesitant to hire Negro pilots for fear of how their Southern passengers and white crewmembers might react, but would henceforth judge applicants only on their qualfications as pilots "without regard to race, creed, color or national origin."[10]

The *Time* article said essentially the same thing, adding that President Eisenhower's Committee on Government Contracts had met with the presidents of eleven airlines and urged them to desegregate the cockpit. Some of the presidents did not deny that a ban against Negro crewmembers existed, "but promised to eliminate it gradually. Last week's statement was one of the first big steps in this direction.... At week's end, the Air Line Pilots Association, the Air Line Stewards and Stewardesses union and the Flight Engineers International Association promised that Negro applicants would be welcome."[11]

Marlon also noted that the article said that Negro pilots seldom had enough training in four-engine aircraft; he had over 3,000 hours!

Marlon was thrilled by the news and began to seriously think about resigning from the Air Force and becoming an airline pilot.

He believed that with his extensive multi-engine experience, and with the airlines and airline-related unions now stating that they would "welcome" Negro applicants, it would not be a matter of beating the bushes in search of employment but of deciding which of the many offers that would undoubtedly come his way to accept.[12]

CHAPTER 7:
ROCKS IN HIS JAWS

As IN SO many other areas of endeavor, African-Americans found acceptance in the world of aviation akin to flying into a very stiff headwind—of hurricane velocity.

Although the Wright Brothers succeeded in powered flight in 1903, the first license for a Negro pilot in the United States was not issued for two more decades. Surprisingly, perhaps, it was issued to a woman, Bessie Coleman, from northeastern Texas.

Born into poverty in 1892 in tiny Atlanta, Texas, the ambitious Bessie (she was primarily self-taught) graduated from high school and attended one semester at the Colored Agricultural and Normal University (now Langston University) in Langston, Oklahoma.

A lack of finances forced her to drop out and she moved to Chicago in 1915 where she shared an apartment with two of her brothers. She attended beauty school and found work as a manicurist in a barber shop. But she had seen a newsreel about aviation and began to dream about a career in the skies. Her brother John, who was a soldier in the American Expeditionary Force in France, told her stories about French women learning to fly. As a result of his prodding, Bessie decided that anything French women could do, she could do better. She applied to numerous flight schools across the U.S. but, due to her race and sex, no one was willing to admit her. Based on the advice of a friend, she found a better-paying job and began saving up for a move to France, all the while teaching herself French. After also talking several sources into funding her dream, the gutsy young woman, in November 1920, sailed for Paris.

Within seven months, she had completed the ten-month course at the *Ecole d'Aviation des Frérès Caudron* (Caudron Brothers' Flying School) in Le Crotoy, the Somme, where she quickly learned to do loops, barrel rolls, and spins in a Nieuport over the same cratered battlefields that had been the scene of years of ferocious fighting during the Great War. She received her license on June 15, 1921—the only

Bessie Coleman, first African-American to earn a pilot's license
(Courtesy Smithsonian National Air & Space Museum)

woman out of the sixty candidates to graduate from the *Federation Aeronautique Internationale* during a six-month period, and the first Negro American aviator to earn a pilot's license.

Once back in the U.S., she hoped to open the first flight school for Negroes and make her living in aviation, but the racial barriers were too high. Becoming a barnstormer—an aerial daredevil—seemed to offer her a way to fly and make money. She flew in her first air show in Garden City, New York, in 1922; her beauty, style, and grace (and some crafty promotion by air-show operators around the country) helped her become a celebrity. She not only broke down gender barriers but also racial ones, refusing to perform in Texas unless both black and white spectators were allowed to enter the air-show grounds through the same admission gate (the audiences, however, remained segregated in the bleachers).

Her career was cut tragically short on April 30, 1926. While testing a stunt plane before an air show in Jacksonville, Florida, her mechanic, who was piloting the JN4D "Jenny" from the front seat, lost control and the plane flipped. During the ensuing seconds of violent maneuvers, Bessie, who was not strapped in, fell out of the open cockpit to her death; the mechanic also crashed and died. But her legacy did not die with her; several Bessie Coleman Aero Clubs were established where Negroes learned to fly. [1]

Another early Negro aviator to gain fame was Hubert Julian, born in either 1897 or 1900, and nicknamed "The Black Eagle." Two years after Charles A. Lindbergh's historic 1927 trans-Atlantic flight, Julian duplicated the feat. In 1931, he became the first Negro pilot to make a transcontinental flight across the United States. He later trained with the Tuskegee Airmen but did not see combat.[2]

After Julian came August H. "Augie" Martin, who trained pilots in World War II. Finding the cockpit doors of commercial airlines barred to him after the war, Martin was hired, according to author Stan Solomon, by "low-prestige 'non-scheds' or supplemental carriers such as World Airways. In 1949, he became a captain, but not with a U.S.-based airline. The fledgling El Al, national airline of the new Jewish state of Israel, hired him. Then came a job as a test pilot for Lockheed and finally, in 1955, the job he kept until his death—flying for Seaboard and Western Air (later Seaboard World), a cargo carrier eventually absorbed by Flying Tigers." Martin was killed in 1968 when his plane crashed while on a mercy flight delivering emergency medical supplies to war-torn Nigeria.[3]

On February 5, 1957, Perry H. Young, Jr., the first American Negro pilot generally credited with carrying passengers on a commercial flight, flew into history. At the controls of a twelve-passenger New York Airways helicopter, Young, who had been an instructor at Tuskegee in World War II, made the nine-minute trip from La Guardia Airport to Idlewild.* Like Orville Wright's flight in 1903, Young's journey was short, but its historic implications were enormous.[4]

Still, despite the abundant proof that Negro pilots could fly just as competently as white pilots, no major American airline was willing to become a pioneer and integrate the cockpit.** The airlines *did* hire Negroes—to clean the planes or handle the baggage—but not for the cockpit or passenger cabin positions. When it came to pilots, each and every major airline closed the cockpit doors to any Negro pilot who dared apply for a job.

---

* The airport's name was changed to John F. Kennedy International in December 1963.

** Nor were airlines in any rush to integrate the cabin. It was not until 1958 that the New England regional carrier Mohawk Airlines became the first airline to hire a black flight attendant—Ruth Carol Taylor. (*Jet*, May 12, 1997)

MARLON PONDERED THE difficult choice confronting him: Should he quit the Air Force which, in spite of its faults, had trained him to fly, was giving him the opportunity for advancement (he had once envisioned himself becoming a general like Benjamin O. Davis), was mostly shielding him from overt racial discrimination, and was providing him and his family with security and the opportunity to see the world on the government's dime? Should he abandon all of that and, in effect, leap into the unknown without a parachute from a craft that wasn't in trouble, bouyed only by the slim hope of landing a job with one of the major airlines—none of which had ever hired a Negro pilot? The decision was agonizing and Marlon paced back and forth in his mind, trying to decide which way to turn.[5]

At this point, something fundamental in Marlon changed—something Eleanor has never quite understood. "In Japan," she said, "Marlon became sullen and angry. I hesitate to use the word 'depressed,' but I began noticing the anger and difference in his behavior. He never talked about his feelings and he has never talked about what the anger was, but I know it had something to do with the fact that some officers in the squadron were leaving the Air Force and getting well-paying airline jobs. He realized he didn't want to stay in, that he wanted a career in commercial aviation." Marlon began taking out his anger and frustration on the children—not physically, but verbally—belittling them and putting them down.

When Eleanor wrote to her sister Paula—who had been a flight attendant with American Airlines but at that time was working in American's Flushing, New York, office—and told her about Marlon's desire to change careers, Paula was aghast. She hurriedly wrote back, telling Eleanor that the scuttlebutt in the office was that the airlines really had no intention of hiring Negro pilots—Harriman's statement was just a political ploy designed to curry favor with minorities prior to the election. Paula implored her sister to try and talk Marlon out of resigning his commission.

Eleanor enjoyed Japan and did not want to leave—certainly not if Marlon had no firm prospects for employment. After all, they now had four young children, with a fifth on the way. But Marlon would not be dissuaded; he had his heart set on piloting airliners and earning substantially more money than the Air Force was paying him.

When Marlon wouldn't listen to her, Eleanor went to the base chaplain

Eleanor's sister, Paula Gallagher, photographed in the late 1950s while she was a flight attendant for American Airlines
(Courtesy Green archives)

to express her concerns and to show him the letter her sister had sent. Eleanor said, "The chaplain agreed with me that it was risky for Marlon to think that he could get a job with the airlines. The chaplain was a friend of the commanding general of Johnson Air Base, so he talked to the general and the general called Marlon and said, 'I hear you're wanting to leave the Air Force and become a commercial airline pilot.' Marlon said he was. The general told him to give it more time and think it over, but Marlon wouldn't change his mind." The process of separation from the service went forward.

Before leaving Japan, Marlon sent off letters of application to all the major American carriers, letting them know of his qualifications and upcoming availability; once he returned to the U.S., he would begin following up. (With some irony, Marlon was promoted to captain just before he left Japan.)

In late March, Marlon's application for resignation of his Air Force commission was granted and, in early April 1957, the Greens said their goodbyes, boarded a military transport ship in Yokohama harbor along with their car, a 1955 Chevy they had dubbed "Silver," and sailed back to the States, arriving in Seattle on April 20, 1957.[6]

Two days later, Marlon went in person to United Airlines' Seattle office to apply for a pilot's job. Lloyd Powell, placement interviewer for United in Seattle, gave him an application form to fill out and then administered written aptitude and psychological profile tests; Marlon waited while the tests were scored. Powell then informed him that there were two "soft spots" in his application: his lack of a college degree and a low score on the aptitude test. Powell said that Marlon was rejected on the basis of the tests, stating, "We regret that it was necessary to make this decision in Mr. Green's case but the decision would have been the same regardless of his racial background. Other Caucasian applicants with equal or greater technical qualifications have likewise been eliminated when test information has shown temperamental handicaps similar to Mr. Green's."*[7]

Feeling disturbed by the test results and the United interview, Marlon drove down to Parks Air Force Base in Pleasanton, California, so he could be officially discharged.[8]

Harry and Rose Cox, friends of the Greens, in San Mateo, California, September 1956 (Courtesy Green family archives)

---

* Marlon disagreed, and filed a complaint against United. In November 1957 an investigator for the airline found that "there was no evidence of a discriminatory practice against Mr. Green. The scoring, when checked with the 'master sheet,' has been done correctly. The official who did the scoring states that Mr. Green's test reflects a very positive attitude in matters of personal taste and prejudice and that it reflects a man who would not respond quickly or without panic in an emergency." (Findings of investigator, Nov. 29, 1957, Green family archives)

But bad luck dogged the Greens upon their return to the United States. In the San Francisco area, they stayed in San Mateo at the home of friends Harry and Rose Cox, where they were rattled by an earthquake. Seven-month-old Monica then came down with an infection from an innoculation she was given by a nurse on board the ship as they sailed toward Seattle. Some of the children then got the mumps, which Eleanor, pregnant again, also caught.[9]

Learning that a United Airlines official was going to make a presentation on integration and the airline industry in nearby San Francisco, Marlon drove into the city to attend the public meeting. In a letter to William P. Rogers, U.S. Attorney General, and James R. Durfee, Chairman of the Civil Aeronautics Board, Marlon noted that Russel F. Ahrens, United Airlines' Vice-President of Personnel, said at the meeting, "We, the scheduled airlines, have told the President of the United States that we will not hire Negroes for flight crew duty at this time because we are not ready for integration."

Marlon also said, "Though United has the fewest 'southern' cities on its routes of any of the Big Four (American, Eastern, TWA, and United), Mr. Ahrens said the airlines were fearful that Negro flight crew members would not be served at airport restaurants and hotels in southern cities where their crew assignments might require them to lay over."

Stunned by Ahrens's statement, especially since it came "almost seven months to the day after United had participated in a 'reiteration' of policy on non-discrimination," Marlon then went to check again on his application with United; perhaps there had been a change of heart. There was some hemming and some hawing, and then H. L. Pollard, United's Employment Director in San Francisco, "told me face to face: 'Even if your qualifications were one-hundred-percent perfect, we would not hire you because of your race.'"[10]

Amazed and dismayed by Pollard's forthrightness, the Greens departed California and headed east, only to be stranded overnight in a fierce spring blizzard in South Dakota; a state trooper came to their rescue. After spending several days in Rapid City, South Dakota, with Ed Kammerer, a friend of Eleanor from her days at Xavier, the Greens continued their trek eastward (with Eleanor still recovering from the mumps). The Greens reached New York where, said Eleanor, "We spent perhaps three days looking for a place to stay and briefly checking out options for Marlon's job search. At that point, money loomed as a serious issue, and Marlon decided to call relatives in Lansing, Michigan, to see if they could provide temporary housing."[11]

"They were generous enough to put us up—a horde of Marlon Greens arriving in town," Marlon said. "They sheltered us and helped us with feeding and care."[12] Marlon and Eleanor, hoping they would be in Lansing for just a short while, rented a house at 913 Nipp Street. Eleanor noted, "Marlon's cousin, Mabel French, was a realtor and a wonderful help with our housing issues."[13]

Deciding to visit New York a month later and make the rounds of the major airlines there, Marlon got out his best suit, had it cleaned and pressed, kissed Eleanor and the kids, and headed to the Big Apple. To save their precious savings, Marlon roomed at the Harlem YMCA at 135th Street and Lenox Avenue. For a week in June 1957 he went on a determined quest for airline employment. He filled out applications at Pan Am, United (again), American, Eastern, Western, Northwest, and any place else he could think of that employed pilots. He knew he was more than qualified for any of the airlines; during his nine years in the Air Force, he had logged more than 3,000 hours in multi-engine aircraft. And he knew the airlines always gave first preference to former Air Force pilots. He was full of hope.

But hope proved to be insufficient. Each day, as he plopped himself into stylish chairs in front of receptionists in the Manhattan offices of the major airlines and embarked upon the tedious task of filling out employment application forms, he had the gnawing sense that, despite the receptionists' friendly demeanor, he was never going to get past the gatekeepers, that he was never going to have the opportunity to show anyone who mattered what he could do in the cockpit.

When he reported to United's offices at Idlewild, Marlon had the feeling that the office had been alerted by their personnel office in Seattle to "be on the look out for Negro Captain Green who was heading East."[14] Indeed, as Marlon related, "Upon my arrival in the Idlewild office, it was clearly evident that the personnel who interviewed me knew something about me prior to, and in addition to, the information requested on the form which I completed."[15]

Finally, on June 20, as his discouraging week in New York was about to expire, a bright ray of sunshine in the form of a telegram beamed itself into the Harlem YMCA. It was from Kenneth C. Sorby, Personnel Director for Continental Airlines, headquartered in Denver, Colorado.

Harlem YMCA, where Marlon stayed during his job search in New York City
(Courtesy Green family archives)

Marlon was being invited to come for a personal interview and take a flight test. Perhaps this was the big break for which he had been looking.*[16]

---

* Eleanor speculated that, had Continental known that the YMCA's address was in black Harlem, they might not have sent the invitation.

CONSERVATIVELY ATTIRED, AND with his Air Force honorable discharge certificate and neatly typed resume residing in an attaché case, Marlon landed at Denver's Stapleton Airport on the evening of June 23, 1957, rented a room at the YMCA, and the next day took a taxi to the Continental hangar on Smith Road, where the company had its offices. At that time, Continental was more of a regional carrier than the major, international airline it later became, its routes limited to eight states: California, Colorado, Illinois, Kansas, Missouri, New Mexico, Oklahoma, and Texas.[17] Under the leadership of Robert Forman Six, however, the company, during a period of unprecedented airline industry growth, was beginning to make great strides.

Robert Six was, quite literally, a larger-than-life person. Marlon recalled that Six was tall—at least six-foot-three. "Quite a prominent person in any crowd," Marlon said. "And he was a pioneer or a ramrod in aviation; he was not a bashful or shy person by any means."[18]

Six's biographer, Robert J. Serling,* describes him as:

> resembling the fifth head on Mount Rushmore.... His face looks as if it were sculpted rather than created out of a combination of parental genes. It is long, almost horsey, with a strong jutting jaw that might have been modeled after the prow of an old-style battleship. It is more masculine than handsome. It would be awesome except for the saving grace of his smile—Six is one of those honest, completely open men who smile with their eyes as well as their mouths.... Without question, he is as complex a person who ever headed an airline. He is hard, quick-tempered, profane and dictatorial. He also is soft, warm-hearted, sentimental, deeply religious and generous.[19]

Advertising maven Mary Wells, whose company did the early advertising work for Continental, summed up Six's appearance in just nine words: "He looked like a tall, black-haired, grinning pirate."[20]

Born in Stockton, California, on June 25, 1907, to Dr. and Mrs. Clarence Six, Robert grew up in a family that, if not fabulously wealthy,

---

* Eleanor noted that Robert Serling, author of numerous aviation books and brother of Rod Serling, creator of TV's *The Twilight Zone*, later flew several times as a passenger aboard airliners piloted by Marlon Green. (Per Eleanor Green)

Robert F. Six, the flamboyant president of Continental Airlines for forty years, circa 1960
(Courtesy Denver Public Library)

did not know deprivation. Besides eventually inheriting much of the family fortune, Robert also inherited his father's love for hunting, fishing, and the outdoor life. Although his father wanted him to go into medicine, young Robert had his heart set on attending the Naval Academy and a career in the Navy. The fact that he had mediocre grades and dropped out of high school in his sophomore year precluded realizing that dream.

Shortly after leaving home to find his way in the world, both his parents died. Not knowing in what direction to steer his life, Robert Six bummed around, trying his hand at a variety of occupations, including a bill collector and a seaman on oil tankers. But, after a brief ride in an open-cockpit biplane with a barnstorming pilot, it was aviation that won his heart, and he scraped up enough money to take flying lessons.

Six was a terrible pilot, cracking up on at least three occasions. Still, he was not dissuaded, and in 1929, just before the Great Depression hit, received his pilot's license and bought a plane of his own, a used Travelaire with a Curtiss OX-5 engine. Never lacking in self-confidence, Six started his own one-man, one-plane airline—the Valley Flying Service—in California. He made charter flights, sold rides on weekends, did a little barnstorming, and taught others to fly. He hung on for four years but realized he was never going to make big money. The major airlines, too, fared little better during those rough Depression years, and the red ink on their balance sheets could be measured in gallons.

With few prospects for pilot work in the U.S., Six looked to China, where he had a friend who hinted that he might be able to hook him up with China National Aviation; the job fell through. Discouraged, he returned home after eighteen months, then used up the last of his inheritence on a year in Europe. Returning broke to the Bay Area, Robert Six found work driving a truck for the *San Francisco Chronicle*, then met and married Henriette Erhart Ruggles, the divorced daughter of William Erhart, the chairman of the huge and hugely successful Pfizer drug corporation.

In 1935, Robert Six traded in the truck-driving job for something a bit more respectable: He and a partner became the Northwest District distributor for the Beech aircraft manufacturing company. His extroverted style helped him enormously as a salesman. The following year he set his sights higher and, with some wheeling and dealing, became a forty-percent owner of Varney Air Lines, a small, struggling carrier operating primarily in the western and mountain states. Boeing Air Lines, which had joined two others to form United Air Lines, also bought a piece of the company, and in 1937 Robert Six changed the name from Varney to Continental—a name with more hope than reality in it at the time.

Gradually the little airline added more planes and more routes and actually started to show a small profit. Also in 1937 Six moved the company's headquarters and all sixteen employees from El Paso, Texas, to Denver, Colorado. The next year Six was named president of Continental, at thirty-one the nation's youngest airline head.

With only half a dozen airplanes and twenty-nine employees, everyone at the company wore two or three different hats. To Six, "vacations" and "days off" were foreign words; at Continental, Saturdays and Sundays were indistinguishable from Mondays and Tuesdays. It was a schedule that would have crushed a lesser man. Six drove himself just as hard, if not harder, than he drove any of his employees or other company officers. Only on rare occasions would he escape into the Colorado mountains for a day of hunting or fishing to help alleviate the stresses and strains of the job.

Bills and problems mounted, but Six would not be deterred, and no detail of the operation was too small for him to become personally involved. Despite a charming manner and effusive smile for public consumption, Six could turn into a tyrannical monster in an instant. A letter of complaint from a customer, the spilling of a few drops of expensive fuel, or a sloppily applied graphic to the fuselage of one of his planes would set him off into an apoplectic rage. If someone did something wrong, no matter how insignificant, he would receive a royal ass-chewing from the boss. Six's biographer, Robert Serling, writes, "Some believe Six may have either deliberately or subconsciously assumed his fire-eating role because Continental probably couldn't have survived without his domineering and demanding strength."

To stay in business, the airline cut costs ruthlessly, borrowed heavily, and even slashed executive salaries when necessary just to keep the employees fed and planes in the air.

When the U.S. became embroiled in World War II, the government snapped up several of Continental's pilots and half of the company's airplanes, impressing them into military service. Continental's survival became day to day. Salvation came at last in the form of a contract for the airline to do modification work on B-17 "Flying Fortress" bombers—modifications to improve the bombers' range and firepower—at the company's Denver Stapleton Airport facility. The war saved Continental.

With the company's existence assured, at least for the duration, thirty-five-year-old Robert Six volunteered for military service. In August 1942, he was commissioned a captain in the Army Air Corps and, after earning a multi-engine rating, assigned to lead a transport squadron within the Air Transport Command in the Pacific theater. He personally ferried only one plane, a modified B-24 bomber known as a C-87 cargo plane, from California to Australia, then spent a couple of months "flying a desk" in New Caledonia, an island east of Australia. He was subsequently stationed at Hamilton Field in San Raphael, California.

After a year in uniform, Six developed health problems; his weight ballooned, his blood pressure skyrocketed, and he suffered a mild stroke. He was taken off flying status and sent back to Denver, where Continental's Modification Center had fallen seriously behind schedule; the Air Corps ordered him to straighten it out. Six also learned that his temporary replacement at the helm of Continental, Terry Drinkwater, was secretly plotting to take over the company permanently; in February 1944 Six put down the palace coup.

So valuable was Robert Six to the war effort at the Modification Center that, in June 1944, the Air Corps discharged him (with the rank of lieutenant colonel) and let him return to civilian status so that he could more fully oversee the Center's operations. Six also ousted Drinkwater and resumed his role as head of Continental. Under his leadership, in spite of wartime restrictions and the ongoing pressure to modify bombers, the airline continued to grow, adding routes throughout the West.

When the war ended in 1945, Six could point with pride to the fact that his Center had modified over 2,000 B-17 "Flying Fortresses," 400 B-29 "Super Fortresses," and a couple dozen P-51 fighter aircraft during its existence. Less happy was what had happened on the home front; Six's marriage to Henriette had lasted for eighteen years, but the war, her unhappiness with living in isolated Denver, and his all-consuming obsession with the airline had badly eroded their relationship. They divorced amicably and childless in 1952.

At that time one of Broadway's hottest stars was sassy, brassy Ethel Merman, who could belt out a song like no one before or since. Robert Six first met the dynamic diva in 1938 and became mesmerized by her. Now single, he was again attracted to her—or her stardom—when they were reacquainted at a dinner party in New York thrown to celebrate the one-year anniversary of her hit musical, *Call Me Madam*. She apparently felt the same, for they began a secret courtship and were married in Mexicali, Mexico, on March 9, 1953.

Even though his elegant, Tudor-style home at 245 Race Street was in the posh Denver Country Club area, it was not posh enough for such a famous performer, nor for a rising airline president. In June 1953 he purchased for $79,000 the eleven-bathroom mansion formerly owned by Denver attorney J. Churchill Owen, within Cherry Hills, Denver's wealthiest and most exclusive enclave. For her part, Merman promised to give up show biz soon and be a good housewife and mother to her two children from a previous marriage.

Financially the airline was doing well, and the Six family's income was bolstered not only by the sales of Ethel's recordings but also by Robert's shrewd investments in uranium, chemicals, and oil (he owned a few oil wells with actor Jimmy Stewart). The tall, striking, gregarious airline president and his vivacious Broadway-star wife were a glamorous addition to Denver's otherwise moribund social scene; the parties they

Robert Six's and Ethel Merman's home at 245 Race Street, Denver (Author photo 2005)

The gated Six estate in the exclusive Denver suburb of Cherry Hills (Author photo 2005)

threw at their Cherry Hills estate were covered regularly by the local society columnists.[21]

——•••—

ONE OF MARLON Green's earliest memories of Continental was that the airline was fairly small: "I remember that General Motors, to which I had applied in Detroit, had more airplanes—more flyable instruments—than Continental did in 1957. Continental had, I think, ten or eleven airplanes and General Motors had twenty-something, executive-type airplanes, varying in size.

"When I got to Denver, I went to the Continental hangar on the north side of Stapleton Airport. While there, I engaged in conversation with another applicant named Bryant—pilot talk, shop talk—and I became aware that, objectively speaking, his qualifications did not equal mine."

While at Stapleton Airport for his interview, Marlon was introduced to Captain George E. Cramp, Continental's assistant chief pilot, who then checked Marlon out in a Link Trainer—a cockpit mock-up that simulated flight and responded to the pilot's commands. With the Link Trainer check successfully completed, Cramp invited Marlon into his office to discuss his flying record. After going over some of the questions, Cramp asked Marlon why he had not answered the "Race" question on the employment application; Marlon was evasive. Cramp directed him to add the word "Negro" during their meeting and return the next day for the check flight. The interview ended and Marlon went back to the YMCA.

The following day, Cramp turned Marlon over to Bill Greunke, who was the pilot instructor and check pilot. "He's the one who gave me my flying check in a DC-3," Marlon recalled. Marlon was not yet qualified or licensed to be captain, or first pilot, in a commercial airliner so, for the purpose of this examination, Greunke went along, taking off and flying the aircraft for safety purposes. Once airborne, he gave the controls to Marlon to test his handling skills and put him "under the hood"* for an instrument check. "I think I did well, and after we landed,

---

* To assess a pilot's ability to fly solely by instruments and not rely on what is visible from the cockpit windows, a pilot being assessed must literally wear a hood that restricts vision to just the panel of instruments.

Greunke said everything was satisfactory."

Cramp and Marlon then went over to the Continental cafeteria and had a brief chat with Ken Sorby, the personnel director, who promised Marlon, "We'll contact you in ten days."

Marlon returned to Lansing, bursting with eager anticipation. For the next ten days, each time the phone rang, he thought it was Continental calling, and whenever the postman delivered the mail, Marlon expected there to be a letter from the airline, welcoming him to the fold and asking him to report for duty. But there were no calls from Continental, and no letters or telegrams, either.

Two weeks after his flight test with Continental, he decided to take the initiative and call the airline. "It was the fourteenth day when I called them," he said, "and talked to somebody in Personnel to let them know I hadn't heard anything."

The bad news was then dropped on Marlon. "I was told I hadn't been selected. I was hurt and disappointed, of course, that during that ten-day period I hadn't been notified, and fourteen days had come and gone and nobody had realized that I hadn't received the word of whatever their decision was. I found out subsequently that, of those other pilots from that group who had been there at the interview with me, *all* of them had been hired."

Marlon's brother James has an expression for people who are angry, which was perfectly applicable here: He's got rocks in his jaws. "Well, I had rocks in my jaws over this development by Continental," said Marlon.

A horrible thought went through Marlon's mind: Maybe Eleanor's sister Paula was right, after all. Maybe the news articles that said the airlines had all "restated their policies of non-discrimination" were just a political ruse to keep Averill Harriman off their backs and help him win re-election.

Now what was he going to do? He couldn't get hired by the airlines and he couldn't very well go back into the Air Force. To do so would be like admitting defeat, that he had made a terrible mistake—and the Air Force didn't like pilots who were uncertain or made mistakes or admitted defeat.

Marlon gave a brief thought to joining an Air Force Reserve unit just to have some income, but swiftly abandoned the idea. "It was a 'Catch 22' situation," he explained, "or a contrivance of fate—whatever you wish to call it. The airlines were in a position to say, looking at my blackness but not acknowledging it, 'Mr. Green, we're impressed with your qualifications, but we can't consider entertaining your service until you are free of your military obligation. If you have *any* military obligation, we won't consider you a very high prospect.'"

The opportunities that had once looked like unlimited super-highways from his vantage point on the other side of the world were suddenly turning into dead ends.

But he had to do something—and soon—for their fifth child, Paula Clare, was due in July.[22]

CHAPTER 8:
A VICTIM OF HAPPENSTANCE

IT ALL SEEMED so obvious and clear cut to Marlon Green.

Continental Airlines and United Airlines and Capital Airlines and Francis Aviation and General Motors and Abrams Aerial Survey Corporation and, by Marlon's count, several hundred other companies to which he had applied had all turned him down simply for one reason.

They had not refused to hire him because he wasn't any good as a pilot or because he didn't have enough experience or because there was some blot on his personal history or a serious flaw in his character. His eyesight was perfect, and his health was excellent. He never touched alcohol or took illegal drugs. He had never been in trouble with the law. He had served his country honorably in uniform for over nine years, and had stood ready to put his life on the line if the need had arisen. Except for that minor flap about mittens at Lockbourne Air Force Base, there were no negatives on his Air Force record.

Had he exhibited any number of other deficiencies, he could have taken steps to correct them. But he had the hours, the multi-engine experience, and a clean record. There was not a single *legitimate* reason he could see for the airlines not to be falling over themselves trying to hire him.

Of course, he knew *exactly* why he had not been hired. There was one glaring, obvious, *screaming* reason that disqualified him from becoming a commercial airline pilot—something over which he had no control: He had been born black, and there was absolutely nothing he nor anyone else could do to change or alter that fact of life.

So he determined that since *he* could not change, the *system* would have to change.

But where to begin? Because Continental was the only airline to have given him a flight test and then passed him over for less-qualified applicants, Marlon decided to lodge an official complaint against Continental.

Marlon was acquainted with Ramon Rivera, the executive director of the New York City branch of the Fair Employment Practices Commission (FEPC), and Rivera informed Marlon "that Colorado had an agency that might deal with this area of law."

Marlon contacted the Colorado Anti-Discrimination Commission* and they sent him a form to fill out so he could detail his complaint. "I filled it out on August 13, 1957, and sent it in. They responded with a notice that the matter would be investigated, and in some number of days they would have some information for me about their investigation."

———·•·↓·•·———

IN MICHIGAN, MARLON finally caught a break. The story of his struggle to find an airline pilot's job was picked up by Frank Hand, the aviation writer for the *Lansing State Journal*. Marlon said that Hand "wrote a story [published on August 4, 1957] about how it seemed unusual that Marlon Green—with all his qualifications and his flying history and having served in the Air Force for nine years and three months—can't get a job with the airlines. His article was sympathetic and got a lot of publicity."[1]

Perhaps *too much* publicity. Harrold W. Bell, Jr., Continental's Vice-President of Personnel, had a copy of the article which apparently had been sent to him by someone in the company. On a clipping of the article was the penciled notation: *"Green may have a big chip-on-shoulder; perhaps not interested enough in flying; too many personal problems on his mind."* Now, in addition to being a Negro, Marlon was being labeled by people at Continental as a trouble-maker and publicity hound, neither of which would stand him in good stead with the airline nor improve his chances of being hired.[2]

In addition, Ben King, Vice-President of Public Relations for Continental, later noted, "We wanted cockpit harmony.... We didn't want anybody with a *cause* in the cockpit."[3]

Three weeks after the article appeared, the Democrats, who were in power in Michigan at that time, responded by offering Marlon a job as

---

* The Commission was established earlier in 1957 with the passage of Colorado's Anti-Discrimination Act. The first director of the Commission was Roy M. Chapman, a blind World War I veteran, who had owned a bookstore in Grand Junction, Colorado. (*Denver Post*, Feb. 19, 1925)

pilot for John Mackie, the state highway commissioner. Marlon said, "Mackie's job was to design and build highways, primarily the new interstate system, and the other state roads as necessary. He was not too enthusiastic about flying but seemed impressed with my qualifications. He said he would be willing to have me on his payroll as his pilot."*

Marlon began work for the Michigan State Highway Department on August 28, 1957, at a salary of $228.00 a month (a year later he received a raise of $44.00 per month; by comparison, in August of 1957, a Continental Airlines pilot made $390.00 a month; the following August, the base salary was raised to $500.00 per month).[4]

Marlon, Eleanor, and their five (with the birth of Paula Clare in July) children had outgrown their rental home on Nipp Street and in the fall of 1957 moved into a larger one at 608 North Logan Street, the sale arranged by Mabel French, Marlon's cousin. Eleanor set about turning the house into a home, filling it with the furnishings they had acquired over the course of their marriage. A little paint here, a little fixing up there, and it was beginning to shape up. It had an awning and a screened-in front porch and, although the bedrooms needed a bit of refurbishing, the living room and dining room were fine. The attic ran the full length of the house and, according to Eleanor, had a good "atticky" smell. The basement was small but clean, dry, and useful; laundry could be hung down there during the winter. The back yard was heavily shaded by foliage. A garage stood close to the rear of the house and was accessed by a driveway; the Greens' 1955 Chevrolet fit snugly into the garage.[5]

———·-·●-·-———

---

* Eleanor noted that Marlon's cousin, Mabel French, who helped the Greens get their house in Lansing, was a political activist and knew Jane Briggs Hart, wife of Philip Hart, then the Lieutenant Governor of Michigan, and later a U.S. Senator. Jane's father was Walter O. Briggs, who owned the Detroit Tigers baseball club and Briggs Stadium, and Jane was one of the top female pilots in the U.S. Eleanor said, "I am reasonably certain that this connection is why Marlon got the job flying for the Michigan State Highway Department." In 1960 Jane Hart qualified to be a female astronaut, but NASA canceled its women-in-space program the following year. (Eleanor Green interview, May 17, 2004; *West Catholic Alumni Emissary*, Winter, 2004-2005)

The Green family home, now gone, at 608 N. Logan in Lansing, Michigan
(Courtesy Green family archives)

ON SEPTEMBER 2, 1957, the Supreme Court ruling known as *Brown v. Topeka Board of Education* got its first trial by fire—not in Topeka, but in Little Rock, Arkansas. In May 1955, the Little Rock Board of Education decided to gradually apply the Supreme Court's 1954 ruling and begin to integrate the city's schools starting with the 1957-1958 school year. Nine Negro students, based on their character and academic performance, were selected to attend Little Rock's previously all-white Central High School.

The news was not well received by the white community, and several "citizens' councils" opposed to the plan vowed to physically block the school's entrances. Arkansas Governor Orvil Faubus sided with the segregationists and stood ready to call out the Arkansas National Guard to prevent any Negro students from entering the building.[6]

On September 4, 1957, when the nine students arrived to attend classes, they not only found their way blocked by armed soldiers but also by hundreds of white students and parents hurling racial epithets and death threats at them. With no other choice, the Negro students retreated. The whole sorry incident was captured by news photographers, the images broadcast and published around the world.

Anger not seen since the War Between the States quickly boiled up between Washington, D.C. and the South. One Alabama newspaper editorialized, "If Faubus persists [in defying Eisenhower and the Supreme Court], the only way in which the Federal Government can overcome him is to order Federal soldiers to march on Arkansas soldiers—civil war."[7]

President Eisenhower became personally involved and summoned Governor Faubus to meet with him, where he warned the governor not to interfere with the Supreme Court's ruling. Still, Faubus was defiant. Only after a federal court issued an injunction for Faubus to withdraw the National Guard troops did he back down. The troops marched away on September 20 but the angry white parents did not.

On Monday, September 23, 1957, local police quietly slipped the "Little Rock Nine," as the Negro students were now known, into the school. When the white parents learned of this, a riot nearly ensued; the nine were escorted out of the building.

Woodrow Mann, the mayor of Little Rock, fearing for the community's safety as well as the safety of the students, asked President Eisenhower for federal troops—a request that was granted. On September 24, 1957, "Ike" ordered the 101st Airborne Division into the city and federalized (i.e., put the unit under federal, not state, control) the ten-thousand-man Arkansas National Guard. With this overwhelming show of force, the Little Rock Nine were finally able to attend classes even though hundreds of segregationists continued to protest outside the school.

For an entire year, the Little Rock Nine were subjected to taunts and physical abuse by white parents and their fellow students, but their quiet bravery won the admiration of a nation.*[8]

Eisenhower's biographer, Michael Korda, writes,

> Ike has received very little credit for his efforts on behalf of civil rights, but that is largely because he regarded himself as a "moderate" on the issue, and was not ashamed to say so, and also because he avoided rhetoric and dramatic gestures, instead quietly insisted on enforcing the law. He had always believed in

---

* For their steadfast courage, the Little Rock Nine have been honored over the years. A statue depicting the group stands today in front of the Arkansas State Capital, and in 1999, all were awarded the Congressional Gold Medal by President Bill Clinton. (en.wikipedia.org/wiki/Little_Rock_Nine)

"the right to equality before the law of all citizens...whatever their race or color," and during World War II he had moved to desegregate Red Cross clubs in his theater of command, and taken the more radical step of sending "Negro replacements" into "previous all-white combat units," four years before Truman's order to desegregate the United States armed forces....

He acted with more energy—and in a more straightforward way—than either President Kennedy or President Johnson.[9]

———•◆•———

ALTHOUGH HE HAD a job flying for the State of Michigan, Marlon continued to make himself known and available to the rest of the nation's airlines.

Said Marlon, "At one point somebody told me that the president of TWA, Carter Burgess, was going to be in the Los Angeles area, speaking to some group, maybe an airlines meeting. So I got on the same flight that he was on just to give it another shot—you know, to have a captive audience. He was courteous—a Virginia patriarch, if you want to call him that. I think he recognized, looking at me, that there's something unusual about this applicant. I don't recall if I had earlier written to him personally, but I approached him for personal consideration of my qualifications and interest in being a pilot for TWA. He was kind and not abusive at all. The result was—it didn't pan out."[10]

In fact, *nothing* panned out. There was no imminent, or even hinted, prospect of airline employment for Marlon Green. With few other avenues to pursue, he filed charges of discrimination with the New York Fair Employment Practices Commission (FEPC) against Eastern and Pan American Airlines to go along with the ones against United and Continental. But at least he had a job flying; perhaps that could lead to something better.[11]

———•◆•———

THE COLORADO ANTI-Discrimination Commission continued to work on Marlon's behalf. Members of the Commission met with Continental executives on four occasions; they also contacted President Eisenhower's Committee on Government Contracts, but Jacob

Seidenberg, the Committee's Executive Director, told them that the President's Committee "could find no grounds granting them jurisdiction over airline complaints filed by Green." Marlon must have wondered that, if a presidential commission had no jurisdiction over the airlines, who did?[12]

On January 13, 1958, Roy Chapman, head of the Colorado Anti-Discrimination Commission, met with Continental officials who gave him a "tale of woe"—the carrier's financial situation was not good; only three of the fourteen pilots who applied for jobs the previous July were hired, and 211 employees were on furlough; Continental hoped that, if the financial climate improved, they would be able to recall some of the furloughed employees by mid-1958, but there would be no recruiting of new pilots before 1959.* Most damning of all was Continental's bald assertion that they would not hire Marlon because he was a "trouble maker," that he had already acquired a

Roy Chapman, the first head of the Colorado Anti-Discrimination Commission, photographed in 1935, was a blind, World War I veteran. (Copyright, Colorado Historical Society, Photo Subject Collection, scan 7331)

---

* The airline was also spending a lot of money to upgrade. Robert Six was working on a deal to purchase fifteen Viscount prop-jets from the British manufacturer Vickers and $60 million worth of Boeing 707s. (Serling, 115)

reputation within the airline industry of being a "publicity seeker" and "too aggressive" in pursuit of a job.

The airline told Chapman, however, that they *had* offered Marlon a position as either a sales or passenger agent at $275-$390 a month, or a mechanic at $2.63 an hour. (Marlon later said he knew nothing about these offers, and would not have taken them even if he had known.)[13]

———•••———

WHILE IN LANSING, Marlon applied to three Michigan-based companies he knew employed pilots: General Motors, Abrams Aerial Survey, and Francis Aviation (the latter two based in Lansing). He was turned down by all three. "General Motors claimed military pilots are unacceptable," Marlon told a *Lansing State Journal* reporter, "because they are trained to accomplish a mission without regard to hazard. That's a lot of nonsense. The other two outfits claimed they weren't hiring, but both have hired pilots since I applied."[14]

Believing that the three firms had discriminated against him solely because of his color, he filed a complaint with the Michigan Fair Employment Practices Commission. His complaint soon attracted the attention of the Lansing chapter of the National Association for the Advancement of Colored People.

Marlon said, "To this day, as far as I know, the NAACP does not view my case with pleasure because of Stuart Dunning, Jr., a black lawyer who was the head of the Lansing chapter at the time the article appeared in the *State Journal*. I don't want to treat his history wrong, but I recall him approaching me with this proposition: If you will let us use your facts to pursue this case, and with the agreement that the airline would not be required to hire you—a proposition or a position that was never appealing to me—we will pursue the discrimination and the violation of the law. And when I refused the offer, I think he was nonenthusiastic about pursuing the case in Michigan.

"In other words, if I dropped my suit against Continental, and let them pursue only the discrimination and the violation of the law, they would...well, I'm not aware that they were offering me *any* goody at all. I wasn't going to become the corporate pilot for the NAACP, or anything like that. There was no benefit. I think they were in a position of not wanting to press the airlines any more than the State of New York, when it made its 'reiteration publication,' was in a position to pressure the airlines or force them to obey the law.

"What I interpreted of the Lansing NAACP's stance was, 'We don't expect a better outcome than New York as far as getting you to sit in the cockpit of anybody's airliner.' I don't know if they used the word 'test case.' But I had never been disposed to any action in this matter that did not involve the prospect of my becoming a pilot with the airline involved. So I told them clearly that I would not agree to any such pursuit of my relief if the assistance of the NAACP was based on that requirement."

Disgusted, Marlon left Dunning's office. He had just slammed headlong into another roadblock. If the NAACP wasn't willing to assist him, who was?[15]

ON SEPTEMBER 10, 1957, the Colorado Anti-Discrimination Commission's director Roy Chapman met with Kenneth Sorby and Harrold W. Bell, Jr., Continental's Personnel Director and Vice President of Personnel, respectively, to discuss Marlon's complaint in detail.

At certain points in history, an individual, a company, a nation has the opportunity, with a word or gesture or brave act, to make a decision that changes the world for the better. These seminal moments are the guideposts of civilization, the exact point when human life on this planet is forever altered for the good. On September 10, 1957, the executives of Continental Airlines were handed just such an opportunity. They *could* have stood up and said, "Gentlemen, I believe that our company, Continental Air Lines, is wrong. The entire airline industry is wrong. We have *all* been guilty of racial discrimination. Racial discrimination is wrong. It is an evil that is corrosive to the human spirit and a disgrace to the Constitution. It goes against everything for which this nation stands—or *should* stand. We do not want our company to be accused of wrong and evil acts. We are better than that. Therefore, we're willing to go out on a limb and say that we will take personal responsibility for hiring Marlon Green and making him Continental's first Negro pilot."

They could have gone even further. They could have gotten down on bended knee, embraced Marlon's hands in theirs, and said something like, "And to you, Mr. Green, we wish to make our most humble and earnest apology for the way in which you have been treated by our company, and by our race. Please forgive us, and please forgive Continental Air Lines."

But September 10, 1957, the midst of the so-called "Eisenhower Era," was the height of conformity in buttoned-down, gray-flannel-suited corporate America. High-ranking, well-paid company officials who wanted desperately to keep their jobs and their big-finned cars and their split-level homes in suburbia did not stand up (or kneel down) and make such cinematic declarations. They had not risen to positions such as Vice-President of Personnel by walking out onto flimsy limbs.

Instead, they played Yes-Men. They crouched behind walls of old fears and prohibitions and hide-bound tradition. They kept their noses above the placid corporate waters, hoping to avoid making waves. They hunkered down deep inside the bunkers of lock-step mind-set and covered their ears and shut their eyes, hoping the uncomfortable moment was only momentary and would soon pass them by. It goes without saying that Continental's executives did not seize the opportunity, defy their boss, and alter the course of aviation and civil-rights history.

According to notes that were taken at the meeting, Bell did, however, concede that Marlon was a "fully qualified pilot; that he met all of Continental's other qualifications from the standpoint of such things as age, height, weight, pilot experience and ability; and that his appearance, character, personality, attitude, and aptitude were fully acceptable. It is Continental's claim that subsequent to his interview, and out of fourteen original applicants, they accepted him as one of the six applicants who were fully qualified for pilot training."

Marlon did not make the next cut, however, when four of the remaining six—all of whom were white—were accepted for training. No one at Continental would admit responsibility for the decision, however. Both Bell and Sorby disclaimed any involvement in the ultimate selection of the final four candidates. "The substance of the testimony," concluded Chapman's report, "was that it just happened, or was a coincidence, that Green was not one of the four selected for the next class [July 1957]." In other words, Marlon D. Green, pilot, was simply an innocent victim of happenstance.

As it turned out, the fifth acceptable candidate, originally passed over, was enrolled in the September class, while ten other applicants were admitted to the August class. Marlon was supposedly kept on the list of acceptable applicants until August, when Bell directed Sorby to remove his name solely because his case had made headlines in the August 4, 1957, edition of the *Lansing State Journal*. Marlon Green was becoming troublesome, and Bell wanted no troublesome pilots.

Bell had told Chapman that his airline's minimum requirement for a person to be accepted as a candidate for pilot training was at least 2,000 flight hours, "with as much multi-engine experience as we can get." Bell also testified that *a minimum of one hundred hours of multi-engine experience was required* [author's emphasis]. Marlon Green was far and away the most qualified applicant, with 3,071 total flight hours, almost all of which were in multi-engine aircraft.

The applications of the other hopeful pilots were introduced as evidence. The results are revealing:

1. Applicant Stearns: Total flight hours: 1,234; Multi-engine hours: 934.
2. Applicant George:* Total flight hours: 2,100; Multi-engine hours: 897.
3. Applicant Bryant: Total flight hours: 1,000; Multi-engine hours: five.
4. Applicant Dresser: Total flight hours: 1,031; Multi-engine hours: None.
5. Applicant Cole: Total flight hours: 1,000, almost all in single-engine aircraft.

The Commission, in its findings, scolded Continental for overlooking Green, who had well over twice the total flight hours as four of the five other candidates, and almost triple the number of multi-engine hours of the next leading candidate. Chapman upbraided Continental because "some of those selected in preference to Green did not have the minimum qualifications which Bell stated were required." The Commission found that Green was qualified in every other respect—in addition to

---

* Pilot S. Clark George, age 34, was at the controls of a Continental Airlines Vickers Viscount 812 coming from Midland, Texas, when it crashed late on the icy night of January 29, 1963, while trying to land at Kansas City Municipal Airport. The crew of three and all five passengers were killed.

flight experience—such as personality, aptitude, attitude, character, appearance, etc. Yet, of those five eligible but less-experienced applicants, all were offered employment.

The Commission also took Continental to task for Sorby's brief "interview" of Marlon at the airlines' airport cafeteria. Said the report, "Green's interview with Sorby consisted of a chat for a few minutes in the company cafeteria, and ended there. He was not given an interview in the Personnel Office, three and one-half miles from the airfield, nor at the Hangar Office, although Sorby testified that he conducted Denver interviews at one or the other of these places." And: "Green was instructed to write 'Negro' on his application" in the blank marked 'Race.'"

The Commission came to the inevitable conclusion: "Upon all of the evidence and also in view of the above-recited facts and circumstances, this Commission cannot believe that the four successful applicants were selected in preference to Green by the method, or lack thereof, claimed, particularly when the company's own Policy Manual required selection of the best-suited person or persons. Upon all the evidence, it is the finding of the Commission that Green was better qualified as to pilot experience, and at least as well qualified in other respects, for the job sought by him than the other applicants, and that he was not selected for the July or August training classes because of his race."

Chapman determined that there was "probable cause" to find that Continental had indeed discriminated against Marlon Green and had thereby violated Colorado's fair employment laws. (For one thing, state law prohibited a prospective employer from asking a person's race or requiring a photo on a job application.) Although more than six months had passed since Chapman's initial investigation, on March 28, 1958, the Commission gave Continental thirty days in which to respond to the investigator's charges and/or admit Marlon Green to a pilot training class.[16]

Continental's lawyers went into crisis-control mode and requested the hearing be delayed until May 1958—a delay that was granted—in order for them to adequately prepare their response. It took the lawyers and Continental eight months before they were ready to face Roy Chapman and the Commission again. This formal hearing took place on May 7, 1958, at the Commission's offices at 655 Broadway in Denver, and Marlon flew in for the hearing.[17]

IT SHOULD BE noted that Colorado does not have an unblemished reputation when it comes to racial tolerance and civil rights. From 1925 to 1927, under the governorship of Clarence J. Morley, a former Denver District Court judge and active member of the Ku Klux Klan, the Klan wielded more influence over Colorado than any other state west of the Mississippi. The Denver mayor's office, too, was Klan-influenced, Benjamin F. Stapleton* having been elected with strong KKK support; he later repudiated the group, but held the mayoral post for twenty years.

Negroes who crossed the Klan's carefully drawn lines of social conduct felt the organization's wrath. In 1921, a Negro postal worker who moved into a white Denver neighborhood had a bomb explode in his yard. At the time, however, the Klan reserved most of its intimidation for Catholics and Jews.[18]

Much progress had been made in the intervening three decades, but attitudes are harder to change than governmental administrations, so it is impossible to say that hostility in some quarters toward minorities did not still exist beneath Colorado's otherwise welcoming exterior.[19]

MARLON FLEW INTO Denver in a borrowed plane to attend the May 7, 1958, hearing. Representing him was another of Colorado's Assistant Attorneys General, Wendell Sayers.[20] Representing Continental were Patrick M. Westfeldt and William C. McClearn, two of the best young trial attorneys from the powerful Denver law firm of Holland and Hart.

Holland and Hart was formed eleven years earlier when thirty-nine-year-old Denver attorney Stephen H. Hart, unhappy that the staid Lewis and Grant law firm for which he had worked for thirteen years declined to make him a partner, went to see a colleague, forty-seven-year-old Josiah Gilbert Holland (not to be confused with Abraham Lincoln's biographer of the same name), a mining law expert who owned his own successful legal firm.

"Joe" Holland, as he was known to his friends, was born into a wealthy family in Denver on October 1, 1900, schooled at Phillips

---

* Denver Municipal Airport changed its name to Stapleton Airfield in 1944, then to Stapleton International Airport in 1964—a name in use until Denver International Airport opened in 1995.

Exeter Academy in Exeter, New Hampshire, studied at the University of Colorado, graduated from Yale, then received his law degree from the University of Denver in 1925. He was socially active and belonged to numerous clubs, including the Denver Country Club. In 1931 he was elected to the Colorado legislature.

Impressed with Hart, Holland immediately offered him a partnership and the two launched what would soon become one of the largest and most prestigious law firms in the Rocky Mountain region.

Holland and Hart quickly attracted a strong line-up of important corporate clients, including millionaire Claude K. Boettcher's Ideal Cement Company, multi-millionairess Helen G. Bonfils's *Denver Post*, the National Livestock Tax Committee, and numerous other, well-heeled clients.

Patrick Westfeldt joined Holland and Hart in January 1948 and became a partner three years later; McClearn, a World War II Army veteran, joined the firm in the mid 1940s after obtaining his law degree from the University of Colorado. He also served a stint in the Air Force during the Korean War before returning to the firm.*[21]

By the late 1950s Holland and Hart was one of the most respected law firms in Colorado, and its partners and associate attorneys were well paid for their services. Joe Holland lived in a large, Santa Fe-style adobe home on several wooded acres near Robert Six's mansion in the ultra-exclusive south Denver suburb of Cherry Hills, while Steve Hart resided at the northeast corner of Ellsworth Avenue and Colorado Boulevard in a multi-storied brick home whose horizontal lines showed a mild Frank Lloyd Wright influence. William McClearn resided in a more modest blond-brick ranch-style home a few miles farther south of Hart, in a toney neighborhood known as Bonnie Brae. Patrick Westfeldt, a bachelor, lived in a sixth-floor apartment at Eighth Avenue and Clarkson Street in an area packed with the mansions of Colorado's gold and silver barons known as Capitol Hill, just a block or two from the Colorado governor's palatial home.[22]

Perhaps as a result of being Robert Six's next-door neighbor (his home was one-tenth of a mile from the eight-foot-high stone wall that surrounded the Six estate), Joe Holland and his law firm came to

---

* When asked by the author for an interview for this book, Mssrs. Westfeldt and McClearn both declined.

handle the airline's legal business; Holland also served on Continental's board of directors.

The true story of why Continental wanted to keep Marlon Green off its payroll is a mystery to this day. No one at Holland and Hart wanted to discuss it, and the public relations department at Continental claimed that they had no files that went back to the late 1950s. The matter of exactly who fought against the hiring of Marlon, therefore, is left to conjecture. Robert Serling, Six's biographer, makes no mention of the Green matter, nor of the years of litigation that followed the ruling by the Colorado Anti-Discrimination Commission.

However, one can conclude from Serling's biography that Robert Six was the epitome of the "hands-on" manager. By all accounts, he had trouble delegating authority. Nothing escaped his attention. He even scrutinized invoices and questioned outgoing checks for the tiniest expenses before personally signing them. It seems entirely plausible, therefore, that the decision not to hire Marlon Green was made at the very top. One can almost picture Six in his spartan office (he saved lavish furnishings for his Cherry Hills home), when told by someone that the Colorado Anti-Discrimination Commission was demanding that Continental hire a Negro pilot, bellowing out, "Not only '*no*,' but '*hell, no!*'"

It is also likely that his lawyer and neighbor Joe Holland even warned him that a lawsuit and negative publicity for the airline would probably follow any refusal to employ Green. But Six had dug in his heels. He was not the type of individual who was easily cowed by the threat of lawsuits; bad press was another matter. The answer, however, was still no. He probably told Holland to have his law firm look into ways Continental could legally defend his position.

Robert Six was an industry leader and a maverick in many ways, but becoming a pioneer and defying the color barrier—and risking a backlash from bigoted customers—was a step he was apparently unwilling to take.

————◆————

I T IS NOT often that one gets *two* opportunities to stand up, take a position, and do the right thing. But Continental, once again, had that opportunity within its grasp on May 7, 1958, at the Colorado Anti-Discrimination Commission hearing.

However, instead of taking the high road and blazing a trail toward racial equality and integration within the airline industry, Westfeldt's and McClearn's response to the Commission—probably at the behest of Six himself—came in the form of a Motion to Dismiss.

In their Motion, Continental's lawyers argued that the airline was a duly authorized and certified commercial air carrier, and that it had "inadvertently" given Marlon an out-dated job application form that contained the box for "Race" to be filled in, whereas their current application forms no longer had that box.

Continental also claimed that the Colorado Anti-Discrimination Act of 1957 did not prohibit an employer from requiring a job applicant to include a photograph of himself or herself with their application.

Most importantly, Continental stated that, because it was engaged in interstate commerce, only the federal government—not individual states—had the authority to regulate or control the activities of businesses engaged in such commerce. Continental's lawyers made the point that if states were allowed to become involved in the regulation of interstate commerce, it would "constitute an undue burden on interstate commerce, in violation of Article I, Section 8 of the Constitution of the United States."

In conclusion, Continental rejected the Commission's demands that it immediately enroll Marlon Green in a training class with the ultimate goal of hiring him, saying that its interpretation of the law was that the Colorado Anti-Discrimination Commission had no jurisdiction in matters related to firms engaged in interstate commerce.

Another matter that apparently stuck in the craw of Harrold W. Bell, Jr., Continental's Vice-President of Personnel, was the media attention that was beginning to grow regarding the case. The *Denver Post* reported that Bell testified during the hearing that the airline "was not interested in pilots who make the front page, for whatever reason." The newspaper further noted that Bell "admitted Green met other requirements, but that Continental learned Green had filed cases against other airlines in his attempt to break the color barrier." Bell said, "We want a person who is a good, normal, quiet, self-respecting individual, who is going to be careful of his passengers by being careful of himself."[23]

The airline's lawyers made a motion that the complaint be dismissed; the Commission denied the motion but gave the Attorney General, Marlon's legal representative at the hearing, as well as Continental's attorneys, ten days in which to research, prepare, and submit a ruling on the constitutionality of the Commission's jurisdiction in this matter. The Commission also called upon the airline to submit the original applications of the five other pilots who had applied for jobs at about the same time as had Marlon and had been hired.[24]

The meeting was adjourned and Marlon walked out into the bright Colorado sunshine that held no warmth for him.

The following morning, before returning to Michigan, and with his soul deeply troubled, Marlon left the downtown Denver YMCA and saw the twin gray-granite spires of the Cathedral of the Immaculate Conception on Colfax Avenue, two blocks from the State Capitol, beckoning to him. He decided to stop in for some spiritual comfort.

As it happened, Mass was about to be said. It would be a Mass that would change his life.[25]

CHAPTER 9:
THE FASTEST GUN IN DENVER

AFTER MARLON ENTERED the huge cathedral, genuflected, crossed himself, and found a seat in one of the pews, it became obvious to him that something was amiss.

The priest—Monsignor [later Bishop] George R. Evans—came out to say Mass, and Marlon saw that he didn't have an altar boy. "He was carrying the cruets of water and wine up to the altar himself," noted Marlon. "Normally they're off on a little side table and the altar boy goes to get them when necessary. Immediately I got up and let him know that I would serve as his altar boy and take the wine and water to where they should be.

"We went through the complete service and afterward he invited me into the sacristy and expressed his gratitude for my coming forward to assist him. He was impressed with having someone—especially a black Catholic—volunteer to do it. He didn't respond to my blackness, or express it overtly, but I think it was a source of interest to him."

The two men entered into a conversation about who Marlon was and why he happened to be there. After Marlon told of his concerns about being shunned in his search for an airline pilot's job, Evans, a canon or church lawyer, said he needed an attorney. Marlon said, "He recommended one right off the tip of his tongue—T. Raber Taylor."

Attorney T. Raber Taylor was highly regarded in the Denver Catholic community because of his and his wife's many charitable, church-related involvements. "He was a high-ranking official in the international St. Vincent de Paul organization that provides services to the needy," Marlon said. "He was a prominent attorney in Denver and had a long-standing practice, mainly with wills and trusts, but also labor law in general and discriminatory trade-union practices in particular."

Evans placed a call to Taylor, and Marlon was invited to stop by the lawyer's office in the American National Bank Building at 17th and Stout Streets; Marlon practically flew the one mile between the church and the office building, his spirit bouyed by renewed hope.

The Cathedral of the Immaculate Conception, where Marlon sought spiritual comfort during his May 1958 visit to Denver (Author photo 2006)

Monsignor George R. Evans, the Denver clergyman who helped Marlon find the lawyer he needed (Courtesy of the Denver Catholic Register, Archdiocese of Denver, reprinted with permission)

Taylor's secretary greeted Marlon and said he could meet with Taylor as soon as he was free. Marlon sat in the small waiting room and leafed distractedly through a couple of magazines before Taylor appeared, introduced himself, and shook hands. The lawyer was tall, about Marlon's height or a little taller, with a solid build and a firm handshake. Marlon always appreciated firm handshakes, which he felt gave an indication of the strength of character of the man wielding it; perhaps it was something he had learned in the Air Force. Taylor invited Marlon into his private office and closed the door.

As Marlon's tale unfolded, T. Raber Taylor jotted down notes and seemed to become visibly upset by the gross injustice and blatant racism he saw being perpetrated by Continental.

Marlon's attorney T. Raber Taylor, circa 1963 (Courtesy Mary Taylor Hassouna)

At the end of the discourse, the lawyer apologized, telling Marlon that his hands were tied for the moment. "He said he couldn't get involved in the case immediately," Marlon recalled, "because it was still with the Anti-Discrimination Commission, and he would have to wait until the Commission made its decision before he could step in." Marlon thanked him and returned to Lansing, a small seed of optimism germinating inside.[1]

In 1958 the Holland and Hart law firm was located in the Equitable Building (foreground) on Seventeenth Street in downtown Denver. T. Raber Taylor's office was located in the American National Bank Building, just beyond the Equitable. (Author photo 2005)

THE COLORADO ATTORNEY General's office submitted its interpretation on the constitutionality of the Commission's jurisdiction in the Green case within the ten-day deadline. Marlon was informed by Roy Chapman that there would be a slight delay while the Commission reviewed both sides' arguments.

Trying to retain his confidence in the rightness of his cause, Marlon continued on the offensive. He again made headlines in Lansing on August 13, 1958, when he accused the Michigan Fair Employment Practices Commission (FEPC) of "failing to press discrimination cases to the full extent of the law" in his claims of racial bias by General Motors* and others. He accused the Commission of being "active in a program to prevent the enforcement of the FEP law of 1955 by refusing to make a thorough investigation of complaints; refusing to state its findings when an investigation *is* made; and dismissing cases in which the evidence demands full prosecution of the law."

Marlon recalled that John G. Feild, the Executive Director of the Michigan Fair Employment Practices Commission, told him, "Suppose we do find that General Motors *has* discriminated against you illegally; what do you expect *us* to do about it? This commission will brand no company as having violated the laws."[2]

If the Michigan Fair Employment Practices Commission wasn't willing to go to bat to ensure fair employment for him, who was?

NEWS ITEM:

(New York City, September 20, 1958) During a book signing at Blumstein's Department Store in Harlem to promote his new book, *Stride Toward Freedom: The Montgomery Story,* the Reverend Martin Luther King, Jr. was stabbed with a seven-inch letter opener wielded by a deranged Negress, Izola Ware Curry, who was also carrying a loaded pistol at the time of her arrest. King was rushed to Harlem Hospital where doctors removed the letter opener from his chest.

During police questioning, Curry said that she believed the NAACP and King had been "boycotting" and "torturing" her, and that she thought the civil rights leader was planning to kill her.[3]

---

* Dorothy Reid, wife of George Reid, the Michigan State Highway Department photographer, and a friend of the Green family, noted that General Motors had been interested in Marlon's qualifications "until they saw him, at which time they began to go frantically into reverse." (Letter, Dorothy Reid to John A. Hannah, June 20, 1961)

—·—•·•·•·—

ALTHOUGH DWIGHT D. Eisenhower "deplored" the practice of racial segregation while he was the Supreme Allied Commander in Europe during World War II, he refused to upset the social applecart by demanding that the armed forces in the European Theater integrate. The same held true while he was president of the United States. With racial tensions slowly rising to a boiling point, he listened sympathetically to the views of civil-rights leaders, made a few statements, but Negro leaders felt he did very little of substance to advance the cause of integration and racial harmony.[4]

—·—•·•·•·—

"BOB SIX SLINGS Fastest Gun in Denver," read the headline in the October 27, 1958, edition of Denver's *Rocky Mountain News*. The writer, columnist Pasquale Marranzino, extolled the gun-slinging skills of the airline president who practiced on a regular basis with his six-guns in the basement shooting range of his Cherry Hills home. An electronic timer recorded the swiftness of Six's reactions. Marranzino reported that Six could draw from his holster and fire at a target fifty feet away at just under two one-hundreths of a second. His wife, Ethel Merman, reportedly also enjoyed blasting a few of her husband's hand-made paraffin rounds herself, having learned how to handle a shooting iron while playing the role of Annie Oakley in *Annie Get Your Gun*.[5]

All the seemingly harmless gunplay and the publicity surrounding it was yet another example of Robert Six's flamboyant lifestyle—a flamboyance that Continental's executives did not want to see from any of their pilots.

—·—•·•·•·—

AS THE AUTUMN of 1958 turned into winter, Marlon, still in Lansing, heard nothing from Roy Chapman and the Colorado Anti-Discrimination Commission. It was apparent to Marlon that the Commission was delaying, for whatever reason, its decision until after the 1958 elections. "I was hurt; I knew that this was giving up my last possibility of having anything at all regarding the airlines," he said.[6]

Marlon was more than hurt; the Greens' financial situation had become even more precarious with the birth in September of their sixth child, Philip Lawrence Green.[7]

Angry and frustrated at the Commission's foot-dragging, Marlon fired off a telegram to the Commission on December 14, 1958, telling them to drop his complaint against Continental. "I told the Commission that if you are not willing to render your decision in my case, then withdraw my complaint." James Reynolds, a member of the Commission, persuaded Marlon to rescind his withdrawal request. Marlon did but, as he would learn later, his telegram would have serious repercussions.

Five days after receiving Marlon's telegram, the Commission announced its decision: Continental Airlines must enroll Marlon Green in the next pilots' training class. Six refused, and Continental's legal team filed in Denver District Court an appeal to the Commission's decision. The battle lines were drawn. The war was about to begin.[8]

———•———

ELEANOR WAS ALWAYS just as invested in her husband's quest for a pilot's job as he was. On November 2, 1958, she wrote to America's most famous aviator, Charles A. Lindbergh, then employed as technical advisor to Pan American World Airways:

> For several months now I have considered writing to you about a problem in the field of commercial aviation that has confronted our family. Because we have been disappointed so often in our search for help with this problem, we have become increasingly pessimistic, but today is one of those days when I have hope that somewhere there is a person of sufficient prestige in the field of aviation who is interested in this area of human relations and has the moral courage to do something about it.

Eleanor went on to tell Lindbergh about Marlon's lack of success in finding a pilot's job, ending with, "Unfortunately, Pan American has been among the many [airlines] who have discriminated against him. So, in my husband's case, merit alone is not enough. His skin color has cancelled out merit and he needs some special intercession. I wonder if you can help him."[9]

Apparently not even Charles Lindbergh could—or would—help Marlon; he never responded to Eleanor's plea.

———•••———

DURING THE WINTER of 1958-1959, Marlon met several times with Richard J. Brake, a partner in the Lansing law firm of Sinas, Dramis, Brake and Werbelow, to see if that firm could be of any assistance to him.

In a 2007 letter to the Green family, Brake noted, "It was in the early stages of the firm that Marlon Green came to me seeking to correct a grave injustice. Continental Airlines had blatantly discriminated against him because of his race. Having personally suffered the indignities and humiliations of being an enlisted man in the Army with a seven-year college education, I obviously had empathy with and outrage at

Richard J. Brake, Marlon's lawyer in Lansing, Michigan, circa 1960 (Courtesy Richard J. Brake)

Marlon's plight. Unfortunately, there was nothing that I, or as a Lansing lawyer, could do to right the injustices of a Denver corporation. All I could do was to encourage Marlon to pursue his dream in Denver."

Knowing that Marlon had earlier talked with T. Raber Taylor, Brake wrote to Taylor, telling the Denver lawyer,

> It is my feeling that his personal interest is such that he should have individual representation to work in conjunction and cooperation with the commission.
>
> Unfortunately, as you know, Mr. Green is the father of six children and is not in a financial position to undertake a lengthy

and expensive legal battle. He could afford some fees but, in all probability, could not afford the true value of the services required.

However, because of the merits of this particular case and the important rights involved, I would be willing to make some concession insofar as our fees are concerned and I am in hopes that we could retain local counsel who would feel the same. Would you be able to undertake representing Mr. Green locally on the basis that I have outlined?[10]

T. Raber Taylor mulled over Brake's letter. What Brake was asking him to do was to drastically reduce his fees in order to help Marlon in his legal battle in the Colorado courts—a battle that would undoubtedly involve hundreds or thousands of hours of work with no assurance that he would be successful—or even paid. The case might drag on for years and be a drain on the small law firm's time and finances.

Taylor wrote back to Brake, saying that he feared Marlon's telegraphed demand in December that the Anti-Discrimination Commission drop the complaint "may have irreparably damaged the case."

But Taylor went on to mention that he had already spent many hours researching the case and would consider representing Marlon if Marlon agreed to several conditions, one of which was an advance of $150.00 to cover out-of-pocket expenses, stating, "Mr. Green has six children, I have seven. I am willing to make some sacrifice in his regard but unless he is willing to make a commensurate personal sacrifice, it would not be fair for me to sacrifice my children's interest in his behalf.... I think we will all be in accord that a case of this type warrants a fee of several thousand dollars and that Holland and Hart is undoubtedly being paid at least that amount by Continental Air Lines."

Taylor averred that he would be amenable to a $750.00 retainer and indicated that he had already notified the Greens of same. Marlon had agreed to the terms and sent a "down payment" of $150.00 to Taylor.[11]

At the end of March 1959, Taylor began putting together the material he would need to file the Green case for Duke W. Dunbar, the Attorney General of Colorado, who had expressed an interest in joining the case against Continental. Taylor asked the AG's office to consider including in their petition that the Commission's order regarding the hiring of Marlon be enforced and that the District Court enter an order for temporary relief or a restraining order against Continental.

In a letter to Marlon, Taylor said, "You and I both know that this is a difficult case. I assure you that I will do my best for you. Please be patient and pray that all goes well."

It was an incredible understatement. Taylor had no idea how difficult it would truly be, nor how much patience (and how many prayers) he and Marlon and Eleanor would need to expend.[12]

FAMILY FRIENDS PITCHED in on the Greens' behalf. After Eleanor told her former Xavier roommate, Joan Stanley, now living in Berkeley, California, with her husband Marvin Chachere, that T. Raber Taylor had agreed to take the case, Joan wrote to the lawyer, saying, "Because of the very special nature of this case, we wish to extend to you our congratulations and will offer daily our fervent prayers that your effort will be blessed with success. We will be anxiously awaiting the outcome of the hearing and we will pray daily that great good, even if hidden or narrowly seen for awhile, will come from your deeds."[13]

George and Dorothy Reid, too, sent a letter expressing their gratitude to Taylor for championing Marlon's cause. It read, "We have been deeply concerned for some time about the plight of our friends, the Marlon Greens. Since we first met them over a year ago, we have become increasingly impressed by their courage and faith in the face of crushing disappointments and humiliation. Whenever a path they have taken leads to a dead end, they bravely try another. Marlon Green is a man who has had the integrity to stand up against terrific opposition and not only say what he believes in, but fight for it.

"The fact that you have agreed to represent Marlon, at a sacrifice to yourself, is in our opinion an indication of your integrity. We are very happy that this good fortune has come to the Greens."[14]

Norbert ("Norb") and Sheila Wiley were graduate students at Michigan State University and were close friends of the Greens. Norb recalled, "Sheila and I had been introduced to the Greens through a mutual friend, Father Joseph Fichter. Our two families would get together for cookouts and just hang around socially; our kids and their kids played together. We talked a lot about his problems with the airlines. Marlon is not a passive person. He was quite aggressive—he never just sat back and ignored anything."[15]

The Wileys, too, sent their own praiseworthy letter to the Greens' lawyer: "It is very gratifying for us to see a lawyer take a case which will be tough and, I suppose, not very lucrative—yet of great moral significance. We have known the Greens throughout their struggle to get fair treatment from the airlines, and we know of nobody (or no cause) more worthy of help. We give you then our thanks, admiration, and prayers, knowing that your efforts will help, perhaps notably, the cause of racial justice in America."[16]

Norb and Sheila Wiley, graduate students at Michigan State University, and close friends of the Greens, with their children (Courtesy Norb Wiley)

DESPITE TAYLOR'S WORDS of assurance that he would do his best for Marlon, and the letters of support that came from friends, Marlon refused to pin all his hopes on the Continental matter being resolved in his favor; he continued to press the other airlines in his bid to win a seat in the cockpit. In a letter to C.R. Smith, president of American Airlines, he pulled no punches:

> On February 24 [1959]...I decided during my waiting time [in Chicago] to go to the American employment office at Midway [Airport] to see about my application which had been on file there since November 1957. At the receptionist window I asked about pilot employment and the young lady, thoroughly briefed on such answers to Negroes, said, "I'm sorry, sir, but I have nary a thing to offer you. You can fill out an application and we will notify you if any openings occur in the future."
>
> As she spoke these planned and deceptive lines, Mr. Smith, three young men were sitting in the same room in preparation for a [pilot's] class to commence on March 16.... I took the form she gave me and sat down in the reception area to fill it out. While doing so I could not help overhearing the conversation going on beyond the partial partition to my left. Almost within arm's length of me an American [Airlines] official was interviewing new pilots (as distinguished from the furloughed pilots) for a class to start on March 16th or possibly for subsequent classes....
>
> As this conversation developed I almost cried in shame and resentment that, in spite of a letter promising notification...this recruitment had commenced and applicants had been notified and called in for processing.

Marlon went on for another page and a half, detailing his frustrations at the string of broken promises for an interview and a flight test he had received from American Airlines' Director of Personnel, a man named Kistler, before finally receiving a letter of rejection that stated Marlon was "substandard by comparison" to other applicants.

Marlon closed by saying the runaround he had received from American Airlines:

confirms my suspicion that the failure to notify and the rejection are based on the same factor: I am a Negro applicant! Mr. Smith, I plead with you for fairness. Review these events and exercise your executive responsibility where necessary to rectify the tragic effects of racial selection. When this is done, I am sure that I will be among the top ten of the new pilots selected for the March 16th class.*[17]

To bolster his chances of overcoming corporate racism, Marlon began to enlist the help of influential friends. Prentiss M. Brown, Jr., an attorney, a fellow pilot, and the son of a United States senator from Michigan, thought very highly of him, and when Marlon let him in on his thus-far unsuccessful attempts to be hired by an airline, Brown went to bat for him. Writing to C.R. Smith on March 23, 1959, Brown was fulsome in his praise:

> I have known Marlon Green for the last two years, having become acquainted with him as a fellow pilot here in the State of Michigan.... I have had the pleasure of flying with him in Highway planes and also in my own airplane, at which times he has taught me some things that I should know about radio navigation. I have found him at all times to be a gentleman, a man possessed of a natural skill in flying, and certainly a pleasant person to be associated with. I have also found in Marlon a sort of inner confidence within him which keeps him smiling and always looking at the brighter side of things.
>
> The reason I mention this is because he had had, as you know, some difficulties with certain other airlines in his attempt to become a pilot for them. One would think after having so many bitter experiences in the last four or five years, that he himself would become embittered. I have found this not to be the case in Marlon's situation. In other words, he keeps smiling,

---

* On April 7, 1959, Taylor warned Marlon about the Smith letter, saying "I am not certain that it is good and it might be bad for you to be pressing the American Airlines application at the same time as we are trying to press the Continental Airlines anti-discrimination order. I don't blame you for applying to American Airlines but your letter to Mr. Smith might well be used against you at some later time. Letter writing is an easy sport but it can prove hurtful. It shows the opposition the fullness and weakness of our hand."

continues to be pleasant with an inner confidence in himself that apparently keeps driving him to pursue his one desire in life, that is, to be gainfully employed with a commercial airline....

I mention this inner confidence or peace that I find in Marlon Green to try to demonstrate that he genuinely seeks employment as an airline pilot not because his employment would be a precedent maker but because he loves to fly, because he is qualified to fly, and because he wants this to be his life's work. A lesser person in his position could pursue the course that Marlon has taken merely for the purpose of trying to be the first negro to be employed by a commercial airline. In my belief this [is] certainly far from the interest of Marlon Green.

I understand that Marlon has applied once again to American Air Lines for employment.... It is my hope that Marlon Green can be considered.... It is also recognized that there are probably additional reasons that you must mull over in your mind before a negro is employed as a pilot by your company, most of which revolve around what the public is going to think of this unprecedented move. I think we both recognize that there really shouldn't be any reason why a negro or a Japanese or a South African should not be hired as well as any other person for commercial pilot if he has the qualifications. But public reaction is something that is a factor, and you most certainly are interested in that for the protection of your company.

Brown went on to compare Marlon's attempts to break through the airline color barrier to Jackie Robinson's historic arrival on the major-league baseball scene: "My reaction...was that he must really be an outstanding person, both physically and mentally, to be selected as the first negro...."*

Brown closed with, "I believe American Air Lines should take this important step and hire Marlon Green.... It is my opinion that by hiring Marlon Green you would be getting a man of great ability, of good character, and a man who is a gentleman all the way through."[18]

---

* On April 10, 1947, Jackie Robinson broke major league baseball's color barrier when he was signed to play for the Brooklyn Dodgers. The Boston Red Sox were the last major-league team to integrate—in 1959. (Tygiel, passim)

The letter evidently had no effect. American Airlines did not hire Marlon Green, nor even give him an interview or flight test. The rocks in Marlon's jaws were turning into boulders.

CHAPTER 10:
MOST UNSOUND

THE HEARING BEFORE the District Court—*Colorado Anti-Discrimination Commission v. Continental Air Lines, Inc.*—was set for June 11, 1959, in the Denver City and County Building, just to the west of the Colorado State Capital, with District Judge William A. Black presiding. Present were T. Raber Taylor and Marlon Green, along with Colorado Assistant Attorneys General Robert Nagel and Charles S. Thomas, representing the Anti-Discrimination Commission. Representing Continental were Patrick M. Westfeldt, Warren Tomlinson, and William C. McClearn. With Marlon was his oldest son, six-year-old Joseph.[1]

Continental's lawyers based their argument on the 1878 Supreme Court decision in *Hall v. DeCuir* (95 U.S. 485), a legal precedent. This case was first appealed to the U.S. Supreme Court by the owner of a Louisiana steamboat engaged in the transporting of freight and passengers between New Orleans and Vicksburg, Mississippi. The Louisiana Supreme Court earlier had awarded damages to Josephine DeCuir, a Negress who was denied access to a cabin set aside for white passengers, but the U.S. Supreme Court held that the Louisiana law did not apply because the steamboat was a business involved in interstate commerce, the regulation of which was the sole responsibility of the U. S. Congress; states could not require carriers engaged in interstate commerce to provide integrated facilities even for trips that took place only within state borders.

Additionally, the Court pointed out that if each of the ten states bordering the Mississippi River were free to regulate every carrier and to provide for its own passengers and freight, the resulting confusion would produce great inconvenience and unnecessary hardships. The Court's opinion, delivered by Chief Justice Morrison R. Waite, clearly preserved "existing racial customs" and provided a rationale that was eventually used to support the "separate but equal" doctrine later used by segregationists in all sorts of applications.

Waite's Court concluded that: "Commerce cannot flourish in the midst of such embarrassments. No carrier of passengers can conduct his business with satisfaction to himself, or comfort to those employing him, if on one side of a state line his passengers, both white and colored, must be permitted to occupy the same cabin, and on the other be kept separate. Uniformity in the regulations by which he is to be governed from one end to the other of his route is a necessity in his business."[2]

After deciding that Continental's lawyers were right—*Colorado Anti-Discrimination Commission v. Continental Air Lines, Inc. was* more of a case involving interstate commerce than one centered around racially discriminatory hiring practices—Judge William Black remanded the case back to the Commission for the purpose of answering three questions: (1.) Is Continental operating in interstate commerce as far as the Green case is concerned? (2.) Does the job sought by Green involve interstate commerce and, perhaps most importantly, (3.) Is Continental, if they are shown to be an interstate carrier, subject to the Colorado Anti-Discrimination Act? He further told the Commission that it could make any other findings it thought relevant to the case.

Colorado Assistant Attorney General Robert Nagel asked Black

"whether the remand order was broad enough to have findings made in support of the conclusions on discrimination." Black said that the Commission *did* have the jurisdiction to make such findings.

"Therefore," Taylor told Marlon, "the order that is being submitted to the Commission [by the Court] will make findings of fact and conclusions of law and enter a new order. On its own motion it is proposed that the Commission will vacate its old order, which was found defective, so there will

Denver District Court Judge William Black, circa 1961
(Courtesy Associated Press)

be a clean complete fresh start."³ The hearing was postponed to June 26.⁴

Following the inconclusive hearing, Marlon and Joseph flew on to Aspen. "We had a Cessna 180 that an attorney friend [Prentiss M. Brown, Jr.] from St. Ignace, Michigan, loaned us to go to Denver," said Marlon. "Joseph and I spent three days in Denver, and a wealthy woman who was interested in the case—Barbara Poindexter—invited us over to her place in Aspen, where we spent the night."⁵

Barbara Poindexter was a wealthy, well-connected woman who counted as some of her closest friends Aspen's greatest benefactors, Walter and Elizabeth Paepcke of Chicago. The multi-millionaire Paepcke was the founder of Container Corporation of America, a generous philanthropist and supporter of the arts who had, in the late 1940s, transformed Aspen from a nearly abandoned Colorado mining town into a posh ski resort and cultural center. With his wife (who was the sister of diplomat Paul Nitze), Walter Paepcke created the Aspen Institute for the Arts. (The Paepckes were also good friends with statesman and former presidential candidate Adlai Stevenson, the humanitarian and theologian Albert Schweitzer, the philosopher and educational theorist Mortimer Adler—all of whom were major shareholders in Continental Airlines.)⁶

Surrounded by the sublime summer beauty of the alpine setting, Marlon began to unwind a little, and even got in some trout fishing in a mountain stream. "On our fishing trip," Marlon told T. Raber in a letter, "Joseph was the hero. He sat on a rock, the very image of Izaak Walton,* and excelled by catching two fish while our host-guide and I could only manage one each. I saved my face by the fact that my catch was the largest—a nine-inch trout.... Our daily prayer to St. Thomas More for your success continues. Yours in Christ, Marlon D. Green."⁷

Barbara Poindexter, like the Paepckes, also owned stock in Continental Airlines. Eleanor said, "Mrs. Poindexter had adopted a non-white child and was therefore acutely aware of and involved in matters of racial justice and equality. She was also friends with Eleanor Roosevelt, the widow of the former president, and persuaded Mrs. Roosevelt to write to Continental in support of Marlon but even this

---

* Walton, 1593-1683, is considered the "father" of angling and in 1653 published his book, *The Compleat Angler*.

letter yielded no results."*[8]

Barbara Poindexter also informed the Greens that she had talked with a friend about Marlon's situation and told him, "It was absurd that there are no Negro pilots. He said, 'Passengers wouldn't stand for it [i.e., being flown by a Negro]—they'd walk right off the planes.' I told him he was wrong."[9]

Mrs. Poindexter also made a point of bringing Continental's discrimination to Walter Paepcke's attention, indicating that Six refused to answer her letters. Paepcke assured her that he would talk to Six about Marlon at the airline's next board of directors meeting. "I have a feeling Six's secretary has instructions to throw out letters on this subject," she wrote Eleanor. The Aspenite also sent letters to the syndicated newspaper columnist Drew Pearson and letters to the editors of the major newspapers in Chicago, New York, Los Angeles, San Francisco, and other cities. "I am hoping to shame Six into the proper action," she proudly told Eleanor.[10]

———•—•—•••———

IN HIS JUNE 15, 1959, letter to Marlon, T. Raber Taylor expressed his feeling that Judge Black's ruling was "a blessing rather than a disadvantage," because it allowed him more time in which to fully research cases involving interstate commerce, which seemed to be Black's main point. Taylor felt that Continental's attorneys "failed to introduce into evidence an abundance of fact that Continental Air Lines is an interstate commercial air carrier and that your job would always have involved interstate flights. We all know that Continental Air Lines is an interstate carrier but unless this knowledge is reflected in the record as fact, the Court cannot consider the commerce question."[11]

In other words, the case hinged not on whether Continental had committed an act of racial discrimination by refusing to hire a Negro pilot but on whether or not the Colorado Anti-Discrimination

---

* Eleanor Roosevelt's letter said, in part, "I hardly think my endorsement [on Marlon's behalf] will carry much weight but of course it would be a great step forward if Continental were to find it possible to open up the pilot's training course to qualified Negro pilots." She was right; her endorsement carried no weight. (Letter, Eleanor Roosevelt to Robert Six, Jan. 2, 1959, courtesy Franklin D. Roosevelt Library)

Commission had authority over an airline involved in the conduct of interstate commerce. Marlon just shook his head; as far as he was concerned, the legal waters were getting muddier by the day.

Meanwhile, Taylor was working well into the night on Marlon's behalf, poring over volumes full of case law and legal journals, looking for precedents to counter *Hall v. DeCuir*. On some nights he skipped dinner and did not return home from the office until after 2:00 a.m. *Colorado Anti-Discrimination Commission v. Continental Air Lines* was no longer just a legal case; to T. Raber Taylor, it had taken on the trappings of a holy crusade.[12]

———•··•··———

IN THE MEANTIME, the Colorado Anti-Discrimination Commission withdrew its December 19, 1958, findings of fact, conclusions of law, and order. Mort Gitelman, who studied the case as a Master of Laws graduate student at the University of Illinois, wrote in his thesis, "Then, without notice to either party or hearing of any kind, the Commission entered new findings and a new order (approximately nineteen pages long, compared with the original document of five pages). On June 25th the Commission presented its new findings and order in the district court. Judge Black decided that the new findings and order was void as it had been entered without notice and hearing, that the original order was non-existent having been withdrawn and, because there was nothing for the court to review, the case would be dismissed."[13]

———•··•··———

"THIS LETTER BRINGS sad news," wrote T. Raber Taylor to Marlon on June 25, 1959. That morning, he said, during a hearing on motions before Judge Black, the judge "announced that the [Green] matter before the Court became moot by the Commission's vacation of its December 1958 order."[14]

Taylor explained that on June 22 Judge Black made a strange ruling that basically threw out the Colorado Anti-Discrimination Commission's complaint against Continental.[15] The Commission, per the judge's original directions, had withdrawn its five-page complaint and entered a new, nineteen-page complaint. Judge Black reprimanded the

Commission for doing what he had told it to do, and dismissed the case against Continental. It was as though a college professor had told his English literature class to prepare for a true-false quiz on the works of Jane Austen and then had given them an essay exam on quantum physics, flunking them when they did not do well.

According to an article in the *Denver Post,* Assistant Attorney General Robert Nagel had argued during the June 25 hearing that the Commission "had the power to enter the new order because it was based upon the same findings that the Dec. 19 [1958] directive had been based upon. But Judge Black told Nagel that the new complaint was 'the most unjudicial [complaint] I have ever received in seventeen years on the bench.'" Black gave Nagel and Taylor thirty days in which to correct the errors.[16]

Taylor's sad letter to Marlon went on: "[Judge Black] further stated...that the Commission could not under the law make new findings without a new hearing.... In view of all of the prayers and efforts that have gone into this case thus far, disappointment is the word which describes our feelings. Disappointment is often accompanied by a sense of shock."[17]

Marlon *was* shocked. And incredibly angry. Judge Black's ruling meant, in effect, that the whole case had to start over from square one.

THOMAS RABER TAYLOR was not a man to be easily defeated by a judge's adverse ruling. He was not unaccustomed to hardship or setback. He had worked his way through Denver's Regis College in 1933, and by waiting on tables at a sorority house while completing his law degree at Harvard, from whose law school he graduated in 1936. He had seen combat duty as a lieutenant commander with the Navy in World War II in the deadly cauldron of the Mediterranean Theater during the invasions of North Africa, Sicily, Italy, and southern France. He had married Josephine ("Jo") Reddin in 1938, started a family, had seven daughters, and threw himself into not only his career but also the Society of St. Vincent de Paul, where he rose to international prominence.

His professional interests covered a variety of areas including taxation, wills, federal administration, and medical-legal problems. He was especially well-known for his work in union discrimination issues. He also had many legal publications to his credit, including "Equal Protection of Religion: Today's Public School Problem," which appeared in the April 1952 issue of the *American Bar Association Journal*.[18]

If a District Court judge thought he could change the rules in the middle of the game and throw out Taylor's and the Commission's carefully crafted case, there were remedies—such as appealing Judge Black's ruling to the Colorado Supreme Court.

T. Raber told Marlon that he was ready to prepare an appeal that would be based on two main points, the first being that Judge Black had erred when he sent the case back to the Commission to make findings of fact on an immaterial issue (i.e., interstate commerce); and the second being his belief that the Colorado Supreme Court must enforce the Commission's original order of December 1958 that directed Continental Airlines to enroll Marlon in the next training class.

But such an appeal would not come cheaply. Taylor said that he expected the cost of preparing an appeal to the Colorado Supreme Court could be anywhere from $1,800 to $3,000. "I know you were strained to raise the money to pay for the representation and preparation of the answer to the Denver District Court," he told Marlon. "In fairness to my family I am not in a position to continue contributing my services without some payment. If you want me to represent you and prepare a brief for presentation to the Colorado Supreme Court, please send me an air mail letter. You might suggest your present feelings about the entire case and what financial support you can get and give to the case."

Taylor went on to explain that appealing to the Colorado Supreme Court did not guarantee that the Court would reverse Judge Black's order: "It is equally possible that the Colorado Supreme Court can dismiss the whole case or that it could send the case back to the Commission or to the [District] Court to take action in keeping with what the Supreme Court would feel."[19]

Marlon was staggered by the potential cost of an appeal and, on July 20, 1959, he replied to Taylor, "I am most regretful that the money necessary to retain your services is not available to me. Like you, I fear success before the Colorado Supreme Court is far from probable. In spite of this I would be anxious to pursue the faintest hope if I were financially sound. I am most unsound." He did not, however, tell T. Raber to drop the case. That decision he and Eleanor would need to mull over.[20]

Marlon was caught in that proverbial spot between a rock and a hard place. The possibility that Taylor's fee could be as high as $3,000—with no assurance of victory—was daunting in the extreme for a man making $2,736.00 a year.* He agonized over what to do.[21]

———•—•—•••———

IN COLORADO, EFFORTS were still being made on Marlon's behalf, even without Marlon's knowledge or consent. Charles S. Thomas, another assistant attorney general, informed T. Raber Taylor and Roy Chapman of the Anti-Discrimination Commission that he was moving forward with the appeal to the State Supreme Court, at no cost to Marlon.[22]

Nor had T. Raber Taylor put the case on the back burner, awaiting Marlon's decision. He evidently had searched the depths of his soul and the tenets of his faith for guidance as to which direction to turn. He was much involved with charitable causes, even if they proved to be time-consuming and financially unrewarding. Could he, as a devout, practicing Catholic and reasonably well-off attorney, turn his back on the plight of Marlon Green, a member of an oppressed minority, and expect to feel right about it? He could not.

On August 15, 1959—the Feast of the Assumption, a day important to Catholics—Taylor summoned every ounce of charity within him and gave Marlon the good news: "Since I received your July 20 letter I have continued my interest in your case and have been working for the preparation of a brief to be filed for the Colorado Supreme Court in your behalf....

"In my July 17th letter I told you that in fairness to my family I was not in the position to continue contributing my services without some payment. Therefore, I ask you to make whatever payment for my services on a weekly, monthly, or other basis as your limited resources will permit....

"I would appreciate your sending me a letter telling me what you feel you can do to bear the burden of this appeal. I think you mentioned that some of your friends had contributed some money to you and that

---

* Taylor would later estimate that he devoted $27,000 worth of time to the Green case.

other friends were going to support you. Whatever they would be able to contribute would be helpful.

"An injustice has been done to you. Now is the time when the step must be taken to rectify this error or it must be abandoned. If you feel that you would prefer to have the case dropped please let me know and I will also inform Mr. Chapman."[23]

Had he not been so deeply invested in obtaining justice for himself, it might have been possible for Marlon to simply thank T. Raber for all his efforts and ask him to drop the case. Yet giving up would mean that the ardent followers of Jim Crow would have won; that one more Negro with a legitimate grievance against the system would have been pushed back down into the mud; that the Orval Faubuses and Marvin Griffins— soon to be followed by the Ross Barnetts and George Wallaces*—of the world could smirk with self-satisfaction; that airline executives and attorneys could clap each other on the backs of their expensive, well-tailored suits, hoist a few glasses of champagne, and congratulate each other on their great triumph over a financially burdened Negro pilot whose only crime was his deep desire to fly commercial passenger planes.

But the battered ghost of Emmett Till hovered in the air, attended to by the spit-streaked faces of the students at Little Rock Central High; the humiliated, egg-splattered Autherine Lucy at the University of Alabama; the insulted ears of Rosa Parks on a Birmingham bus; the dangling corpses of countless victims of lynchings. There was no way Marlon DeWitt Green was going to back down now, no matter what it cost in money, time, energy, or heartbreak to go forward.

---

* Orval Faubus was governor of Arkansas from 1955-1968, and is perhaps best known for calling out the state's National Guard to prevent the integration of Little Rock's Central High School in 1957. Marvin Griffin served as governor of Georgia from 1955 to 1959; his term in office was marked by corruption and his steadfast refusal to abide by the Supreme Court's ruling in *Brown v. Board of Education*. Ross Barnett, governor of Mississippi from 1960 to 1964, personally blocked Negro college student James Meredith from enrolling in the University of Mississippi in 1962. George Wallace, governor of Alabama, followed Barnett's lead and personally barred Negro students from entering his state's flagship university in 1963.

CHAPTER 11:
GUIDED BY DIVINE PROVIDENCE

AS SOON AS he received T. Raber Taylor's August 15, 1959, letter, Marlon phoned the lawyer, then followed up with a note: "I will not try to improve on my wife's description of your letter. Startling! Startling! She was happily excited as we talked on the telephone at noon. Thank you for giving us this wonderful occasion to thank God.

"As you probably realize, my earlier letter was occasioned by my inability to commit myself to any *definite* financial obligation. Your heroic (I know it is a considerable sacrifice) charity and Mr. Chapman's generosity bind me to respond in some similar though meager manner. Enclosed is a check for $150.00. Some time late in September a monthly raise amounting to about thirty-one dollars will commence. This increase will be promptly forwarded to you each month." Marlon went on to say that he would obtain a $400.00 loan from his credit union and send it to Taylor.

He closed with, "I am most desirous that this matter be pursued. Thank you for making pursuit possible. Sincerely in Christ, Marlon."[1]

THE WHEELS OF justice turned with glacial speed as the summer of 1959 changed into autumn colors. Besides the developments in the Marlon Green case, 1959 had proven to be a most eventful year. Alaska had become the forty-ninth state; the Soviet Union had sent a lunar probe to photograph the dark side of the moon; and Marlon's favorite ball team, the Los Angeles Dodgers, was in the process of defeating the White Sox in the World Series. Cuban President/Dictator Fulgencio Batista had fled from the encroaching insurgents and was replaced by President/Dictator Fidel Castro. Movie director Cecil B. DeMille, architect Frank Lloyd Wright, actor Errol Flynn, General George C. Marshall, Baseball Hall of Fame player Mel Ott, and singers Buddy Holly, Richie Valens, and the Big Bopper (J.P. Richardson) all passed into history. The

Cold War simmered; the United States declared a moratorium on nuclear weapons testing; and Soviet Premier Nikita Krushchev met with President Eisenhower and toured the United States. The possibility of world peace seemed at hand.[2]

In terms of racial matters in America, however, the report was as mixed as ever. In April 1959, Jackie Robinson, Harry Belafonte, A. Philip Randolph, Daisy Bates, Roy Wilkins (head of the National Association for the Advancement of Colored People), and other prominent African-Americans led some 25,000 high school and college students through the nation's capital in the second Youth March for Integration.[3]

Many public schools in the seventeen Southern and "border" states were still in various stages of non-compliance with the 1954 U.S. Supreme Court's *Brown v. Board of Education* ruling. In Prince Edward County, Virginia, as an example, the County Board of Supervisors took the draconian measure of closing *all* the public schools rather than admit *any* Negro students; at the same time, a private foundation was set up in the county to give tuition grants and tax breaks so that white students could attend private schools.[4]

For its part, the North could claim no moral high ground. In New York City in 1959, for example, a judge declared that the city's public junior high schools were neither integrated nor equal. According to the January 9, 1959, issue of *U.S. News and World Report*, Judge Justine Wise Polier of the Children's Court Division of the Democratic Relations Court found that there was "a city-wide pattern of discrimination against junior high schools with 85 percent or more Negro and Puerto Rican students as compared with schools which have 85 percent or more white students. A far greater percentage of positions in the schools with heavy Negro and Puerto Rican attendance were not filled by regulatory licensed teachers."[5]

A growing undercurrent of racial discontent was beginning to rumble throughout the land. As the Negro population at large was at last starting to see some glimmer of hope in their centuries-old struggle against oppression, some began to speak out forcefully for even more radical change—a forcefulness that began to frighten the white majority.

In the late 1950s, a nascent Negro militancy movement emerged, led by former Marine Robert F. Williams, a thirty-eight-year-old African-American and head of the Monroe, North Carolina, chapter of the

NAACP. Williams had grown up seeing black women raped and sexually degraded by white men and he vowed to redress such grievances, despite being targeted for death by the local Klan. In 1957, Williams and his well-armed para-military group of Negro veterans fought off an armed Ku Klux Klan motorcade with "a hail of disciplined gunfire" when the Klan attacked the home of a fellow NAACP official who had attempted to integrate the local swimming pool.

The following year, Williams and the Negro community of Monroe became outraged when two young boys, David "Fuzzy" Simpson, seven, and James Hanover Thompson, nine, were jailed after someone reported that they had been kissed by a seven-year-old white girl; Williams, with the help of the Socialist Workers Party, turned the incident into an international issue.*

Then, after a court found two white men not guilty of raping Negro women, Williams declared "it was time to meet violence with violence"—a declaration that forced Roy Wilkins to expel him from the NAACP. Williams knew his weapons. As head of the Monroe chapter of the National Rifle Association, he disavowed Martin Luther King, Jr.'s policy of non-violent resistance and began advocating armed struggle by Negroes against the Klan and other enemies. As might be imagined, Williams became a lightning rod at a time when many southern Negroes preferred to keep a low profile and do nothing that would attract the ire of segregationists.**[6]

—··+··—

---

* One of the boys was sentenced to fourteen years in prison for attempted rape; the other was sentenced to twelve years. After President Eisenhower learned of this miscarriage of justice, he applied pressure that eventually freed the boys.

** Williams, wanted by both the Klan and FBI, fled the U.S. in 1961 and moved to Cuba. After five years in Castro's "Communist paradise," and finding racism just as onerous there, Williams returned to the United States in 1969 to face FBI charges of kidnapping a white couple in Monroe. Shortly after his return, Williams obtained a Ford Foundation-funded position at the Center for Chinese Studies at the University of Michigan and briefed Henry Kissinger's State Department on Chinese diplomacy. The charges against him were eventually dropped, but his militancy inspired both Huey Newton and Bobby Seale, founders of the Black Panthers organization of the 1960s. (Zinn, 203)

WHILE MARLON WAITED to learn if the Colorado Supreme Court would hear the appeal, he sent out his own appeals for financial assistance to friends and relatives.[7]

Eleanor indicated that friends of theirs gave what they could. "Norbert Wiley and his wife Sheila did give us money. Norb was a doctoral student at Michigan State at the time. My mother also gave us money at intervals. We are talking here of very, very small sums of money, certainly not the thousands needed to cover the legal costs. It enabled us to pay for food and gas, period."[8]

———•••———

FOR NEARLY THREE years, from 1957 to 1960, Marlon and Eleanor managed to scrape by on his salary as pilot for the Michigan State Highway Department. In February 1958, he was even featured in a photo and short write-up in *Ebony* magazine, the Negro community's version of *Life*.[9]

"Whenever there was a need for the commissioner or a group of engineers to visit a Michigan structure, in the Upper Peninsula or wherever," Marlon said, "then the Highway Department rented a Rockwell Aero Commander, an airplane that would accommodate the anticipated group. We had one Aero Commander that was available at Pontiac that accommodated me and up to six people. It was the same type of plane that Eisenhower used. This plane was pretty popular with corporate executives who couldn't afford their own DC-3 or something bigger. It was kind of a precursor to the Lear jet."

In addition to the highway commissioner, Marlon also spent considerable time flying George Reid, the Highway Department's official photographer, to various parts of the state. Reid's job was to photographically document—in motion and still pictures—the progress of the interstate highway system that was then being constructed across Michigan.

Marlon recalled, "We rented a little Cessna, took the door off, and George would lean out with his own courage and skill and take the shots he wanted while I was maneuvering over the particular area that he was shooting."[10]

George and his wife Dorothy befriended the Greens and were among their closest supporters in Lansing. Reid said that flying with a Negro pilot caused him no problems. "I was already mentally prepared for

Marlon shown while employed as the pilot of the Michigan State Highway Department, 1960 (Courtesy Green family archives)

Four of the Green children — Peter, Monica, Joseph, and Maria — watch their dad taxiing in the Highway Department Cessna, Lansing, Michigan, Airport, July 1958. (Courtesy Green family archives)

George and Dorothy Reid, friends of the Greens in Lansing, circa 1960
(Courtesy Green family archives)

people of different cultures," he said, "as my wife and I had invited Japanese exchange students into our home. The fact that Marlon was a Negro was not an issue for me, even though I had never really known any Negroes. I just assumed he was a competent pilot, or he wouldn't have gotten the job."

Reid recalled a time when he thought Marlon's race might have caused some problems. The two of them were renting a hotel room in the Upper Peninsula. He said, "We were in Houghton, an ex-mining town, and wanted to get one room with two beds, because we needed to talk over the shoot that would start early the next day. The clerk said he'd rent us two rooms, but I said no—Marlon's my pilot and we had business to discuss. Two men in the office were looking at us strangely. I'm normally kind of shy, but I was upfront and direct and ready for them in case they had any 'rules.' Marlon didn't say anything; he just stood off to the side and let me handle it."

Reid said, "The thing that really impressed me about Marlon was how personable he was—very friendly. He had a manner about him that was very relaxing. He was really more than just a pilot—he was a friend. We had to work very closely to get the action and the angle just right, and he was very cooperative and skillful in maneuvering that light plane just the way I needed it. And he always made sure that I was strapped in before we took off, so I didn't fall out of the open door."

Reid also recalled that Marlon always made the sign of the cross just before they headed down the runway. "He might also have said a little, inaudible prayer before we took off," Reid mentioned. "I had never seen any other pilot do that. It was comforting and inspiring that this was important to him."[11]

The prayer Marlon always uttered before taking off was, "St. Thérèse of the child Jesus, protect us on our flight."[12]

Years later, George Reid's stepdaughter, Kate Emmons, also recalled how Marlon's skill and easy, professional manner at the controls won her over: "I was already living in New York City when the Green family became good friends with my parents in Lansing. I remember that George often said how safe he felt when hanging by a strap from the open door of a small plane if Marlon was the pilot. It was a giddy thought—the two of them up there swooping around while George filmed footage of Michigan Highway Department construction.

"A great memory I have is of a trip that Marlon, George, and I took to the Upper Peninsula on a freezing cold day. I sat in the co-pilot's seat and felt very safe—the only time in my life I enjoyed flying. We landed on a frozen lake dotted with little ice-fishing shacks. Marlon and I hung out with the fishermen while George did whatever, and then went into the big general store there and bought smoked whitefish to take home. It was a lovely sunny day and George took some pictures in the plane and outside when we got there."[13]

NEWS ITEM:

(Greensboro, N.C., Feb. 2, 1960) Four Negro freshman from North Carolina Agricultural and Technical College protesting segregated accommodations, today staged what they called a "sit-in" at the segregated lunch counter at Greensboro's downtown Woolworth's store and refused to give up their seats to white patrons. The store closed without the students being served, and the four were arrested.[14]

THIS FIRST "SIT-IN" was just the beginning. Seeing this as a perfect non-violent tactic to gain national attention to the plight of the Negro, the Congress on Racial Equality (CORE) and Martin Luther King, Jr.'s Southern Christian Leadership Conference (SCLC)* began to organize more student sit-ins. Over the next two months, following Harlem Congressman Adam Clayton Powell's call for a national boycott of Woolworth stores, similar sit-ins took place at Woolworth, Kress, and McLellan stores and bus terminals in fifty-four cities across nine Southern states.[15]

Sit-ins were picking up momentum, creating a life of their own. For the most part, students sat silently at the counter, taking up all the available seats, while they endured the jeers, racial epithets, and some-times food and hot coffee being deliberately dumped on them by white patrons.

On February 8, 1960, in Durham, North Carolina, Negroes protested against being denied seating at a lunch counter and packed the place with bodies. Protests, riots, and arrests also took place at lunch counters in Portsmouth, Virginia; Chattanooga, Tennessee; and Montgomery, Alabama, and Martin Luther King, Jr. made news by being jailed on February 17 for his part in the Birmingham bus boycott. In Nashville, Tennessee, a peaceful protest at the Woolworth's on February 27 turned violent when a group of white teens attacked the protesters; eighty-one Negro demonstrators were arrested.[16]

March witnessed no end to the protests or the disturbances that accompanied them. At the Tuskegee Institute, students began a boycott of white merchants as a way of protesting a 1957 Alabama law that redrew Tuskegee's city boundaries so as to prevent nearly all Negroes from being considered as residents—or voters.[17]

Sit-ins and protests were suddenly taking place everywhere across the South. A thousand Negroes taking part in a lunch-counter sit-in in Orangeburg, South Carolina, on March 15 were attacked by police using fire hoses, tear gas, and truncheons; 388 students were arrested. Atlanta, too, was shaken by lunch-counter protests; a young man by the

---

* The SCLC was formed in the wake of the Montgomery bus boycott. Inspired by its suc-cess, and seeing no coordinated effort to combat racism, activist Bayard Rustin sought to form a coalition of persons willing to confront the status quo; King picked up the gauntlet and organized a group of Southern Negro ministers that soon became known as the Southern Christian Leadership Conference. (www.stanford.edu/group/King)

name of Horace Julian Bond* was one of the organizers. In the east Texas town of Marshall on March 30, police used fire hoses to disperse a peaceful Negro crowd at a lunch counter.[18]

On April 19, the home of Z. Alexander Looby, a Negro Nashville city councilman and a lawyer who represented jailed protestors, was destroyed by a bomb; neither he nor his wife were injured. More than 2,000 persons marched upon city hall to protest Nashville's failure to halt racial violence. Such reported acts were only the tip of the iceberg; throughout March and April 1960, demonstrations, protests, counter-protests, arrests, and beatings of Negroes by whites were taking place across the South at an ever-increasing pace.[19]

The United States Congress was getting the message that something needed to be done before the country descended into total chaos. On April 21, 1960, the U.S. House of Representatives, responding to the growing unrest, passed the Civil Rights Act of 1960, 288 to 95.**[20]

The passing of an act, however, did not ensure domestic tranquility. On April 24, 1960, a group of 125 Negro bathers attempted to hold a peaceful "wade-in" of a "whites-only" beach along the Gulf Coast at Biloxi, Mississippi. They were set upon by a mob of angry whites wielding clubs, chains, and blackjacks. That evening gunfire broke out and eight Negroes were hospitalized.[21]

The month of May began to show a modicum of progress when Eisenhower signed the Civil Rights Act of 1960 into law and Nashville

---

* Better known simply as Julian Bond, the Morehouse College junior was a founding member of the Student Non-Violent Coordinating Committee (SNCC) and in 1961 he and Morris Dees founded the Southern Poverty Law Center (SPLC). In 1965 he was elected to the Georgia House of Representatives but that body refused to seat him because of his vocal opposition to the Vietnam War; the U.S. Supreme Court ruled that such action violated Bond's freedom of speech and ordered the Georgia House to admit him. (*New York Times*, Jan. 11, 1966) He served in the Georgia House until 1975, when he was elected to the Georgia Senate. At the Democratic National Convention in 1968, he was nominated to run for vice-president, the first black to be accorded that honor. However, being only 28, he was too young to qualify for the office and withdrew his nomination. He was elected national chairman of the NAACP in 1998, and has been a professor at the University of Virgina.

** The bill, filibustered for over 125 hours by Southern Democrats—the longest filibuster in history—created federal inspection of local voter registration rolls and established penalties for anyone who attempted to obstruct another person's right to register or to vote. (en.wikipedia.org/wiki/Civil_Rights_Act_of_1960) integrated six lunch counters; a U.S. District Court judge ordered Atlanta to begin desegregating its schools the following September; the Justice Department filed suit to force Biloxi to open a beach that Negroes could use; and Martin Luther King, Jr. was acquitted of perjury charges in the Montgomery bus boycott trial.

June, too, brought continuing hope. Trailways Bus Lines and several Southern department-store chains announced that they would desegregate their lunch counters. The federal government began looking closely at voter-registration records in numerous Southern counties to see how many Negroes were registered to vote. In July, Harper Lee's race-consciousness-raising novel, *To Kill A Mockingbird,* was released to critical acclaim.[22]

With so much progress being made in 1960, it was just a matter of time before Continental Airlines invited Marlon Green to join the fold.

Or was it?

ALTHOUGH HE WAS employed as a pilot for the state of Michigan, Marlon wasn't flying for an airline, and the snubs by the major carriers, the delays in his court case, and his low state salary were all eating away at him like Prometheus' vulture, devouring him bit by bit. He became more irritable and moody, snapping at the children for the noise, the messes, the slightest breaches of his strict family rules.

Also throughout much of 1960, Marlon grew increasingly unhappy at work. One of the issues weighing on him was the type and condition of the aircraft that the Michigan State Highway Department was leasing from the Michigan Department of Aeronautics. He said, "The planes we were renting were not well equipped with the radio equipment that I desired for safety and the weather conditions that sometimes were experienced."[23]

Marlon wanted the state to rent a rugged Twin Beech Model 18 "bush plane" with two R-985 Pratt and Whitney engines rather than continue using the outdated aircraft from the Michigan Department of Aeronautics; Marlon much preferred the updated electronic capabilities of the Twin Beech. On October 4, he went out on a limb to request that the Department lease a Model 18 from a local company, Francis Aviation, but his superiors vetoed his request, citing budgetary problems.

Family friend Ed Kammerer took this snapshot of the Green clan and friend
Cleo Moran in Lansing, Michigan, July 1958.
(Courtesy Green family archives)

Although he had discussed the matter several times with Howard E.
Hill, Managing Director of the Michigan State Highway Department,
Marlon felt he was getting nowhere—a feeling that was leading him
toward action.[24]

—··✈··—

THE COLORADO SUPREME Court fixed from 10:00 until 10:15 A.M. on
June 6, 1960—Marlon's thirty-first birthday*—as the time and date
when they would hear the appeal of Marlon Green, who had waited
two years for his day—or, rather, fifteen minutes—in court.

Marlon had hoped to attend, but it would have meant borrowing
money from one of his brothers, and the funds did not come through.
He noted to Taylor, "We pray for a favorable (heroic) ruling by the
Colorado Supreme Court. In advance, I thank you for your preparation

---

* At the time, the major airlines' upper age limit for hiring new pilots was thirty.

Colorado Supreme Court justices, 1960

Edward C. Day

William E. Doyle

Albert T. Frantz

Frank H. Hall

Francis Knauss

O. Otto Moore

Chief Justice Leonard Sutton

(All photos courtesy of Colorado State Archives)

and presentation in my behalf. I wish you could have more than fifteen minutes." He enclosed a check for forty dollars.[25]

T. Raber Taylor, as was his custom, rose early on June 6 to avoid the traffic jam in the bathroom he knew would be caused by his wife and seven daughters. He showered, shaved, put on his best suit, downed a quick breakfast, and headed out the door to attend 6:30 a.m. Mass at St. John the Evangelist Catholic Church, just a couple of blocks from home to, as he put it, "pray to the Holy Spirit that I would be an effective instrument in the cause of justice." Spiritually fortified, he then drove to the Colorado Supreme Court chambers downtown and readied himself for his presentation to the justices.

Taylor had spent twelve hours of his weekend preparing for his fifteen minutes of oral argument. Once he was permitted to address the justices, he focused on three concepts: First, that Continental had discriminated against Marlon solely on racial grounds; second, that Continental had denied the allegation of racial discrimination; and, third, that the airline had introduced the question of the Anti-Discrimination Commission's jurisdiction in the matter strictly as a "red herring" ploy in order to gain delay. Taylor hammered home the fact that the Court needed to enforce the Commission's ruling that Continental must admit Marlon to a training class as soon as possible.

The majority of justices, however, had some serious concerns with Taylor's line of reasoning. Justice Edward C. Day brought up the fact that Marlon's December 14, 1958, telegram to the Commission to withdraw his complaint had been a voluntary act—Day's implication being that Marlon must not have really cared about pursuing the matter. Taylor responded to Day that Marlon had been discouraged by the delays of the Commission "almost to the point of despair," and told the Court the reason was because Marlon had hoped that, by threatening to withdraw the complaint, he would prod them into a speedier decision.

Justice Day, apparently viewing Marlon as a civil-rights "crusader," then asked if an employer would be obliged to hire a crusader like Carrie Nation, the prominent Prohibitionist, who would be pre-occupied with the crusade rather than the employment. As Taylor relayed to Marlon later, "I pointed out that an employer would have a sufficient reason *not* to employ a Carrie Nation but that you were not a Carrie Nation. I explained that when you were in the Air Force, you made application to many of the airlines, just like college students today must make application to many colleges with a desire to be admitted by one."

Justice Day pressed on, accusing Marlon of engaging in several known instances of anti-discrimination litigation. Taylor pointed out to the judge that it was true—Marlon *had* tired of being turned down or ignored for pilot jobs he knew he was qualified to hold, and felt his only relief was through anti-discrimination commissions.

Justice Frank H. Hall then asked whether it was illegal for a prospective employer to require an applicant to disclose his race on an application form. Taylor explained the Colorado statute on such requirements, telling the justices that requiring an applicant to reveal his race or religion or to include a photo was just a tool some employers used to screen out "undesirable" applicants without having to consider their qualifications.

Taylor closed his argument by bringing up the matter of why Continental had refused to hire Marlon in the first place—because he was a Negro. As to the excuse that Marlon was not hired because, according to Harrold W. Bell, Jr., there had been "too much publicity" about the case, Taylor explained that Marlon had not even known until the September 10, 1957, hearing that this was a concern to Bell and Continental, and that Marlon was also unaware that he had been considered qualified and might be hired later. To Marlon, Taylor wrote, "I pointed out that after you were interviewed, twenty-three other pilots were employed" by Continental.

Finally, Taylor told Marlon, "No one can guess what the Justices of the Colorado Supreme Court are going to decide.... With a case of this importance, I expect the Court will either take weeks or months before a decision is rendered. In the meantime, therefore, let us pray that the Justices will be guided in their deliberations by Divine Providence. Regardless of the outcome, all things have a purpose in God's plan for us."[26]

THE WAIT FOR the decision was excruciating, but unavoidable; courts run on their own timetable and there was nothing Marlon nor Eleanor nor T. Raber Taylor could do to speed up the process.

At last, on August 15, 1960, the phone rang in the Greens' home. It was James Danahey, an attorney in Taylor's office; T. Raber was in

Philadelphia attending his eldest daughter's vows as a Medical Mission Sister. Danahey did not have favorable news to report; the Colorado Supreme Court had decided, by a 4-3 vote, to send the case back to Denver District Court for a re-hearing. Although Chief Justice Leonard Sutton, Justice Albert T. Frantz, and Justice William E. Doyle had concluded that there was "ample evidence" to support the Colorado Anti-Discrimination Commission's findings that Continental had discriminated against Green, they were out-voted by Justices Day, Hall, Francis Knauss, and O. Otto Moore. "Justice delayed is justice denied," wrote a bitter Justice Doyle, quoting nineteenth-century British Prime Minister William Gladstone.[27]

Marlon thanked Danahey and hung up, feeling as though he had just been run over by a bus. Three years of agonized waiting for Continental—or some other airline—to do the right thing had just gone spinning down the drain. Three years of praying and expecting that justice would be served; three years of barely being able to manage financially; three years of hoping that, by some miracle, the heavens would part and the scales would fall from the eyes of Robert Six and Harrold Bell, Jr. and all the others at Continental and they would hire him and beg his forgiveness, were all for naught.

Marlon's dream of becoming an airline pilot had just been told to go to the end of the line and start over again. But how could he? How could he summon up the emotional strength to start over? And where would he ever find the money to keep sending to T. Raber Taylor—a good, decent man trying to do the best for the Greens, no doubt about that. But the case was a bottomless pit into which all of the Green's expendable income was being thrown.

Eleanor worried that her husband's unhappiness might lead to desperate measures: "One night Marlon tried to take the Michigan State Highway plane up alone at night—why, I don't know. But, luckily, the plane was locked and Marlon didn't have the key."

Marlon's burden was Eleanor's burden as well, and it was becoming almost too much for her to bear. She gave a moment's thought to leaving him, but then what? She had put too much effort into the marriage and into Marlon's quest for justice to quit now. She sensed, too, that "the whole case would have blown up and Taylor would have absented himself; we would have been in an even worse financial situation" if she left Marlon.[28]

T. Raber Taylor did his part to bolster his client's spirits. He wrote to Marlon on August 24, 1960, telling him that he planned to submit a Petition for Review to the Colorado Supreme Court.

Taylor explained his reasoning: "Three of the judges would immediately enforce the first order. If, on re-hearing, we would persuade one of the four majority-opinion judges to change his vote, we would have a majority decision and the first order would be immediately enforced, or at least enforceable. This would involve some additional delay. This delay, however, would be, if successful, much less than going back to the District Court for a hearing on the merits and then having another appeal to the Colorado Supreme Court." Taylor mentioned that it might take until some time in October before the State Supreme Court would rule on the Petition for Review. But, seeing no other recourse, two days later he filed the Petition.[29]

Despite his emotional pain, Marlon wrote a note thanking his lawyer. "You have proceeded beyond the Court's decision without hesitation about a further retainer. I cannot offer a further retainer and I feel reluctant to accept your services because the prospects for speedy justice are so remote and my ability to compensate you is even more remote. I boldly ask that you continue to represent me because your counsel is necessary, the injustice of racial discrimination is grievous and widespread, and because victory will be a boon to me and a credit to your legal spirit and ability." Marlon enclosed his customary forty dollars.[30]

Two weeks later, Taylor had news for Marlon—bad news. The Colorado Supreme Court had denied the Petition for Review and said the matter would have to go back to Denver District Court and Judge Black. Marlon's reaction is not recorded, but it could not have been pleasant.[31]

———•——•♦••———

MARLON GREEN'S FRUSTRATIONS and unhappiness on the job finally got the better of him, and the battles with his boss came to a head. "On October 4, 1960," he said, "I told them that if they weren't interested in leasing a better aircraft, then I wasn't interested in flying for the Highway Department any more. They did not respond positively, so I tendered my resignation and became jobless again."

With no other prospects on the horizon, Marlon bounced around, doing whatever odd jobs he could find to bring in money. For two months he tried selling Cutco cutlery door to door. "All it proved was that I am not a salesman," he confessed.[32]

Norb Wiley recalled that after Marlon resigned from his flying job with the state, he mentioned to the Greens that he was working on his Ph.D., part of which involved interviewing about 150 people in three small Michigan towns. "These were towns where a black person, maybe even today, could not be an effective interviewer. I told Marlon and Eleanor that I needed to hire a grad student to help me with the interviews and Marlon said, 'Well, hire *me*—I need the money!' But I said, 'No, I think it'll ruin the study.' He and Eleanor were so pissed off at me that I did that. They thought the right thing to do was to ignore the fact that he was black, and it is, but I wanted my Ph.D.!"[33]

Wiley later observed, "My impression was that Marlon and Eleanor, as pioneers, had half the world's troubles on their backs. The two issues of interracial marriage and fighting the airlines may have been too much at that time and place. In a way, the issues may also have fought each other. Getting that job required a lot of intensified, black-American consciousness, a consciousness that may have rubbed against integration and interracial marriage."[34]

DEEPLY DISCOURAGED AND still unemployed, Marlon could no longer afford a lawyer, which meant he could no longer afford to pursue justice in the courts. On October 10, he wrote to Taylor, requesting the termination of the lawyer's services. He enclosed a check for forty dollars to help defray accumulated expenses.[35]

T. Raber's optimistic letter of October 11 crossed in the mail with Marlon's gloomy one of the day before. In his missive, Taylor mentioned that their nemesis, Judge Black, had lost his bid to be elected to the Colorado Supreme Court and, after having had his decision to throw out the Commission's case reversed by the higher court, was feeling "mellowed."

"In order to avoid the necessity of having the case delayed any longer," Taylor wrote, "and having it sent back to the Commission to make any findings with regard to interstate commerce, I pointed out to

Judge Black that the Colorado Supreme Court majority opinion invited him to take judicial notice that Continental Air Lines was engaged in interstate commerce...and then found it was irrelevant. Therefore, it will be stipulated by me as your attorney, by Charles Thomas as attorney for the Commission, and by William McClearn as attorney for Continental Air Lines, that Continental Air Lines was engaged in interstate commerce and that the job for which you applied would have involved interstate operations."

Taylor said he had emphasized to Judge Black that, in his opinion, the Commission *did* have the jurisdiction to hear the complaint, and all the judge needed to do was to "determine under United States Supreme Court cases, whether the Colorado Anti-Discrimination Commission, on the facts, did have jurisdiction."

Taylor also noted that "we can be thankful that the case has not been sent back to the Commission for a correction of the form of the order, and for the findings on interstate commerce," which would have likely delayed it even further. The case, Taylor said, was set for October 25, 1960, for a hearing solely on the questions of law.[36]

Marlon wondered if "a hearing solely on the questions of law" was just another delaying tactic by Continental.

CHAPTER 12:
A KNIFE IN HIS HEART

ON THE DAY following the October 25, 1960, hearing in Denver District Court, which also lasted halfway through the 26th, Taylor reported back to Marlon that both sides had engaged in making oral arguments and that the judge had given both sides ten days in which to file briefs; the tone of the letter was hopeful.[1]

A week later, while still awaiting the judge's ruling, Marlon thanked Taylor for all the efforts in his behalf:

> Considering that your service is, in fact, a gift to me, it is unfortunate that contrived delay in this matter should impose such additional work on you. I do appreciate your generosity and patience. Perhaps we are commencing to see some reward for all the pain, labor and prayer: witness Judge Black's mellowing and, as I conclude from your recent letters, his intent to get to the heart of this matter and act promptly on its merits.
>
> God owes us nothing, of course, but let us hope that even greater "miracles" are imminent; that I may enter into a stable employment situation as pilot for Continental and that the bright light of your charity and professional preeminence may be seen by all for the greater glory of God....
>
> Our monthly payments will resume as soon as my employment situation permits.

Marlon also told Taylor that he was placing a small ad in the *Wall Street Journal,* offering his services as a pilot.[2] The responses to Marlon's advertising are unknown; suffice it to say that there were no takers to his offer.

Next, he tried a direct-mail campaign, sending out over two hundred letters (starting off with "I am a Negro and a pilot...") to companies he felt might be in need of someone to fly their corporate planes; again, the response was underwhelming.[3]

At one point, Father Hilary Hayden, a monk at St. Anselm's Abbey in Washington, D.C., and a friend of Marlon, tried with tongue in cheek to lighten the burden by suggesting that Marlon make his job hunt known by flying over Manhattan trailing a half-mile-long banner that said "Marlon Green wants to fly for you." The suggestion brought a smile, but he did not follow the advice.

"NEGRO PILOT LOSES Conair Suit," read the headline in the Sunday, January 8, 1961, edition of the *Denver Post*. "A Denver judge ruled Saturday that Colorado's racial policies may not be extended to interstate carriers and he refused to order Continental Air Lines to hire a Negro pilot who claimed illegal discrimination."

So began the article that sounded the latest death knell to Marlon's hopes for a positive outcome. The reporter noted, "Judge William A. Black held that Congress has 'legislated extensively' in the area of racial discrimination in interstate air transportation and has thereby withdrawn this field from state regulation. He said the law for more than 100 years has been that any regulation attempted by a state on interstate carriers is an illegal burden because federal uniform law is required 'to promote and protect national travel....' Whether or not Continental discriminated was not decided in Judge Black's ruling." Black cited forty-four federal court decisions, dating from 1824 to 1959, in his thirty-four-page decision.[4]

In a letter to Marlon the next day, with newspaper clippings summarizing the judgment, T. Raber Taylor said, "I would much prefer you to have a job with Continental than to see you establish the leading precedent in the United States that State anti-discrimination commissions have jurisdiction over interstate carriers. Nevertheless, your courageous action has made a contribution to race relations in the United States."[5]

The Marlon Green case was one of Judge William A. Black's last official acts as district judge; a few days later, he retired.[6]

With Judge Black's rejection of the Commission's findings, Marlon D. Green was once again subjected to another setback, another judicial slap, another crushing blow to his spirits and his dreams of flying. Eleanor Green, too, was distraught and could remain publicly silent no longer. On January 12, 1961, she rolled paper into her Underwood typewriter and clacked out the following letter to Palmer Hoyt, editor of the *Denver Post*, in which she took issue with the January 8 article's characterization of Marlon's quest to become an airline pilot as a "test case":

> He did *not* file the complaint as a test case nor did he participate with the Commission in making it so. In May 1957 my husband left the Air Force hoping to obtain a job flying with one of the commercial air carriers. Though he was and still is well qualified, he has in the past three and a half years been refused by every major air carrier in this country. After almost four months of unemployment in 1957, during which period he was refused by Continental, he finally obtained a job as a pilot with the Michigan State Highway Department.... Since the current period of unemployment beginning this past October, he has sent out more than 260 letters to business firms applying for a pilot job. There have been no offers forthcoming, though a number of firms have expressed good-will and the intention of giving him future consideration. The one job opportunity he has came from an agency: Cuba needs pilots!
>
> ...We have received help from no organization and have borne the financial burden of the court fight as best we could. But now we have come to the end of our resources. Each day our children recite the pledge of allegiance in school and say: "...with liberty and justice for all." For my husband I feel there has been neither liberty (in the sense of being able to obtain equal job opportunity) nor justice. This is the common lot of Negroes in this land of ours.
>
> To suffer the burden of discrimination in patience has great Christian merit. But patience does not preclude speaking out and fighting a great evil. It is unfortunate that the great number of people of good will in our country are, for the most part, silent and sometimes unseeing spectators of the human anguish produced in their neighbors by discrimination.*[7]

In a cover note to T. Raber Taylor that accompanied a carbon copy of her letter to the *Post*, Eleanor said,

---

* The *Denver Post* published Eleanor's letter a week later.

I am deeply grateful to you, to your wife and children and to your good secretary, all of whom in some way, have made sacrifices as a result of your taking Marlon's case. Please convey my thanks to them. Your great charity has been a real inspiration to us in our darkest moments.... Marlon has mentioned to you that he has asked someone for financial help. It is very doubtful if he will receive it. It's pretty difficult to find a combination of Christian charity and wealth....

I write to you tonight with great sadness. The enormity of the suffering experienced by Negroes in this Christian country of ours overwhelms me.... I find it rather ironic that the other state anti-discrimination commissions might file a brief *amicus curiae* ("friend of the court") before the [Colorado] Supreme Court. None of them has been diligent in pursuing any of Marlon's complaints. With all of them it has been a series of inadequate investigations, procrastination and delay.

It is very difficult not to become bitter under the circumstances, Mr. Taylor. The hope of Marlon ever achieving his ambition of flying for an airline is almost certainly dead. The possibility of another flying job is very remote. It is God's will that we suffer so, and I am sure He will give us the grace to bear it.[8]

The same day that Eleanor was writing her letter, T. Raber Taylor was sending a note to Marlon, indicating that the appeal to the Colorado Supreme Court was moving forward and that he had no intention of giving up.[9] In fact, he was already working on a new angle. He had contacted his old friend, Byron S. "Whizzer" White, a Colorado lawyer who had joined the administration of President John F. Kennedy as Deputy Attorney General,* and inquired as to whether or not "the Attorney

---

* White would later be a justice on the U.S. Supreme Court. In the 1930s, he had been a standout on the University of Colorado football, baseball, and basketball teams, and set many records which still stand. He also played professional football for Pittsburgh in 1938, then quit to attend Oxford College in England. He returned to the U.S., played professional football for Detroit and led the league in rushing. In the off-season, he attended Yale Law School. When World War II broke out, he became a naval officer, served in the South Pacific, and became friends with another Navy officer, John F. Kennedy. The future president invited White to be a part of his political campaign in 1960 and, after winning the election, appointed him to be Deputy Attorney General under his brother. On March 30, 1962, Kennedy named White, 44, to be an associate justice on the Supreme Court. (www.thedailycamera.com)

General of the United States would be willing to enter its appearance on behalf of the United States as *amicus curiae?*"[10]

On February 16, 1961, Taylor followed up with a letter directly to the president's younger brother, Robert F. ("Bobby") Kennedy, Attorney General of the United States, and repeated his request that the Attorney General "petition the Colorado Supreme Court for leave to appear as *amicus curiae* and file a brief on behalf of the United States, setting forth its position on the question of pre-emption."*[11]

A week later, T. Raber Taylor received a brief note from Bobby Kennedy, acknowledging receipt of Taylor's request. "The Marlon D. Green case is important to all interested in seeing that equal job opportunity is assured," Kennedy wrote. "I appreciate your bringing this to my attention, and we will be in communication with you further as soon as we have looked into the matter."[12]

DENVER POST EDITOR Palmer Hoyt, probably inspired as much by Eleanor's heartfelt letter as by the gross injustice being done to Marlon, wrote, or caused to be written, an editorial in the January 24, 1961, issue of his newspaper, under the headline, "Green Case: National Handicap Exposed":

> There is, in the Colorado courts, a case that furnishes a remarkably apt lesson in why the Communists so often beat us in the competition for winning friends in the world....
>
> Aside from the fact that some of our leaders and many of our citizens fail to recognize the urgent need to *win* the competition, the major problem is that we have saddled ourselves with some unnecessary handicaps.
>
> We are handicapped by our acquired prejudices, particularly prejudices against non-white persons (who may constitute a minority in the United States but who are the majority in the world), and prejudices in favor of the status quo, whatever it happens to be.

---

* The right of one law to take precedence over another in circumstances where the rights or remedies of the one law conflict with another. Federal laws generally pre-empt state laws.

When we as a nation miss golden opportunities abroad, our people seem justifiably angered. But when we show the same lack of sense at home, the anger fails to materialize. Yet, we won't be able to act wisely abroad until we are prepared to do so at home.

Therefore, any domestic example is worth studying. And the Colorado case is one at point. Before us in Colorado we have a case in which a Negro pilot, Marlon Green, whose competence is not an issue, was turned down for a flying job by an airline operating here because he is a Negro....

Now, ordinarily, this would be the end of an old familiar story. Except that an outside source has helped furnish an interesting moral. According to a letter from Green's wife that appeared in Sunday's *Denver Post,* he could go to work right away at a flying job. He could, if he wanted to work for Fidel Castro's government. He has got an offer from Cuba!

Presumably, Green has reasons of conscience to keep him from accepting a hand from those who oppose Uncle Sam. But, then, he isn't getting the kind of help he needs most from his fellow citizens.

It's something for Americans to think hard and long about.... The best place to practice the techniques of successful world leadership is on our home ground.[13]

———◆———

BY FEBRUARY 1961, Marlon estimated that he had sent out 375 letters seeking employment, but there had been no positive offers of employment. He had even gone to Toronto for an interview with De Havilland Aircraft of Canada, but received no assurances of a future job.

To help supplement the family finances, Eleanor had applied to both the Lansing Public Library and Holy Cross School, the local Catholic

NEWS ITEM:

(Washington, D.C., Mar. 6, 1961) President John F. Kennedy today issued Executive Order 10925, which created the Committee on Equal Employment Opportunity and required that projects financed with federal funds must "take affirmative action" to ensure that hiring and employment practices are free of racial bias.[14]

school operated by the parish and where Joseph, Maria, and Peter were students. Both offered her jobs; she took the lower-paying, temporary substitute-teaching position with the school, thinking, as she told Taylor, "of the gospel for the fourteenth Sunday after Pentecost."* She also felt the longer hours at the library would mean more time away from the children. "Despite the lower income, my choice seemed to be the better one for our family as a whole," she said.[15]

Marlon mentioned to T. Raber that the publication of Eleanor's letter in the *Denver Post* and Hoyt's subsequent editorial had resulted in no job offers.** [16]

———·•·•·———

THE LEGAL SITUATION for the Greens began to look more promising in the spring of 1961. Besides the president's Executive Order, the Anti-Defamation League of B'nai B'rith and the American Jewish Congress both asked the Colorado Supreme Court for permission to file briefs of *amicus curiae*. Bobby Kennedy also came through, indicating that the Justice Department would file a similar brief on Marlon's behalf.[17]

In spite of this glimmer of hope, Marlon's mood remained sour and his spirits low, and five weeks went by before he was able to write to his attorney. "I think you are aware that my life is full of sorrow, suffering and anxiety while I continue to be unemployed," he told Taylor on April 14. "Under these circumstances I am most reluctant to write letters. I apologize if I have offended you by being remiss in correspondence. I feel incapable of assisting you in any way but by prayer. I wish we could spend a few minutes or hours in personal conference. We are all well and abiding in desperate hope that God will soon whiten the black list which controls our employment future."[18]

Marlon and Eleanor continued to worry about the future and ache over the injustices being perpetrated. To escape their woes briefly, the

---

* Eleanor explained, "I'm paraphrasing, but the Gospel narrative for the fourteenth Sunday after Pentecost, the gospel of Matthew 6, 24-33, reminds us of the virtues of trust: God feeds the birds, clothes the naked and the lilies of the field, and brings consolation to people in need."

** The stack of rejection letters in the Green family archives is easily three inches high. Many more were discarded or destroyed.

St. Meinrad Archabbey, Indiana (Courtesy St. Meinrad Archabbey)

family took a short trip to southern Indiana in April for a retreat at the St. Meinrad Archabbey, a Benedictine monastery founded in 1854 by monks from the Einsiedln Abbey in Switzerland, with which they, as Lay Oblates, were affiliated. The Greens' brief visit was a spiritual tonic for them.

While driving home after the four-day stay at the abbey, six-year-old daughter Maria asked, "Daddy, do you think we can spend four days a week at home and four days at St. Meinrad?"

Marlon said, "In order to keep a schedule like that, I would need not only a private airplane but an eight-day week!"[19]

Once back home, he informed Taylor by letter, "We returned safely from our pilgrimage to St. Meinrad's. Our material necessity, employment, has not yet been God's will for us but the equally essential resignation has resulted from our sacrifice and prayers. All of us enjoyed the change in routine.... For my wife it was a welcome vacation from meal preparation."[20]

DESPITE PRESIDENT KENNEDY'S executive order that established the Committee on Equal Employment Opportunity, 1961 was not a good year for race relations in America, and May was an especially harsh month. In a 1960 ruling (*Boynton v. Virginia*), the U.S. Supreme Court declared segregation within interstate travel illegal; buses, terminals, waiting rooms, restrooms, and restaurants were to be integrated. Although the new federal law prohibited segregation of passengers in interstate travel facilities, the Congress of Racial Equality (CORE), led by James Farmer, planned to test the law by sending student volunteers, known as "Freedom Riders," into the South on Greyhound and Continental Trailways buses. Farmer said they would not be breaking the law, "merely doing what the Supreme Court said we had a right to do."[21]

In the spring of 1961, two Negro college students, John Lewis and Bernard Lafayette (both of whom were later major figures in the civil-rights movement), tested the law on their own by refusing to move to the back of an interstate bus. Impressed with the young men's courage, Farmer asked the two if they would take part in a wider test of the law. Lewis accepted the challenge but Lafayette's parents, afraid for their son's safety, refused to let him participate.

On May 4, 1961, John Lewis, along with a twelve-person interracial group of Freedom Riders, which had been intensely trained in non-violent tactics, departed Baltimore in two buses and headed for New Orleans; it was hoped that the riders would reach New Orleans on May 17, the seventh anniversary of the Supreme Court's *Brown v. Board of Education* decision. More than being just a symbolic ride, Farmer's main motive for the trip was to provoke the racists into a violent clash with the non-violent Riders that would gain widespread publicity and force the Kennedy administration to take action. Farmer got his wish; when two Negro riders attempted to use a whites-only restroom at the bus station in Rock Hill, South Carolina, they were badly beaten. But it was just the beginning.

When the buses reached Atlanta, the riders met with Dr. Martin Luther King, Jr., who told Simeon Booker, a reporter for *Jet* magazine who was along on the trip, that he was worried that they would never make it through Alabama to their destination; King was right.[22]

—··•··—

NOT ALL WHITES in the South had antipathy toward Negroes and the civil rights movement. Under its courageous publisher, Coleman Harwell, Nashville's leading newspaper, *The Tennessean*, was a progressive voice for change in the South. On its staff were such journalistic luminaries as David Halberstam, Tom Wicker, Fred Graham, Wallace Westfeldt, Dick Harwood, Creed Black, and John Seigenthaler, Sr., the weekend city editor.

Seigenthaler, a native of Nashville, told this author about his early, heady days at the paper: "We covered the civil-rights movement across the South. If there was a problem in Little Rock or elsewhere, we had a reporter and photographer there. It was an exciting news room. Somewhat competitive, but very congenial and very collegial.

"But there came a time when a new publisher, Silliman Evans, Jr., came in. He wanted a new editor, and he brought in someone who said that the staff had been manipulated by the students in the sit-in movements, and that there was going to be a change in the policy of covering civil rights: that the Associated Press could cover it outside of Nashville."

The new management and new policies did not sit well with some on the staff and, within a five-month period, they resigned. Seigenthaler left journalism briefly to go to work for U.S. Attorney General Robert Kennedy. Seigenthaler had spent eight months working with RFK in 1959 on his book, *The Enemy Within* [about Senator John L. McClellan's committee's investigations into Teamster boss Jimmy Hoffa and corrupt labor unions from 1956 to 1959, at which Kennedy was McClellan's chief counsel]. "I lived with Bobby Kennedy for four months," Seigenthaler said. "We'd work five days a week, and on the weekends he'd go home to his family in Hyannisport and I'd go home to Nashville. When the 1960 presidential campaign came along, he asked me if I'd come to work in the campaign."

At first, Seigenthaler was reluctant to leave journalism, but when he realized that Evans' new policy at *The Tennessean* about covering (or not) civil rights was cast in concrete, he joined the campaign two weeks after the Democratic convention. Because of his knowledge of the civil-rights movement and many of the people within it, he served as Robert Kennedy's administrative assistant.

Seigenthaler had grown up in a home where his parents were good, decent people but, like so many in America, oblivious to the racial injustice that was rampant all around them. As was the case with nearly

U.S. Attorney General Robert F. Kennedy (left) and John Seigenthaler, Sr., confer about civil-rights matters, spring 1961. (Courtesy John Seigenthaler, Sr.)

every other "white son of the South," the younger Seigenthaler was totally blind as a boy and as a teen to the fact that many injustices were being perpetrated against Negroes. Black people used "colored only" drinking fountains and toilets and church pews, sat in the back of the bus, rarely spoke up, and refrained from appearing "uppity" to whites. It was almost as though slavery had never been abolished.

It was only later that Seigenthaler finally saw the evil corruption of segregation. He recalled that one of his earliest epiphanies came while he was an Air Force control-tower operator at MacDill Field in Tampa, Florida, before Truman integrated the services. "I remember thinking how bizarre it was to look down on that field early in the morning," he said, "and see black troops fall out on one side for roll-call and then go off to a black mess hall, and see the same identical thing happen with white troops on the other side. We all took the same oath to defend the Constitution and the country against its aggressors and, yet, here we were.

"Ralph Ellison, in his book, *Invisible Man*, said, 'They don't see me.' It's tragic that he's feeling the pain and I'm not even aware that my blindness, my indifference, is inflicting the pain. It's difficult to understand how thoughtful, sensitive, caring people could have been that insensitive and uncaring—to not even have an inkling of the injustice of it." Seigenthaler would go on to devote much of his life to combating racism and fighting for justice—a stand that nearly got him killed in 1961.

"A few days before the Freedom Riders started out from Baltimore," Seigenthaler recalled, "Simeon Booker, a friend of mine, came in to see me, and he and I and Bobby Kennedy talked. Simeon said, 'I'm getting ready to do this and I'm afraid there's going to be trouble. Is there anything you can do?'"

Seigenthaler and Kennedy knew that local law enforcement agencies in the South were infiltrated by, and working closely with, the Klan, effectively tying the FBI's hands. Seigenthaler said, "We knew that the FBI agents had to work with the local law enforcement on federal matters—bank robberies, kidnappings, transporting of stolen goods—and that those agents didn't want trouble with the Klan. J. Edgar Hoover didn't acknowledge that civil rights was an issue over which he had jurisdiction—he thought it was better for him and the FBI if local law enforcement would handle things like riots. It was a real dogfight to get Hoover to recognize that this *was* a matter that he had to investigate. Hoover was equally arbitrary about not having the FBI do much about cases of police brutality against Negroes; he thought it would rupture his agents' relationships with local law enforcement. He and the FBI were a problem from the beginning."

Before Simeon Booker left for the Freedom Rides, Bobby Kennedy told him that there wasn't much the Justice Department could do without an active FBI. But Kennedy also told Booker that if there were any problems, he should call him or Seigenthaler at home; the two men gave Booker their home telephone numbers.[23]

———•••———

ON SUNDAY, MAY 14, 1961—Mothers' Day—as the Freedom Riders reached Anniston, Alabama, on their way to New Orleans, a surly mob of several hundred people was there to meet them—and beat them. The local police in Anniston had decided to "look the other way" and allow the Klan to have "a little fun" before stepping in to "protect" the Riders. As one of the buses pulled into the Greyhound station, the white driver, a "good old boy," leaned out the window and smiled at the crowd. "Well, boys, here they are," he yelled. "I brought you some niggers and some nigger-lovers." The group was set upon by a mob of pipe-wielding thugs.

As the second bus, some miles back, approached the town, it was halted by a road block, pelted with stones, and had its tires slashed. The driver stopped to change tires but someone threw a fire bomb into the bus and set it alight.[24] The Riders—men and women, Negro and white—escaped with their lives but ran directly into the waiting arms of a mob, who severely beat them. Replacement buses arrived and both groups of Riders fled to Birmingham, but the white drivers, fearing for their own safety, refused to go any farther.

Birmingham was no more hospitable to the Riders than Anniston had been. After arriving in Police Chief T. Eugene "Bull" Connor's town, they were attacked again. He claimed that he could not provide officers at the bus terminal because of a shortage of officers due to the Mother's Day holiday. The governor of Alabama, John Patterson, also shrugged. "When you go someplace looking for trouble," he said, "you usually find it," adding, "You just can't guarantee the safety of a fool, and that's what these folks are—just fools."[25]

On that Sunday, May 14, Seigenthaler received a call from a shaken Simeon Booker in Anniston, who told him about the attacks and that the Riders had decided to abandon the trip; to continue on was suicide. "Simeon said they had been badly beaten," Seigenthaler recalled. "Some of them had skull fractures, broken bones, and were bloody and mauled and, frankly, frightened. They were courageous but frightened. They were lucky not to have lost their lives. Simeon said that they had voted not to continue, but that they couldn't get out of town by either bus or plane because there were bomb threats against the airplanes."

The next morning Bobby Kennedy and Seigenthaler met to talk about Alabama. The president was scheduled to leave for a diplomatic trip to Canada, but he and the attorney general discussed the situation before he left and they decided to send Seigenthaler down to assist the Riders. Seigenthaler flew into Birmingham on May 15 to meet with Delta Airlines officials there and get the Riders safely out on a plane to New Orleans.

He was shocked at the Riders' condition. "They were all hurting and they were really grieving," he said. "Part of the grief was not just the physical pain from the beatings they had taken but also the knowledge that they hadn't been able to continue their trip by bus."

Seigenthaler worked out the arrangements to evacuate the Riders, but it was a tense time. The group was booked on a regularly scheduled flight from Birmingham to New Orleans, but Delta was worried about bomb threats. To avoid receiving bomb threats, Seigenthaler told the Delta officials simply not to answer the phone. Nevertheless, all the passengers' bags were thoroughly searched to make sure there was no bomb on board. "It was relatively easy to get them to New Orleans by nightfall," Seigenthaler said, and the flight went off without incident.

Emotionally exhausted, Seigenthaler fell into a motel bed at about two A.M., but was soon roused by a call from Bobby Kennedy. "The attorney general said, 'There's another wave of Freedom Riders starting down from Nashville. Do you know a woman named Diane Nash?'* I said I knew a young student named Diane Nash and she probably knew me. The attorney general said, 'Look, she is apparently directing this. Would you please call her and tell her what you've seen? Tell her to call it off.'"

Seigenthaler phoned George Barrett, a Nashville civil-rights lawyer, and asked him to contact Nash and "sort of soften her up." Then Seigenthaler called her. He first tried to persuade her softly, then sternly, then "almost indignantly." "I said, 'Young woman, you're about to get some of your friends killed. I just deposited some people here last night who were lucky to escape with their lives. What you are doing is going to result in somebody getting killed.'"

In spite of his tough stance, Nash was even tougher. "She was like a tree by the water," he recalled. "She would not be moved. She said, 'Sir, we all signed wills last night and left all our worldly goods to our beneficiaries. We're not going to be turned around. We are not going to let violence overcome non-violence.'"

Realizing that he had no more chance of stopping her and the second wave of Riders than he did of stopping the sun from rising, Seigenthaler asked Bobby Kennedy to call Alabama Governor Patterson

---

* Nash, a Fisk University student, had played a major role in organizing the Nashville sit-ins.

and arrange for a meeting. Seigenthaler said, "I had tried to call Patterson but he wouldn't talk to me. He wouldn't take the attorney general's call, either."

The second wave of Freedom Riders reached Birmingham on May 17, 1961, and was immediately arrested by Police Chief Bull Connor and his troopers, then driven up to the Alabama-Tennessee state line and dumped on the side of the highway in the middle of the night; they somehow found rides back to Birmingham, 120 miles to the south, and showed up the next day. Connor was livid.[26]

Meanwhile, Patterson finally agreed to meet with Seigenthaler and discuss providing safe passage for the Riders. "At one point in the meeting," said Seigenthaler, "Patterson made the mistake of saying to his commander of the Alabama State Highway Patrol, Floyd Mann, 'Floyd, tell this man we can't protect them.' Mann said, 'Governor, I've been in law enforcement all my life. If you tell me to protect them, then they'll be protected.' And that changed the dynamic. They worked out an arrangement whereby Bull Connor would protect them in Birmingham, Commissioner [Lester B.] Sullivan, Connor's counterpart in Montgomery, would do it in Montgomery, and Floyd Mann would protect them on the highway."

Seigenthaler then drove to Montgomery to observe and assist in case anything happened.[27] He did not know that Sullivan had proclaimed, "We have no intention of standing police guard for a bunch of trouble-makers coming into our city."[28]

Under pressure from the White House, Greyhound Bus Lines agreed to carry the Riders between Birmingham and Montgomery, which are ninety miles apart. Arrangements were also made to have Mann's patrol cars stationed at intervals along the route and have a State Patrol plane circle above the bus. Everything seemed calm and under control.

The Freedom Riders left Birmingham on Saturday morning, May 20, 1961, but, as the bus entered Montgomery, Sullivan's police escort vanished. Seigenthaler, who had been trailing behind the bus in a car, had a bad feeling. He said, "Commissioner Sullivan had decided to give the mob half an hour."[29]

The bus pulled into the terminal, which was deserted and eerily quiet. "Then, all of a sudden, just like magic, white people everywhere," said Rider Frederick Leonard.

All hell broke loose. Jim Zwerg, a white Rider, was first off the bus and was attacked unmercifully by members of the Klan. William Barbee, a Negro Freedom Rider, was thrown to the ground and beaten with a club as the mob yelled, "Kill him!" John Lewis was so badly hurt that he required hospitalization.

Upset that his promise of a peaceful journey had been so rudely broken by forces beyond his control, Alabama State Highway Patrol Commissioner Floyd Mann rushed into the maelstrom, drew his pistol, and warned the crowd that he would shoot if they didn't obey his order to disperse.[30]

Seigenthaler said the scene at the bus station "was bloody and brutal. It started a couple of minutes before I arrived. The bus station parking lot was like a teeming ant hill of violence."

The majority of the action was taking place around the bus, but there were two white students, women, who were being attacked by a sort of "satellite" mob of about two dozen people who had surrounded them. Seigenthaler said, "They had tried, with some of the young women who were African-American, to get away from there in a cab driven by a black driver, but he was scared out of his wits and said he'd go to jail if he carried white women. So these two white women were on their own."

Seigenthaler braked the car and jumped out to help the two, Susan Wilbur and Susan Herman. "I yelled at one to get into the back [of my car] and jerked the other one, Susan Wilbur, around to my side and told her to get in. She resisted. If she had just gotten into the car, we could have gotten away and I wouldn't have been hurt and," he added with a chuckle, "wouldn't have been in the history books."

The mob suddenly turned on Seigenthaler. "They spun me around," he said. "I made the mistake of saying the magic words: 'Get back—I'm from the federal government.' "

Somebody clobbered Seigenthaler with a pipe behind his left ear and he went down hard, losing consciousness. While he was out, the mob backed off momentarily—a break which allowed the two women to dash to the safety of a nearby church. Meanwhile, Seigenthaler lay under the car, out cold, for some twenty-five minutes before a policeman appeared and had him transported to Bartlett's Clinic.

"I had never been knocked unconscious before or since," Seigenthaler said. "I came to on the table as they were x-raying me. Dr. Bartlett was talking on the phone with Byron White, the deputy attorney general, telling him that I was injured but that I would be all right. I was heavily sedated; they put me in a private room and surrounded the place with state police. Late in the afternoon I woke up and Robert Kennedy called. We talked about what had happened. He told me he had dispatched U.S. marshals to Birmingham, which I regretted."[31]

On that day, May 20, President Kennedy issued a statement that said,

> The situation which has developed in Alabama is a source of the deepest concern to me as it must be to the vast majority of the citizens of Alabama and other Americans. I have instructed the Justice Department to take all necessary steps based on their investigations and information. I call upon the Governor and other responsible state officials in Alabama as well as the mayors of Birmingham and Montgomery to exercise their lawful authority to prevent further outbreaks. I would also hope that any persons, whether a citizen of Alabama or a visitor there, would refrain from any action which would in any way tend to provoke further outbreaks.[32]

Seigenthaler recalled that later that evening, as soon as he was able to walk, he was released from the hospital and driven to the airport. He left town on the same plane that had just brought Martin Luther King, Jr. to Montgomery. That night, King held a meeting of Negro community leaders in the First Baptist Church, which was surrounded by 300 federal marshals who, in turn, were surrounded by several thousand angry whites. The whites—men, women, and children—began jeering the marshals and the Negroes inside the church and hurling rocks through the windows. The stand-off continued until three A.M. when, at the urging of Robert Kennedy, Governor Patterson, against his will, declared martial law and called out the state police and Alabama National Guard.[33]

———•·•◆•·•———

ALTHOUGH DEEPLY TROUBLED by the unrest tearing at the fabric of the nation, Marlon knew he could do nothing to heal the nation's wounds. Besides, he barely had the strength to fight his own battles. But he was not shy about reacting to anything and anyone who displayed any sort of insensitivity toward matters of race and equality.

In a letter dated July 2, 1961, for example, he did not hesitate to excoriate the Bishop of Lansing, Joseph H. Albers, for giving in to local, vocal Catholics who did not want Mexican immigrants worshipping in their midst, and thus established a parish exclusively for Spanish speakers:

> Dear Bishop Albers,
>
> It must be boldly stated that the decision *to segregate* [Marlon's emphasis] was made not in Little Rock or Montgomery (where unchristian race hatred is a common, though sinful, fact) but in Lansing, Michigan, which hypocritically prides itself on being "better than the South." Bishop Albers, you are aware that your motives in establishing a segregated parish for Mexicans are not at all unsimilar to those of job discriminators, school segregators and other actuators of white supremacy.
>
> I would not write this letter to you if the above considerations were my only basis of appeal. No. Fortunately, you and I are Catholics and can speak, at least between ourselves, of loftier, more sacred and binding reasons for resisting the thoughtless clamor of the majority to segregate. Fortunately, neither the date on a calendar nor the accident of geography determines your grave duty to resist. Christ is your Master. Christ is your Judge. [34]

—————•—————

SINCE MARLON WAS unable to find a job as a pilot, he thought he might be employable with the Federal Aviation Agency as an airline inspector. T. Raber Taylor assisted with a letter to Burke Marshall, special assistant to Bobby Kennedy, requesting the attorney general's office apply whatever leverage it could to get Marlon hired by the FAA. Nothing, apparently, was done.[35] On May 31, 1961, Marlon also wrote directly to Najeeb Halaby, head of the FAA but, again, without result.[36]

On June 8, 1961, Marlon wrote another letter, this time to Stanley Gewirtz, Vice-Chairman of President Kennedy's Task Force on Aviation Goals at the FAA, and outlined his complaints. Said Marlon, "Between December '56 and May '57 my applications had been reviewed by several airlines. During '57 and early '58 pilot recruitment was at its most active since World War II, minimum requirements for pilot entry were at their lowest since World War II, and airlines were even hiring pilots who did not have the minimum requirements. I have not been hired. I am a Negro."

He pointed out to Gewirtz that he had applied for a job with the FAA to be an airline inspector but the FAA had informed him that, since the airlines would not hire Negro pilots, they would not look favorably upon Negro inspectors. He also mentioned that, after he traveled at his own expense to the FAA's offices in Washington, D.C., to inquire as to why he had not heard from the agency regarding his application, he was informed that he did not qualify for the job because he had not flown airline-type aircraft in the last three years—a "Catch 22" situation if ever there was one.

Marlon emphasized to Gewirtz that, since resigning from the Michigan Highway Department in October 1960, he had still been unable to find any airline—or anyone else, for that matter—willing to employ him. "I have not been able to get any work, even driving a taxi here in Lansing or hauling garbage for the city," he said, noting that 316 pilots had been hired by the FAA since July 1, 1960, but he had not.

He closed with, "I don't know what you can do about the situation or to help me. I hope you will do whatever you can to eliminate such inconsequentials as race and religion from their current dominance in aviation employment."[37]

Gewirtz evidently made no effort to redress the grievance, or even to reply to Marlon's letter.[38]

Next, Marlon began looking overseas in even the most unlikely spots for support and possible employment. To Tengku Abdul Rahman, the Prime Minister of Malaya, he wrote on June 8:

> Your Excellency,
>
> Mr. Shaw [Ralph Shaw, editor of the *Borneo Bulletin* and an acquaintance of Marlon] has suggested that a need for qualified pilots may exist with Malayan Airways, the Flag Carrier of your nation. I appeal to you, Your Excellency, for the opportunity to work as a pilot for Malayan Airways....[39]

If a need for qualified pilots existed with Malayan Airways, it didn't extend to Lansing, Michigan, and to Marlon Green. He was not offered a job.

———•••┃•••———

ON JUNE 15, 1961, a spark of good news greeted the Greens. On that date the United States Justice Department aligned itself with Marlon's attempts to be hired by Continental when it filed a fifty-two page "friend of the court" brief with the Colorado Supreme Court. No date was set for the start of oral arguments since Continental needed time to study the brief and prepare answers.[40]

The brief did not put bread on the table, however, and so, with Marlon still jobless, the Greens were forced to go on public assistance. "We would get bulk provisions from the government—peas, powdered milk, peanut butter, yellow American processed cheese in three or four-pound blocks," Marlon related. "The 'surplus' foods were free from the government for anyone who could demonstrate need. Although we were never on food stamps, it was pretty lean."

There was a further humiliation. On the hot, humid day of Friday, July 21, 1961, while Marlon was standing in a long line in Lansing to receive government-surplus food, he heard that Gus Grissom, his former classmate from Randolph, and now one of the acclaimed Project Mercury astronauts, was about to be launched into space in an orbital shot called "Liberty Bell Seven."

"The day when Grissom was about to make his first attempt," Marlon reflected, "I was standing in line in Lansing, Michigan, waiting for the handout of surplus food. On this particular day, they had had an 'abort' or a 'hold' or something, while Grissom was attempting to make his launch in the Mercury capsule, and I remember composing a letter—not blaming Grissom for being white or myself for being black—but it was emotional and almost poetic: 'While Grissom is on his way to the stars, Marlon is standing in line for surplus foods.' Something like that. There was an element of hurt and disappointment in it."*[41]

Eleanor watched with growing concern as her husband sank deeper

---

* Marlon's note actually read, "On March 24, 1951, Virgil Grissom and I became pilots. Today he literally strives for the moon. I 'shoot for the moon' when I dare hope that I can even earn my living as a pilot in the United States."

Grissom died on January 27, 1967, at the Cape Kennedy launch pad when fire swept the Apollo 204 space capsule during a training run. Astronauts Roger Chaffee and Edward White also perished in the blaze. (history.nasa.gov/apollo204/grissom) and deeper into an emotional morass. "One evening," she said, "Marlon declared he was going to hitch-hike to New York. He left and I sat on the porch all night, wondering what I was going to do. He came back the next afternoon."[42]

Marlon acknowledged this need to escape, physically and mentally, from all the pressures crushing him: "There was one time, after I had burned all the responses from the airlines, that I thought was the low point of my depression about the airlines' response. I felt there was nothing else I could do in Lansing, and I wanted to try to make my way someplace else. I think I got as far as Jackson, Michigan, on that hitch-hiking thing, but it may not have been that far. It was an act of desperation for change. I'm not sure that did it, because I don't think anything came within reasonable proximity of it. It was just a moment that had to be responded to by getting away. Once it was over, it didn't help any, but it was done."[43]

Marlon's growing herd of personal demons continued to attack him. On August 3, T. Raber Taylor received a strange and disturbing letter from his client. It appeared that Marlon had lost all hope, for he declared that he desired to end their relationship once the Colorado Supreme Court had made its final decision, whatever that decision might be. In the note Marlon said, "Litigation as I have known it in this case is not an effective instrument against the prevailing injustice. I need to be free to take whatever action possible in opposing racial discrimination. For this reason I feel I must dissociate myself from the counselor-client relationship we have known. My actions may be of such directness and acerbity as to embarrass you or hurt your legal reputation."[44]

What was Marlon planning to do, Taylor wondered. *Was he going to shoot someone at Continental? Burn down their hangar? Commit suicide on the steps of the Colorado state capitol?* The possibilities were frightening. Taylor wrote back, "Your August 1, 1961, letter surprises me. I do not understand it.... In view of the fact that I have been striving so long to act in your best interests, I cannot understand why you would be contemplating any action to embarrass me or hurt my legal reputation.... Do your thoughts of acerbity mean that you are now displeased with the way the case is being presented to the Colorado Supreme Court? I would like to have a clear, open and frank statement from you as to what is troubling you.... If it is against me, I want you to speak frankly."[45]

A partial clue to Marlon's mental state came to Taylor in an August 6, 1961, letter from Eleanor. "I, too, am very disturbed about Marlon's welfare," she began. "As you may have inferred from the letter he wrote you last week, there has been no success in getting a job with the FAA or anywhere else.... The picture is very dismal, Mr. Taylor. I fear that Marlon may be close to the breaking point. He is full of anger and frustration and it is bottled up inside him.

"We all attend daily Mass together and the grace of God keeps us going from day to day with some measure of peace, but I am afraid it cannot last much longer.

"Marlon has had some respite in taking the children fishing, but the place where they fish is close to the airport and planes constantly fly overhead. I think each plane is a knife in his heart as it goes over."

Eleanor also related instances of overt discrimination in Michigan, times when Marlon was refused a cup of coffee, or asked to eat his meal *outside* a restaurant, or ignored by clerks in department stores, or refused accommodations at motels.

She went on to mention that her mother, although not overly sympathetic to Marlon's struggle for justice, nevertheless was sending enough money each month to keep the family going. Eleanor also indicated that she was not having much luck finding even temporary work herself, but hoped to land another teaching job the next month, September.

She ended her letter with, "I am truly sorry, Mr. Taylor, that taking Marlon's case has been such a burden to you. We are deeply grateful for your great charity and continue to keep you in our daily prayers."[46]

Clearly, Marlon Green had reached the tipping point. Could anything bring him back from the precipice?

Marlon and three of the Green children fishing in Lansing, Michigan
(Courtesy Green family archives)

CHAPTER 13:
OFFICIALLY A PAUPER

CONTINENTAL AIRLINES HAD other matters on its corporate mind in the early 1960s besides its ongoing legal battle with Marlon Green and the Colorado Anti-Discrimination Commission.

Robert Six was in the process of expanding his business by adding both new airplanes and new routes. He cut fares drastically to attract new customers, lured high-powered airline executives away from other carriers, and attempted to acquire another regional carrier—National Airlines—a merger deal that eventually fell through. He did not, however, hire any Negro flight crew members.

There was also tension and tragedy. On August 2, 1961, Continental Flight 54, a Boeing 707 bound from Los Angeles to Houston, was hijacked by a father-son team; they wanted the plane to take them to Cuba. When the 707 made a refueling stop in El Paso, federal agents shot up the tires, then stormed the plane and subdued the two men.

The following year, on May 22, 1962, Continental Flight 11, from Chicago to Los Angeles, was blown out of the sky near Unionville, Missouri. Forty-five passengers and crew died when a bomb planted in an on-board lavatory exploded; investigators believed it may have been a suicide-for-insurance plot, but the suspected bomber died along with everyone else. It was one of the first known cases of airliner sabotage. Ironically, the aircraft was the same 707 that had been hi-jacked by the father-son team a year earlier.[1]

ON AUGUST 14, 1961, T. Raber Taylor wrote to the Greens and said that he had a hunch the Colorado Supreme Court was going to rule in Marlon's favor. He advised Marlon "to get himself in physical and emotional shape to pass the physical and psychological tests" he was certain Continental would require him to take.

Taylor recommended Marlon find some outdoor work—gardening,

landscaping, or some other healthy, physical labor. "So many of us find that as we work with the things of God, our mind is freed of tension and care," he counseled, almost as a priest would. "Often, as we work with our hands, it gives the blessing of balance. I am not unsympathetic to Marlon's feelings of resentment. Each of us, however, is called upon to imitate Him who did not condescend to come to earth, but came to earth for love of us, the lowly, to work with His hands as a carpenter, and to show us the Way."[2]

On the same day Taylor was writing his letter to the Greens, Marlon, with his soul wandering through thickets of despair, wrote to the Trappist monk Thomas Merton at the Abbey of Gethsemani, near Bardstown, Kentucky.

Thomas Merton's star had been rising within the American Catholic community for some time, and he had aligned himself with the nascent civil-rights movement. In a sense, Merton became Marlon's last best hope of finding inner peace. Merton's *Thoughts in Solitude* echoed much of Marlon's pain:

> My Lord God, I have no idea where I am going. I do not see the road ahead of me. I cannot know for certain where it will end. Nor do I really know myself, and the fact that I think I am following your will does not mean that I am actually doing so. But I believe that the desire to please you does in fact please you. And I hope I have that desire in all that I am doing. I hope that I will never do anything apart from that desire. And I know that if I do this you will lead me by the right road, though I may know nothing about it. Therefore I will trust you always though I may seem to be lost and in the shadow of death. I will not fear, for you are ever with me, and you will never leave me to face my perils alone.[3]

Marlon had just read, and been deeply impressed by, Merton's "Letter to an Innocent Bystander" from the book, *Raids on the Unspeakable*, and decided to contact the monk to seek his advice and solace. Merton responded:

> Thanks for your very good letter and the enclosures which give me at least some idea of your difficulties and where you

The Trappist monk Thomas Merton (Photograph by Sibylle Akers.
Used with permission of the Merton Legacy Trust and the Thomas Merton Center, Bellarmine University)

stand.... What can I do for you in a concrete way? You are always welcome here on retreat.... In the meantime, you certainly should do all that you can to get the just treatment you deserve. There is no question that you should go ahead and employ all rightful means to secure employment and at the same time to resist the unfair treatment meted out to you as a Negro. In this you can also help others.

From your letters it seems you are more or less alone. In the matter of employment this is logical.... The man for you to follow, as you know, is Martin Luther King. His tactics seem to me to be perfect and admirably Christian....[4]

Marlon was heartened by the response, and said that Merton was a comfort to him. "It was spiritually helpful," Marlon said, "to find a white person willing to say that racial justice is a thing to be sought and a thing to be worked for, and that injustice is a thing not to be tolerated. In those days, it was very meaningful to have it put in the name of God. So, yes, Father Merton was very meaningful to me." He resolved that he would one day visit the monk.[5]

———·•·———

WHILE MARLON WAS seeking spiritual uplift as well as justice and an end to his financial woes, Robert Six's personal life was taking a different turn. After divorcing Ethel Merman, he married Audrey Meadows in Hawaii on August 24, 1961.*[6]

———·•·———

THE DAY AFTER writing to Merton, Marlon finally gathered enough emotional strength to answer Taylor's letter of August 7, in which the lawyer asked him to be straightforward about his reasons for wanting to drop out of the case.

The answer was simple: "*I am convinced that there is no solution to my need and quest for equal opportunity.* [Marlon's emphasis] Since I see no solution to an urgent, basic need, I am desperate. Desperate men are never restrained by niceties and often not even by adverse laws which themselves help create the desperation."

Marlon apologized for making Taylor expend "further time and money in a lost cause." He went on to say that he would, if the court ruled in his favor, wait fifteen days for Continental to comply with the

---

* Meadows was a glamorous actress who was turned into the frumpy and harried Alice Kramden in the "The Honeymooners" segment of the Jackie Gleason television show, one of early TV's most popular and enduring variety programs.

order. "If Continental does not comply, non-continuance [of the case] becomes effective on the 15th day after the ruling and our dissociation becomes effective by the 25th day after the ruling. If Continental *does* comply, I will wash your feet on the Statehouse steps and (smile) mortify myself by accepting the job."

He added, "I *do* have a grievance. It's against 'the system.' 'The system' nullifies my equity, encourages the wrong-doers in racial matters and makes the efforts of able, heroic men such as yourself worthless except in futile witness against the evil. I have no grievance against you. Totally to the contrary, I am...grateful for your magnanimous and charitable assistance since March of 1959 and your benevolence and prayers since we met on the morning of May 8th, 1958."[7]

Marlon closed with a passage from Thomas Merton's "Letter to an Innocent Bystander":

> ...whether we "act" or not, we are likely to be destroyed. There is a certain innocence in not having a solution. There is a certain innocence in a kind of despair; but only if in despair we find salvation. I mean despair of this world and what is in it. Despair of men and of their plans, in order to hope for the impossible answer that lies beyond our earthly contradiction, and yet can burst into our world and solve them only if there are some who hope in spite of despair.[8]

—·—·—◆—·—·—

IN LATE AUGUST 1961, Marlon's brother-in-law, Winfield Reynolds, husband of his sister Jean, stopped by to visit the Greens in Lansing. Eleanor recalled that Winfield was in a graduate program at Wayne State University in Detroit and was on his way back home to Arkansas. Eleanor said, "Because Marlon hadn't seen his parents in a long time, Winfield invited Marlon to drive down to Arkansas with him." Since Winfield wasn't returning to Michigan right away, Marlon realized that he would need to ride a bus back to Lansing.

Buses, of course, had been a focal point of much of the civil-rights movement. There was Rosa Parks' bus in Montgomery, Alabama; the segregated Trailways and Greyhound waiting rooms and lunch counters across the South; the bus torched in Anniston; the attacks on Freedom

The pinney worn in September 1961 by Marlon Green as a silent protest against segregation on his bus ride through the South (Courtesy Green family archives)

Riders in Birmingham and Montgomery. There were many bad reasons for Marlon to ride a bus, especially in the South, and two good ones: First, he could not afford to fly and, second, he could use the opportunity to make a personal statement about race in America.

Before Marlon left Lansing, he had a seamstress make a sleeveless vest known as a pinney for him to wear over his clothes. On the front it said, "I am not a Freedom Rider" and "And I am not free" stitched onto the back.

He sat in the back of the bus and put on the pinney when the bus crossed the Mason-Dixon line,* and also wore it into the southern bus stations. "I cannot recall any comments or reactions to it," he said. "The experience was mine alone."

After he reached his parents' home in El Dorado, Marlon called Eleanor to let her know of his return plans. She encouraged him to stop at the monastery in Kentucky and try to meet personally with Merton.

---

* The Mason-Dixon line was regarded before the Civil War as the dividing line between the free and slave states.

The meeting with Merton was brief—only twenty minutes—but it did much to salve Marlon's emotional wounds. Marlon said, "I liked him and he seemed to be impressed by my history."[9]

The meeting, apparently, was also significant for the monk, who commented in Volume IV of his book, *Turning Toward the World: The Pivotal Years*, a collection of the monk's journal entries from 1960 to 1963: "September 5, 1961... Another visitor. Marlon Green, a negro and a remarkable person. He is fighting for the right to be hired as a pilot by the passenger air-lines, which said they would hire negroes but in fact refuse to."[10]

Marlon and the monk continued their correspondence over a two-year period.*

On the same day he met with Merton, and before reboarding the return bus to Lansing, Marlon found a typewriter and wrote a letter to the president of the Continental Trailways bus line: "I urge you to practice your belief in the equality of your customers by ending the odious custom of racial segregation on buses, in waiting rooms, toilets, and in all other terminal facilities operated by Continental Trailways. Bus riding is miserable enough at its best. Segregation because of race makes people of all colors want to avoid riding buses whenever they can."[11]

———•———

MARLON TOOK TAYLOR'S earlier advice to heart and tried to find employment of an outdoor, physical nature—cutting down trees, chopping wood, or doing farm work, but without success; a recession and severe downturn in the Michigan economy caused by layoffs in the automobile industry had put the squeeze on the job market. He managed to find a few lawns to mow and a few cars to wash, but that was about it. He also applied for a job as a vehicle mechanic at the local post office but heard nothing about his application. He and Eleanor both feared that the rust which his flying skills had accumulated since leaving the Michigan Highway Department job would wipe out any hope that someone would hire him as a pilot.[12]

---

* The 53-year-old Merton died tragically on December 10, 1968, when he was accidentally electrocuted in Bangkok, Thailand, while attending an international conference on Christian and Buddhist monasticism. (www.merton.org)

With Marlon having no income and Eleanor making very little as a temporary substitute teacher at Holy Cross School, they scraped by on their meager savings—Marlon's overtime pay which became available to him when he left the Highway Department. They also exhausted the remnants of Marlon's state retirement account, into which he had paid for more than three years. They took a loan on a small life-insurance policy Eleanor owned and dropped their health insurance. Through the spring, summer, and fall of 1961, the Greens continued to struggle. Their financial situation was tight and was about to become tighter; Eleanor's substitute-teaching job was scheduled to come to an end on March 30, 1962.[13]

ON OCTOBER 23, 1961, T. Raber Taylor and David Rubin, a lawyer from the U.S. Department of Justice, Gilbert Goldstein of the Anti-Defamation League of B'nai B'rith, and Charles Rosenbaum of the American Jewish Committee all presented their arguments to the Colorado State Supreme Court. Justice Doyle, one of the three judges who had earlier supported Marlon's cause, was no longer on the Court; replacing him was Justice Robert McWilliams, an unknown commodity. It was now a matter of waiting for the decision.[14]

While he waited, Marlon wrote to Taylor, "Thank you for your notice that the oral arguments have been heard by the Colorado Supreme Court. At your recommendation, my family and I have commenced to recite the prayer 'Come, Holy Ghost' at the conclusion of our evening meal for the intention of enlightenment for the Supreme Court judges. Too, during dinner we light a special candle for this intention. The candle is approximately seven inches high and 1-1/2 inches in diameter. We hope it will last."[15]

DECEMBER 1961 MARKED Marlon's and Eleanor's tenth wedding anniversary. Much had happened to them during the past decade. Not only had Marlon resigned his secure position as an Air Force officer to follow his dream of becoming an airline pilot, but he and Eleanor had become parents of six children during that period—Joseph, Maria,

---

NEWS ITEM:

(McComb, Miss., Nov. 29, 1961) A mob of a dozen cursing white youths and adults, shouting "Kill 'em! Kill 'em!" attacked five Negro Freedom Riders—three males and two girls—at the Greyhound bus station here, beating them savagely. The Negroes were attempting to integrate the terminal's lunch counter.

The angry crowd chased the Negroes around and over the counter and tables, tossing one youth in the air and striking and kicking him repeatedly after he hit the floor. An elderly white man had tried to block the entrance to the terminal's cafe but the Negroes disregarded his warnings and entered anyway. The manager of the lunch counter, Mr. A. P. McGehee, reportedly told the five, "Greyhound does not own this building; Greyhound does not own this restaurant. You get out of here."

After the assault, the Negroes fled from the premises while police looked on.

The Riders, who were members of the New Orleans chapter of the Congress on Racial Equality (CORE), had come to McComb from New Orleans to test the city's compliance with a Federal order to halt segregation at the nation's bus and rail terminals.

The mob action repeated on a smaller scale the larger riots directed at Freedom Riders in Anniston, Birmingham, and Montgomery, Alabama, last May. The F.B.I. is investigating.[16]

Peter, Monica, Paula, and Philip—children who needed to be fed, clothed, and housed.

Marlon had pinned the entire future of his family on the vague assurance by the airlines in some news articles that the airlines would welcome Negro pilots with open arms. The oft-stated dream of equality was turning out to be nothing but empty promises, and the reality of his situation was like bitter ashes in his mouth.

Christmas 1961 was a gloomy holiday in the Green household, with few gifts for the children under the tree. The only bright spot was a chess set that Eleanor gave Marlon; it started him on a lifelong devotion to the game.*

---

* Chess became Marlon's passion. He taught himself the game and, as his children grew older, he taught them as well. The Green children took part in many chess tournaments in the Lansing area.

It was also an appropriate gift; the new year seemed to offer nothing but stalemates and checkmates.[17]

———•·•♦•·•———

ON FEBRUARY 13, 1962, the Colorado State Supreme Court, by a four-to-three decision, upheld the lower court's ruling that the Anti-Discrimination Commission had no jurisdiction over a company engaged in interstate commerce. The court would not force the airline to hire Green.[18]

Marlon and Eleanor were, of course, devastated by the Colorado high court's decision, but not particularly surprised; rejection and bitter disappointment had taken up permanent residence in the Green household.

Despite the court's ruling, Eleanor expressed her deep appreciation to Taylor for his generous donation of time and effort on their behalf. "Where we shall go from here," she wrote, "I have no idea. Many times I am tempted to say: 'My God, why have You forsaken us?' Yet I know He has not! We have gone through periods of great mental suffering, and it is a miracle that we have retained our sanity in the face of this enormous injustice. In these times of terrible trial, He has given us sustaining grace."

She told Taylor that, aside from him, no one with any real power had made an effort to aid Marlon in his struggle. Family and friends were supportive but did not have the will, the money, the training, nor the prestige to provide any sustainable assistance. She felt that her substitute-teaching job, which was due to end shortly, would help them get by for the next few weeks but, for Marlon, "there seem to be no job opportunities at all in this city. Our present situation is becoming increasingly intolerable.... May God have mercy on us all, the oppressors and the oppressed!"[19]

T. Raber Taylor, too, was discouraged but he did not know the meaning of the word "quit." After spending many hours seeking guidance in prayer, and consulting with Roy Chapman of the Anti-Discrimination Commission, he decided to pick up the gauntlet that had been thrown down by the Colorado State Supreme Court and by "the system," and press onward.

———•·•♦•·•———

AN ARTICLE IN the March 5, 1962, edition of the *Denver Post* carried the news—the Colorado Anti-Discrimination Commission announced that it would appeal the decision to the U.S. Supreme Court.

Jim Ritchie, the *Post* reporter, stated, "The U.S. Supreme Court's decision—either upholding or reversing the Colorado court—would have national significance, possibly matching in importance the Supreme Court's 1954 decision outlawing segregation in public schools, legal experts said."

The article went on to say that the earlier 4-3 decision by the Colorado State Supreme Court "held that the state anti-discrimination act does not apply to employers engaged in interstate commerce. The decision seriously hinders the Colorado [anti-discrimination] commission and similar agencies in 18 other states from enforcing statutory prohibitions against discrimination in employment, commission officials said. The Colorado court said only the federal government can prevent discrimination in hiring for interstate commerce."[20]

"I do not think your case has ended in dismal failure," a confident Taylor wrote to Marlon the next day. Events were moving ahead; this was no time to think about giving up. "I feel that from our disappointment will come a firm foundation for equal job opportunities for all men regardless of race, creed, or national origin. I look forward to the day when the U.S. Supreme Court will vindicate your position as you so ably expressed it in your February 27th letter."[21]

As luck would have it, out of the blue on March 7 Marlon got a job—washing out milk cans at the Sealtest Dairy in Lansing. It wasn't a glamorous, high-paying pilot's job, but it was a job with a paycheck attached. And it was also a civil-rights breakthrough of sorts; the local Sealtest plant had never before hired a Negro.

"I have not been able to learn precisely who or what it was that prompted the company to terminate its old policy by hiring *me*," he mused in a letter to T. Raber. "I had not applied to any dairy in the area, for as far as I know none hire Negroes. Monday night a man in our parish (another Mr. Taylor) whose daughter babysits for us and who works at the dairy as a salesman, came by to ask if I were still looking for a job. Evidently at a recent union meeting there was some discussion about why there were no Negroes employed by the dairy." The babysitter's father recommended that the plant hire Marlon; he was interviewed, passed the physical, and was hired at $2.47 an hour—

about the same as he made when he became a pilot for the Michigan Highway Department.

"In any case a Negro was desired and deliberate steps were taken forthwith, not to make it known that the opportunity was available as by public advertising for applicants or by letting the word to the 'Colored' grapevine, but to locate and hire a Negro. I do not mean to imply that I am not happy that I was the object of this favorable decision, but this action confirms that non-routine actions by companies like Sealtest and Continental are not handled routinely nor accidentally, as Continental would have us believe."[22]

Marlon later elaborated, "Sealtest still used the old metal milk cans at that time. The milk was good, but Sealtest Dairy at three o'clock in the morning had some *stinky* milk cans. The job was unpleasant and I grew to hate it. I recall thinking, 'Boy, if I were white, I would not be limited to this situation.' To put it another way, if I weren't black, I wouldn't be limited to this situation."[23]

The stresses and strains of the situation were also wearing on Eleanor. The children, of course, were too young to truly understand what was happening. Daughter Marie remembered that there was something unusual about her family but she had a hard time putting her finger on it: "When we were kids, people stared at us all the time and we didn't know why. When we lived in Michigan, I realized that when I went someplace with my mother I was treated differently than I was when I went someplace with my father. I couldn't figure it out for the longest time, and then I got it—he was a different color."[24]

ABOUT THIS TIME, Eleanor began to lose hope that Marlon would ever be hired by an airline and began pressing him to consider other alternatives, such as using his G.I. Bill education benefits and studying for an advanced degree. But, much to Eleanor's dismay, Marlon discounted the idea, for flying was all he really wanted to do. Dismissing the fact that he had been valedictorian of both his grade school and high school, Marlon said, "I am not an 'education person,' and I was not interested in the time it would take me to get a master's degree. It just wasn't an item of interest to me because I'm not a 'student.' I'm not prone to think of a formal education as something I want to do.

Plus, I didn't want any action of mine to take away the possibility that an airline would be in a position to respond favorably. My feeling at the time was that Continental had given me many excuses for not hiring me; I didn't want to give them any additional excuses because of any action of mine.

"The feeling I had in those days, and I think it was a genuine reality, was that if you commit yourself to anything that the airlines can use as a justification for not hiring you—if I went and re-enlisted in the Air Force, for example, and after fulfilling the four-year enlistment—then I would have been over the airlines' age limit, which was thirty, and I don't think anybody was hiring pilots over age thirty until the big crunch for pilots came along in the middle sixties and the Vietnam War. Basically, my feeling was, I don't want to do anything to give them another excuse for not hiring me."[25]

———·—·—●—·—·———

THE SEALTEST JOB notwithstanding, in March 1962 Marlon D. Green officially became a pauper. T. Raber informed him that the costs of taking the case to the United States Supreme Court were mounting and would continue to do so. "A petitioner's docket fee is $100.00 with an additional $50.00 if oral argument is permitted," he told Marlon. In addition, Taylor noted there were other fees and costs for the printing of forty copies of the record and the printing of briefs. Taylor said that Marlon could avoid most of these costs if he were to declare himself, in an affidavit, a pauper. "Lawyers who have an interest in your case have made the unsolicited suggestion that your appearance as a poor person would strengthen your case. Nevertheless, I do not want to humiliate you, but rather to assist you. If you do not wish to file the affidavit, it will make it harder to work for you, but I will still do so."[26]

Marlon swallowed his pride and told Taylor that he would "humbly and happily sign the affidavit as a poor person. I am usually compelled to view poverty as relative; if things could be worse, then I am not in bad shape. I often avoid the word poverty and think of myself as in a state of *unjust economic deprivation* [Marlon's italics], temporary variety. As I see it, this was my condition even prior to my protracted unemployment because, as a result of the sin of racial discrimination by employers such as Continental Air Lines, I was denied the right to participate normally in a common occupation of life which occupation would have afforded economic security aplenty for me and my family.

"We have and always have had the routine essentials: Nourishing food in sufficient quantity, adequate clothing and finances to pay for household utilities, but security and savings have been denied us because of my efforts to enjoy the right of equal employment opportunity.... I am not constantly frugal. Now and then, to my wife's dismay, I indulge myself by buying a pack of cigars or a carton of whole milk to avoid the repugnance of our usual powdered milk.

"We want to make the sacrifice necessary to pay $75.00 of the docket fee. Our friends in East Lansing, George and Dorothy Reid, see the case as very significant and want to participate by subscribing to a portion of the docket fee. Their check for $25.00 is enclosed along with ours. I trust that this 'partial payment' will not constitute a violation of my status as a poor person. I assure you I still am."[27]

IN APRIL 1962, Taylor's efforts to take the case to the United States Supreme Court were moving forward. He had submitted a Petition for Certiorari (a writ of a superior court to call up the records of a lower court), Marlon's "Petition for Leave to Proceed *in Forma Pauperis*," and other necessary documents required by the clerk of the Supreme Court.

Taylor also began asking prominent individuals, such as New York Congressman Adam Clayton Powell[28] who, in 1944, became the first Negro from an inner-city district to be elected to the House of Representatives;[29] Louis Buckley, Regional Director of the U.S. Department of Labor;[30] Harvard Law School Dean Erwin Griswold;[31] and others for any advice or input they might have on Marlon's case. Edward Terrones, the Acting Director of the Colorado Anti-Discrimination Commission, informed Taylor that he had formally requested the states of Michigan, Ohio, Massachusetts, Connecticut, New Jersey, and Pennsylvania to join Colorado in the appeal to the Supreme Court.[32]

Slowly but surely, Marlon's case was gaining national attention; the law journals of the law schools at Harvard, Columbia, and Notre Dame had written notes on the Colorado Supreme Court decision, and Stanford was planning to use the case as the basis of its Moot Court

Arguments in the fall.*[33]

Things began to look up when, on June 15, David Rubin, an attorney with the Civil Rights Division of the Department of Justice, called T. Raber Taylor to inform him that in three days Bobby Kennedy would file a memorandum with the U.S. Supreme Court in support of the application for certiorari—an important step in convincing the Court to hear the case.[34]

On that same day, June 15, the Green case received another boost when the State of California's Fair Employment Practice Commission agreed to file a "friend of the court" brief on Marlon's behalf.**[35] On June 18, Bobby Kennedy and the Department of Justice, as promised, filed their all-important *amicus curiae* brief with the Supreme Court.[36]

Although some noteworthy supporters were beginning to line up on Marlon's side, the question still remained: Would the United States Supreme Court, under Chief Justice Earl Warren, be willing to hear the case?

Meanwhile, the complaint Marlon filed in late 1957 with the Michigan Fair Employment Practices Commission regarding General Motors' refusal to hire him, went unresolved.

> **NEWS ITEM:**
>
> (Lansing, Mich., June 19, 1962) The Michigan Fair Employment Practices Commission ruled that Northwest Airlines had discriminated against Marlene White, a Negro applicant for a stewardess job, and directed the airline to hire her upon the satisfactory completion of stewardess training.
>
> Miss White had been trying without success since 1959 to obtain a position as part of a flight crew with Northwest. A week later the airline announced that it would comply with the commission's order.[37]

---

* The November 17, 1958, issue of *Time* mentioned that Father Theodore M. Hesburgh, president of Notre Dame University from 1952 to 1987, was a charter member of President Eisenhower's ad hoc U.S. Committee on Civil Rights. He was also a long-time friend and bridge partner of American Airlines' president C.R. Smith. When Eleanor learned of this, she wrote to Father Hesburgh and asked him to intercede with Smith on Marlon's behalf. The priest responded, saying, in effect, that he did not have the kind of relationship with Smith that would make such a conversation possible.

** Later, the American Jewish Congress, the Anti-Defamation League of B'Nai B'rith, and the Catholic Council on Civil Liberties would also file briefs of *amicus curiae*.

Marlon, on the advice of his attorney, wrote on July 9, 1962, to Archibald Cox,* the Solicitor General at the United States Department of Justice, thanking him for his support of the case:

> Mr. T. Raber Taylor of Denver has kept me informed of your interest and participation in the protracted Continental Discrimination Case. From time to time Mr. Taylor has expressed gratitude in his own name and mine for your legal assistance. The reading of your memorandum in support of the Petition for Certiorari prompts me to tell you directly that I am grateful.
>
> The voice of the United States Government has been too long silent about the right of citizens to equal economic opportunity. When it has been heard its message was usually equivocal. Your memorandum before the U.S. Supreme Court departs far from both silence and equivocation.
>
> I am heartened. I am grateful. I thank you.[38]

But Marlon could no longer stand washing out the stinky milk cans at Sealtest, and after just four months on the job, on July 10, 1962, he gave his notice, citing a cut in pay as his reason for resigning. "Sealtest decided to reduce the hourly wage of my job," he told T. Raber. "This was negligible (3 cents per hour) but neither company nor union officials notified me that the reduction was being considered, nor that it had been effected on July 1st.... The reduction had been one of the bargaining points in negotiations which were concluded in mid-June."[39]

———•———

THE LONG MONTHS of waiting to hear if the United States Supreme Court would hear *Colorado Anti-Discrimination Commission v. Continental Air Lines, Inc.* finally came to an end on October 8, 1962, when the Court announced which cases it would consider for the next term. Taylor received a telegram from the court clerk announcing that

---

* Archibald Cox became famous in 1973 as the Watergate Special Prosecutor during the Nixon Administration.

NEWS ITEM:

(Oxford, Miss., October 1, 1962) Six United States marshals were wounded by gunfire and three bystanders were killed today in rioting sparked by the decision of U.S. Attorney General Robert Kennedy to send white-helmeted federal marshals in flak jackets to the University of Mississippi in order to prevent James Meredith, a Negro, from being lynched.

Meredith, 29, had just been admitted to the all-white institution and was scheduled to enroll today when the unrest, started to a large extent by outside agitators, broke out.

The rioting began about 7:30 P.M. and the federal marshals attempted to quell the disturbance by a show of force and the heavy use of tear gas. The mob, estimated at about 1,000 persons, refused to disperse and fought back with rocks, bottles, and guns. Some rioters advanced against the 300 marshals behind a bulldozer that had been taken from a campus construction site but the tear gas forced them back. Military units—federalized Mississippi National Guard and regular Army troops—were called to the scene but did not arrive until after midnight.

During the disturbance, the mob heckled the marshals, calling them "Nigger lovers" and shouting anti-Bobby Kennedy slogans. Mississippi state troopers looked on in amusement, refusing to come to the aid of the besieged federal force.

Two of the three dead were identified as Ray Gunter, 23, of Abbeville, Miss., and Paul Guihard, 30, a French newspaper reporter. The identity of the third dead victim was not immediately available. Another reporter was wounded by birdshot and several other newsmen were beaten during the melee.

Declaring that his state had been "physically overpowered" by the federal government, Governor Ross R. Barnett appealed for calm and asked everyone to "preserve the peace and avoid bloodshed."

Just prior to the arrival of troops, however, Barnett issued another statement, saying that he would never surrender or give an inch in his determination to preserve segregation in Mississippi.

Meredith's attempts to register as a student at the all-white state university have been opposed by state officials and students for over a year. Twice rejected by the school in 1961, Meredith filed a complaint with the District Court on May 31, 1961.

Meredith's allegation that he been denied admission because of his color was rejected by the District Court. However, on appeal, the Fifth Judicial Circuit Court reversed the District Court ruling. By a 2-to-1 decision the judges decided that Meredith had indeed been refused admission solely because of his race and that Mississippi was maintaining a policy of educational segregation.[40]

the Petition for Certiorari would be granted. In other words, the U.S. Supreme Court *would* hear the case.

Taylor immediately called Marlon in Lansing with the good news and explained that he would be given two hours to present oral arguments. If the Court approved, others representing "friends of the court" could also give oral arguments. Continental's lawyers, too, would be allowed to present arguments for their side. No date had yet been set for the hearing, but Taylor assumed it would be in late 1962 or early 1963.[41]

To be sure, Marlon and Eleanor were elated at the news but reality had taught them not to be too trusting that the scales of justice would tip in their direction. After all, both the Denver District Court and the Colorado Supreme Court had already let them down; who was to say the United States Supreme Court wouldn't do the same?

Nevertheless, the *Lansing State Journal* interviewed Marlon and reported that he had expressed "great joy" at the announcement. "My family and I have waited for this for a long time. It has been so long expected."[42]

—··•··—

IN OCTOBER 1962, Marlon's legal problems, and racial tensions at the University of Mississippi and elsewhere, suddenly took a back seat to other national concerns as the world lurched toward the brink of nuclear catastrophe during what became known as the Cuban Missile Crisis.

Through overflights by spy planes, the United States learned that the Soviet Union had installed in its puppet state, Cuba, a number of missiles with nuclear warheads capable of reaching the United States. President John F. Kennedy demanded that the Soviets remove them; Soviet Premier Nikita Kruschchev refused. In response, American warships stopped Russian ships heading for Cuba with more missiles, launchers, equipment, and technicians. The two nations ratcheted up their military readiness and stood eyeball to eyeball, unblinking, each waiting for the other to draw first.[43]

Some former Air Force pilots, now working for airlines, were called up from inactive reserve status and told to report for duty in the event the U.S. and the Soviet Union went to war. Marlon notified his lawyer on October 30, "On the possibility that the Cuban crisis might precipitate some brightening of my employment prospects as a pilot, I have hastened to renew my Aviation Medical Certificate, First Class."[44]

Taylor wrote back, "When it was announced on the radio that a large number of [former active-duty Air Force] pilots were being ordered to duty, I immediately thought of you. This is a serious and tense time in our national history, and we will need many men who have had your training and determination."[45]

Finally, Kruschchev blinked, removed the missiles, and the crisis went off the boil. The world breathed a huge sigh of relief.[46]

————•————

ON DECEMBER 17, 1962, Marlon sent a check for $405 to Taylor, noting that $400 of it was for T. Raber's anticipated travel expenses to Washington for the hearing and the additional five dollars for "your postage fund. (Big deal!)"[47] Fortunately, Eleanor had found a one-year, full-time job teaching in the Lansing Public Schools; they would not starve.[48]

In January, the Supreme Court notified Taylor that the case would be heard during the week of March 25, 1963.[49]

Navy Chaplain Father/Lieutenant Commander John F. Carr, the friend of the Gallagher family who visited the Greens in Japan following the death of Eleanor's father, was now stationed at Quantico Marine Base, thirty miles south of Washington, D.C. When he learned that the Greens might be traveling to the nation's capitol, he invited them to stay at the base's V.I.P. guest quarters.

"Our base is just 45 minutes driving time to the federal buildings," he told Eleanor, "and the homey, quiet atmosphere of Marine Corps Schools will be a pleasant retreat from a trying day in Washington. I am expecting an affirmative answer—no excuses will be considered valid."[50]

With free lodging in hand, Marlon contacted T. Raber to let him know that he and the entire Green family would be in attendance as spectators, no matter what. Marlon said, "Cleo Moran, a friend in Detroit, offered us her car for the trip (she is sure our '55 Chevy just won't make it) and a former schoolmate of Eleanor's, Father Carr, now a Naval chaplain at Quantico Marine Base in Virginia, has offered us accommodations at the base.... If it's any help, you'll have a jury of Greens behind you."[51]

It seemed to Marlon that 1963 was already starting out to be considerably better than 1962 had been. And it was about to improve even more.

CHAPTER 14:
NINE WHITE MEN IN BLACK ROBES

THE DATE FOR oral arguments before the United States Supreme Court—dubbed the "Warren Court,"* after its chief justice, Earl Warren—in *Colorado Anti-Discrimination Commission v. Continental Air Lines, Inc.* (the parallel Colorado case, *Marlon D. Green v. Continental Air Lines, Inc.*, was consolidated into one case for U.S. Supreme Court purposes a few months earlier) was set for Thursday, March 28, 1963.[1]

The battle lines were clearly drawn. United States Congressman Adam Clayton Powell, a Negro from New York, had also entered the fray and championed Marlon's cause by hinting that unless Continental hired Marlon, he would hold up Continental's application to be a carrier for the lucrative Military Air Transport Service (MATS) contract. The hint seemed to fall on deaf ears, and the case went to the highest court in the land.

On the afternoon of March 22, Marlon and Eleanor packed up their suitcases and six children into "Silver," the family's 1955 Chevrolet, and headed east for Detroit, where they had dinner and spent the night with Cleo Moran, Eleanor's friend and former roommate in New Orleans.

The next morning, after exchanging cars (Cleo had a Nash Rambler of newer vintage), the Greens motored on toward Virginia, arriving at the Marine base at Quantico on the 25th.[2]

Marlon said, "At that time, Eleanor and I were acquainted with two people of significance in our history who lived in the Washington, D.C., area. On the Benedictine side there was a priest at St. Anselm's Abbey—Father Hilary Hayden. It used to be St. Anselm's Priory—famous as a finishing school for young boys in the Washington area. St. Anselm's Priory became, through expansion and growth, an abbey. Father Hilary was a close acquaintance of ours who had been interested in the case since the start. Whenever I was in the Washington, D.C., area, Father Hilary always allowed me to stay at the Priory.

---

* The various U.S. Supreme Courts have traditionally been identified by the names of their chief justices, i.e., the Taney Court, the Warren Court, the Roberts Court, etc.

Father Hilary Hayden of St. Anselm's Priory, Washington, D.C., hosted Marlon on several occasions.
(Courtesy Green family archives)

"The other person was a friend of Eleanor's who was a diocesan priest from Boston—Father John Carr—who visited us in Japan after Eleanor's father passed away. It was he who made arrangements for all of us to stay in guest quarters at Quantico. I think he was a lieutenant commander but to pull this off, you'd think he'd have to be an admiral! Those two members of the cloth were responsible for our being comfortable in Washington. It certainly was a relief to have that facility at Quantico available for us for the two or three days when we were in town."[3]

On March 28, 1963, with four of their children in tow (Paula and Philip were too young to be admitted and stayed in Washington, D.C., with a friend of Marlon's brother James), the Green family headed for the heart of the District of Columbia in their borrowed car. There stood the Supreme Court building, a blindingly white marble edifice, its imposing west entrance facing the Capitol Building. It is a building designed to inspire respect for the judicial system of the United States.

The Greens, along with their attorney, T. Raber Taylor, plus other members of their "friends of the court" entourage—Taylor's wife and several daughters, James Green, Joan Stanley Chachere, Father Hilary Hayden, and family friends Dick and Mary Brown—climbed the long stretch of broad marble steps and passed between the majestic fluted columns supporting the soaring portico, the architrave of which has the words "Equal Justice Under Law" carved into it. The group, along with

United States Supreme Court Building (Author photo 2007)

countless others before and after them seeking equal justice, then entered through the set of large bronze doors.

They crossed the highly polished marble floor of the imposing, column-lined Great Hall, then the Middle West Hall, and finally were admitted to the inner sanctum—the main courtroom where they found seats in the gallery section at the rear. Bobby Kennedy sat nearby. Ahead of them, behind the nine empty, high-backed chairs on a raised dais, stood four more columns, and behind them, set into an alcove, a wall of deep-red curtains. People spoke in hushed tones, as though in a cathedral. The whole atmosphere was calculated to inspire the type of reverence that Chief Justice Charles Evans Hughes referred to on October 13, 1932, when he laid the cornerstone for the building: "The Republic endures and this is the symbol of its faith."[4]

Little Maria Green, all of eight years old, recorded in a small notebook her impressions of the eventful visit to the Supreme Court: "You will find that it is a very strict place. You may not take anything in the Court except your purse, your coat and of course yourself.... I felt very hopeless that my father would get a job, but there is a chance. A very weak one."[5]

Her seven-year-old brother Peter also kept a diary. In it he wrote, "In the Supreme Court. It was a marble building. But my sister Maria said it would look better if it was made of wood."[6]

Although Marlon was about to have his day in court, he would not actually be allowed to speak. That burden fell to T. Raber Taylor, along with Floyd B. Engeman, an Assistant Attorney General of Colorado, the two of whom presented the main argument; Shirley Adelson Siegel, an Assistant Attorney General of the State of New York, and Howard H. Jewel, an Assistant Attorney General of California, were given permission to speak on Marlon's behalf as "friends of the court." Arguing for Continental was Patrick M. Westfeldt. Marlon was calm. "I wasn't nervous," he said, "because I knew they weren't going to ask *me* to speak."[7]

"All rise," ordered the chief bailiff, and the assembled spectators and attorneys got to their feet as the nine justices entered through a doorway, their somber black robes lending even more gravity to the setting. The associate justices were Hugo L. Black (an Alabaman who had been a member of the Ku Klux Klan in his younger days but who had since renounced racism and become a passionate champion of minority rights), William J. Brennan, Jr. (of New Jersey); Tom C. Clark (Texas); William O. Douglas (Washington state); Arthur J. Goldberg (Illinois); Chicago-born John M. Harlan II (known as the "great dissenter of the Warren Court," but whose grandfather had also served on the U.S. Supreme Court and argued against segregation, especially in the 1896 *Plessy* v. *Ferguson* case*); Potter Stewart (Ohio); and Colorado's Byron R. "Whizzer" White (who had been elevated from United States Assistant Attorney General to the U.S. Supreme Court in April 1962 by President Kennedy). The group was led by Chief Justice Earl Warren.

---

* This case essentially established the principle of "separate but equal," a system that justified segregation by providing different races separate facilities or services as long as the quality of each group's public facilities remained equal. The case stemmed from a lawsuit brought by Homer Plessy after he was jailed in 1892 for sitting in a "whites-only" railroad car of the East Louisiana Railroad. (Plessy was seven-eighths white and one eighth black but, under Louisiana law at the time, was legally considered a "Negro.")

After the judge for the state trial, John H. Ferguson, ruled that the Lousiana law did not, as Plessy's attorney had argued, violate the Thirteenth and Fourteenth Amendments to the U.S. Constitution, the case was appealed to the U.S. Supreme Court (the "Fuller Court"), which in 1896 agreed with the lower court. The lone dissenting Justice was John Harlan. The concept of "separate but equal" remained until struck down by the Warren Court in the 1954 *Brown v. Board of Education* case. (www.watson.org/-lisa/blackhistory/post-civilwar/plessy)

Earl Warren, Governor of California
(1943-1953) and Chief Justice of the
U.S. Supreme Court (1953-1969)
(Courtesy National Archives)

The seventy-one-year-old Earl Warren was a complex and controversial figure—a Republican by party affiliation, a liberal by nature, a libertarian by deed, and someone who confounded those who tried to pin any particular label on him.

Formerly the governor of California, Warren strongly advocated the interning of Japanese-Americans living on the West Coast during World War II (later contritely apologizing for the action). On the liberal side, he proposed in 1945 that California create a state medical insurance program. In 1948, he was Thomas Dewey's running mate against Harry Truman for the presidency. In 1952, he hoped to be the Republican Party's nominee for president, but the honor went to Dwight D. Eisenhower, a national war hero, who won in a landslide.

Warren could also be vindictive. A story is told that in exchange for delivering the California vote to him at the Republican convention, Eisenhower had promised Warren a seat on the Supreme Court as soon as a vacancy occurred. When that vacancy, upon the death of Fred M. Vinson on September 8, 1953, turned out to be that of the chief justice, Eisenhower balked. Furious, Warren threatened to tell the nation that Ike was not someone who kept his promises; Eisenhower relented and appointed Warren to the top spot despite the fact that he had never served as a judge at the state or federal level.

In 1954, Warren became a lightning rod for every segregationist in America when he spearheaded the unanimous verdict in the *Brown v. Board of Education* case that overturned *Plessy v. Ferguson* and outlawed

racial separation in schools. The "Warren Court" soon acquired a reputation as a liberal, activist, pro-civil rights group—much-hated by those
who did not share its and the chief justice's views. Although Warren
had been an ardent anti-Communist while governor of California,
Robert Welch, head of the right-wing John Birch Society, accused
Warren and the Court of being part of a Communist conspiracy.
"Impeach Earl Warren" stickers soon sprouted on bumpers across the
land, while some thought impeachment was too mild a sentence;
according to them, the chief justice should be lynched.[8]

If Marlon and T. Raber Taylor thought Earl Warren and his Court
might be pre-disposed to favor their case over that of a side that felt
interstate commerce trumped civil rights, they kept it to themselves;
there is simply no way of knowing in advance how a court will vote.
Everything, it seemed, hinged on T. Raber's oral presentation of the case.

———•••———

No WRITTEN TRANSCRIPT of the hearing was produced. All that
exists is a CD made from a reel-to-reel recording of the session and provided as a courtesy to the Green family by the National Archives.* The
quality of the recording was spotty; it contained the actual voices, with
all their inflections, of the key players (most of whom are now dead)
but, because of the imperfections of recording technology in 1963, not
everything spoken was captured. There apparently were only two microphones in the courtroom—one at a podium for the lawyers arguing the
case and one in front of the chief justice, which meant that anyone
seated more than one chair away from Warren was virtually inaudible.
The justices can be heard interrupting the lawyers from time to time and
asking their questions but, aside from a stray word or two, the actual
questions are missing.

And interrupt they did! No sooner had the lawyers begun to launch
themselves down an important legal route than one or another of the justices side-tracked them; no doubt the questions were important, but the
constant interruptions wrecked the flow and pace of the presentations.

---

* At the time, written transcripts of the Supreme Court proceedings were not provided
by the Court. If an attorney or law school thought a case would be important for future
reference, they paid to have a transcript done. The author created a transcript from the
recording for this book.

The Warren Court, 1963: Front row (left to right): Tom Clark, Hugo L. Black, Earl Warren, William O. Douglas, John M. Harlan. Back row: Byron R. White, William J. Brennan, Jr., Potter Stewart, Arthur J. Goldberg

(Photograph by Abdon Daoud Ackad, Collection of the Supreme Court of the United States.)

Soon, another problem presented itself. Earl Warren was apparently suffering with a head cold that day, and his frequent coughs and clearing of his throat often obscured a key word or phrase by one of the lawyers or associate justices.

There was a further disappointment. While one might expect the type of impassioned speech worthy of Gregory Peck as Atticus Finch in the 1962 film *To Kill a Mockingbird*—a speech that would have the audience leaping to its collective feet at the end and applauding whichever lawyer made the most dynamic delivery—there was, sadly, none of that. The language, instead of impassioned, was legalistic, dry, dull, wandering off into backroads of "pre-emption;" and "jurisdiction;" and "burden on commerce;" and "interstate operations;" and which case and which federal act is going to be considered "controlling;" and endless other arcane references to ancient legal precedents.

Taylor started out strongly, but about a minute into his laying out of the case he was interrupted by a justice; one can surmise by his tone of voice that Taylor was a bit perturbed. But he pressed onward, giving the Court a tidy summation of Marlon's background: his nine-year career in the Air Force; his fruitless attempts to be hired by every airline in the country; the reasons why he brought the case against Continental specifically; and the runaround that the airline gave him.

Taylor then ticked off a litany of complaints against the carrier—the brief "interview" in the cafeteria instead of a more formal and dignified meeting at Continental's offices; the failure to be notified of Continental's decision in a timely manner; the other, less-experienced pilots hired in his stead; the alleged retribution against him by Harrold Bell, Jr. for allowing his complaint to gain national publicity.

Taylor's best moment in his initial argument came when he pointed out, "It was in June of 1957 when [Marlon] was being interviewed in Denver [by Continental]. There was a July 1957 [training] class; the other men were found qualified and ordered to that class. Mr. Green was *not* ordered to that class [and] was under the impression that he would be told one way or the other [if he were accepted]. Not having received word, he called Continental Airlines and was told he was still being considered. However, he was not accepted for the July class and in August 1957 he filed a complaint with the Colorado Anti-Discrimination Commission."

Taylor went on, "I think here it is important to point to the record as to the reason why, or one of the reasons why, Continental says Mr. Green was not employed. In the record on page 183 is a newspaper article from the *State Journal* of Lansing, Michigan, of August 4, 1957, entitled 'Job As Airline Pilot Eludes Lansing Negro—Claims Racial Bias.' I think it's important to also point out that in the record...an official of Continental [Bell] said that the reason that Mr. Green was not selected for the July class was 'happenstance'.... And they discussed the article in the newspaper telling of Mr. Green's qualifications and difficulties in trying to get the job.... [T]here's a stipulation that the article appearing in the Lansing, Michigan, *Journal* is substantially identical to a news release which was seen by a Continental officer in an Albuquerque newspaper."

Taylor then went into a long discourse on the Denver District Court's and Colorado Supreme Court's rulings against Marlon, and on the various federal laws that he felt were precedent-setting in this case, and the number of states that had anti-discrimination statutes. The justices, however, kept interrupting to ask Taylor questions that didn't quite make it onto the recording, but Taylor more than held his own, discussing at some length such precedents as *Railway Mail Association v. Courtney,* and the Lloyd La Folette Bill of 1912.

Floyd Engeman, one of the Assistant Attorneys General of Colorado, was then granted permission to address the Court. He waded bravely into *Hall v. DeCuir, Portland Cement v. Detroit, Kelly v. Kramer, Morgan v. Virginia,* the 1875 Colorado Enabling Act, et al, in the hope of scoring some points, but his argument just seemed to be stirring up muddy waters.

After surviving a barrage of questions, Engeman handed off to a "friend of the court," California Assistant Attorney General Howard Jewel, who began, "As I make it out, airline pilots are only distinguishable from other employees of interstate commerce carriers in that there is a rather particular and specified group of federal regulations which have to do with safety. And since in this case Mr. Green has been certified by federal authorities and, so far as I know, there has been no word in this record to the effect that Mr. Green was in any way an unsafe pilot or was in any way uncertificated, that issue, so far as the limitation of this problem to airline pilots, seems to be questionable."

Jewel then touched on legal precedents which, to the non-legal mind seemed to have little bearing on the matter at hand, such as the Railway Labor Act, the Federal Communications Act, and more.

At one point Justice Stewart became almost angry, upbraiding Jewel with, "We're not talking about federal law generally—we're talking about the airline industry in the United States and the very pervasive federal regulations over it. We're not talking about generalities; we're talking about pre-emption in this field. So I hope you'll address yourself to *that. I* have been talking about it, but I haven't heard that much from *you*."[9]

Moments later, Jewel was released from his hotseat and turned the podium over to Shirley Adelson Siegel, an assistant attorney general of the State of New York, who latched onto the Court like a terrier onto a pants leg. Marlon recalled that Siegel was "a cross between Loretta Young, Joan Crawford, and Katherine Hepburn. There seemed to be no spark until she got up to speak. She had an effect on the whole courtroom; no one seemed to buoy the spirits like she did."[10]

Forty-three years later, Shirley Adelson Siegel still remembered that March 28, 1963, was a very important day—the first time she had argued a case before the United States Supreme Court. "I felt very

Shirley Adelson Siegel, Assistant Attorney General of New York, circa 1963 (Courtesy Shirley Siegel)

strongly about the case," she said. "As soon as we learned of the case, we decided we wanted to come in as *amicus*. We had to apply to the [Supreme] Court, and then we asked the attorneys general of other states to come along."

Since the 1940s, the New York Attorney General's office was one of the nation's leading state A.G.s when it came to civil-rights issues. Whenever a case was accepted for argument by the U.S. Supreme Court, the New York Attorney General's office noted that.

Siegel's thirteen-year-old son was also in the spectators' gallery for the hearing; he had come to Washington, D.C., on a field trip with his classroom teacher while on spring break. "I was very interested in his reactions afterwards," said Mrs. Siegel. "He said he was very scared. He was afraid I wouldn't be able to answer the questions. The stress on him—wondering if his mommy would know what to say."[11]

During the hearing, she told the justices in her peppery, rapid-fire delivery, "I want to get to the burning question of pre-emption, but first I want to state very vigorously [that] I'm here today on behalf of the State of New York, which sets the standards for these laws. We are the 'grand-daddy state' from which all others follow, and I represent also a group of well over a dozen other states that have anti-discrimination agencies and are broadly concerned over the outcome of this case—not over petty jealousies for their jurisdictions, but [because] they are vitally concerned that a verdict for the respondent here [Continental] might create a very serious vacuum in the matter of protection against racial discrimination in employment, and also unsettle the foundations of our jurisdiction."

It was obvious that she had quickly shaken up the sleepy solemnity of the court. One of the Justices, perhaps Brennan, a New Jerseyite, interrupted with a witticism: "Would New Jersey be a 'co-grand-daddy?'" he asked, and laughter was heard on the recording.

"New Jersey very quickly followed on our heels to make us more effective," she replied, deftly picking up the thread, "but we had developed more as the result of a traveling commission proposing bills that affected one end of the state for a period of a year or so, and so—"

Another interruption, again indecipherable. "They may have done that, too, your honor," she replied to the unheard Justice. "I believe that New Jersey would be the first to yield to us the honor. They certainly are in touch with us about our administrative construction often enough." More laughter.

Then she forceably reined in the light-heartedness that was threatening to gallop off with her presentation, letting the Justices know in no uncertain terms exactly who had the floor. "I regret that my valuable time may be slipping in this give and take," she said.

She went on to describe the New York A.G.'s office's experience in matters involving racial discrimination in employment: "Approximately seven percent of these have involved interstate carriers. In the early years there were many railroad cases, and in these dozens and dozens, in fact a couple hundred of these railroad cases, the railroad perhaps then squirmed—I don't know what went on behind their calm exteriors —but they accepted the conciliation procedures of the state commission—the first Negro brakeman was put on one railroad, and so on. And these breakthroughs—each of them, although maybe only a handful of persons were concerned—had an enormous significance, as I'm sure this Court will appreciate.

"In the case of the airlines, we have, to date, done business with twenty-five airlines, all of them interstate, in New York alone. Now these airlines haven't gone screaming to the Civil Aeronautics Board with a statement of pre-emption to bail them out."

She rocketed through her presentation, words tumbling out in a torrent, almost as if through forcefulness alone she could make the nine white men in black robes understand the historic importance of her material to the case.

"Not only is it in our experience in close to a hundred cases involving airlines, almost half of those involving flight crews—pilots as well as hostesses—and we perhaps had the dubious honor of having been responsible for the first Negro hostesses or stewardesses on airlines [to be hired] in our region."

A Justice asked, "Was that Mohawk?" evidently recalling the Ruth Carol Taylor hiring in 1958.

"Mohawk, right. Not *one* of these airlines had gone to court about this," Mrs. Siegel continued. "We've had no litigation on the question about jurisdiction over interstate employees, and no litigation over the question of pre-emption in the case of (indecipherable). Now, on the pre-emption point, I'm sure it's in the back of the minds of all of you, but I must state it again—that even if the Civil Aeronautics Act or the Railway Labor Act, which would have also brought the question here, should create a right in this field—there certainly is a great deal of precedent in this Court for permitting state regulation which does not burden commerce and is in harmony with the national policy to proceed."

Shirley Siegel then fielded several questions from the Justices, all of them too faint to be heard on the recording. But she heard them, and they became like dry logs to throw on the fire of her argument: "This is about discrimination in the Civil Aeronautics Act which reflects, in our opinion, the time-worn common-law right of equality of opportunity for service. It's an integral part of our tradition going way back before there *was* a statute—that common carriers should not discriminate.... And the language in air transportation, the language in service, appears everywhere in the Civil Aeronautics Act where you have language about discrimination. Section 406-B declares, 'The promotion of adequate economic and efficient service by air carriers without unjust discrimination.' Section 4-A, 4-B provides, 'No air carrier shall subject any particular person in air transportation to any unjust discrimination....'

"In an area like this," she went on, hitting her stride like a well-tuned marathoner, "where the police power of the state has such a strong interest in the enforcement of the regulation, unless there's a clear Congressional indication that our jurisdiction has been displaced, such displacement would not take place. On the contrary, there's perfect harmony here. [Indecipherable] is very similar to the railroad cases, where a man, a locomotive engineer, who drives for an interstate railroad, has the nation's safety in his hands in the same way as an airline pilot. The railroads are very heavily regulated by the national government. And yet this court, again and again, has sustained local regulations and acted under the police power which, for example, required all locomotive engineers to take an eye exam, or who said that men who were driving trains would have to have an examination and said that if there were intemperate habits, they would be disqualified."

She continued on and closed with: "The federal government has acted in such a clear way and demonstrated so unmistakably its right to pre-empt in this field. We have a growing pattern of state laws which are doing a job. They have not resulted in turmoil in interstate transportation. On the contrary, they have been doing an *effective* job, and have worked in accordance with the highest national policy. We earnestly urge this Court to reverse the decision of the Colorado Supreme Court. Thank you."*[12]

Marlon recalled that when Shirley Siegel spoke, "for maybe eight minutes, no more than ten, she was so forceful about what was taking place, I think she made the most emotional impact upon the members of the court—if anyone can ever accuse them of being emotional. It was her presentation before the Supreme Court on our behalf that was the most spirited part of the Supreme Court hearing."[13]

———•—•—•———

SHIRLEY SIEGEL'S PRESENTATION was the closest thing to an ovation-evoking moment—no doubt the highlight of the entire proceeding—but its fire was soon doused by Patrick Westfeldt's argument on behalf of Continental.

In a clear and confident tone that matched Taylor's, Westfeldt began,

---

* Shirley Siegel's presentation drew praise from a number of quarters. Sol Rabkin, a lawyer, civil-rights advocate, and director of the Anti-Defamation League of B'nai B'rith, had attended the hearing and wrote to Louis J. Lefkowitz, New York's Attorney General, Seigel's boss. He told Lefkowitz in a letter dated April 2, 1963, "Her...argument was not only lively and interesting, exciting reactions from the judges, but was also terse and effective. In her argument she gave flesh to what had seemed, on the basis of the presentation of the other counsel on her side, an essentially bloodless issue." (Letter, Rabin to Lefkowitz, Apr. 2, 1963)

"May it please the Court, I believe that it is inescapable and it is not disputed that in this case we have an order of a state commission, which is unskilled in the field of aviation, that has ordered a federally-certified commercial airline to hire a particular person as a pilot to fly its aircraft. Now, how did the commission get to that point?"

Westfeldt went into detail about Marlon being invited to come to Denver to interview for a pilot's job, and take the flight test, and the Link Trainer test. He continued, "Continental's decision, after [the tests and interview] was that Green was eligible and was qualified. He was wired by one of the other supervisory people, Wyler, on July 5 that he hadn't been included in the July class. Wyler's telegram went to his [parents'] home in Arkansas instead of his Michigan address so that Mr. Green, on the eighth, called Continental, talked to Mr. Bell, Vice President of Personnel. Bell told him that he was eligible and was qualified but that he hadn't been included in the July class."

Westfeldt noted that on August 6, 1957, Continental executives saw the interview Marlon had given the *Lansing State Journal* and which various newspapers picked up from the wire services. "At that point, Continental—Mr. Bell—exercising its judgment that here's a man with not only nationwide notoriety, but he also had fair-employment-practices cases pending against other aviation employers—[stated]: 'We don't like this notoriety; I don't know if it's good for him or not, but we don't like it. If he's going to plow ahead with these cases, it's going to interrupt his training and service in Colorado.'

"So it was at this point, and upon the receipt of that information [i.e., the newspaper article] that the company decided that Green was not qualified for the position. There was no question about his ability to fly. We never said that."

Justice Goldberg asked Westfeldt an indecipherable question, which apparently was, "What was the reason why Green was not included in the July class?" to which the lawyer replied, "The record...shows that the Continental people and even the investigators [from the Colorado Anti-Discrimination Commission] had not been able to determine a specific reason.... I would say that the reasons were that there were at least six, and maybe more by that time, names in the file, and the first four that came off the top were employed and put into the regular program, which first includes pilot training and then during the first-year mandatory probationary employment."

Justice Stewart then asked, "Don't we have to assume that [Green] was refused employment by your company on the basis of his race? Whether or not this turns out to be true is a matter for your non-discrimination—whatever your Commission is called—as reviewed by your state courts. But as the case is presented to us now, there's no issue at all, is there? Unless the only basis on which he was refused employment was because he was a Negro?"

Westfeldt responded that, while the Anti-Discrimination Commission concluded that Green was denied employment solely on account of race and not for some deficiency as a pilot, the Colorado courts did not. He said, "The basis of one of the necessary elements in the conclusion of the Commission that Continental discriminated on account of race was *its* decision as to pilot qualifications, which not only made a decision that he *was* qualified but that he was *better* qualified than any of the other applicants."

Chief Justice Warren broke in. "Was there any contention on the part of Continental that the others were better qualified than this man?"

Westfeldt: "The contention, Mr. Chief Justice, was that no 'rating' was made as to who *was* better qualified and who *wasn't* better qualified. And I really believe that that goes to the heart of the matter. Because I don't believe that it is the policy of Continental Airlines or any other airline to really grade finely on initial pilot flight checks."

The Justices and Westfeldt went back and forth on the matter for a few minutes as the lawyer tried to convince them that Continental's decision was based not on race but on other factors. Besides, he pointed out, the Commission had no authority to tell a private company who it could and couldn't hire, especially since the airline was involved in interstate commerce—a field not subject to state laws.

Westfeldt made the point that a Commission established by the Colorado State Legislature to look into matters of discrimination had no authority to question any actions, or make any rulings against, a company operating within the state that is engaged in interstate commerce. This was certainly not the point of view espoused by Taylor, Engeman, Jewel, or Shirley Siegel—but resolving divergent points of view is what the Supreme Court is for.

After dealing with some other points of law raised by the Justices, Westfeldt moved on to another important facet of his case—Supreme

Court rulings in cases involving discrimination against Negro passengers using public interstate modes of travel—rail and bus.*

Justice Goldberg asked a question, apparently regarding whether or not the Civil Aeronautics Act or Interstate Commerce Act covers discrimination against employees, and Westfeldt admitted, "I know of no case where it has been applied to an employee."

After an exchange of questions and answers between Warren and Westfeldt about the Civil Aeronautics Act, the Chief Justice asked, "Do you have any response to what the [assistant] attorney general of New York, Mrs. Siegel, had to say, both about the way they handled it with twenty-five different airlines in their state, without a point of this kind being raised?"

Before Continental's lawyer could respond, the gavel sounded for the lunch break, and the Court was in recess.[14]

---

* In December 1954, on their way to perform several scheduled concerts in Australia, the famous jazz singer Ella Fitzgerald and members of her band were bumped from a connecting Pan American Airways flight in Hawaii for what she claimed were racially motivated reasons. Fitzgerald and her entourage had to wait three days before they could continue their journey. Pan Am officials said it was an "honest mistake" caused by a mix-up in reservations, but the singer sued the airline for $270,000. (*New York Times*, Dec. 31, 1954)

CHAPTER 15:
HOPEFUL

THE AFTERNOON SESSION seemed afflicted by the same torpor and wrangling over legalistic minutiae that marked the end of the morning session. Patrick Westfeldt went on in a nearly unbroken monologue, citing various federal acts and one case law after another which may either have represented an important precedent or may have been just thrown into the stew to obfuscate; it was impossible to tell which.

If nothing else, Westfeldt should be credited for being supremely well prepared; he obviously knew his case law, which rolled off his tongue the way a die-hard baseball fan can rattle off World Series statistics: the Lucas Flower case, the Dowd case, the Central of Georgia case, the Morton case, the Garner case, *Dreiner v. Teamsters, Richardson v. the Texas-New Orleans Railroad, Southern Pacific v. Arizona, Bethlehem Steel v. the New York Labor Board*, et al. If trials could be won by just the sheer number of cases cited, then Westfeldt would be unbeatable.

But the effect of his presentation—piling on the "burden" argument *ad nauseum*—was so leaden that one could almost hear the eyelids of the justices, weighed down by the lunch digesting in their bellies, slowly closing like eighteen tiny garage doors.

Somewhere about three-quarters of the way through the recording Westfeldt repeated something he had previously touched upon: "I want to point out that I don't think that there's any need for any more evidence on *burden*. Earlier in my argument this morning...I did start discussing the fact that the Colorado Commission *did* make a determination of Green's qualifications. They made that determination that he was qualified, therefore the alleged discrimination was on account of race. *That is in error.*

"In the Colorado [Anti-Discrimination] Act, a decision by the commission on qualifications *has* to be made. I think that's really all that has to be said about it. I do not think that it is possible to permit twenty or thirty commissions around the [United] States, with persons unskilled in matters of aviation, to determine qualifications of pilots.

"For the sake of argument, suppose the facts in this case were a little bit different. Suppose Mr. Green, instead of having three thousand hours, had *one* thousand hours; could they [the commission] then still have determined qualifications?"

Warren: "I thought they based their determination on the grounds that you yourself had found this man to be qualified."

This observation momentarily seemed to fluster Westfeldt. "Uh, Mr. Chief Justice, they *did*, in part, and then they dismissed our conflicting judgment which arose at the time of the publicity that occurred. At that time—Continental had first decided that Green *was* qualified; at the later date, when the publicity occurred, Continental took the position that he was *not* qualified. So they made the decision in conflict with our judgment—the judgment that was exercised in early August of 1957.... The company felt that this would cause a lot of notoriety and that it could interfere with his training."

Westfeldt's argument seemed specious: If Marlon *had* been hired by Continental and *was* in training, the whole issue of him continuing to *try* to be hired would be moot—he would no longer be involved in seeking justice, because he would already be employed!

But none of the Justices brought this up and Westfeldt plowed onward: "Other pilots had been discharged for becoming involved in controversial public things [although Westfeldt did not elaborate or present evidence to back up this statement] and this was their view that they wanted someone that was less in the public eye—a 'quieter' type of person." [Of course, it hardly needs restating that Robert Six, the president of Continental, was himself a rather flamboyant character— with his revolvers, lavish lifestyle, and marriages to prominent show-business figures—not exactly a "quiet" type of person.]

Arthur Goldberg then asked a question to which Westfeldt responded, "Well, at that particular time, Justice Goldberg, *he had already been admitted to the first training course* [author's emphasis]; he was told that he was eligible and his name was held with the other eligible pilots for subsequent employment. And this appears in the record of the telephone conversation between Mr. Green and Mr. Bell."[1] [Marlon was asked about this assertion, to which he replied, "That's news to me. I don't recall that at all."][2]

Then Chief Justice Warren spoke up. "It's possible, I suppose, for a person to be unqualified for reasons which might stem indirectly *from* his race but not be *because* of his race—assuming that somebody who was a follower of the tenants of the Black Muslims who hated white people so badly that he was likely to get so infuriated that he might shoot one. I suppose you wouldn't want somebody like that as a co-pilot with a white flight crew, for safety reasons. And if a person were born a white man instead of a colored man, chances are he would not have become a Black Muslim."

Westfeldt replied, "My feeling on that is this: That the initial judgment on whether to hire or *not* to hire—qualifications, and things like that—must *first* reside with the carrier. *There's* where the responsibility is. *That's* the organization that performs the interstate transportation, that runs the risk, makes the gains, things of that nature. But, if its judgment is going to be limited, it must be limited according to the intent of Congress and by one single federal agency—a single authority prescribing uniform regulations."

Warren responded, "It's not your position, though, that as to racial discrimination that the federal standard is a *different* standard from that imposed by Colorado in any way?"

Westfeldt said no, and added, "We're dealing with this high-speed transportation industry with commissions all over and officials all over.... And I do believe that the airlines—so regulated from top to bottom—*must* be regulated in this field also by the federal government. I think that a decision by a state commission in conflict with the carrier's judgment [as to what pilot] is qualified is a *direct intrusion* into something that is very national in character and must be regulated." He went on to say that he felt that the Civil Aeronautics Board, and not state anti-discrimination commissions, should be the one to be in charge of determining and regulating pilot qualifications.

After several more questions and answers, Westfeldt ended his presentation and thanked the court. Taylor then once again took his place at the podium and argued that existing laws about discrimination in the transportation field dealt solely with passengers and not employees, pointing out that "We are here concerned with whether or not the Civil Aeronautics Act should be converted into a Fair Employment Practices Act."

After a few more minutes of back-and-forth dialogue between Taylor and the justices, the recording suddenly and mysteriously ends.

Whether there was some final, fiery, impassioned plea on the part of T. Raber Taylor for justice for Marlon Green is unknown.[3]

The unexpected ending leaves one wondering: Did Taylor make his case strongly enough? Did Westfeldt, with his avalanche of cited case law, do a better job of swaying the justices? There was nothing new that hadn't already come out in previous hearings, no "Perry Mason moment."*

Once the recording concluded, there was a nagging feeling that neither side had landed a knock-out blow. A few quick jabs here and there, a couple of bloody noses, but nothing to send the other side reeling into the ropes; nothing to compel the Justices to say, while deliberating in their chambers, "Ah, hah! Mr. (fill in the blank) certainly had the strongest argument! I therefore cast my vote for (fill in the blank again)!"

———•—•—♦—•—•———

UNFORTUNATELY, NOTHING WAS immediately resolved. Unlike at the end of most ordinary court trials, a judgment was not rendered; it would take the Justices several weeks to reach and announce a decision. Their deliberations are not a matter of public record. No one knows what wrangling, arguments, and arm-twisting—if any—went on behind the scenes.

So Marlon and Eleanor and T. Raber and Floyd and Howard and Shirley filed out of the imposing white marble edifice in a state of limbo, wondering if they had given it their best shot, wondering if their side would prevail, or if Continental would be declared the winner.

Asked about the mood of his side once the hearing was over, Marlon said, "Hopeful." The Greens and their counsel separated and the Greens returned to Quantico. "We did not do anything with the Taylors in D.C. before or after the hearing," Eleanor recalls. Son Joseph remembered that on the drive back from Detroit to Lansing his father "showed a very rare instance of emotion when he broke down into tears at the wheel of 'Silver,' our Chevrolet station wagon."[4]

---

* A popular television series in the 1950s, starring Raymond Burr as the intrepid lawyer. Mason always seemed about to lose his case until some unexpected development at the last moment rescued him and his client.

NEWS ITEM:

(Greenwood, Miss., Mar. 29, 1963) Policemen in this small Southern town loosed a snarling dog on a group of forty-two Negroes marching home after having registered to vote, while other policemen used their batons on the marchers; the Reverend D. L. Tucker was bitten on the ankle by the dog.

Greenwood's Mayor, Charles E. Sampson, stated the reason for the police action was because the police suspected that the group was going to conduct a sit-in at the Alice Cafe.

A CBS cameraman, shooting film of the event, was arrested and had his film confiscated.[5]

BACK IN LANSING, time hung heavily in the Green household. March gave up its chilly grip on Michigan and April claimed its annual birthright. Tulips and crocuses pushed their heads up from the verge of the Greens' yard, and buds began to swell on the ends of the bare tree branches. Robins sang cheerily and scrounged for food.

Marlon's mind was on food, too—his favorite bean soup with potatoes, onions, and black pepper that he was preparing in a pot on the stove. It was April 22, 1963, a Monday. The Supreme Court hearing had been over for three weeks. Eleanor was off at her teaching job, the older kids were in school, and only four-and-a-half-year-old Philip was at home with Marlon.

As was his lunchtime habit, Marlon had the kitchen radio tuned to WJR in Detroit, the CBS affiliate. "The eleven o'clock news with Richard C. Hottelet came on," he recalled, "and Hottelet announced something to the effect of, 'The Supreme Court had rendered a unanimous decision today in the case of the Negro pilot trying to become an airline pilot. Continental was ordered to admit him to a training class.'"

Almost as soon as the newscast was over, Marlon's phone rang. It was Bill Sheehan, the news director at WJR Detroit, asking for Marlon's reaction. "He had interviewed me before," Marlon said, "shortly after Frank Hand's first article had appeared in the *Lansing State Journal*. He was familiar with the case and my efforts to find employment with an airline, and was very enthusiastic when the Supreme Court decision came out. He asked for my response—'WOW' is what I said to him.

That was certainly the elation that was in all of my being."

After he hung up, Marlon realized that he had this wonderful good news and nobody to share it with. He dialed the number at Eleanor's school and asked the secretary there to have her call him back as soon as possible.[6]

When she finally got the news, Eleanor was, as she recalled, "incredulous, unbelieving, numb! I knew full well, however, that the decision did not mean Marlon would actually get a job. On the one hand, it was a blessed relief; on the other hand, it did not dispel our then-desperate financial and psychological issues, plus the emotional cost to our children because of the uncertainty of our economic struggle to survive."[7]

Next, Marlon called T. Raber Taylor in Denver but was informed that he was in Paris attending the annual international meeting of the Knights of St. Vincent de Paul. Marlon had no sooner hung up the phone than it rang again; it was CBS News in New York, then NBC, then *Time* magazine, the *Lansing State Journal, Denver Post, New York Times*, the Associated Press, *everyone*. They all wanted interviews, photographs, film, the *story*. Marlon obliged, and soon the news was flashed around the country.[8]

The *San Francisco Chronicle* picked up the story and in an editorial on April 24, 1963, said, "It should be noted in this sorry history of one man's encounters with racial discrimination, that its 600-odd episodes [the total number of job applications Marlon submitted] occurred not in the benighted, intolerant, racist South; they occurred mainly in the North, the liberal, unbigoted North, which works itself into fits of self-righteous indignation and clucks incredulously when racial prejudice tramples on American principles in the South."[9]

On the evening of their victory, the Greens had a simple, quiet meal with the children at the dining room table. No champagne corks were popped, no fireworks were shot off or happy dances held on the front lawn, no grand dinner at a local restaurant was scheduled. Marlon and Eleanor did not even go to church to light a candle and give thanks for the Supreme Court's decision. While it seemed that the Greens' long nightmare was finally over, they refused to allow themselves the luxury of celebration. Their hopes had been dashed so many times, and the victory was still so new, so tenuous and unbelievable, that it seemed almost inappropriate to rejoice.[10]

———•••———

FOR THE NEXT couple of weeks, congratulatory letters and telegrams poured into the Green home. In one, Father M. James, O.C.S.O., the Abbot of the Abbey of Gethsemani, wrote,

> We saw your picture in the paper, and that you had won your case with the United States Supreme Court. The hearts of all us monks here at Gethsemani go out to you, and to Eleanor, and to your dear Family, in these days of trial and crisis. To think that for seven years you have had to struggle and work for this wonderful victory. It just seems incredible to me, the whole business.
>
> Somebody sent us a picture of your beautiful Family on the steps of the Building of the Supreme Court in Washington. God has blessed you with a wonderful Family. You are like one of the pioneers blazing the trail for many who will come after you.
>
> Be assured, dear Marlon and Eleanor, that whenever you need prayers, just let us know. Meanwhile, realize that you are remembered in the daily round of our Trappist life of prayer and sacrifice here at Gethsemani.[11]

The Trappist monk Thomas Merton followed his abbot's letter with one of his own:

> Great news. Congratulations. This is a very big step forward and you deserve a great deal of credit for the patient struggle you have gone through. I hope now that decision will "take." God bless you for it. I am sure one day a lot of people will have reason to be very grateful to you.
>
> The news from Alabama is nasty, at least what gets through to me. But I think the spirit and courage of the non-violent demonstrators there is magnificent. At the moment the people that Americans can be most proud of are the Negroes. They are the ones who are really living up to the ideal to which the whites, especially in the South, are more inclined to pay lip-service. I hope that gradually rights will finally get recognized

and that the situation will change. But you know better than I do that it is not going to be easy.

We are living in a time of crisis, in which people do not want to change, and yet they are being forced to change in a million ways that nobody can control. I believe more and more that Freud was right when he said that civilization was a kind of sickness. It certainly proves to be that, in our day. The whole world is ill, and the worst of it is that they all think they are sane. If only more of us could realize how nuts we really are....

Meanwhile, I keep you and your fine family in my prayers.[12]

Many years later, family friend Norb Wiley told the Greens, "Your family did a whole lot to make this country a better place, but you gave too much, suffered too much. You all gave (or had taken from you) too much of a normal, healthy life. You all were kind of lynched. You gave up about half of your lives, because Marlon and Eleanor fought racism so persistently and heroically. You are right up there with King, Malcolm X and the other race heroes. There should be monuments to your family in Washington, D.C., and the other major cities. And Marlon deserves his own holiday. I am really proud to have been slightly involved and I wish I had done a lot more to help you out."[13]

———•·•◆·•·•———

MARLON AND ELEANOR were forever grateful for everything T. Raber Taylor had done for them. Marlon said, "He was a man of high standing. It was a pleasant experience when he so generously gave of his time and expertise to benefit my life."[14]

Eleanor said, "It was a magnificent *grace* that enabled T. Raber Taylor to take the case *pro bono*. I consider him *the hero*. He made an enormous financial commitment at a time when he had seven children himself. For a number of years, on the anniversary of the Supreme Court decision, I would stop by the Taylor home with banana bread or flowers, sometimes by myself and occasionally with sons Joseph or Philip, to thank them."[15]

The T. Raber Taylor family in August 1999. After a sixty-five-year career as a lawyer, the family patriarch passed away on March 31, 2004; his wife followed two years later.
(Courtesy Mary Taylor Hassouna)

CHAPTER 16:
A BLACK THUMB

WHEN FLOYD DOMINY learned of Marlon's Supreme Court victory, and, realizing that it might take some time before Continental actually allowed Marlon to climb into a cockpit, he was intrigued. Perhaps Marlon could be useful to him.

Floyd Elgin Dominy was the controversial, outspoken Commissioner of the Bureau of Reclamation in Washington, D.C., and water was his game. Having been born and reared on a Nebraska "dry farm" that relied solely on rainfall for its irrigation, he knew firsthand the value of water and the problems farmers faced scraping out an existence in the arid West. He had also been county agent in one of the most drought-stricken areas of the West during the dustbowl days of the Great Depression. He was appointed to the Bureau of Reclamation in the early 1950s as a land-development specialist, then was elevated to Assistant Commissioner in 1957, and finally Commissioner in 1959.[1]

"I've got a[n office] building [at the Federal Center in Denver] where icicles practically form in winter and a plane where ice *does* form, right in the carburetor," Dominy once said, justifying his need for a new building and a new airplane.

"My people need a decent place to work, and I need a plane that isn't going to fall out of the sky." He also needed a pilot.[2]

Floyd E. Dominy, Commissioner of the Bureau of Reclamation, circa 1963
(Courtesy National Archives)

IN HIS 1986 book *Cadillac Desert*, an unflattering portrait of Dominy, the late author Marc Reisner writes, "Dominy's reputation and legacy are...problematical—at least as complex as the man himself. In *Encounters with the Archdruid*, John McPhee portrays him as a commissioner who led Reclamation on a terrific binge, plugging western canyons [with dams] as if they were so many basement leaks. His reputation, even today, is outsize; he is often talked about in Washington, and in the conservationists' annals of villany he remains a figure as large as, if not larger than, Ronald Reagan's Interior Secretary... James Watt [who eventually fired Dominy]."[3]

As befitting his hard-charging personality, Dominy seemed to delight in controversy, and nothing pleased him more than a good fight, whether with underlings or superiors (first Stewart Udall, Interior Secretary, and, later, Watt). He relished battling with environmentalists over dams in the West and with Congress over appropriations the way a linebacker craves contact with running backs.

As might be expected for someone so outspoken, Dominy had many critics. In the late 1950s, Dominy was locked in a pitched battle with his leading nemesis, David Brower, head of the Sierra Club, who was up-in-arms about Dominy's pet project—the Glen Canyon Dam—that would control the flow of the Colorado River through the Grand Canyon and back up to form Lake Powell on the Utah/Arizona border.

Described by a biographer as the "archdruid" (defined as a zealot who would sacrifice people in order to save trees) and the most militant conservationist in the world (at least in the 1960s), Brower was a passionate, obstinate defender of wild spaces. Floyd Dominy's and the Bureau of Reclamation's efforts to "despoil" these wild spaces by damming rivers made the commissioner and the Bureau, in Brower's eyes, Public Enemy Number One. Brower had won many victories before he encountered the indomitable Dominy. Brower had helped create Redwood National Park; spearheaded the landmark Wilderness Act, which set aside millions of acres of public land; and placed the oil fields and forests of Alaska off-limits to drillers and loggers. But it was the fight over the Glen Canyon Dam project that became Brower's toughest battle and bitterest defeat.

An avid outdoorsman since childhood, Brower had joined the Sierra Club in 1933, served with the 10th Mountain Division in World War II, and returned from the alpine battlefields of Italy to immerse himself completely in matters of conservation. He became the editor of the Sierra Club's magazine and, in 1952, was elected executive director of the group that grew from a small coterie of 2,000 nature lovers in the 1930s to the nation's most-powerful environmental force with 77,000 members by the 1990s.

Brower's consciousness was forever raised by the spectre of Hoover Dam, constructed on the Colorado River in 1935 to capture the run-off from the Rocky Mountains and provide water and electrical power for southern California's Imperial Valley farms and the growing megalopolis of Los Angeles. Hoover Dam was an environmentalist's worst nightmare—the world's biggest concrete structure and, behind it, Lake Mead, the world's largest man-made reservoir. Brower vowed that he would do whatever possible to prevent another Hoover Dam. Picking up the gauntlet dropped upon the 1914 death of John Muir, founder of the Sierra Club, Brower set out to save not only the unspoiled West but, if he could, the entire planet.

Therefore, when plans for damming the Colorado River at the northern end of the Grand Canyon and thus flooding Glen Canyon were first publicized in the mid-1950s, Brower was outraged. He knew he had but one course of action: going to war with Dominy, the Bureau of Reclamation, and Colorado's Congressional Representative, Wayne Aspinall, a pro-dams Democrat who, according to *Counterpunch* magazine, "ruled the House Interior committee with an iron fist during the great fights over the fate of the river."[4]

Donning his shining activist's armor, Brower decided to slip into the enemy's camp and make a deal with them. In 1956, he took Dominy on a raft trip down the Colorado River in an effort to convince the commissioner that damming the river would cause a great environmental catastrophe. Brower knew that the Sierra Club could not match the power of the federal government, so he made Dominy an offer: The Sierra Club would not fight the building of the Glen Canyon Dam if the Bureau of Reclamation would drop plans for building the Echo Park Dam on the Green River inside Dinosaur National Monument that straddles northeast Utah and northwest Colorado, as well as other dams within the Grand Canyon. Surprisingly, Dominy agreed. Immediately afterward Brower felt as though he were Dr. Faust, who had just sold his soul to the devil.

John McPhee writes in *Encounters with the Archdruid*, a book about the war between Brower and Dominy, "David Brower believes that the dam in Glen Canyon represents the greatest failure in his life. He cannot think of it without melancholy, for he sincerely believes that its very existence is his fault."[5]

As much as he loved nature, Brower hated the hard-drinking, cigar-smoking Dominy and others who were enamored of dams, bridges, mines, highways, ski areas, and anything man-made that interferes with nature—pure, stark, unspoiled nature. As Dominy himself once told McPhee, "Many people have said of me that I never met a stranger. I like people. I like taxi-drivers and pimps. They have their purpose. I like Dave Brower, but I don't think he's the sanctified conservationist that so many people think he is. I think he's a selfish preservationist, for the few. Dave Brower hates my guts. Why? Because I've *got* guts. I've tangled with Dave Brower for many years."[*][6]

For his part, Dominy was equally confident of the righteousness of his cause. In an August 2000 interview for *Radio High Country News*, he said, "I was in the federal government for thirty-seven years, in water and land development, but I expect the Glen Canyon Dam and the creation of the most wonderful lake in the world, Lake Powell, is my crowning jewel....

"I was a dominant man, no question about it. As a matter of fact, some people said my name should be 'Dominate,' not 'Dominy.' I was dedicated. I knew that we needed to develop the waters of the West if we were going to develop the West....

"I don't think we destroyed the Gunnison River (in Colorado) by building three wonderful hydroelectric dams. Before, it was a closed river. Now the public has access to those three reservoirs, with far more fishing and boating and recreational activities than was ever there in its natural state. Glen Canyon Dam, for example, in addition to its main function of providing the regulated water supply for the upper basin projects, it also has opened up for three million visitors a year a land that probably had twenty or thirty visitors before. Rainbow Bridge gets

---

[*] Brower was ousted from leadership of the Sierra Club in 1969; he formed a more activist environmentalist organization, Friends of the Earth, with chapters around the globe. He was voted out of that organization in 1986 and returned to the Sierra Club. Brower died in 2000. (www.sierraclub.org)

300,000 or more a year now, when it had only 15,000 in fifty years. The Colorado River float trip was limited to about a six-week period, haphazardly, when it was available in the flood season. Now you've got 20,000 people going down it every year.

"Sure, we've changed the environment of the river, but that doesn't mean we've made it worse. I happen to think that *Homo sapiens* is what the Endangered Species Act ought to be addressed to. I'm no fan of the Endangered Species Act. The thing that they're talking about now is that we've destroyed the humpback chub, because he can't live in clean water. Well, hell, all the archaeological digs around the world prove every day that various species—flora and fauna—have been evolving and expiring over the years."[7]

It seemed only right that a man so pugnacious and combative as Floyd Dominy would want as his personal pilot another man who was not afraid to challenge the status quo.

———————

FLOYD DOMINY'S BUSY schedule called for him to make frequent speeches around the country and frequent trips to Utah and Arizona during the construction of the Glen Canyon Dam project. He, therefore, required his own plane and pilot, but was unhappy with the pilot currently assigned to him. In May 1963, after learning of Marlon's Supreme Court victory, he thought Marlon might make a suitable replacement.

Dominy told this author, "I read about Marlon and his problems with Continental Airlines—that they refused to hire him because he was black. I had a pilot at the time that I was not overwhelmed with. He had an all-weather certificate and all that stuff, but he wouldn't use it, so I immediately asked my people to check out this guy [Marlon] to see if he still had a pilot's license; I knew that if he'd been a captain and a pilot in the Air Force, he knew damn well how to fly a plane."

The background check came back positive and Dominy's office contacted Marlon. Dominy said, "If he wanted to take a chance on employment, he'd have to come to Washington at his own expense to interview with me personally—which he did. And, of course, in those days before the Civil Rights Act [of 1964], there were very few places where I could take a black man to lunch in Washington. But there was a Chinese restaurant [the China Inn, an inexpensive establishment in the Chinatown section of Washington, D.C., located at 629-31 H Street NW] that I patronized that I knew would allow me to bring in anybody I wanted to."

Dominy was in the midst of his annual jousting match with Congress for money, a battle he dearly relished, just as he loved sparring with David Brower. "I was testifying before Congress that week; it was appropriations time and I only had about an hour and a half free, so my staff told Marlon to come down there to that Chinese restaurant. We had lunch together and had a good visit. I was overwhelmed with the guy. He was personable, highly intelligent, and well groomed.

"Finally I said, 'I have two questions, Mr. Green, and then I'll make up my mind whether I'm going to offer you a job or not. The first question is, with this airplane we have—with dual radio and transponder and all this equipment—would you as the pilot, and no co-pilot, be prepared to fly me under all weather conditions and into any airport in the United States that the commercial airlines are using under those same conditions?' He said, 'Yes, I'm confident I can do that.' I said, 'Good— you passed that one hundred percent.'

"Then I said, 'The second question is a little more delicate. You're black. You're positively black. You're *shiny* black. That doesn't bother me a minute. But suppose I'm scheduled into a southern city for a speech and I make reservations in advance for myself and my pilot; we show up at the hotel and they won't take you. They'll honor *my* reservation but they won't honor *yours*. What do you want me to do about that?' Well, he said, 'I'll pick up my bag and say, "Mr. Commissioner, I'll find a place to stay and let you know where I am."'"

"I said, 'Fine. Privately, I'll raise hell about that, but publicly, I can't make an issue out of it. I'm there to make a speech and I'm going to have to make my speech.'"[8]

At the conclusion of the lunch, the two men shook hands and Marlon returned to Lansing to take part in his accustomed state of being: waiting while others decided his fate.

Meanwhile, Dominy decided he would make Marlon a job offer. Dominy liked the idea; being the only government official with a black pilot was just part of his persona—Marlon Green would be a black thumb that Floyd Dominy could apply to his white nose to annoy and confound his critics.

At THE END of April 1963, Marlon Green received great news. The Bureau of Reclamation was offering him the job as pilot for Floyd Dominy, at a salary of $9,475 a year. The only condition was that the Greens would need to move to Denver, where the Bureau's aircraft was hangared. Marlon jumped at the offer.[9]

Then another piece of good news arrived:

NEWS ITEM:

(Denver, Colo., May 8, 1963) Continental Air Lines announced that it has offered Marlon D. Green, Negro pilot, a job with the airline following a unanimous ruling by the U.S. Supreme Court that states may forbid discriminatory hiring practices by interstate carriers.

Mr. Green stated that he would wait until his attorney, T. Raber Taylor, returned from a trip to Europe before making any decision about whether or not to accept the offer. "I want to work for Continental," is all Green said.

A Continental spokesman said Green would be treated exactly as any other newly hired co-pilot, except that he would be given a priority status of June 24, 1957....

Continental said in a statement that it initially rejected Green's application because of what it termed complaints he had filed against other airlines. The airline said it "doubted that a man in this position could become one of the dedicated, professional pilots."

"If Green accepts the job offer," a Continental official said Tuesday, "he will be assigned to the next aircraft qualification class when it is formed during the next three months."[10]

MARLON DID NOT immediately resign his new job with the Bureau of Reclamation, pack his bags, and head for Denver to enroll in Continental's next class. There were myriad details of the Court's decision that first needed to be worked out, plus many contract clauses and provisions and exceptions that needed to be argued about and agreed to. And, of course, Continental wanted to delay for as long as possible the admittance to their previously all-white cockpits the Negro pilot who had caused them so much time, trouble, expense, and negative publicity. In truth, it would be nearly two more years before Marlon joined the ranks of Continental's pilots.

"There was what we might call a 'wiggle session' to work out the conditions of employment," Marlon said. During that period, one of the things to be considered was how he was to be compensated for the wrong that had been done by Continental's discrimination. "The biggest benefit I got from this negotiation, if you want to call it that, was that my 'seniority date' would be retroactive to June 24, 1957, which was the date that everyone eventually agreed was the date when I should have been hired. I think that date was determined by the Colorado Anti-Discrimination Commission."

There was no award of back pay, but there was a "consideration" of it. Marlon said, "Continental resisted the idea of back pay, and T. Raber Taylor did not feel it was worth fighting for, because the calculation was that the back pay would be the difference between whatever a co-pilot for Continental might have earned during that seven- or eight-year period and what had been earned from other sources.

"Now mine had not been great but, likewise, most of the pilots who had been hired during that time had been laid off by Continental in the interim, and Taylor didn't think it was worth the effort to try to squeeze out this item by itself. Things that *were* considered as greater objects to be sought were the seniority date, which I just mentioned, and the conditions of that seniority that could be put into effect."

A permanent pass was one of the perks that Marlon asked for and received; if someone had been employed by Continental for more than five years, that employee and his or her family were entitled to a permanent pass that allowed them to fly for free. He also noted, "Vacation was one full month after five years, and that became part of the award on the day I went to work. Those two were big. Seniority entitled me to a position based upon the needs of the company for upgrades or demotions. You were protected by seniority. The higher your seniority is nearly always thought of as a benefit. And that date being fixed for June 24, 1957, was in my favor throughout my working years with Continental. If there was a furlough of pilots due to a downturn in the company's financial situation, you'd be furloughed in reverse sequence—last hired, first fired."

Marlon also reflected on the changes in the airline industry since 1963. "Back pay is a standard now, I think, in almost every discrimination case. Where discrimination is found, an award of back pay is one of the penalties, if you want to look at it that way, for efforts to achieve equality. But I have never argued with Taylor's recommendation [to not pursue back pay] in that regard. I agreed after a while—I think it was October 1964—that was about the time that everything was settled."[11]

NATURALLY, MARLON'S VICTORY attracted considerable national attention. The May 17, 1963, issue of *Time* magazine published a letter from Father Joseph Fichter of Loyola University in New Orleans, in which he praised *Time*'s interest in the Green case and the Supreme Court for its decision to make an historic ruling on discrimination in the workplace.

Not everyone, of course, applauded the Supreme Court's decision or wished Marlon well. Below Father Fichter's letter appeared one from Mario L. Caluda of Baton Rouge, in which he castigated the Supreme Court for dictating which job applicants private companies could and could not hire.[12]

Hate mail also arrived at the Green household. There were several, mostly unsigned, letters that spewed nothing but ugly, racist sentiments—all of it too vile and disgusting to repeat here.[13]

WHILE HE WAITED for T. Raber Taylor to work out the details of the contract with Continental, Marlon went to work as Floyd Dominy's pilot.

"The plane was there in Denver long before I was," Marlon said, "and its being there had nothing to do with me. His office was required by Congress, I think, to be in Washington D.C., but the Commissioner's duty was mostly in the West. Seventeen states in the West are primarily the area of responsibility of the Bureau of Reclamation, as opposed to the Corps of Engineers, which works all over the U.S. and its territories. When Dominy had any activity, usually he would fly commercial to wherever he wanted to be in the West and then, depending on his schedule, he'd put together dates, appearances, and personal visits to occupy his time until he wanted to go back to Washington; I would fly him back to Washington.

Marlon Green and members of the Bureau of Reclamation near the Flaming Gorge Dam in Utah, 1963. Floyd Dominy is third from left.
(Courtesy Green family archives)

"So, the Bureau's airplane and I were located in Denver, and whenever we were needed by the commissioner, we would go wherever he wanted to go to take care of his needs. Upon conclusion of those duties I would return him to Washington in the airplane, or take him to some other place where he could catch a commercial flight back to Washington.

"When he had a need, his priority was Number One. And at other times, people within the Bureau of Reclamation, the chief engineer's office especially, would need to use the airplane. My duty was to accommodate whatever need there was. Whenever the commissioner called, he would become priority Number One. Like *Air Force One*, in that regard—when the President wants to go somewhere, his requirements come first."[14]

After moving to Denver, the Green family rented several homes, including the left half of this duplex on Ivy Street. Eight people lived in a space of less than 1,000 square feet.
(Author photo 2005)

MARLON, ELEANOR, AND their six children packed up all their belongings, said goodbye to friends in Lansing, and moved the thousand miles to Denver. With no money for even the cheapest motel rooms, the family spent their nights on the road sleeping in the car.

The journey took four or five days, ending when the majestic panorama of the snow-capped Rocky Mountains spread itself across the horizon from north to south. Abutted up against the mountains, Denver seemed to be an oasis on the flatness of the plains. Marlon and Eleanor hoped that it would be a place where they and their children could find friends and acceptance and live without fear.

First came the task of finding a place to live in the Mile High City; the Greens moved into half of a single-story rental duplex in north Park Hill. The mixed-race neighborhood was convenient to Stapleton Airport, located just over a mile to the east where, in a corner of the Gates Rubber Company hangar, the Bureau of Reclamation's Aero Commander was housed. The convenience was offset by the day-and-night roar of aircraft taking off and landing nearby—a roar that was music to Marlon's ears. They also found a nearby Catholic church— Cure d'Ars. After only a couple of months, the Greens moved and rented a slightly larger home on Ivy Street.[15]

—·—·—·—

LIKE MOST AMERICAN cities, Denver has a long history of racial discrimination in housing. During the first quarter of the twentieth century, African-Americans in Denver were not free to live wherever they wanted. The practice of "red-lining"—the unofficial demarcation line between white and minority neighborhoods—was strictly enforced by realtors, buyers, and sellers. If a Negro family wanted to buy or rent a home, it was the common practice to shunt them into a mile-square area just north of the downtown core known as "Five Points." There the Negro population had its own safe enclave of stores, schools, clubs, restaurants, churches, parks, doctors, dentists, sports teams, a newspaper (the *Denver Star*), and even its own all-Negro fire department. It was a place of collegiality among racially homogeneous folk, and they prospered, relatively speaking, within their own community.

Denver's first African-American secondary-school principal, Bess Turner, played down racial animosities: "We [blacks] have too long a history in Denver to have any concerns. We never had any problems."

The surrounding white community, however, was less friendly to those Negro persons or families who transgressed the physical boundaries or spoke out against segregation and intolerance. They were quickly brought up short by beatings, intimidations, and front-lawn cross-burnings, courtesy of the local KKK chapter. Negroes quickly learned where their "place" was, and it wasn't mixing with white Denverites, unless it was strictly a master-servant relationship. Whites, on the other hand, were free to enjoy themselves in the Five Points jazz clubs, listen to Ella Fitzgerald or Duke Ellington at the Rossonian Hotel, or dine cheaply at the many barbeque establishments.

But discriminatory covenants were an "immovable object" colliding with the "irresistible force" of integration and social change. With the Five Points neighborhood burgeoning to the exploding point, expansion beyond the "red line" was inevitable. Soon Negro families broke out of their Five Points cage and pushed eastward, across the once-sacred dividing line of Downing Street. The boundary line was again pushed farther east to York Street, then into the area north of City Park known as "Struggle Hill."

In a vain effort to keep out Negroes (and, in some cases, Hispanics and Jews), "Neighborhood Improvement" associations were formed that drew up covenants which the homeowners signed, essentially forbidding them from selling to "undesirables" unless every homeowner on that block agreed.*

Holly Wasinger, in an article in *Colorado Heritage* magazine, notes that George L. Brown, the first African-American staff writer for the *Denver Post* and later Colorado's lieutenant governor (1975-1979), "wrote a series of articles about segregation in Denver in 1951. He revealed that twice he tried to swim in the Lakeside Park pool but was denied entrance by the manager with the explanation, 'They might throw rocks at you.' In another article, Brown described 'a most dehumanizing day' in which he took his family to twenty-five separate lodging facilities, such as hotels and trailer courts, and was denied lodging by each one on the basis of his race. At Crestview Trailer Camp he was told: 'We have no restrictions on pets, but we draw the line on Negroes.' That day he also heard, 'We're not prejudiced, we just don't take Coloreds because of the custom,' and 'No, we don't accept Negroes. I know God loves you as much as He loves me, but I'm sorry.'"

Brown also tried to have his family served at forty local restaurants; thirty-eight turned them away. At one of the two restaurants that did serve them, angry white patrons revolted, leaving without paying and declaring to the managers that they would not return.

Housing and dining weren't the only problems faced by Negroes; interracial marriage was also illegal until 1957, abolished by the passage of Colorado's Anti-Discrimination Act.

In the late fifties and early sixties, the inexorable eastward movement of Denver's Negro population then crossed Colorado Boulevard into an all-white neighborhood called "Park Hill," where something rather remarkable happened.

Instead of fleeing to the suburbs as the white residents of other parts of Denver had previously done, the white residents of Park Hill stayed and, for the most part, welcomed their Negro neighbors. There were no riots, no burning of crosses, no bricks thrown through windows. Instead, pastors spoke out from their pulpits about the need for calm, acceptance, and love. White housewives, perhaps nervously at first, baked cookies and cakes and brought them over to the new arrivals.

---

* The covenants were not abolished until the late 1950s.

Block parties were organized where the long-established whites could meet and mingle with the Negroes. A tenuous peace known as racial harmony seemed to break out spontaneously, and held. Park Hill became one of the nation's first successfully integrated residential neighborhoods.[16]

MARLON HAD NOT been on the job with the Bureau of Reclamation for very long when the discrimination Floyd Dominy had warned him about during their initial interview at the China Inn came to pass.

"It happened in Austin, Texas, and it happened in Amarillo, Texas," said Dominy. "This motel in Amarillo took him in as a guest, but the restaurant was under private contract management, and he went into the restaurant and they wouldn't serve him. Another time in Columbia, Missouri, we went into a restaurant for breakfast together and they wouldn't serve him, either. Of course, I walked out with him; we went without breakfast that day. But these things were happening all over at that time."

Perhaps worried that Brower's arch-conservationists, or someone who didn't like the fact that Dominy had employed a Negro pilot, might try to sabotage the Bureau's plane, Dominy said, "Whenever we were in the South, I wouldn't let him leave the airplane when it was being refueled. I said, 'I'll get you a sandwich and bring it back, but you're going to stay with that airplane and make sure somebody doesn't put salt or sugar in the Goddamn gas tank.'"[17]

DOMINY AND GREEN enjoyed an easy relationship in which race and racism played an almost comic role. For example, Dominy recalled the time that he and Marlon were flying from Minot, North Dakota, back to Washington with Senator Quentin Burdick on board.

Dominy said, "I asked the Senator, 'On this line of flight, are we going to fly over your ranch, by any chance?' He said, 'Well, as the crow flies....' I said, 'In this airplane, we don't talk about how the crow flies; we just let him fly.' Old Doc was laughing up a storm up there in the cockpit."

Marlon chuckled when reminded of this incident, noting that such banter did not hurt his feelings. "He and I had thrown that imagery around for a long time," Marlon said, recalling, "He would always begin a trip by asking me, 'How far is it as the crow flies?' And I always kidded him that his initials foretold his career path: 'F.E.D.'"[18]

———•··•··———

DESPITE MARLON'S U.S. Supreme Court victory, the racial climate in the country in 1963 seemed to be changing for the worse.

In early May of that year, following a week of speeches and marches by thousands of demonstrators, both black and white, protesting the oppressive segregationist policies in Birmingham, Alabama, the city police chief, T. Eugene "Bull" Connor, unleashed police and firemen on the demonstrators. The nation, glued to its collective television sets, watched as the scenes of police dogs attacking Negroes and high-pressure fire hoses sending them tumbling down streets like so much trash being washed into the gutter flickered across their screens.[19]

On May 11, 1963, hard-core segregationists in Birmingham bombed both the motel at which the Reverend Martin Luther King, Jr. was staying and the home of his brother, the Reverend Alfred Daniel King.[20]

Southern Negroes continued to suffer injustices—and worse. Just after midnight on June 12, 1963, civil-rights activist Medgar W. Evers was gunned down in the driveway of his home in Jackson, Mississippi.*[21]

These three events—plus the numerous other civil rights demonstrations, marches, protests, and boycotts that were occurring in virtually every major American city from June through August 1963—were precursors to one of the largest public demonstrations ever seen in the United States.

———•··•··———

IN AUGUST 1963 the news media were full of stories about the upcoming "March for Jobs and Freedom," organized by A. Philip Randolph

---

* It was not until 1994 that white supremacist Byron De La Beckwith was convicted of the murder and sentenced to life imprisonment. (www.stanford.edu/group/King)

Marlon and the Bureau of Reclamation Aero Commander aircraft in
Washington, D.C., August 1963 (Courtesy Green family archives)

and Bayard Rustin, that would take place in the nation's capital on the
twenty-eighth of the month. The Reverend Martin Luther King, Jr. was
scheduled to deliver the keynote speech, and Negroes from across the
country were planning on being there, coming by bus, car, train, and
plane. It was anticipated that this would be the largest civil-rights
march and rally ever held.[22]

"Floyd Dominy did not mention the march to me specifically,"
Marlon said, "but he suggested that I stay in Washington for the weekend instead of returning home to Denver."

Marlon took Dominy's advice. He initially planned to join the contingent from Colorado, but their hotel was too far away; he decided
instead to march with the NAACP group from Elizabeth, New Jersey. "I
marched with them till we got to the assembly area. I then made my
way to the Lincoln Memorial," he said.

The day of the march was ennervatingly hot and humid. A quarter
of a million people, predominantly black but with a sprinkling of white
faces, ringed the Reflecting Pool between the Washington Monument
and the steps of the Lincoln Memorial, where the speakers' stand had
been set up.[23]

The Lincoln Memorial had been the site of several other historic gatherings, including that Easter Sunday in 1939 when Marian Anderson, after being barred by the DAR from singing at Constitution Hall (an act which prompted Eleanor Roosevelt to resign from the DAR), performed a concert before an integrated crowd of 75,000. Ms. Anderson told a reporter, "I am not surprised at Mrs. Roosevelt's action, because she seems to me to be one who really comprehends the true meaning of democracy."[24]

Another important occurrence at the memorial took place on June 29, 1947, when President Harry S. Truman addressed several thousand delegates attending the annual conference of the National Association for the Advancement of Colored People. Truman had already created the President's Committee on Civil Rights, and in this speech said:

> We cannot be content with a civil liberties program which emphasizes only the need of protection against the possibility of tyranny by the Government. We cannot stop there. We must keep moving forward, with new concepts of civil rights to safeguard our heritage. The extension of civil rights today means, not protection of the people against the Government, but protection of the people *by* the Government. We must make the Federal Government a friendly, vigilant defender of the rights and equalities of all Americans. And again I mean all Americans.
>
> As Americans, we believe that every man should be free to live his life as he wishes. He should be limited only by his responsibility to his fellow countrymen. If this freedom is to be more than a dream, each man must be guaranteed equality of opportunity. The only limit to an American's achievement should be his ability, his industry, and his character. The rewards for his effort should be determined only by these truly relevant qualities.
>
> Our immediate task is to remove the last remnants of the barriers which stand between millions of our citizens and their birthright. There is no justifiable reason for discrimination because of ancestry, or religion, or race, or color. We must not tolerate such limitations on the freedom of any of our people and on their enjoyment of the basic rights which every citizen in a truly democratic society must possess.[25]

———•••———

THE AREA AROUND the Lincoln Memorial was a veritable sea of people on that hot August day in 1963—young, old, rich, poor, hopeful, hurting, curious, concerned, angry, aimless—an ocean of humanity that rippled in the sunshine like a dark tide. When King advanced to the podium bristling with microphones, the tide surged toward him, wanting to embrace him and his every word. Marlon was not far from the speaker's podium—he estimated 150 feet—and had a good view of the proceedings.

Necks craned and hands shaded eyes in order to capture a glimpse of the man many Negroes regarded as their Messiah. Slowly, with carefully chosen words, Dr. King began his "I Have a Dream" speech—one of the greatest orations in human history.

King made reference to Lincoln's momentous freeing of the slaves, which served as a beacon of light that illuminated the path of freedom. Such a move, however, was merely a prelude to the many decades of oppression, segregation, and discrimination which the slaves and sons and daughters of slaves continued to endure.

King talked about the thousands who had come to the memorial as a way of symbolizing the fact that the Negro still was not free, that a century after the Emancipation Proclamation was issued, "the Negro lives on a lonely island of poverty in the midst of a vast ocean of material prosperity. One hundred years later, the Negro is still languishing in the corners of American society and finds himself an exile in his own land."

Telecast to a nationwide audience, it was the first time many whites had heard King speak, and the first time many became fully aware of the depths of Negro discontent.

King went on, painting a portrait of a white America as having resisted for decades giving the Negro his promised due, of working overtly and covertly to hold down people of dark skin. The crowd reacted, applauding and murmuring "Amen" at many of King's inspiring phrases.

For five, ten, fifteen minutes King continued on, his amplified voice becoming more passionate with each passing sentence. There were colorful, stick-in-the-mind references to America having defaulted on the promissory note contained within the Constitution: That all men are created equal. There were references to the evils of "gradualism," in

The huge civil-rights rally which Marlon attended at the Lincoln Memorial in
Washington, D.C., August 1963 (Courtesy National Archives)

which each generation of white leaders would gradually dole out small bits of equality without pouring out the full measure which was every American's rightful portion, regardless of color.

There were references to police brutality, to Negroes being denied the right to eat in any restaurant or sleep in any motel or hotel; to Negroes being consigned to ghettos and slums; to being prevented from voting; to being barred from attending the schools of their choice; to the destiny of both black and white Americans being inextricably linked.

There were not-so-vague warnings of trouble to come if the blessings of liberty continued to be denied to the Negro: "Those who hope that the Negro needed to blow off steam and will now be content will have a rude awakening if the nation returns to business as usual. There will be neither rest nor tranquility in America until the Negro is granted his citizenship rights."

King then seamlessly and fervently launched into the references for which the speech will forever be known: *I Have A Dream*. These dreams included black and white children holding hands and attending the same schools together; of freedom ringing from every hill and mountain, every town and valley.

King concluded his stirring speech with the thundering words, "When we let freedom ring, when we let it ring from every village and every hamlet, from every state and every city, we will be able to speed up that day when all of God's children, black men and white men, Jews and Gentiles, Protestants and Catholics, will be able to join hands and sing in the words of the old Negro spiritual, 'Free at last! Free at last! Thank God Almighty, we are free at last!'"[26]

A great roar rose up from the throats of a quarter-million Americans assembled in the shadow of Abraham Lincoln's memorial that day, a roar that was heard across the country and around the world.

Deeply impressed with King's words, and with the size of the crowd gathered to hear them, Marlon realized that he and Eleanor were not alone in their struggle. There were millions just like him who cried out for freedom, justice, and equality, and he lifted his voice and joined in the joyous roar.[27]

CHAPTER 17:
THE LONG, HOT SUMMER

HUNDREDS OF MILES away in Birmingham, Alabama, the roar of the crowd in Washington was also heard by three Klansmen—Robert E. Chambliss, Thomas Blanton, Jr., and Bobby Frank Cherry. They had their own loud response to King's speech.

At 10:19 a.m. on Sunday, September 15, 1963, a little more than two weeks after King told the world about his dream, the equivalent of ten sticks of dynamite, planted by Chambliss, Blanton, and Cherry, exploded in the basement of the Sixteenth Street Baptist Church in Birmingham, Alabama, killing four young Negro girls who had been, at that moment, pulling on their choir robes. The dead were Addie Mae Collins, Carol Denise McNair, Carole Robertson, and Cynthia Dianne Wesley. Twenty other persons in the congregation were also wounded by the mighty blast.

September 15, 1963, was black America's 9-11. The Sixteenth Street Baptist Church became black America's World Trade Center, Pentagon, and a field in Pennsylvania, all wrapped up as one.

Much of white America was also shocked and outraged, rudely shaken awake from its sleep of benign neglect. Just as everyone today can recall exactly where he or she was when the twin towers of the World Trade Center fell, virtually every black American who was older than six in 1963 remembers where he or she was when they learned that the Sixteenth Street Baptist Church had been dynamited.

A tearful Reverend King gave the eulogy at the girls' funeral, which was attended by over 8,000 mourners, both Negro and white.[1]

The day following the attack, a visibly moved President John F. Kennedy issued a solemn statement:

> I know I speak on behalf of all Americans in expressing a deep sense of outrage and grief over the killing of the children yesterday in Birmingham, Alabama. It is regrettable that public

disparagement of law and order has encouraged violence which has fallen on the innocent.

If these cruel and tragic events can only awaken that city and State—if they can only awaken this entire Nation—to a realization of the folly of racial injustice and hatred and violence, then it is not too late for all concerned to unite in steps toward peaceful progress before more lives are lost. The Negro leaders of Birmingham who are counseling restraint instead of violence are bravely serving their ideals in their most difficult task—for the principles of peaceful self-control are least appealing when most needed....

This Nation is committed to a course of domestic justice and tranquility—and I call upon every citizen, white and Negro, North and South, to put passions and prejudices aside and to join in this effort.[2]

Four days after the church bombing, President Kennedy met with King and six other Negro leaders, who told the President that the black citizens of Birmingham (re-named by many "Bombingham") were "almost on the verge of despair as a result of this reign of terror." Kennedy promised to do everything he could about the criminal tragedy.[3]

After the meeting, the president issued another statement:

I have received reports from the leading Negro citizens concerning the situation. Next Monday I will confer at the request of [Birmingham] Mayor [Albert] Boutwell with white civic leaders who want to give us information concerning the steps which the city has taken and plans to take to reestablish the confidence of everyone that law and order in Birmingham will be maintained.

In addition, I have today appointed General Kenneth Royall and Colonel Earl Blaik as a committee to represent me personally in helping the city to work as a unit in overcoming the fears and suspicions which now exist. They will go to Birmingham in the next few days to start on this work of great importance.

In the meantime, the Federal Bureau of Investigation, as well as local authorities, is making massive efforts to bring to justice the persons responsible for the bombing on Sunday and previous incidents*.... I urge all citizens in these next days to conduct themselves with restraint and responsibility.[4]

THE WORLD *WAS* taking note of the struggle going on in the "land of the free." On October 15, 1963, the Reverend Dr. Martin Luther King, Jr., was notified that he had been awarded the Nobel Peace Prize for 1964. He immediately announced that "every penny" of the $54,000 cash award would be donated to the civil-rights movement.[5]

Naturally, not everyone was overjoyed by the news. Bull Connor, the Birmingham, Alabama, police commissioner, declared that the Nobel committee had hit a new low in their selection of Dr. King.

Virgil Stuart, the police chief of St. Augustine, Florida, a city that underwent unrest when King led civil-rights demonstrations there during the summer, echoed Bull Connor's sentiments, declaring King's selection to be nothing more than a joke.[6]

IF MUCH OF America was reeling from the terrible events that took place in Birmingham on September 15, 1963, it was shaken to its core a little more than two months later when, on November 22, President John F. Kennedy was killed while riding in a motorcade through the streets of Dallas.**

Reflecting upon the death of JFK, Marlon said, "I was about to say I felt 'shattered' when I heard he was assassinated, but it wasn't quite

---

* The FBI was, in fact, doing very little to bring to justice the persons responsible. Finally, after the 1972 death of FBI Director J. Edgar Hoover—who had done everything possible to undermine Martin Luther King, Jr., and who had for years obstructed the investigation into the Birmingham bombing case—Ku Klux Klan member Robert Chambliss was tried in 1977 for his role in the bombing, convicted, and sentenced to life imprisonment. In 2000, the two other Klan members, Thomas Blanton, Jr. and Bobby Frank Cherry, were also indicted for the act of domestic terrorism. Both men were subsequently tried, convicted, and sentenced to life in prison. (www.crimelibrary.com/terrorists_spies/terrorists/birmingham_church)

** A special commission, headed by Chief Justice Earl Warren, looked into the assassination, and concluded in 1964 that a lone gunman, Lee Harvey Oswald, was responsible. (Warren Commission Report, passim)

that severe. This was more likely my sentiment: *Camelot* had been shattered, but not in the *frivolous* sense of Camelot.

"I had thought of Kennedy as a boon or a God-send compared to what I knew, with as much sophistication as I had in those years. He was a man of good will, with regard to all those things that were so meaningful for me—civil rights, voting rights, preventing the growth of the Ku Klux Klan, and any illegal expressions of hatred. So, generally, I saw Kennedy in a happy light, knowing that in order to become president he had to make concessions—such as overcoming his 'Catholicity'—to win the prize, and I was greatly pleased when he won the prize. I didn't think that his death meant the end of the gains that had been made. But it *was* a severe set-back."[7]

———•———

SOMEHOW THE NATION slowly recovered from its collective grief, but Negroes and others with a stake in the outcome of the burgeoning civil-rights movement cast a wary eye at the new president—Lyndon Baines Johnson—a Southerner, possibly a redneck, and wondered if he would turn back the clock on everything that had been gained during Kennedy's brief tenure.

Gradually the deep wound caused by JFK's assassination began to heal, and those in the country who believed in equality looked forward with guarded optimism that the nation, especially after the passage of the Civil Rights Act of 1964,* was headed in the right direction. Civil rights became the national focus; in 1964, a far-off place called Vietnam was little more than a tiny blip on the national radar screen.

———•———

MARLON PONDERED PRESIDENT Johnson's apparent commitment to civil rights and affirmative action, and wondered if it was sincere or merely a "political act." "Of the two," Marlon noted, "I would say it

---

* The major provisions of the Act, considered the most important piece of civil-rights legislation since Reconstruction, prohibited discrimination in public accommodations, in government, and employment, essentially sweeping away the "Jim Crow" laws. (en.wikipedia.org/wiki/Civil_Rights_Act_of_1964)

NEWS ITEM:

(Washington, D.C., June 4, 1964) In a speech today to the graduating class at the all-Negro Howard University, President Lyndon B. Johnson explained the philosophy that underlies his and the nation's commitment to affirmative action, asserting that civil-rights laws alone were not enough to remedy the effects of past discrimination.

Said the President, "You do not wipe away the scars of centuries by saying, 'Now, you are free to go where you want, do as you desire, and choose the leaders you please.' You do not take a man who for years has been hobbled by chains, liberate him, bring him to the starting line of a race, saying, 'You are free to compete with all the others,' and still justly believe you have been completely fair....

"This is the next and more profound stage of the battle for civil rights. We seek not just freedom but opportunity—not just legal equity but human ability—not just equality as a right and a theory, but equality as a fact and as a result."[8]

---

was an act. Lyndon Johnson was a segregationist and maybe a racist, but it's my thinking that, as the times changed, the circumstances required that his behavior be subdued and transposed. That's what I think happened with his career and the Civil Rights Act of 1964, and it makes you wonder if a leopard can change its spots. If it *was* an act, he sure deserved an Academy Award for everything after '64.'"[9]

NEWS ITEM:

(Denver, Colo., July 15, 1964) Denver District Court Judge Neil Horan ruled Tuesday that Continental Airlines must hire Negro pilot Marlon D. Green.

In a 15-page ruling, Judge Horan dismissed the airline's petition and affirmed the January 1959 order of the Colorado Anti-Discrimination Commission, which required the airline to hire him and give him priority status.

Horan ordered the Commission to consult with Continental as to the problems involved in granting relief to Green, citing "the difficulty in determining the relief to be granted," caused by the long delay between the time of the Commission's order and Tuesday's ruling. The judge gave the Commission 20 days to submit a written judgment to the court.[10]

THE SUMMER OF 1964 earned infamy as "the long, hot summer," as several cities across the nation literally erupted in a series of race riots and disturbances.

It started with a riot that began on the sultry night of Saturday, July 18, in New York City's Harlem district, and raged until the 23rd. The unrest was sparked by the shooting death of James Powell, a Negro teenager, by a white policeman two days earlier.

A peaceful gathering to protest the killing smoldered for two days until, following a Saturday rally sponsored by CORE, it exploded into an orgy of burning, looting, and vandalism, with bottles, bricks, and other missiles thrown at the 500 policemen who had been called out.

Jesse Gray, a leader of a Harlem rent strike, inflamed the situation when he called for a hundred "black revolutionaries" willing to die to correct what he called "the police-brutality situation in Harlem." A third night of violence spilled over into the Bedford-Stuyvesant neighborhood. When the rioting was finally over, scores of people had been either injured or arrested.[11]

On July 25, 1964, police in Rochester, New York, attempted to make an arrest for disorderly conduct during a street party in the city's predominantly Negro "Crescent" area. The situation quickly grew out of control and soon a fifty-square-block area was teeming with battles between police and rioters. Hundreds of white troublemakers also rushed to the area to do battle with the Negroes. Stores were looted and torched. So severe was the uprising that Governor Nelson Rockefeller was compelled to call out the New York National Guard—the first time Guard troops were thus used in a northern city.[12]

Jersey City was next to experience several days of racial confrontations. On the night of August 2, a Negress was arrested for being drunk and disorderly; a Negro who came to her assistance was also arrested, and the pair was taken to the police station. Soon a crowd of about forty demonstrators surrounded the station, claiming police had beaten the two. The crowd dispersed then later re-formed in even larger numbers. Police in riot gear held them back until the mob barraged them with bricks, bottles, garbage-can lids, and other debris. White motorists driving unaware into the area were attacked and beaten, and businesses in the area were looted. Dozens of rioters were arrested.[13]

Two more cities—Paterson and Elizabeth, New Jersey—were then wracked by racial strife. On August 11, 1964, trouble began in the

NEWS ITEM:

(Philadelphia, Miss., Aug. 4, 1964) The bodies of three civil rights workers were discovered today buried in an earthen dam on a farm near this rural, east central Mississippi town. There was evidence that the three had been beaten and shot to death. The trio reportedly had been participating in the "Freedom Summer" project to help Southern Negroes register to vote.

The three young men, two white and one Negro, had been missing since June 21. They were identified as Michael Schwerner, 24, and Andrew Goodman, 20, both white, and James Chaney, 21, a Negro from nearby Meridian. A spokesman for the FBI said white segregationists murdered them the night they disappeared. Nineteen whites, including several police officers, were charged with conspiracy to deprive the victims of their civil rights.*[14]

run-down Negro section of Paterson when a group of black youths began pelting passing cars with rocks and bottles. Fifty police moved in to quell the disturbance, which then provoked a larger response from the Negro community. By the next day, however, calm had been restored, but the anger was still palpable.

A larger battle broke out the same night in Elizabeth, a port city about twenty miles north of Paterson, with Molotov cocktails being tossed and at least one motorcycle cop pulled off his bike and beaten by a Negro mob. The reasons for the outbreak of violence were not immediately clear.[15]

The Chicago suburb of Dixmoor underwent a two-day spasm of violence that came to be known as the "Gin-Bottle War." It started on August 16 when Mike Lapota, a white liquor-store owner, attempted to apprehend a Negress whom he claimed had stolen a bottle of gin. In response, a group of Negroes began picketing the store and the confrontation quickly escalated. More demonstrators showed up, as did more police. Bricks and bottles were thrown at the cops, and the police in turn threw tear-gas grenades and fired over the heads of the rioters to disperse them.[16]

---

* In 1967, the nineteen indicted white men went on trial for the crimes. Former Ku Klux Klansman James Jordan testified that sawmill operator and part-time Baptist minister Edgar Ray "Preacher" Killen was the main person responsible for the kidnapping and murders. The nineteen were freed, but Killen was indicted by a grand jury in January 2005 and was ultimately convicted in June 2005 of three counts of murder. (www.law.umkc.edu/faculty/projects/ftrials/price&bowers/Killen)

A section of an American city destroyed during the race riots of 1964
(Courtesy National Archives)

Parts of Philadelphia, Pennsylvania, were then engulfed by rioting that began late on the sweltering Saturday night of August 28, 1964. Police had been called to investigate a stalled vehicle that was blocking an intersection in the predominantly Negro neighborhood of North Philadelphia—a section known to locals as "the Jungle." A sullen crowd showed up and a confrontation between police and residents ensued. More police were called as more residents arrived and began flinging objects from nearby rooftops. At the height of the battle, it was estimated that 400 patrolmen fought a throng of about 300 Negroes.[17]

IN SEPTEMBER 1964, with the Bureau of Reclamation job secure and the prospects of Marlon finally landing a high-paying airline job with Continental looking more solid than ever, the Greens felt they were safe in moving to larger quarters. They looked at several houses in the Park Hill neighborhood and settled for a substantial, two-story brick home that faced Denver's City Park Golf Course. They mortgaged the home for $24,500.[18]

Paula Green, then seven years of age, vividly recalled that, one night before the family moved in, they all drove to the City Park Golf Course at dusk, got out of the car, then plopped down on the grass of the sixth tee "to 'spy' on our new house. Magical!"

After moving in, the Greens also changed churches and found one closer to their new home: Blessed Sacrament Catholic Church, located on Montview Boulevard.[19]

Most of the Park Hill neighbors were friendly, and soon the Green children were playing with a large assortment of kids their own ages. The only problem came from, as Marlon said, "A mean French woman who lived in the house just to the north. When the boys were playing basketball in our driveway and making too much noise for her, she would set her sprinkler to hit our driveway." Marlon went over to her yard one day and shut off her sprinkler; she called the police. Marlon reported the "Hedge Row Row" to the *Denver Post,* which ran the story. Shortly thereafter the woman and her husband moved and were replaced by a friendlier, more understanding family.[20]

———•–•—♦—•–•———

ON NOVEMBER 3, 1964, Continental Airlines at last made Marlon an acceptable offer, confirming the date of his seniority to his job interview and flight test in Denver in June 1957. He and T. Raber Taylor took some time to study the offer.[21]

———•–•—♦—•–•———

AS MARLON CIRCLED in his personal holding pattern and waited patiently for Continental to invite him to the "next" pilot training class, he and Bureau of Reclamation Commissioner Floyd Dominy shared many adventures. Marlon found himself flying Dominy, and sometimes Dominy's boss, Secretary of the Interior Stewart Udall, around the western half of the country.

At the end of November 1964, Doc and Dominy flew from Washington, D.C., and stopped overnight in LaCrosse, Wisconsin, where the commissioner had a speech. They left LaCrosse early the next morning so Dominy could make another speech at a luncheon with the North Dakota Chamber of Commerce in Minot.

NEWS ITEM:

(Washington, D.C., Nov. 18, 1964) After Rev. Martin Luther King, Jr. criticized the FBI's failure to protect civil rights workers in Albany, Georgia, because the Bureau's agents were Southerners, the agency's director, J. Edgar Hoover, 69, denounced King in a rare news conference as "the most notorious liar in the country."

Still smarting from the Warren Commission's stinging criticism of the FBI for failing to inform the Secret Service that Lee Harvey Oswald was a threat to President Kennedy before the assassination a year ago, Mr. Hoover dismissed Rev. King's charges and countered that the majority of FBI agents assigned to the South were born in the North.

The day following Hoover's outburst, Rev. King responded that he was still dismayed that no arrests have been made in Albany, Ga. of persons who assaulted Negro civil rights workers there, nor had the FBI brought to justice anyone involved in either the Birmingham church bombing which killed four little girls in Birmingham nor the Mississippi case of the three murdered civil-rights workers. [22]

On the way, Dominy and Green flew into a raging snowstorm. Dominy recalled that there were "Terrible winds from the west. We finally had to get right down on the deck [flying at a very low altitude] in order to make any progress at all because, upstairs, the wind was so strong we could hardly fly. It got worse and worse and, finally, it was a blizzard—an absolutely terrible snowstorm. All of a sudden—I'm sitting in the back, going over the notes for my speech—Doc says, 'Commish, would you take a look at that right engine? I'm losing oil pressure.'

"I glanced out the window and, hell, oil was streaming out of it everywhere. So I said, 'Feather it, Doc; we don't want the damned thing to catch fire.' He feathered the prop, of course, and said in a calm voice, 'I'm going to detour into Bismarck.' I said, 'But, Doc, my speech is in *Minot.*' Of course, you can't tell the captain of the ship what to do, but he worked for me, and he wanted to accommodate my wishes.

"He said, 'Minot field is at minimum.' I said, 'Is it threatening to go *below* minimum?' He said, 'Well, no.' So I said, 'We're only about an hour out of Minot; why don't we go on? The reason we bought this new plane [a Grand Commander] was because it has good performance on one engine.' So he said, 'All right; we'll proceed.'

"Well, about ten minutes later, Minot announces that the commercial field is closed. So Doc says, 'What do you suggest now, Commish?' I said, 'Call the SAC air base at Minot. They've got two-mile-long runways and they've got radar assistance, and we're a government aircraft. I'm sure they'll give you permission to land.' So Doc contacted SAC and, sure enough, they said, 'Come on in and land.'

"We had the tower on the radio, and the controller was guiding us in. The controller said, 'You're thirty minutes out; you're five hundred feet above the level of the runway, and change your heading to such-and-such.' We couldn't see a damn thing. I remember the last instruction: 'You're over the end of the runway, you're fifty feet above it, cut your engine and glide on in.' We didn't see anything until we were on the ground. But old Doc didn't sweat it a minute; he was just as calm as could be."[23]

While in Minot, Marlon was interviewed by the local newspaper about his historic Supreme Court victory. The reporter noted,

> A soft-spoken, very articulate and well-educated man, Green emphasized he was not—and had never intended to be—"any Jackie Robinson" among airline pilots.... It is a fact that Green was probably the first Negro to apply for an airline pilot job—but it is not a fact that he will be the first Negro trainee.
>
> "About one year ago," he explained, "TWA accepted a young Negro as a trainee, but a month or so afterwards, for some reason, he committed suicide.* So, you see, I am not the first by any means."
>
> Now 35 years of age, Green is looking forward eagerly to...the start of training for a job he has always coveted. He is not naïve. He knows there may be some who will resent his victory—but, on the other hand, he is extremely grateful.
>
> "Grateful, of course, to those who have helped me all these years and very, very pleased with the opportunity now given me by Continental."

---

* William DeShazor, 28, a resident of Poughkeepsie, New York, was found shot to death in a Kansas City hotel with a pistol in his hand. DeShazor, a graduate of the University of Chicago with a degree in physics and a former Marine Corps pilot with over five years service, was in training to become a pilot with TWA. The coroner ruled DeShazor's death a suicide. (*Poughkeepsie Journal*, Feb. 10, 1964)

He is a man who is looking ahead, not back, on the long years of struggle.

"There is a lot of history behind us, true," he said, "but it is the future that counts now."

And, declared this man, who does not think of himself as "any Jackie Robinson," he is facing that future without bitterness and "without rancor towards anyone."[24]

———•———

AFTER CONSULTING WITH his lawyer, Marlon accepted Continental's offer on December 2, 1964. Now it was a matter of waiting for a training class to open—a wait that would take almost two more months.

Marlon's Supreme Court victory was also beginning to break the ice for other Negro pilots trying to secure posts with other airlines. An Air Force pilot by the name of David Harris saw ads placed in the *Air Force Times* by two commercial carriers and sent them his application, complete with the fact that he was a Negro. Harris was hired by American Airlines on December 3, 1964.[25]

———•———

DOMINY RECALLED A later incident potentially just as serious as the flight into Minot. The Grand Commander had just had its engines rebuilt, and Dominy said, "After the first trip with the rebuilt engines, the mechanics in Denver found metal filings in the oil, and there was a great hullabaloo about it. Even the FAA moved in to check it out."

Dominy suspected sabotage; as far as the Sierra Club and the environmentalists were concerned, Floyd Dominy was Public Enemy Number One. And others may have had reasons to do away with Dominy's Negro pilot.

Dominy said, "The FAA asked Doc to give them a flight demonstration but he refused. He said, 'I've got a pilot's license; everybody knows I can fly.' It became quite an issue.

"I said, 'Doc, you're wrong on this. You go out there and fly that Goddamned airplane for anybody who wants you to fly it under federal supervision. They know Goddamn well you can fly; they're trying to *protect* you. So you just get your gear together and volunteer to take that test flight any time they want to.'"

Green followed his boss's direction and passed without a hitch. There were no more incidents.[26]

———··♦··———

WHEN HE WASN'T flying for the Bureau of Reclamation, Marlon took up the game of golf. Denver's eighteen-hole City Park Golf Course is long but not particularly challenging, but Marlon had his own unique way of tackling the course. On afternoons when there were few golfers on the course, he would start at the sixth tee directly across from his house, play around to the eighteenth hole, go into the clubhouse and pay for his round, then finish with holes one through five.

One day he scored every golfer's dream—a hole in one—but there were no witnesses; he was by himself on the course when it happened. He tried yelling to Eleanor at home, but she was too far away and she didn't hear his cries of joy.[27]

———··♦··———

WHILE HE ENJOYED Floyd Dominy's company and the prestige that came with flying a high-profile government official, Marlon was still making less than $10,000 a year. He knew that the major airlines were paying pilots $3,000-$4,000 a *month*, and he ached to get into a commercial cockpit. Even though the Supreme Court had ruled in his favor and ordered Continental to enroll him in an upcoming pilot training class, the airline was dragging its feet and stalling as long as it could. Marlon began to wonder if he would ever be allowed to fly a commercial passenger liner.

At last, after having received word that he was to report to Continental's training class in late January 1965, Marlon submitted his letter of resignation to the Bureau of Reclamation. In return he received a big going-away party from his friends at the Bureau. Nearly 150 of them signed the oversized farewell card, hand-drawn by someone in the office.[28]

Floyd Dominy especially hated to see him go. The two men had formed a strong bond of friendship over the nearly two years they had flown together, and each had a deep, mutual admiration and respect for the other. But Dominy did not want to hinder Marlon from finally realizing his dream. They shook hands with a hearty grip. Using Green's military nickname, Dominy said, "Doc was a very competent pilot and a wonderful guy."[29]

Marlon reported for training with Continental on January 25, 1965*—over seven years after he had first interviewed with the company, and almost two years after the U.S. Supreme Court had ruled in his favor and against Continental.[30]

The victory, although bittersweet, was a victory nonetheless, and Marlon savored it, at the same time steeling himself for whatever new trials and travails might come his way.

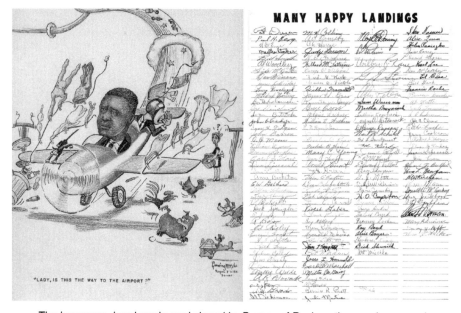

The humorous, hand-made card signed by Bureau of Reclamation employees and presented to Marlon at his going-away party
(Courtesy Green family archives)

---

* Although Robert Six and the Continental headquarters had moved to Los Angeles in July 1963, the training center was, in January 1965, still located in Denver. (Serling, 217)

Marlon in his Continental Airlines uniform in front of his Denver home,
photographed in 1965
(Courtesy Green family archives)

CHAPTER 18:
I PRESUME YOU'RE GREEN

$$\cdot\,\cdot\,\bullet\,\cdot\,\cdot$$

THANKFULLY, CONTINENTAL'S TRAINING sessions were racially uneventful. Marlon felt neither shunned nor ostracized by his instructors or fellow classmates, the latter who numbered six or seven. The camaraderie was nearly the same as he had experienced during Air Force pilot training.

Bernard "Barney" Barnwell was Continental's Director of Training; as he and Marlon were both parishoners at the same Catholic church, they had a nodding acquaintance. George Miller was Chief Pilot but Bill Gruenke did most of the instructing, and he and Marlon got along well.

"There was no tension or negativity," Marlon said. "Those two words did not apply to my experience. It was cordial and routine. That's probably how I would describe it—routine. That was as good as I could hope for."

Like the other students, Marlon initially trained to be first officer, or co-pilot, in the ground school, which lasted six weeks. Near the end of ground school, the students began to get cockpit time, flying with other pilots on actual trips and observing from the right seat.

Marlon recalled, "At that time, Continental was using the British four-engine turbo-prop aircraft, called the Viscount—the Viscount 700, I think it was—with Rolls-Royce engines, and a seating capacity of about seventy passengers."

The classes went smoothly. Flying the airliner was not unlike the multi-engine bombers he had flown during his Air Force days, and soon he was certified to be first officer on the Viscount. The goal for which he had striven for so many years, and for which he and Eleanor had sacrificed so much, had finally been attained.[1]

Not long after Marlon's hiring by Continental, L.D. "Mac" McCloskey, a white pilot with United Airlines and a member of the Air Line Pilots' Association (ALPA), wrote to Marlon and congratulated him on:

> winning one round in the long battle against the sinister forces

A Continental Viscount turbo-prop airliner of the type flown by Marlon Green
(Copyright, Colorado Historical Society, photo by Jim Krebs, scan 87.164.20)

of ignorance and intolerance. I know it must have been a long discouraging struggle and I commend you for the perseverance to see it through. I am embarrassed to live in a country where a citizen must resort to court action to secure a position with a government-franchised public carrier, denied to him because of his race....

Once again let me congratulate you and offer my best wishes in your airline career. I imagine you are very busy now at "Tension Tech," but please let me know if I can be of any help.[2]

Marlon was gratified by McCloskey's letter and hoped that all the other white pilots would feel the same.

Marlon made his first flight as a Continental co-pilot in March 1965 but, surprisingly, he has forgotten the exact destination. "I'll guess it was Kansas City," he said. "If that wasn't it, it was Colorado Springs. Quite often, we had this routine. First trip out in the morning we'd take down to Colorado Springs and then back to Denver. Then you'd get out south-bound again, stopping in Colorado Springs, Albuquerque, and spending the night in El Paso. That was one of the routines I can remember, but I don't recall if my first trip was to Kansas City or down to Colorado Springs. But I do recall that it was in the right seat of a Viscount."

ROBERT SIX DID not go out of his way to welcome Marlon to the Continental family, nor to apologize to him for all the suffering and hardships his truculence had caused.

Marlon finally met the company president at some point during his first year as a co-pilot. "We met for the first time in Continental's operations area under Gate 9 of the C wing of Stapleton," he said. "And if you can appreciate the humor in this, the president of the airline knows that there's only one black man working for his airline as a pilot. He sees me and approaches me in the 'pilot ready room,' if we can call it that, and he says, 'I presume you're Green.' That was almost as bad as, 'Dr. Livingston, I presume?' He presumed I was Green, and he presumed correctly. I thought that was an interesting evasion on his part."

When asked if Six said anything like "Welcome to Continental," or "Sorry about all the trouble," Marlon laughed and replied, "No, he did not say either one of those things. We had what I would call 'minimal pleasantries' for a minute or so, and then he went out to catch his flight. I can't remember now if that was the one I was on to Kansas City. That was the destination for most of the flights I flew as co-pilot."[3]

———•—•◆—•—•———

THE KILLING OF EMMETT TILL, the bombing of the Birmingham church, the John F. Kennedy and Malcolm X assassinations, and all of the other paroxysms and outrages that had rocked America in the 1950s and early 1960s were but a mere precursor to the events that would unfold in the coming decades.

The new string of events began in Alabama, a state long infamous for its successful attempts to frustrate Negroes' efforts to register and vote. Literacy tests and poll taxes, combined with intimidation by the police and Klan, were just some of the tactics used by those in power to maintain the status quo.

On February 17, 1965, a small group of brave voting-rights marchers decided to take on Selma, Alabama, a former slave-trading town more recently notorious for its lynchings of Negroes. The local rednecks were not pleased. One of the marchers, Jimmy Lee Jackson, was shot and killed. To protest this killing, and to press home the need for voting-rights reforms in the state, the Reverend Dr. Martin Luther King, Jr., called on Negroes to gather in Selma on March 6 for an even larger demonstration.

NEWS ITEM:

(New York City, Feb. 21, 1965) Malcolm X, the controversial former spokesman for the Black Muslim movement, was assassinated today in front of 400 supporters at the Audubon Ballroom, 166th Street and Broadway.

Thomas Hagan, a 22-year-old Negro, was arrested and charged with the killing. Eyewitnesses said that Hagan and others began firing seconds after Malcolm X stepped to the microphone. In all, a total of 30 shots were fired, and three other persons were wounded. The bearded militant was hit seven times by bullets. Members of the panicked crowd then attacked Hagan, breaking his leg under a rain of kicks and blows and wounding him with a handgun.

It was believed that other assassins had also taken part in the shooting because the coroner discovered two different calibers of bullets in Malcolm's body, as well as 12-gauge shotgun pellets. Police expressed the opinion that as many as five conspirators may have been involved.

Police speculated that the assassination stemmed from a feud between the Black Muslims, an extremist Negro nationalist movement for which Malcolm had been the highly visible spokesman but left in 1964, and his new group, the Organization for Afro-American Unity.

Malcolm, a slim, reddish-haired six-footer with horn-rimmed glasses and a gift for bitter eloquence against what he considered white exploitation of Negroes, broke in March 1964 with the Black Muslim movement, known as the Nation of Islam, headed by Elijah Mohammed.

A few days before his killing, the 39-year-old Malcolm X, who was born Malcolm Little in Omaha, Neb., told a reporter that he believed he was "a marked man," and that he expected the intense rivalry between his organization and the Black Muslims would likely lead to his death.[4]

King, Reverend Ralph Abernathy, and the other organizers were determined to force a meeting with those who would deny basic civil rights to Alabamans. The group planned to march the fifty-four miles from Selma to the state capital in Montgomery and present their grievances to Governor George C. Wallace. On March 7, a day that became known as "Bloody Sunday," six hundred marchers, both black and white, led by Hosea Williams of the Southern Christian Leadership Conference (SCLC) and John Lewis of the Student Non-Violent Coordinating Committee (SNCC), started out from Browns Chapel AME Church in Selma.

The group was only a few miles into the march when they were set upon by 200 state troopers at the Edmund Pettus Bridge in Selma and beaten savagely with nightsticks, lashed with bull whips, sprayed with tear gas, and trampled by Sheriff James Clark's deputies on horseback. Seventeen marchers required hospitalization.

The situation escalated. Two days later, March 9, under conflicting pressures from Alabama officials and black militants who did not subscribe to King's non-violent methods, King accepted a compromise in which protesters would limit themselves to marching from Browns Chapel and praying at the Pettus Bridge instead of continuing on to Montgomery. Fifteen hundred marchers, however, ignored King and began a second march to Montgomery, but were turned back because of a federal restraining order that barred the protest. The Reverend James Reeb, a white minister from Boston, was beaten to death by four Klansmen in the violence that followed this demonstration.

King and the march organizers regrouped, obtained a federal court order and the protection of the federalized Alabama National Guard, and set out for a third march, this time on March 22, 1965. The group, singing "We Shall Overcome," reached the state capital on the evening of March 25, where King spoke to an assembled throng of some 25,000.

After the rally, Viola Liuzzo, a white housewife and mother of five from Detroit, was driving her 1963 Oldsmobile with Leroy Moton, a young Negro marcher, along Highway 80 when the pair was ambushed by three Klan members—Eugene Thomas, Collie L. Wilkins, Jr., and William O. Eaton. Mrs. Liuzzo was killed by gunfire and Moton wounded; she was the only white woman to be murdered during the years of the civil-rights movement.* Liuzzo's death, and the images of the chaos in the newspapers and on television, convinced President Johnson to sign the Voting Rights Act of 1965.[5]

---

* FBI Director J. Edgar Hoover, in his continuing campaign of harassment and intimidation of King and the civil-rights movement, did his best to smear the reputation of Mrs. Liuzzo by claiming she was a drug addict. (FBI memo, Mar. 25, 1965; www.stanford.edu/group/King; www.alabamamoments.state.al.us; www.emergingpictures.com; www.paperlessarchives.com)

ON AUGUST 6, 1965, the same day that President Lyndon Johnson signed the Voting Rights Act in the presence of Reverend King and other civil-rights leaders,[6] Harrold W. Bell, Jr., Continental's Vice President of Personnel Relations, sent a memo to all of the airline's employees:

> On July 2, 1965, Title VII of the Civil Rights Act of 1964 and the Equal Employment Opportunity Commission became effective. The Commission, headed by Franklin D. Roosevelt, Jr., is responsible for enforcing the provisions of the Civil Rights Act of 1964 which prohibits employers, labor unions and employment agencies from discriminating against a person in matters relating to employment because of a person's race, color, religion, sex or nationality.
>
> *As you know, your Company does not disciminate in its employment and promotional practices and will comply with the Civil Rights Act of 1964 and cooperate with the directives of the Equal Employment Opportunity Commission to their fullest extent. All employees are expected to do the same.*[7] [Author's italics]

———•••———

THE PASSAGE OF the Civil Rights and Voting Rights Acts may have had nothing to do with the next series of wrenching racial eruptions in America.

On August 11, 1965, during another summer heat wave, a young Negro motorist by the name of Marquette Frye was arrested by police in the predominately black south-central section of Los Angeles known as Watts. A crowd of angry onlookers, tired of being the target for the racist animosities of the all-white L.A. police force, gathered about the scene and began taunting the policeman. A second officer was called as back-up. Trying to disperse the crowd, he allegedly struck several Negro onlookers with his baton.

Soon word spread that an incident of police brutality was taking place. Thousands of protesters and agitators flocked to the scene and the traffic stop quickly escalated into a full-scale riot. Unable to handle the mob (which had swelled to over 30,000) that went from taunting to overturning police cars to burning white-owned businesses, the police chief appealed for help. Democratic Governor Edmund G. "Pat" Brown called out the California National Guard, and even Reverend King flew to Los Angeles in an attempt to halt the violence.

The violence was hard to halt. The rioting went on for five days. When the smoke finally cleared on August 21, thirty-four people were dead, more than 1,000 were injured, and nearly 4,000 had been arrested. Property damage in one of the worst episodes of urban violence in the nation's history was estimated at $200 million. Governor Brown later lost his position to Republican challenger Ronald Reagan, partly because many conservative whites felt that the civil-rights movement was moving too quickly for their tastes.[8]

AT SOME POINT during his tenure with Continental, Marlon had cause to be in New York City and paid a surprise visit to the office of Shirley Adelson Siegel, his fiery champion during the U.S. Supreme Court hearing. Although his memory of the meeting is dim, hers is still vivid. "I had a call from the front desk," she said, "and was told that a Marlon Green was there to see me. This was not an appointment that was planned—he just

> **NEWS ITEM:**
> (Hattiesburg, Miss., Jan. 10, 1966) Vernon Dahmer, a 58-year-old Negro, was killed by Ku Klux Klan members in a fire-bomb attack outside his home before dawn today.
>
> According to police reports, Dahmer, a civil-rights activist, held off two car loads of armed attackers with a shotgun while his family escaped from their home. He died from wounds about 12 hours after the assault began.
>
> Police said that Dahmer had been targeted because he was helping local Negroes to register to vote.*[9]

dropped in. I was struck that he should come to see me; I hadn't met him before I argued his case. The case was a principle, and the principle was suddenly personified. He identified himself and we spoke very briefly—I was very busy in those days. He was an attractive man in uniform—his pilot's uniform. I was very gratified to meet the outstanding person this case had been about."[10]

---

* Samuel Bowers, the Imperial Wizard of the KKK, was convicted in 1998 of Dahmer's death. In two previous trials, in 1968 and 1969, all-white juries had been unable to reach a verdict. Bowers was serving a life sentence when he died in prison on November 5, 2006, at age eighty-two. (*Denver Post*, Nov. 6, 2006)

NEWS ITEM:

(Memphis, Tenn., June 6, 1966) James Meredith, whose attempt to be admitted to the all-white University of Mississippi in 1962 sparked rioting and a call-out of federal troops, was shot and wounded in the head, neck, back, and legs by a shotgun-wielding sniper, Aubrey James Norvell, yesterday, shortly after he began a one-man "March Against Fear," from Memphis to Jackson, Mississippi, to protest racism.[11]

NEWS ITEM:

(Memphis, Tenn., June 27, 1966) To honor James Meredith's courage, hundreds of other civil-rights marchers and leaders, including the Rev. Martin Luther King, Jr., Floyd McKissick, and Stokely Carmichael, arrived in Memphis and continued the march in Meredith's name.

When the marchers reached Greenwood, Mississippi, Carmichael called on black Americans "to unite, to recognize their heritage, and to build a sense of community."

He also advocated that Negroes should form and lead their own organizations, and urged a complete rejection of the values of American society.

After being released from the hospital on June 25, Meredith rejoined the march, arriving in Jackson the next day.[12]

AT CONTINENTAL, MARLON quickly made friends with many of the other pilots. One of his favorites was Harlan Miller. Harlan, along with his father Rollie, were the airline's first father-son pilot team. Marlon additionally got along famously with pipe-smoking Tom Frazier, a former World War II aviator, who lived south of Denver in Franktown.

An avid chess player, Marlon also spent many hours engaged in the board game with fellow pilot Ken Brown. Marlon recalled that one day, while whiling away an idle hour in the Stapleton crew lounge, George Miller, the Chief Pilot, strolled by and saw Green and Brown intently engaged in a game. Miller observed quietly for a few moments, then asked, "Who's winning?" Marlon quickly responded: "It's early in the game so it's hard to tell, but at least we know who's black and who's white."

Even someone as personable as Marlon Green, however, will not get along with everyone. One pilot who lived in the Denver foothills suburb of Evergreen had an antagonistic relationship with him; Eleanor recalled Marlon telling her that on his first flight with Continental this

Marlon and co-pilot (and sometimes chess opponent) Ken Brown in the cockpit of a Continental Airlines Viscount II, 1967 (Courtesy Green family archives)

pilot refused to shake his hand. "There was a bit of animosity that arose that I didn't think was based on my performance," Marlon said, "but rather on his disposition. I wrote it off as just a case of personal dislike as opposed to anything more serious than that."

Racially motivated incidents, happily, were few and far between during his years with Continental. To Marlon's knowledge, no passenger ever refused to fly with him. There was one time, however, when someone anonymously emptied the contents of a vacuum cleaner into his mail pouch at the Los Angeles airport, which Marlon viewed as highly suspicious.

And then there was the elderly woman who, mistakenly assuming that the uniformed black man standing at curbside was a Sky Cap, directed Marlon to carry her bags to the TWA counter.

Marlon knew, however, that no matter how well he did his job, there were always people waiting for him to slip up, to make an error, to confirm their suspicions that black pilots could not be good pilots, that Marlon Green did not deserve to fly for Continental. Part of the animosity directed toward Marlon may also have stemmed from the fact that, as a result of the U.S. Supreme Court case, the airline had leap-frogged him over 100 other pilots in terms of seniority.

In the summer of 1966, against the wishes of those who wanted to see him fail, Marlon was promoted from first officer to captain, and earned his certification to fly DC-9s. He flew the Denver-Kansas City-El Paso-Houston routes.[13]

Marlon with his parents at Denver's Stapleton International Airport,
August 1966 (Courtesy Green family archives)

MARLON'S PROMOTION NOTWITHSTANDING, the next year proved
to be another difficult one in terms of black-white relations in America.
In the Central Ward district of Newark, New Jersey, on a steamy July
12 of that year, John Smith, a black motorist, was stopped by police for
a minor traffic offense. Taken to a police station, Smith was reportedly
beaten, and news of the beating spread. The station house was soon
surrounded by an angry mob from a nearby low-income public-housing
project. Seething over poverty, sub-standard living conditions, a lack of
jobs, and years of heavy-handed treatment by the police, the crowd was
ripe for a violent confrontation.

A rumor that Smith had died while in police custody flashed through
the crowd and, even though local civil-rights leaders visited Smith and
assured the crowd that he was still alive and was in a hospital, the
protest got out of hand. Bricks and bottles barraged the police, who

retaliated with clubs and tear gas. The dispersed mob then began rampaging through the neighborhood, looting stores from the Central Ward to downtown Newark. Some of the rioters armed themselves with rifles and machine guns and began picking off policemen and firemen; the police shot back.

Two days later, with the violence and destruction continuing unabated, Governor Richard J. Hughes declared that Newark was in "open criminal rebellion," and called out the New Jersey National Guard; it took four more days before the rebellion was finally put down. By the time order was restored, the death toll stood at twenty-three, over 700 people had been injured, and nearly 1,500 were in police custody. Property damage covered an area of two square miles.[14]

Detroit, too, exploded during that long, hot summer of 1967. Ever since the great migration of blacks from the South looking for work in the war plants of the industrial cities of the North during the economic boom brought on by World War II, whites had fled to the suburbs, leaving the inner cities to fall victim to overcrowding, poverty, crime, and urban decay. And no city exemplified the problems brought about by "white flight" better than Detroit.

During the 1960s, the Motor City was plagued with civic leaders who ignored the festering problems, and by squads of "Barney-Southall-type" racist cops who terrorized black neighborhoods with a campaign of humiliation, degradation, and oppression.

The pressure cooker that was Detroit finally blew its lid on the night of August 23, 1967. People had had enough of police harassment and brutality and, after police raided a club where a celebration was being held for the return of two black veterans from the Vietnam War, a crowd gathered to protest the arrest of the eighty-two people at the party. The frustrated crowd then went on a looting and vandalizing spree that spread through Detroit's mostly black northwest side.

Two days later, with violence increasing, the Michigan National Guard was called out, reinforced by units from the 82nd Airborne Division. Street battles as fierce as anything going on in Vietnam raged through the city, leaving forty-three people dead, 1,189 injured, over 7,000 arrested, and $45 million in property damage. It took a week before the unrest—but not the anger—was finally quelled. The vacant lots where burned-out blocks of homes once stood exist to this day.[15]

NEWS ITEM:

(Orangeburg, S.C., Feb. 8, 1968) A student protest against segregation at a local bowling alley escalated into a bloody confrontation between black students and state patrolmen at South Carolina State College, leaving three students dead and at least 25 others injured.

Reports said that the student mob ignored the order of state patrolmen to disperse, then began throwing objects at the police, who responded by opening fire. When the situation appeared to be progressing beyond law enforcement's ability to control it, a contingent of heavily armed South Carolina National Guardsmen were brought in to restore order.[16]

ON FEBRUARY 27, 1968, following years of racial tensions, bombings, assaults, and riots, the National Advisory Commission on Civil Disorders, also known as the "Kerner Commission" (for its chairman, former Illinois governor Otto Kerner) concluded that the United States was "moving toward two societies, one black, one white; separate and unequal."

The Commission also stated that the main cause of the riots in the United States was "pervasive white racism." President Lyndon B. Johnson rejected that particular finding.[17]

CHAPTER 19:
TURBULENCE AFTER TAKE-OFF

IF THIS BOOK were a movie, this would be a good place to end it. We would see Marlon, handsome in his Continental pilot's uniform, wave jauntily from the cockpit window. Cut to a medium close-up of Eleanor and the six children, all with tears of joy in their eyes and proud, happy expressions on their faces, standing beneath a bright blue sky on the tarmac at Stapleton International Airport, waving back at him. Cut to a long shot of Marlon's plane, with the majestic, snow-capped peaks of the Rocky Mountains in the background, as it lifts off and heads toward the sunset. Music swells to a triumphant chord. Super title: "The End." Fade to black.

Sadly, such a heart-warming, Hollywood ending was not to be.

Although Marlon had finally won his long and arduous battle to become an airline pilot, the fight had taken its emotional toll; by 1968, the Green family unit was disintegrating.

A major source of contention between Marlon and Eleanor centered around the children. Home life for Marlon in early 1968 was becoming less and less satisfying. The children got on his nerves, and the job with Continental was stressful and unbelievably demanding. *He* became more and more demanding, too, and more and more rigid.[1]

Eleanor's friend Cleo Moran insightfully observed, "It has always seemed to me that Marlon got caught up in the glamour of the airline industry. Then he would come home to Eleanor, who was by herself with six little children, and he would try to do all the things that needed to be done with all those children. He'd get off the plane at the airport and drive home and the cold, hard reality [of family life] would hit him. I've always had the feeling that it was very hard for him to make such a quick transition. It was a long way from the glamour."[2]

It was also a difficult time for Eleanor. Most of the family's money worries had abated, but there were new stresses. She said, "By 1968, we had lived in nine different houses or apartments. Obviously, that was another strain. Joseph, the oldest, had been born in Columbus,

Ohio; Maria and Peter in New York; Monica in Japan; Paula and Philip in Lansing, Michigan.

"With the birth of six children during those years and the many moves, plus the stress of the job and legal struggle, it was much too much! Most of the care of the children and the house, etc., etc., was left to me. Also, I did much of the needed typing, problem solving, etc., etc., and taught school for two years. It was exhausting!"

There were also occasional good moments which everyone treasured, like a shared love of music. Eleanor noted, "Joseph had taken piano lessons and we had a collection of other small instruments that the younger children could play. However, in retrospect, I believe one of the problems in our eighteen-plus years of marriage was that we moved so often."[3]

As THE GREEN children matured, it became obvious to Eleanor that each was gifted in various ways. Eleanor reflected, "I enjoyed my children and loved watching them develop. The three boys all showed a flair for music: Joseph played the cello while Peter and Philip played flute. Peter was also an excellent artist, cartoonist, vocalist, mathematician, and budding scientist."

The girls, too, took piano lessons, and Maria played the viola, taking lessons from a violist in the Denver (now Colorado) Symphony Orchestra. As a former teacher, Eleanor wanted them to explore the world and their place in it—a stance that differed widely from Marlon's. "I never discouraged anyone from trying anything," Eleanor said. "I saw their talents and encouraged them. I was open to their creativity. Marlon and I disagreed on that; he wanted to be controlling."

As an example, after Eleanor bought a cello for Joseph and arranged for private lessons, Marlon became angry over her purchase of the instrument.* He also refused to allow Eleanor to buy a viola for Maria.[4]

---

* Joseph's later goal to become a symphony cellist was thwarted by a diagnosis of multiple sclerosis.

AIRCRAFT ENGINEERS HAVE long been aware of a phenomenom known as "metal fatigue." This problem was hammered home in tragic fashion at the dawn of the commercial jet age in 1954 when two British-made de Havilland DH-106 "Comet" aircraft, in separate incidents, disintegrated in mid-air, killing a total of fifty-six people. Crash investigators determined that metal fatigue caused, or contributed to, the catastrophes.

As airplanes take to the sky and are pressurized, the molecules of their aluminum skin expand slightly. As they land, the pressurization is decreased, causing the skin to return to its previous size and shape—factors known as "loading." Plus, the vibrations caused by the engines and the repeated jolts that occur on landings add to the accumulation of stresses and strains on the aircraft's structural integrity, which eventually can lead to cracks and, ultimately, the breakage of the metal.[5]

Marlon Green began to show signs of "mental fatigue." Eleanor had first noticed the tiny, developing fissures while they were living in Japan, but feels the pressures probably began much earlier, back to his childhood and the way he was treated by his mother, then by the director of the Josephite Seminary, then by the Air Force, and then overall by society in general.

"I attribute Marlon's problems to a couple of things," Eleanor said, with a caveat. "Remember that I am just one person making a judgment about a person whom I loved. I think that his relationship with his mother was not good; there were still signs in adulthood of early physical abuse. A bright spot in his life was going to Xavier Prep, and I think he had really high aspirations when he went off to the seminary. But I suspect that there was something racially tinged in the decision-making when the rector of the seminary accused him of having engaged in sexual contact when in fact he had not; a physical examination proved to be negative. Two other black students were asked to leave the seminary shortly after Marlon."

And, despite the military being officially desegregated, and Marlon's positive experiences with white roommates and instructors at Randolph Air Base, there were other incidents that took place beyond the reach of presidential proclamations and Department of Defense directives, incidents that sprang from deep-seated prejudices and even unintentional disrespect.

Eleanor felt that much of Marlon's unhappiness with the military went back to his feeling that he was treated differently while he was stationed in Japan. Then there were the haircut incident at Maxwell and the "mitten problem" at Lockbourne—incidents that might be regarded as minor or inconsequential if they had happened to a white person. To a black person, however, they were slaps at self-respect, and Marlon was sick of being slapped. "He saw himself as being discriminated against because of his color," she said, "and I believe in all probability that he was.

"Marlon had a continuing anger toward the Air Force and the way he was treated," she explained. "There were times when he felt that he was being accepted, and then all of a sudden there would be an episode of some sort and he would be reminded again that he was being treated differently, and he took offense."

But he kept whatever had disturbed him bottled up inside. Marlon never told his wife what might have happened in Japan to sour him on remaining in the Air Force and realizing his dream of becoming a general.

"Unfortunately," said Eleanor, "to this day, Marlon cannot talk about pain and emotional affect. So he limits himself to talking about something concrete, like a movie or a book or a piece of music. If you try to ask him what he *feels* about something, everything closes down."[6]

FOR STILL UNKNOWN reasons, the state of Marlon's mental health continued to crumble. Perhaps it was the pressure of the responsibility for the lives of scores of passengers in his hands every day that he felt. Perhaps it was knowing that he was under the microscope at Continental and that every act he committed and every step he took was being scrutinized by those above him in the "big house" on the "aviation plantation." Perhaps it was the unspoken knowledge that future airline opportunities for others of his race were piled upon his shoulders. Perhaps it was returning after every flight to the role of husband and father to six children that was becoming less enjoyable by the day. Perhaps it was the sandpaper of all the years of racial discrimination that had finally worn away his protective emotional shell.

Whatever it was, the Green family unit finally collapsed like an imploded building.

Eleanor held off saying anything to Marlon about ending the marriage.

Divorce was not acceptable in the Catholic church, and she hoped and prayed that somehow she could salvage the sinking relationship. But the issues grinding away at their marriage went unaddressed, unsolved. They only grew larger and more intractable.[7]

Marlon, too, was unhappy with the predictable routine and responsibilities of married life. Besides his growing emotional estrangement from his wife and children, he was beginning to question and discard his formerly solid embrace of religion in general and Catholicism in particular.

He admitted that he wanted "to step outside my commitment to religion and see if I could breathe; I found out that I could. The idea of responsibility and caring and all that had to be put into a new prism."

In the fall of 1968 Marlon moved out of the family home and into an apartment, recalling that he felt that he just no longer wanted to be married. "I envisioned living alone being better than what I knew at the time," he said. "I think that that vision occurs to every person who is contemplating separation. It certainly did to me. My thought was, 'The grass will be greener on the other side of the fence.'"[8]

Eleanor, of course, was incredibly hurt and angered by Marlon's behavior—and scared by his decision to leave. She was in her mid-forties, now had the sole responsibility for a home and six children, and hadn't worked at a full-time job for a half-dozen years. How would she and the children survive?[9]

———•—•—•••———

BESIDES THE UPHEAVAL in the Green household, the country, too, was undergoing the most difficult period since 1861, the year the Civil War began.

A primary factor in the national paroxysm was the ongoing war in Vietnam. By 1968, a half million American troops were in that Southeast Asian country, battling to keep it from being taken over by the Communists. Whereas a sanitized version of World War II had been presented to the American public by heavily censored news accounts and newsreels of battles that were weeks old, television began bringing the stark horror and reality of the Vietnam war into people's living rooms on a nightly basis. Without a clear-cut victory in sight, the American people had grown disillusioned and restless, and were demanding that the U.S. end its involvement.

Racial tensions, too, were inflamed and fanned by several shattering events. On April 4, 1968, after having given a powerful speech ("I've Been to the Mountaintop") to an assembly of striking sanitation workers in Memphis, Tennessee, the thirty-nine-year-old Dr. Martin Luther King, Jr. was standing with associates outside his room on the balcony of the Lorraine Motel when a bullet, fired from across the street, smashed into his head, killing him.*

In an explosion of collective anger the likes of which eclipsed even the earlier outbreaks of civil disobedience, outraged African-Americans in over 400 cities across America began rioting, burning, and looting to express their anger at the death of their beloved leader. Scores of people were killed or injured during the battles with the police and military troops sent in to restore order.[10]

Two months later, on June 5, Senator Robert F. Kennedy, the slain president's brother and candidate for the presidency, had just delivered a speech during a campaign stop in Los Angeles when he was shot and fatally wounded. A Palestinian Arab gunman named Sirhan Sirhan was wrestled to the floor and arrested. Like James Earl Ray, Sirhan was tried, convicted, and imprisoned.[11]

Another major blow to the national psyche occurred at the Democratic National Convention, held in August 1968 in Chicago. A large contingent of anti-war demonstrators of all persuasions and with varying agendas converged upon the city with the purpose of disrupting the convention and making their views known to the nation and world. Even though Lyndon Johnson had decided not to run for re-election, his vice-president, Hubert Humphrey, was the leading candidate, and the anti-war activists viewed him as cut from the same cloth as Johnson. Even Humphrey's anti-war opponents, Senator Eugene McCarthy and Senator George McGovern, were not radical enough for the radical Left.

In spite of Chicago Mayor Richard J. Daley's promise to the Democratic Party that he would keep the lid on demonstrations, the protests quickly got out of hand. Wild melées took place in the streets—ferocious battles between police and protestors that were photographed

---

* A white man, James Earl Ray, was arrested, tried, convicted, and imprisoned for King's murder. Ray died in prison in April 1998. (history1900s.about.com/cs/martin-lutherking)

and broadcast to the world by the television networks and print media. America suddenly looked like a country on the brink of self-destruction. Although Humphrey won the Democratic nomination, Republican Richard M. Nixon, partly as a backlash to the chaos in Chicago, was elected president in November.[12]

————•—•••—

THE AIRLINE INDUSTRY, by contrast, suffered no major disruptions in 1968. In May, Continental Airlines began service from Hawaii to the islands of Micronesia—Guam, Kwajalein, Truk, Okinawa, and Majuro. And, in 1968, the airline adopted the slogan, "The Proud Bird With The Golden Tail." A large circle with stylized tail feathers was painted in the vertical golden tailfin of every plane in the Continental fleet. Continental actually benefitted from the Vietnam War because the airline was awarded a government contract to ferry troops to and from that country.[13]

Somehow, Marlon was able to separate the turmoil in his personal and family life from his job and continue flying in a consummately professional manner, greeting his passengers with his warm, friendly smile. If any passenger ever thought twice about putting his or her life in the hands of a black pilot, Marlon never heard about it. The fears that the airlines and Robert Six had had about bigoted passengers boycotting their planes were groundless.[14]

————•—•••—

ELEANOR AND MARLON were divorced in 1970. She had already begun job hunting but found it extremely difficult; her resumé was too out-of-date, her skills too rusty. Then a friend who knew of Eleanor's background phoned.

Said Eleanor, "She told me that the Denver office of Altrusa, an organization of professional women committed to working with the mentally ill, was looking for a part-time recreation director who could work with a group of persons living in a group home. She said she thought that the job would be a way to help me step back into the job market. I took the job and worked at it for about a year. It paid very little, but it was something I could put on a resumé."

As Eleanor had hoped, the part-time Altrusa position led to something bigger: a full-time position at Metropolitan State College of Denver (MSCD). The college had recently received federal funding for a program called "University Year for Action" and needed staffing to develop it. Eleanor described UYA as "a Peace Corps program at home" for college students. The students had to commit to the program for a year; they would do full-time volunteer work in the community during the day and attend classes in the evening. During their year's commitment, the students were paid from UYA grant monies.

Eleanor was hired as the program's Community Coordinator and was involved in both teaching and in supervising the students' field work. She said, "It was a challenge to design courses that would relate to the students' work in the field and could be integrated into a degree program," but she loved what she was doing. "The federal government was also putting pressure on the college to hire more women in faculty and administrative positions," she related, "and part of the reason I got the job, ironically, was because of Affirmative Action."

Not only was she working full-time with the program, but she was also studying to complete her doctoral degree (which was completed and awarded in 1983). Subsequently, she became the founding director of the Individualized Degree Program, known in 2008 as the MSCD Center for Individualized Learning.*[15]

———•••••———

IF ANYONE THOUGHT that the 1970s would usher in a major improvement in black-white relations, they were badly mistaken. Widening the gap between the races was the on-going school-integration controversy. Although school districts across the country had promised to abide by the U.S. Supreme Court's 1954 ruling in *Brown v. Board of Education*, many had failed to deliver on that promise. Predominantly black schools remained predominantly black and predominantly white schools remained predominantly white, a situation known as *de facto* segregation, or "segregation in fact."

In 1970, sixteen years after the Supreme Court ordered the desegregation of the nation's schools, some groups and individuals throughout

---

* Eleanor retired in 1997 after twenty-three years at the college.

the country still remained bitterly opposed to what they saw as an unwelcome and unproven social engineering experiment being shoved down their throats.

The point was driven home in Denver on the night of Thursday, February 5, 1970, when thirty-eight school buses—one third of the fleet that the city was using to accomplish court-mandated school integration—were destroyed or damaged in their storage facility by dynamite charges placed by persons unknown; three men were seen running from the scene. Colorado Governor John Love said that he was greatly disturbed that people would resort to "action outside a rational system" to protest social or political conditions. Denver Mayor William McNichols also voiced his dismay at the incident, calling it "one of those manifestations of complete anarchy."[16]

The South, too, remained unhappy at forced school integration. On March 3, 1970, in Lamar, South Carolina, a mob of 125 angry whites, armed with ax handles, chains, and baseball bats, broke through a line of seventy-five state troopers and attacked three buses transporting thirty-two black children to Lamar's formerly all-white high school. The troopers used tear gas to force the mob back while other policemen freed the children from the buses. Even this did not stop the violence, for the mob began pelting the troopers and escaping children with rocks. The attackers then overturned two of the buses and smashed the windows.[17]

Two months later, on May 4, 1970, Ohio National Guard troops that had been called out to put an end to campus disturbances at Kent State University fired a volley of live ammunition into a crowd of student demonstrators who had gathered to voice their opposition to racism, the Vietnam War, the American military incursion into Cambodia, and other issues; four students—all white—were killed.

Ten days later, unrest rocked predominately black Jackson State College in Jackson, Mississippi, over the same issues that had angered the Kent State students. The peaceful protests got out of hand that evening when a false rumor was spread that Charles Evers, the mayor of Fayette, Mississippi, and the brother of murdered civil-rights leader Medgar Evers, had been assassinated. Responding to a report that black students were throwing rocks at cars on campus, the Jackson Police Department turned out in force. In response, students set fires on campus, more vandalism ensued, and reports of gunfire were received by city officials; seventy-five heavily armed Mississippi State Police officers and a unit of National Guardsmen descended upon the school. A line of police began marching toward a large group of chanting students and was greeted by a shower of rocks and bricks. Accounts vary on what happened next, but police opened fire into the crowd and at dormitory windows, scattering the demonstrators. When the firing ended about a minute later, a twenty-one-year-old pre-law student and a seventeen-year-old innocent bystander were dead; more than a dozen other students were wounded by bullets and shotgun pellets.[18]

The autumn of 1970 saw a continuation of racial clashes. On October 5, white and black students at Pontiac (Michigan) Central High battled each other for two days after their school was ordered integrated; the next year the Ku Klux Klan blew up ten school buses in Pontiac that had been earmarked to carry out the desegregation order.[19]

But even in the face of the violence and anger, the U.S. Supreme Court remained adamant. To correct the unequal public school situation and ensure that minority students would have equal access to the higher quality of education that supposedly existed at white schools, the Court in 1971 issued another landmark ruling in the *Swann v. Charlotte-Mecklenburg* [North Carolina] *Board of Education* case: Black students were transported from their neighborhoods and forced to attend schools in predominantly white neighborhoods; similarly, white students would be bused from their neighborhoods to schools in predominantly black neighborhoods.

Naturally, this ruling was greeted with as much vehement resistance by those opposed to integration—and even those who were neutral about integration—as was the ruling in *Brown v. Board of Education*, except that now the ruling wasn't aimed solely at the South but targeted the nation as a whole. Northern cities suddenly felt the impact of the desegregation laws and a new civil war nearly erupted. In the early 1970s, school districts in cities such as Cleveland, Kansas City, Los Angeles, and San Francisco were found by the courts to be segregated and were ordered to immediately enact busing programs to correct the situation. "White flight," a term used to describe the dramatic exodus of white families from racially mixed urban centers into all-white suburbs where the court orders did not extend across school-district lines, went into full swing. Segregation in cities became even more entrenched and, with the steep loss of the middle-class base, increased levels of poverty, crime, and urban decay followed.

Martin Luther King, Jr. had been dead for several years and, although many voices tried to rally the black community, none resonated with the fervent power that the slain civil-rights leader had generated. And, although institutionalized racism was no longer condoned, the attitudes in some people's hearts had not progressed. Instead of following the peaceful path King had forged, an angry black militancy, tired of waiting to be invited to the table of equality, was on the rise; groups such as the Black Panthers, founded in Oakland, California, in 1966, came to the fore.[20]

AFTER LEAVING THE family in 1968, Marlon lived in apartments in Denver until 1969, when he applied for a transfer to Continental's Los Angeles base; his request was approved. He then began a new life for himself in southern California, became certified as a DC-10 pilot, and flew several routes, including the coveted Los Angeles-Honolulu route.

In Los Angeles, Marlon shared a "bachelor pad" with a friend, Tom Newbro,[21] Marlon also stopped going to church completely. Religion, which had dominated much of his life, was now something in the past, a part of his former life. "I don't miss the church," he said later. "I feel better without it. I have come to a point where I find religion pointless as a personal practice. I try to give a name to it—'humanism,' or 'personal responsibility,' or something like that. I can't be sure I've got the right label, but I feel comfortable with my life as a non-religious individual professing no religion, especially none of the 'Western' religions as we know them."[22]

ALTHOUGH HIS DIVORCE from Eleanor was final, Marlon's monetary ties to his family continued, and $250 per child was extracted from his monthly paycheck and sent to Eleanor as court-ordered child support.

Without the responsibilities of family life to restrict his activities, he began to find new outlets to fill his leisure time. He spent considerable time on the golf course and staged the First (And Last) Annual Marlon Green Open in Pomona. He and eight friends and his brother James took part; daughters Maria, Monica, and Paula came out from Denver

Marlon and his second wife, Dolores Taylor, circa 1972
(Courtesy Green family archives)

to award the trophies. After making one particularly spectacular putt, Marlon went into his "victory dance," exclaiming, "I feel like Tom Watson!" One of his unimpressed golfing buddies said, "You may *feel* like Tom Watson but you *look* like Calvin Peete."* The group broke up laughing.[23]

Marlon was also making the Southern California social scene and dating around. After speaking to a UCLA extension class about his experiences in overcoming institutional segregation, he began dating the professor and then, through her, was introduced to Dolores Taylor. He and Dolores were married in 1972.[24]

---

* Peete was one of the few black professional golfers at that time.

> **NEWS ITEM:**
> (Washington, D.C., July 28, 1972) The U.S. Government released shocking information that between 1932 and 1972 the U.S. Public Health service conducted experiments at the Tuskegee Institute in Alabama on nearly 400 black men in the late stages of syphilis.
>
> The study involved 600 subjects—399 men with the disease and a control group of 201 who did not have it.
>
> These men, for the most part illiterate sharecroppers from Macon County, Alabama, were never told from what disease they were suffering, nor of its seriousness.
>
> Told only that they were being treated for "bad blood," the subjects' doctors had no intention of treating or curing them at all. The men, all volunteers, were given free medical check-ups, free meals, and free burial insurance. None was given medication to cure his illness, even though penicillin, which was invented during World War II and was shown to be effective against syphilis, had become available.
>
> Although originally intended to last six months, the study actually lasted forty years.*[25]

THROUGHOUT THE 1970s, Marlon did his job as a pilot and did it well. On one flight, a passenger began choking and Marlon brought the plane down for an emergency landing. There is only one incident he can recall during his years of flying for Continental that was anything less than professional.

In 1973 he had taken off from Los Angeles International and was making the short hop east to the Ontario, California, airport; his schedule then called for him to fly on to Chicago. During the landing at Ontario, Marlon encountered fog—and then some electrical power lines. "There was fog in the area and we just got down too low, too soon," he said. "There was no excuse for it because there were requirements that you stay at or above a certain altitude until after you pass a certain point. If we had done so, we wouldn't have touched the wires. But we didn't, and we did."

---

* On May 16, 1997, President Bill Clinton formally apologized to the nation as a whole and the black community in particular for the experiment, which he labeled "morally wrong" and "clearly racist." (www.npr.org/programs/morning/features/2002/jul/tuskegee)

As a result of the contact with the wires, an electrical circuit in the plane shorted out which prevented the landing-gear from retracting. "The gear wouldn't move at all," Marlon said, "so we left it down and flew back to Los Angeles where I had the tower make a visual check to see if the gear looked sufficient for landing. It did, so we went ahead and landed without incident. Except for the circuits interrupted by the contact with the wire, there was no other damage to the airplane. But we interrupted everybody's day because we were supposed to be in Chicago by that time."

For his mishap, Marlon was docked two months' pay. "I lost about $8,000 and I learned an interesting and expensive lesson."[26]

Eleanor was furious, of course, because it meant her children went without child support for two months.[27]

IN 1974, MARLON and Dolores had a son, Victor, born in February.[28] Besides Victor's birth, 1974 was notable for several other events. In the wake of the Watergate scandal, President Richard Nixon resigned from office. India conducted its first nuclear test. Heavyweight boxers Muhammand Ali and George Foreman staged their famous "rumble in the jungle" championship in Zaire, Africa. The Vietnam War was winding down but the end was still a year into the future. Aviation pioneer Charles Lindbergh, jazz musician Duke Ellington, television newsman Chet Huntley, television showman Ed Sullivan, and Supreme Court Chief Justice Earl Warren all passed away.[29]

ONE OF THOSE who recognized the unrelenting pressure that Marlon was under was Carolyn Shelton, one of the first African-American flight attendants hired by Continental.

Mincing no words, she said, "The racist pilots at Continental called him Captain Midnight. The white pilots asked me, 'Have you met Marlon Green?' and when I said no, they said, 'We call him Captain Midnight.' They hated him. He was very stern and by-the-book because he knew he was under the microscope twenty-four seven. There was also a lot of anger directed toward him."

Carolyn Shelton, circa 1969 (Courtesy Carolyn Shelton)

She sensed that, as the first black pilot in the American airline industry, Marlon had a hot spotlight focused on him at all times. "Whenever he walked into a room, I think he always felt as if he was carrying a basket of rotten eggs and at any moment one would drop." She felt that way, too. "I felt like I was always on stage. Even when I picked up my fork to eat, I felt everyone was watching me to see if I knew how to conduct myself. Marlon had to endure a lot of scrutiny and criticism by people who didn't want to see blacks in the cockpit. Now I know 'another' Marlon Green, but at the time I felt his pain and understood quietly what he had to go through just to survive. Any mistake was magnified."

Shelton was hired by Continental in 1969. A Louisianan, she had been attending college—Texas Southern University in Houston—and was recently married when her young husband was killed in a traffic accident. Deciding to rebuild her life in a new place, she moved to California, where Continental had relocated its headquarters in 1963. The airline industry at that time had a certain aura of high-flying glamour and she decided to apply for a stewardess position with Continental.

Besides being required to wear the company make-up and the company uniform and the company nail polish and the omnipresent company girdle ("We used to have 'girdle checks'* every time we flew," she laughed), she recalled that she was the only black in her stewardess training class. "I was one of the first black women to be hired by Continental up to that time. There might have been only about ten black flight attendants ahead of me."

Like Marlon, Shelton also faced her own battles with racism. "Most of our pilots then were these military crew-cut racist types. I had to endure 'nigger jokes' and a lot of other demeaning things. They'd ask me things like, 'Carolyn, do colored people have dandruff?' Or, this one time I was having dinner with some pilots and one of them came right out and asked, 'Carolyn, is it true that all colored men are hung down to their kneecaps?' I just looked him in the eye and said, 'Every last one of them, honey.' That's the kind of stuff I had to put up with all the time."

Originally based out of Houston, Shelton had to choose a different city because flight crews were required to live within twenty-five minutes of the airport and there was no decent housing for blacks within that radius; she chose Seattle instead.

Her goal was to see the world. "After Seattle, I moved to Guam and lived there for five years," she said. "Sometimes American tourists would see me and think I was a native Guamesian and ask to take my picture. They'd say, 'And what village are *you* from?' and I'd smile and tell them, 'New Orleans.'"

Shelton couldn't remember exactly when she first met Marlon, but it was probably in the early 1970s when she was on the Pacific route and Marlon was flying between California and Hawaii. She recalled being a little scared about meeting him after hearing all the stories about how tough and mean and a stickler for the rules he was.

"Marlon came across to me as so many minorities do," she said. "You have to develop an extra layer of tough skin to deal with a lot of the issues. You internalize them, but they're like a cancer, eating you from within. So you have this exterior of being stern, and maybe some people take it as being rude or mean or whatever. But you have to protect your job and protect your dignity as a man or a woman—especially

---

* Flight-attendant supervisors checked all stewardesses to make sure they were wearing girdles while on duty.

if you were a minority back in those days—and not be like you're on an 'aviation plantation.'

"I didn't socialize with him off duty because that wasn't his M.O. Marlon had to live by a certain set of rules because, as a pilot, he was responsible for so many lives. He was very much 'by the book' when it came to his duties."

Shelton did hear of one amusing incident related to Marlon. Another black Continental stewardess, Jean Hopkins of Baltimore, entered the cockpit during one flight to take the pilots' drink order. Shelton said, "Jean asked Marlon, 'Coffee, tea, or... watermelon?' Everybody broke up over that one."

Shelton is working on a book about her experiences as a black flight attendant and plans to borrow Hopkins' line as her title.

"Among blacks, we still say, 'Racism is alive and well.' It's not blatant racism, but it's still here. Yes, I've seen changes, but the 'n-word' is still here."[30]

———◦—◦—◦—◦———

IN THE EARLY to mid-1970s, according to former Continental pilot David Price, a certified public accountant began promoting to airline pilots a way for them to shelter some or all of their income. All they needed to do was to buy into the CPA's scam, declare themselves chicken farmers, and form small, individual corporations. Hundreds, perhaps thousands, of airline pilots became putative chicken farmers and stopped having taxes withheld from their paychecks.

Although the accountant assured the pilots that his scheme was entirely legal, the Internal Revenue Service was of the opposite opinion. In an effort to avoid the IRS, the accountant moved to Hawaii but was soon located, arrested, tried for tax evasion, found guilty, and imprisoned. The pilots who had participated in the scam, too, were tracked down. Instead of prison, the pilots had their wages and/or their retirement pensions garnished.[31] Although Marlon had heard about the scheme, he did not fall for it.

Eventually, though, he would have his own serious run-in with the Internal Revenue Service.[32]

CHAPTER 20:
TAILSPIN

ANOTHER NORTHERN CITY greatly affected by the Supreme Court's *Swann v. Charlotte-Mecklenburg Board of Education* decision was Eleanor's home town of Boston.

Federal Judge W. Arthur Garrity, Jr. issued a ruling in 1974 that put into effect the state's Racial Imbalance Law which the Massachusetts State Board of Education had passed a few years earlier. The law required that a school with an enrollment of more than fifty percent non-white students be racially balanced, but the Boston School Committee had resisted implementing the order. Judge Garrity ruled that students in mainly black parts of the metropolitan area, such as Roxbury, had to be bused to mainly white neighborhoods, such as South Boston, where Eleanor and her siblings had grown up, and where her mother still lived.

This requirement for cross-town busing, a ruling that satisfied neither the blacks nor the whites, set off a firestorm of protest and violence. While most Boston schools integrated without incident in September 1974, things did not go well in South Boston, described as a "stronghold of opposition to desegregation."[1]

As J. Anthony Lukas writes in *Common Ground*,

> When the school year opened on September 12, 1974, most of the eighty schools affected by the plan were relatively peaceful. But when buses carrying black students pulled up at South Boston High School that morning, groups of angry whites shouted, "Niggers, go home!" And six hours later, as buses from the high school rolled back down Day Boulevard...crowds pelted them with eggs, beer bottles, soda cans, and rocks, shattering windows and injuring nine students. Television flashed the scene across the city and the continent that evening. Whatever the situation at other schools, then and in the future, that image of "busing in Boston" was indelibly stamped on the national

memory, as irrevocable as the scene outside Central High School in Little Rock seventeen years before.[2]

Once South Boston High School became forceably integrated, tensions did not ease as the plan's backers had hoped; if anything, the bitterness escalated. There were daily fights and name-calling in the classrooms, halls, cafeterias, gymnasia, and on the athletic fields. South Boston High's integrated sports teams were pelted with garbage and slurs by their all-white school opponents. Nor was the situation confined to South Boston High. Other neighborhood schools, such as Charlestown, West Roxbury, and the South End, all went through similar anger, hatred, fear, and dislocation. It was an impossible atmosphere for learning.

The acrimony and unrest in Boston lasted for years. White liberals who had earlier moved into black sections of the city in hopes of encouraging integration and racial harmony found themselves beaten and harassed, their cars and gentrified homes besieged by gangs of vandals. The battles and protests and demonstrations spilled into downtown Boston. Somebody fired shots into the offices of the *Boston Globe*, known (and hated by some) for its pro-busing stance. Even Senator Edward "Ted" Kennedy was physically accosted in front of City Hall by a white mob opposed to busing and integration. An enduring image of the ongoing turmoil was a Pulitzer-Prize-winning newspaper photograph by Stanley Forman showing a well-dressed black attorney (Theodore Landsmark) about to be impaled by an American flag on a pole brandished by a white youth (Joseph Rakes). Racial unrest in Boston was ugly and remained that way for two decades.[3]

———·•·———

BESIDES THE SCHOOL-integration questions, relations between blacks and whites in the 1970s remained at low ebb; only in the world of sports and entertainment, or so it seemed on the surface, did blacks and whites get along. Sports remained one of the few arenas where whites would cheer for blacks.

There were small victories, however, and these came in the mass media. "Blaxploitation" films (a combination of the words "black" and "exploitation) such as *Shaft, Cleopatra Jones, Blacula, Superfly, Foxy Brown, Mandingo,* and *Sweet Sweetback's Baadasssss Song,* made primarily by black directors for black audiences, proliferated in the seventies. Some black critics were horrified at the stereotypes and "reverse racism" portrayed in these films but audiences loved them, especially when blacks were portrayed in positions of power and corrupt whites were shown getting their comeuppance.[4]

For too long blacks had been excluded from television, so TV executives, bending to criticism, decided to take a chance and produce television programs, mostly situation comedies starring black actors, aimed at black audiences. Shows such as *Sanford and Son* and *Good Times* became hugely popular in the seventies, although they were excoriated by some critics for perpetuating stereotypes and demeaning black life in America.

There were other programs, such as *All In The Family*, which parodied the race problem through the eyes of blue-collar bigot Archie Bunker. A few shows, such as *Julia* (starring Diahann Carroll) and *The Bill Cosby Show*, attempted to paint a broader picture by focusing on the lives of upper-middle-class blacks—a picture some critics said was unrealistic. Two black entertainers, Richard Pryor and Flip Wilson, had their own comedy shows.

Although certain genres of "black" music such as jazz and blues had long been popular with a wide segment of white audiences, the 1970s saw an explosion of best-selling records by black performers such as The Supremes, the Jacksons, Ike and Tina Turner, and a variety of "soul" performers, that gained wide acceptance by white Americans.[5]

But in spite of this embracing of certain aspects of black culture, large segments of the white population remained non-committal, or even hostile, especially when it came to racial mixing and social integration. Listening to black country-music singer Charley Pride or laughing at Flip Wilson's "Geraldine" character was one thing; living next door to blacks or having one's children attend school with them was quite another.

WHETHER IT WAS the Pilgrims who initially came to the New World, the hardy explorers who first mapped the West, or the original cosmonauts and astronauts who first ventured into outer space, pioneers are always followed by others. The same was true for Marlon Green. Once he, T. Raber Taylor, and the Warren Court had pried open the cockpit door for minorities, there was no stopping them.

After Marlon, Elra "Doc" Ward came to Continental in 1968, followed by Ron Jennings. Gradually the other airlines began allowing black pilots into the cockpit. In 1976, Ben Thomas, a black pilot flying for Eastern, saw the success of two groups—Black Wings and Tuskegee Airmen, Inc.—and decided that African-American airline pilots needed an organization of their own. He set out to create one—the Organization of Black Airline Pilots. At that time, only eighty black pilots were employed by the nation's passenger airlines and freight carriers; nearly half of them showed up at the first organizational meeting in Chicago, and OBAP was born.*

The mission of OBAP was to prepare young blacks and other minorities for a career in aviation and to ensure that the airlines engaged in fair employment practices. OBAP also worked with the Smithsonian's National Air and Space Museum in Washington, D.C., to create the "Black Wings" exhibit, which opened in 1982. The exhibit, which continues to grow and evolve, showcases the often-overlooked contributions of blacks to the field of aviation.

Ten years after OBAP's founding, nearly 400 black pilots were flying commercially. By 2006, that number had jumped to 674, including fourteen black female pilots. Of course, the percentage of black pilots is still miniscule compared to the more than 71,000 pilots working for U.S. carriers. As the OBAP website points out,

> The struggle to expand African-American pilot presence in the faces of unfair hiring/retention practices continues to be an uphill effort, and promises to become increasingly difficult as the generation of black pilots (hired in the 60s) has already begun to reach retirement age. Additionally, the military, which serves as a traditional source of airline pilots, especially black pilots, is rapidly being downsized.[6]

---

* Although Marlon was required to be a member of ALPA, the Airline Pilots' Association, he did not join OBAP, created only two years before he retired. He was, however, honored by OBAP with an award in 2003.

Marlon receives the Lifetime Achievement Award from the Organization of Black Airline Pilots, August 16, 2003. Pictured from left to right: Larry Jackson, OBAP Executive Board; board member Calvin Allen; Marlon; and OBAP President Bob Brown.
(Courtesy Green family archives)

Frank White III, writing in the February 1986 issue of *Ebony* magazine, told the story of the importance of the black pilots' struggle for acceptance with a simple anecdote. An elderly black female passenger at Pittsburgh's airport stopped Sidney Clark, a black pilot flying for USAir, near the baggage carousel.

"Were you the pilot on the plane that just brought us in?" she asked him.

"Yes, ma'am," replied the thirty-two-year-old Clark.

Smiling, the woman beamed at him. "You just don't know what this means to me, young man," she said. "You just don't know."

"Yes, ma'am, I think I do. Being from Mississippi, I think I do."[7]

MARLON'S MARRIAGE TO Dolores Taylor did not last; in 1975, after three years together, the couple divorced.

The following year, Marlon requested and received a base transfer to Honolulu, Hawaii. From 1976 to 1978 he flew the Honolulu to Guam route, via Johnston, Majuro, Kwajalein, Ponape, and Truk Islands. He was also stationed in Guam for awhile, flying local service to Yap, Palau, Rota, Tinian, and Saipan.

While living in Hawaii, Marlon met Sylvia Wells Baldwin Johnson, a real estate agent who sold him his condominium in Kanehoe, Oahu. A divorcée with four children, she and Marlon fell in love and married in 1977.

Marlon and his third wife, Sylvia Wells Baldwin Johnson, in Hawaii, 1975
(Courtesy Green family archives)

IN 1978, AFTER fourteen years in Continental Airlines' cockpits, Marlon decided to call it a career. "Continental was going through some changes at that time," he related. "But the only thing I felt was, I don't want to fly anymore. The schedule was never grueling, but the circumstances of work were becoming less and less 'glamorous,' if that word ever applied—less and less appealing, for sure. There wasn't much difficulty in deciding to retire.

"I was not familiar with the term 'burn-out' at the time," he said. "Now I have no hesitation in labeling my condition as 'burn-out.' Let me see if I can remember the name—'anxiety neurosis' was what the doctor described on my application for retirement. If you ask me if this is the same as pilot burn-out, I would say yes."

Marlon could also perhaps see the writing on the wall of the many problems that were about to slam the airline industry. Before losing his free-travel airline benefits for his immediate family, however, he took his mother and father on a trip to Egypt, the Holy Land, and on an African safari in 1978. He also took daughters Monica and Paula to Spain that same year as his college graduation gifts to them.

In 1979 Marlon and Sylvia divorced. They had no children.[8]

MARLON'S DEPARTURE FROM Continental came just as the airline industry began to shed much of its "glamour." In 1978, with the passage of the Airline Deregulation Act, Congress stripped away much of the protection the large commercial airlines had enjoyed for decades. No longer did the federal government maintain strict control over the airlines' fares, routes, and schedules.

As a result, competition mushroomed and the major carriers saw their market shares eroded by small, low-cost, no-frills, non-union "start-up" airlines such as People Express. Between 1978 and 2001, nine major carriers (including Eastern, TWA, Continental, Pan Am, Braniff, etc.) and over 100 smaller airlines, unable to compete in the new environment, were forced to operate under bankruptcy protection, merge, or go out of business entirely.[9]

Troubles continued to mount for the major carriers. In 1981, the nation's air-traffic controllers went on an illegal strike; President Ronald Reagan fired them all and replaced them with a new crop. Then Frank

"Daddy Kinney" Green at the Wailing Wall in Jerusalem, 1978
(Courtesy Green family archives)

Lorenzo, an investor who owned a small company called Texas International Airlines and was notorious for his cost-slashing tactics, began circling like a shark around the floundering Proud Bird with the Golden Tail, waiting for the right moment to attack and devour the larger carrier.[10]

"Continental didn't have a strike before I left," Marlon said, "but I am certainly glad that I was not there when they did. When Frank Lorenzo came along—along with the mergers with other airlines and the filings for bankruptcy and the strike in the early eighties—I was very happy that I was out of there."[11]

By that time, Robert Six was nearly eighty years old and worn out. In 1982, he retired as president of Continental Airlines and Lorenzo made his move, buying the airline, drastically cutting costs and, with the airline having lost $218 million in 1983, filing for reorganization under Chapter 11 of the bankruptcy laws. Lorenzo also angered pilots and company executives by slashing salaries and benefits. Morale nose-dived.[12]

But Marlon did not have to worry about the turmoil in the airline industry. He was, as the phrase goes, footloose and fancy-free. Receiving a monthly retirement check from Continental and wanting to

Marlon with his fourth wife, Colleen Wiltshire, on their wedding day in
September 1981 (Courtesy Green family archives)

see more of the world, in March 1979 he set off for the Seychelles, an
African country consisting of about ninety tiny islands in the Indian
Ocean southeast of Kenya and north of Madagascar. Of all the places in
the world that he has visited, Marlon says he most loves the Seychelles.

The following March, he returned to the U.S., eventually settling in
Santa Fe, New Mexico. He was only there a few months when the wan-
derlust bug bit him again and he took off for New Zealand. There, in
late 1980, he met his fourth wife, Colleen Wiltshire, a British woman
from the Isle of Man. Colleen was living near Auckland, where she
worked as the night manager of a motel. They married in September
1981—and divorced less than a year later.

Marlon remained in New Zealand for a while, enjoying the natural
grandeur of the country and working on his golf and chess skills. One
of his proudest moments came when, while playing Ortvin Sarapu, an
International Grand Master (and the best man at his wedding to Colleen
Wiltshire), he got his opponent to concede after taking a knight. "If he
had played on," Marlon said, "I'm sure he could have won back the
knight *and* the game."[13]

In 1983, he returned to the United States and settled briefly in Honolulu, Hawaii, then moved to Houston, Texas, went back to Honolulu, then to La Costa, California, Austin, Texas, Honolulu again, and finally, in 1994, to the Miami area—seven moves in the span of eleven years.[14]

He could not have foreseen the new challenges that awaited him, nor the tailspin in which his personal life would be caught.

CHAPTER 21:
NEW BATTLES

NEEDING MORE MONEY on which to live (and to cover alimony expenses and child-support payments for his son Victor), Marlon Green, soon after he retired in 1978, stopped filing tax returns and told Continental Airlines to stop withholding taxes from his monthly retirement checks.

This went on for more than a dozen years before the Internal Revenue Service discovered the situation and, in 1995, began garnishing half of Marlon's retirement checks to recoup tens of thousands of dollars in back taxes—plus a 100% penalty—that was owed to the government. With his financial circumstances drastically reduced, Marlon soon fell to near the poverty level, and the psychological problems that had manifested themselves years earlier began to worsen, resulting in a couple of brushes with the law. Only an intercession (at Eleanor's urging) by family friend Father Hilary Hayden, a sympathetic Florida judge, and treatment at a state mental institution prevented him from serving extended prison time.[1]

IN THE SPRING of 2005, Marlon found himself in another battle—the battle for his life.

On Tuesday, April 5, 2005, Marlon, now seventy-five years old, awoke one morning in his Miami apartment nearly unable to move. "I was incapacitated and frightened," he said, "and unable to stand up."

His right side was paralyzed and he had difficulty speaking. Realizing that he probably had suffered a stroke, he managed to roll out of bed and crawl from the bedroom into the kitchen, where the phone was—but he saw that he had left it on top of the refrigerator. With much difficulty, he was able to reach the cord with his left hand and pull the phone down. He then dialed Eleanor in Denver and told her, with slurred speech, what had happened. She called daughter Paula,

Marlon with one of his physical therapists, Chris Merinkers-Parchment, at the
Veterans Administration Medical Center, Miami, April 2005
(Courtesy Green family archives)

who had power of attorney, who then phoned the Veterans' Administration Medical Center in Miami and had them call 9-1-1.

Within minutes an emergency response team arrived at his apartment. He managed to open the door and, with his one good hand,
threw the key to his outer gate to the paramedics, who then unlocked
it and entered his ground-floor unit.

Rushed to the local Veterans' Administration hospital, Marlon underwent a battery of tests which determined that he had, indeed, suffered
a stroke—a mild, "sub-cortex" type of stroke that affects speech and,
fortunately, not a "cortex" stroke that destroys thinking and language.[2]

He was quickly enrolled in speech and physical therapy at the VA
Medical Center and soon was making good progress. His daughter
Paula reported, "Since his small stroke, he has not regained full speech,

and his right side continues to be significantly weak. However, his comprehension is fine and Dad is loving all this attention at the hospital. He's got two psychologists, two speech therapists, a physical therapist, an occupational therapist, an MD and umpteen nurses, servers and attendants. All the hospital staffers are delighted with him. Even the doctor said today they don't want him to leave; he is the model of everything they hope to achieve in rehabilitation."

On April 25, 2005, Paula provided an e-mail update to friends and family: "He sounds great when we have our daily call in the morning. He has exceeded all the anticipated speech improvement and muscle-strength gains by his team of therapists, but still has lots of work to do; he has very light grasp capabilities with his right hand. So it's highly unlikely that he'll regain enough funtionality to be independent, but he's coming around to accepting that."

Just as Marlon was determined to become an airline pilot no matter what obstacles the airlines and society tried to throw into his path, he was equally determined to overcome the obstacles presented by his medical condition and show the doctors that he would, indeed, "regain enough funtionality to be independent."

As Marlon's condition steadily improved, Eleanor and Paula, as well as his two brothers, James and Allen, flew to Florida to be there when he was discharged from the hospital.

Remarkably, by mid-May he was back in his apartment and living a relatively independent lifestyle—fixing his own meals, taking the bus (rather than utilizing the proffered door-to-door van service for the handicapped) for his transportation needs, using a quad-cane instead of a wheelchair, and generally following the advice of his doctors and therapists. He amazed them all.

Paula said that her mother was still concerned about him: "I can't seem to get her to realize that worry solves nothing and that Dad is just in a new stage of life. If he's OK dealing with it—which is a blessing, for sure—then all we should be doing is providing support."[3]

———•·•·•———

IN THE SUMMER of 2005, Marlon received an invitation to be inducted into the Arkansas Aviation Historical Society's Hall of Fame. He vowed to overcome his disability so that he could be there to receive it.

EPILOGUE:
AUTHOR'S REFLECTIONS

IT IS NOVEMBER 2005 and Marlon is ready for his evening in the spotlight at the Arkansas Aviation Historical Society's Hall of Fame at the Aerospace Education Center in Little Rock. Along with Eleanor, daughters Paula and Monica Green (a history professor at Arizona State University, who has brought her two lovely and lively daughters, Malaika [fourteen] and Kanza [ten]), plus assorted other friends, I have also traveled there to witness the event.

The induction ceremony and dinner is being held on Thursday, November 10, 2005. I am picked up at the airport by Marlon's youngest brother Allen, who lives in Little Rock with his wife Mae. He drives me to my downtown hotel, which is close to the Arkansas River and only a short walk to the President William Jefferson Clinton Presidential Library and Museum. Allen has recently retired after a long career in housing and urban development. We have a very nice chat and I look forward to the "barbeque" that he will be hosting at his home the next day.

The Hall of Fame dinner is completely sold out; I estimate that at least 300 people have filled the museum's glittering lobby, from whose ceiling hang historic airplanes. I get to meet Marlon's other brother, James Zell Green, and two good friends—Bill and Lillian Hopson, who have come all the way from California for this special event.

Marlon, spiffy in a suit and tie, looks as good and healthy as he did when I first met him a year earlier, with no apparent evidence of a stroke—no cane or walker, either. With Marlon, it is mind over matter, and he seems determined to "tough it out." He and Eleanor embrace and kiss. There is evidence of real affection and all the old hurts and anger seem—at least to an outsider—to momentarily melt away.[1]

Marlon tells me that he and Eleanor had shared a remoteness for a considerable time after he left the family. "We didn't speak to each other," he says. "After a while—many years—we were able to tolerate each other's point of view and speak to each other again. As of now, I think we really like each other."[2]

Once the dinner service is over, the evening's festivities begin. Marlon is being inducted along with two other Arkansans who have distinguished themselves in that state's aviation history: Virginia M. Proctor, the first woman to hold the office of Chair of the Arkansas Department of Aeronautics, and Darrell S. Riddell, the longest-serving commissioner of the Arkansas Department of Aeronautics.

Ken Quimby, the Master of Ceremonies and President of the Arkansas Aviation Historical Society, reads off a laundry list of Marlon's accomplishments. A slide show of Marlon's life is presented to the attendees and then Marlon is invited to say a few words. With only the slightest bit of difficulty, he makes his way to the podium and, quite literally, says a few words. In fact, the words come and go so quickly that I don't even have a chance to get them down, but Paula does.

According to her, Marlon said, "When I was young, I told people I wanted to be a bootlegger, because I thought they wore fancy boots. I'm glad life had other plans."[3]

Marlon receives a standing ovation.

The three surviving Green brothers — James, Marlon, and Allen — with pilots Duane Lawrence and Samuel Adeboga of the New Hope Flight Training Academy, who flew Marlon from Miami to Little Rock. Photographed November 10, 2005, at the Arkansas Aviation Historical Society Hall of Fame banquet.
(Courtesy Green family archives)

THE NEXT DAY we take a sight-seeing tour of Little Rock (which includes stopping by Central High School, scene of 1957's infamous school integration events, and a nearby gasoline station which the National Park Service has converted into a civil-rights museum. (It was the only place in the neighborhood that had a pay phone that reporters covering the troop-enforced integration could use). We then attend the barbeque/family reunion/neighborhood party at "Uncle Allen's," which is less a barbeque than a sumptuous catered affair.

The gathering is large and happy, with much food and considerable laughter. Marlon has the "chair of honor" in the living room, and the assembled guests treat him with deference. We view a clip of his ten-second scene in *Escapade in Japan* on videotape and everyone applauds. A professional photographer arrives and a family portrait of the men, their wives, ex-wives, children, cousins, etc. is taken on the lawn outside. I feel very comfortable hanging out with the group, and Allen and James invite me to be an honorary member of the Green clan; I gladly accept.

The following day, Saturday, everyone (with the exception of Allen, who is staying home, and Marlon, who is on his way back to Florida) drives in convoy down to El Dorado, about two hours south of Little Rock. I am driving James (a.k.a. "Uncle Jimmy") in my rental car through mile after mile of pine and oak forests and pecan groves, and for two hours we talk, sometimes frivolously and sometimes deeply. I record his answers to my many questions about growing up black in the South in the 1940s and 1950s, and his considered postulations about the state of race relations in America. It is a pleasant and intellectually stimulating way to spend two hours. We do not solve all the world's ills, but he and I have made considerable progress and agree that we should share the Nobel Peace Prize.

Once in El Dorado, James gives me (along with the rest of the entourage) a tour of the city, pointing out landmarks and places of significance to the family, stopping at the house where the Greens once lived, then at Dr. Rushing's house on the other side of the tracks; at the modern Baptist church that has replaced the Catholic one where the proselytizing Father Marmon once held Mass; at the boarded-up home which was once owned by Fairview Grammar School teacher Mrs. Dunning and her doctor husband; at the large new medical center on the grounds where once stood the ballpark where the El Dorado Oilers

The extended Green family, November 2005, photographed at the
Little Rock home of Allen Green.

(Back row, left to right) David Green (Allen's son); Allen Green; James Green;
Thelma Green (James's ex-wife); Chase Green (Steven's son);
Steven Green (Allen's son); Mark Green (Rudolph's son).

(Middle row, left to right): Josh Green (David's son); Malaika El Hamel (Monica's daughter);
Kanza El Hamel (Monica's daughter); Mae (Allen's wife).

(Front row, left to right): McKenzie Harris (Mae's granddaughter); Marlon Green;
Eleanor Green; Monica Green; Paula Green; Cassandra Green (Steven's wife);
Edwin Green (Allen's son). (Courtesy Green family archives)

played. We stop, too, at the cemetery where Daddy Kinney and Mama
Lucy and son Rudolph are buried. I am informed that the cemetery was
formerly segregated and that Mama Lucy was the first black person
buried there after it was integrated.

Uncle Jimmy also mentions that El Dorado is known as the birth-
place of four future notables: Reese "Goose" Tatum, the "clown prince
of basketball," who starred with the Harlem Globetrotters in the late
1940s and 1950s; Donna Axum, Miss America, 1964; and Lou Brock,
the six-time All-Star outfielder for the Chicago Cubs (1961-1964), the St.

The Confederate monument, El Dorado, Arkansas (Author photo 2005)

Louis Cardinals (1964-1979), and a 1985 inductee into Major League Baseball's Hall of Fame. The fourth notable is his brother Marlon.

I have a real regret when it is time for us to part, for I feel that I have made an historical pilgrimage of sorts, not to *my* past, but back to a time and place which shaped the Green—as well as the Gallagher— family, and the generations that came later, and the face of the airline industry.

Standing in the November twilight of the El Dorado town square, I am suddenly cognizant that the Civil War monument with the Confederate soldier statue is not the centerpiece of the square. The monument has been placed off to one corner of the courthouse so that, from three sides of the square, it can't be seen. I wonder if this is a deliberate act—if the monument has always been here or if it was once moved from a place of greater prominence to its present location of relative insignificance.

I read again the inscription: *Truth crushed to earth shall rise again*, and am puzzled. Of what "truth" does the monument speak? That one race was meant to enslave another? That the South should have been allowed to secede? I wonder how did—and how do—the black citizens of El Dorado view such an inscription, such an implied threat? Would a similar monument in Germany or Russia or Cambodia glorifying the dark deeds and memory of SS troops, Soviet secret police, or Khmer Rouge soldiers be allowed to stand? Does this inscription mean that the long-dead designers of the monument truly believed that the South would, in fact, rise again—complete with all its old, terrible traditions resurrected? Or is the meaning less sinister? Am I reading too much into stone?

In America's Deep South, great stock is placed in symbols, so I can't help but think that the monument's site, off in a corner of the square, says something meaningful, something hopeful, that perhaps the monument—and what it represents—is on a slow, inexorable migration to some less visible part of town, where vines and brush and nature's healing powers will eventually reclaim it.

TIME TO TURN inward and ask myself what I have learned on this journey of discovery. Certainly the profundities are better left to more gifted experts of history, culture, sociology, and race than I. I am merely a writer, an observer, a chronicler of events. When it comes to understanding the complexity of the myriad issues of race in America, I am but a newborn babe, guileless, and without the ability to fully comprehend. I have no solutions, other than to offer a simple word of advice: Listen. Hear what those of different colors are saying. Respect them. Enter into dialogue with them. I guarantee that it will be enlightening.

With this biography of the lives of one family, and my tangential forays into the newsworthy and nation-shaking events surrounding their story, I have only begun to touch the surface of race relations in America. (Indeed, some social scientists have advanced the theory that there really is no such thing as "race" or "races;" that all humans belong to only one race: the *human* race.) The thousands of books, term papers, master's theses, and doctoral dissertations already written and published on the subject have gone into far greater detail than this one volume. Yet, despite the billions of words written and spoken on the subject of race, many of the same old problems persist.

I wonder: Have things gotten better in America since the abolition of slavery? Since Truman's order to integrate the armed forces? Since baseball's color line was broken? Since Ole Miss admitted James Meredith? Since Lyndon Johnson signed the Civil Rights and Voting Rights Acts? Since Continental hired Marlon Green? On one hand, looking at a once-unknown mixed-race senator's spectacular rise to political prominence, we would have to respond with a resounding "Yes!" while, on the other, the answer would need to be a fervent "No!"

While more African-Americans are doing better now than ever before—economically and socially speaking—one need only drive through the crumbling, impoverished areas of our inner cities to see that the "American Dream" remains nothing more than a fading vision for millions of our citizens of color. And, while our cities are no longer burning with rage and hatred, they remain smoldering tinderboxes waiting for the next spark to ignite them (witness the riots in Los Angeles that erupted after black motorist Rodney King's beating by white police on March 3, 1991, was captured on video tape and broadcast).

One thing that sticks with me as I drive the long, tree-lined miles from El Dorado back to Little Rock and the airport and the car-rental counter, is how deeply I've seen the arrows of American apartheid slice into the collective psyche of the African-American community—far deeper than any white person, no matter how sensitive or well intentioned, can ever hope to grasp. I am struck by the searing truth of John Seigenthaler's observation: "It's tragic that Ralph Ellison is feeling the pain and I'm not even aware that my blindness, my indifference, is inflicting the pain. It's difficult to understand how thoughtful, sensitive, caring people could have been that insensitive and uncaring—to not even have an inkling of the injustice of it."

As the "top dogs" in a predominantly white nation, very few of us white folks have any inkling of what the typical black person must go through on a daily basis even now, in the first decade of the twenty-first century—the slights, the slurs, the snubs, the furtive glances, the overt insults, the rejections, and, ironicially, the *invisibility*.

I am aware that many whites feel that blacks are overly sensitive about the race issue and wish "they" would just "get over it," while many blacks wish we whites would be more sensitive and "get a clue."[4]

In a *Washington Post* article from 1981, Charles King, who has conducted numerous race-relations seminars, says, "Blacks are paranoid because of past experiences, and whites don't have any insight into that paranoia."[5] I agree.

Harold Field, who moderates a monthly race-discussion group in Denver,* said, "Not everybody agrees with the need to come to terms with past injustices. Whites are taught to be a-historical. Blacks are weighed down by history. To white folks, racism is viewed mostly as individual and interpersonal. For blacks it goes beyond that and remains in the patterns and practices of policies and social institutions. This is what I like to call the deep 'infrastructure of racism.' It is difficult to understand something that almost never happens to you."[6]

I am also struck by something that Swedish lawyer Gunnar Myrdal wrote. In 1938, Myrdal, a Nobel Prize-winning professor of economics,

---

* According to Eleanor Green, the group was started jointly in 1997 by Joyce Meskis, the owner of the Tattered Cover Book Store in Denver, and Clara Villarosa, who then owned the Hue-Man Book Store in Denver (she has since relocated to New York City and opened the store there), after President Bill Clinton asked black historian John Hope Franklin to form a commission and travel the country for a year to write a report on the state of race relations in the U.S. Franklin's report never received the attention it deserved because the Monica Lewinsky scandal broke at about the same time the report was issued. As of 2008, the Denver group is still going strong and continues to meet on a monthly basis. (Eleanor Green, note to author, Dec. 6, 2007)

was commissioned by the Carnegie Corporation to make an exhaustive study of racism in the United States; in 1944 he published his findings in *An American Dilemma: The Negro Problem & Modern Democracy*, perhaps the single most objective and comprehensive look at the racial issues tearing at the fabric of America. In the final chapter he writes,

> ...the Negro problem is not only America's greatest failure but also America's incomparably great opportunity for the future. If America should follow its own deepest convictions, its well-being at home would be increased directly. At the same time America's prestige and power abroad would rise immensely. The century-old dream of American patriots, that America should give to the entire world its own freedoms and its own faith, would come true. America can demonstrate that justice, equality and cooperation are possible between white and colored people.
>
> In the present phase of history this is what the world needs to believe. Mankind is sick of fear and disbelief, of pessimism and cynicism. It needs the youthful moralistic optimism of America.... If America in actual practice could show the world a progressive trend by which the Negro became finally integrated into modern democracy, all mankind would be given faith again—it would have reason to believe that peace, progress and order are feasible. And America would have a spiritual power many times stronger than all her financial and military resources—the power of the trust and support of all good people on earth. *America is free to choose whether the Negro shall remain her liability or become her opportunity.*[7] [Mydral's italics]

What Gunnar Myrdal wrote over six decades ago is still true. And the opportunity is still there, waiting to be seized.

IN MARCH 2008, his health stabilized, Marlon moved from Florida to Denver, closer to his family. Although private demons no doubt continue to bedevil him, Marlon maintains the ability to present a mostly happy face to the world. He is a survivor, a warrior, his armor dented by his many battles but his head unbowed. As Eleanor says, he has learned how to bury his true feelings and hide his wounds and his pain.

When asked if he would, given the opportunity, live his life the same way, with hardships and all, he responds, "You would have to assume that all the conditions are the same. I think that if all the previous conditions were the same, I would make the same decisions and conclusions. I think of myself as being the same Marlon, the same individual all through my existence.

"I hope that what I went through never happens to anyone else. The whole seven-plus years of litigation was a situation I couldn't avoid. If I had had some other skills, I could have walked away and pursued some other alternative. But I couldn't get out of it, and that's the way it happened."[8]

IT IS THE night of Tuesday, November 4, 2008. The television set in Marlon Green's Denver apartment is on, and the man who made history by becoming the first African-American pilot is watching another African-American man make history: Barack Obama. The election results are pouring in and it is clear that Obama is being enthusiastically swept into the office of President of the United States by millions of Americans of all colors. Afterwards, Marlon reflects, "I'm happy about it. It's history-making in itself but, as far as any consequences are concerned, we'll just have to wait and see. But the nature of the changes are earth-shaking."

One is tempted to say that the victory of Marlon Green and the victory of Barack Obama, although separated by nearly a half century, are somehow inextricably linked. Jackie Robinson resides along that continuum, too, as do Bessie Coleman, Chief Anderson, Benjamin O. Davis, Rosa Parks, Emmett Till, James Meredith, Martin Luther King, Jr., and so many, many more. As a refreshing wave of hope and optimism washes over America on election night 2008 and spirits soar, it is not hard to visualize a similar sense of joy felt over four decades earlier by First Officer Marlon DeWitt Green when he lifted off from the tarmac in the cockpit of a Continental Airlines Viscount turbo-jet and climbed up toward a clear, sunny sky full of boundless opportunities.[9]

APPENDIX A

United States Supreme Court Decision

Colorado Anti-Discrimination Commission v. Continental Air Lines, Inc. 372 U.S. 714

No. 146. Argued March 28, 1963 - Decided April 22, 1963* - 149 Colo. 259, 368 p.2d 970, reversed.

*Together with no. 492, *Green v. Continental Air Lines, Inc.*, on certiorari to the same court.

After administrative hearings, the Colorado Anti-Discrimination Commission found that respondent, an interstate air carrier with headquarters in Colorado, had, within that state, rejected the application of a Negro for a job as a pilot solely because of his race and that this was an unfair employment practice prohibited by the Colorado Anti-Discrimination Act of 1957, and it ordered respondent to cease and desist from such discriminatory practices and to give the complainant the first opportunity to enroll in its training school in its next course.

On review, a state court held that the Act could not constitutionally be applied to the flight crew of an interstate air carrier, and it set aside the Commission's findings and dismissed the complaint. The Supreme Court of Colorado affirmed. Held: The judgment is reversed and the case is remanded for further proceedings. pp. 716-725.

(a) The judgment below does not rest upon an independent and adequate State ground but upon the State Supreme Court's application and interpretation of the Federal Constitution, Federal statutes and executive orders, and this court has jurisdiction on certiorari. p. 718.

(b) Colorado's requirement that respondent refrain from racial discrimination in its hiring of pilots in that state does not unduly burden interstate commerce. *Hall v. DeCuir*, 95 u.s. 485, and *Morgan v. Virginia*, 328 u.s. 373, distinguished. pp. 718-722.

(c) This field has not been so pervasively covered or preempted by the Civil Aeronautics Act of 1938, now the Federal Aviation Act of 1958, the Railway Labor Act or executive orders as to prevent Colorado from applying its Anti-Discrimination Act to respondent, as it did here. pp. 722-725.

Colorado Anti-Discrimination Commission et al. v. Continental Air Lines, Inc.

Certiorari to the Supreme Court of Colorado.

Mr. Justice [Hugo] Black delivered the opinion of the court.

Petitioner Marlon D. Green, a Negro, applied for a job as a pilot with respondent Continental Air Lines, Inc., an interstate air carrier. His application was submitted at Continental's headquarters in Denver, Colorado, and was later considered and rejected there. Green then made complaint to the Colorado Anti-Discrimination Commission that Continental had refused to hire him because he was a Negro.

The Colorado Anti-Discrimination Act of 1957 provides that it is an unfair employment practice for an employer "to refuse to hire, to discharge, to promote or demote, or to discriminate in matters of compensation against, any person otherwise qualified, because of race, creed, color, national origin or ancestry." (fn1) After investigation and efforts at conciliation, the Commission held extensive hearings and found as a fact "that the only reason that the complainant was not selected for the training school was because of his race." (fn2)

The Commission ordered Continental to cease and desist from such discriminatory practices and to "give to the complainant the first opportunity to enroll in its training school in its next course...." On review the District Court in and for the City and County of Denver set aside the Commission's findings and dismissed Green's complaint. It held that the Anti-Discrimination Act could not "constitutionally be extended to cover the flight crew personnel of an interstate air carrier" because it would impose an undue burden upon commerce in violation of Art. i, sec. 8, cl. 3, of the United States Constitution, which gives Congress power "to regulate commerce...among the several states...," and because the field of law concerning racial discrimination in the interstate operation of carriers is preempted by the Railway Labor Act, (fn3) the Civil Aeronautics Act of 1938, (fn4) and Federal executive orders.

The Supreme Court of Colorado affirmed the judgment of dismissal but discussed only the question of whether the act as applied placed an undue burden on commerce, concluding that it did. (149 colo. 259, 368 p.2d 970 (1962)). The obvious importance of even partial invalidation of a state law designed to prevent the discriminatory denial of job opportunities prompted us to grant certiorari. (371 U.S. 809 (1962)).

First. Continental argues that the State Supreme Court decision rested on an independent and adequate nonfederal ground. For that argument, it relies on the Trial Court's statement "that the Colorado legislature was not attempting to legislate concerning problems involving interstate commerce" and the statement of the Supreme Court of Colorado that: "The only question resolved was that of jurisdiction. The Trial Court determined that the Act was inapplicable to employees of those engaged in interstate commerce, and the judgment was based exclusively on that ground." (149 Colo., at 265, 368 p.2d, at 973.)

We reject this contention. The Trial Court itself did not rest on this ground. Instead, it clearly and unequivocally stated that the case presented a constitutional question of whether the Act could legally be applied to interstate operations.

Nor did the Supreme Court of Colorado rely on this ground. It interpreted the Trial Court's opinion as having held that the Act was invalid insofar as it regulated interstate air carriers. The Court further stated that the question was whether the act could be applied to interstate carriers, which it answered by concluding that under the Federal Constitution the state legislature had no power to deal with such matters. We are satisfied that the courts below rested their judgments on their interpretation of the United States Constitution and the preemptive effect of Federal statutes and executive orders.

Second. In holding that the Colorado statute imposed an undue burden on commerce, the State Supreme Court relied on the principle, first stated in *Cooley v. Board of Wardens of the Port of Philadelphia*, 12 how. 299, that states have no power to act in those areas of interstate commerce which by their nature require uniformity of regulation, even though Congress has not legislated on the subject. (fn5) The State Court read two prior decisions of this Court, *Hall v. DeCuir*, 95 U.S. 485 (1878), and *Morgan v. Virginia*, 328 U.S. 373 (1946), as having established that the field of racial discrimination by an interstate carrier must be free from diverse state regulation and governed uniformly, if at all, by congress. We do not believe those cases stated so encompassing a rule.

The line separating the powers of a state from the exclusive power of Congress is not always distinctly marked; courts must examine closely the facts of each case to determine whether the dangers and hardships of diverse regulation justify foreclosing a state from the exercise of its traditional powers. This was emphatically pointed out in *Hall v. DeCuir*, supra, the very case upon which Continental chiefly relies: "Judges not unfrequently differ in their reasons for a decision in which they concur. Under such circumstances it would be a useless task to undertake to fix an arbitrary rule by which the line must in all cases be located. It is far better to leave a matter of such delicacy to be settled in each case upon a view of the particular rights involved. (95 U.S., at 488.)

The circumstances in *Hall v. DeCuir* were that a Louisiana law forbidding carriers to discriminate on account of race or color had been applied so as to hold a steamboat owner liable for damages for assigning a colored passenger to one cabin rather than another. This was held to violate the commerce clause, but only after a careful analysis of the effects of the law on that carrier and its passengers.

Among other things, the Court pointed out that if each of the 10 states bordering the Mississippi River were free to regulate the carrier and to provide for its own passengers and freight, the resulting confusion would produce great inconvenience and unnecessary hardships. The Court concluded that: "Commerce cannot flourish in the midst of such embarrassments. No carrier of passengers can conduct his business with satisfaction to himself, or comfort to those employing him, if on one side of a state line his passengers, both white and colored, must be permitted to occupy the same cabin, and on the other be kept separate. Uniformity in the regulations by which he is to be governed from one end to the other of his route is a necessity in his business...." (95 U.S., at 489.)

After the same kind of analysis, the Court in *Morgan v. Virginia*, supra, held that a Virginia law requiring segregation of motor carrier passengers, including those on interstate journeys, infringed the commerce clause because uniform regulation was essential. The Court emphasized the restriction on the passengers' freedom to choose accommodations and the inconvenience of constantly requiring passengers to shift seats. As in *Hall v. DeCuir*, the Court explicitly recognized the absence of any one, sure test for deciding these burden-on-commerce cases. It concluded, however, that the circumstances before it showed that there would be a practical interference with carrier transportation if diverse state laws were permitted to stand.

The importance of a particularized inquiry into the existence of a burden on commerce is again illustrated by *Bob-Lo Excursion Co. v. Michigan*, 333 u.s. 28 (1948), where the Court had before it a state statute requiring common carriers to serve all people alike regardless of color. The Court upheld the law as applied to steamships transporting patrons between Michigan and Canada. Following the rule that each case must be adjudged on its particular facts, the Court concluded that neither *Hall* nor *Morgan* was "comparable in its facts, whether in the degree of localization of the commerce involved; in the attenuating effects, if any, upon the commerce...; or in any actual probability of conflicting regulations by different sovereignties." (333 U.S., at 39.)

We are not convinced that commerce will be unduly burdened if Continental is required by Colorado to refrain from racial discrimination in its hiring of pilots in that state. Not only is the hiring within a state of an employee, even for an interstate job, a much more localized matter than the transporting of passengers from state to state (fn6) but more significantly the threat of diverse and conflicting regulation of hiring practices is virtually nonexistent.

In *Hall* and in *Morgan* the Court assumed the validity both of state laws requiring segregation and of state laws forbidding segregation. Were there a possibility that a pilot hired in Colorado could be barred solely because of his color from serving a carrier in another state, then this case might well be controlled by our prior holdings. But under our more recent decisions (fn7) any State or Federal law requiring applicants for any job to be turned away because of their color would be invalid under the due process clause of the Fifth Amendment and the due process and equal protection clauses of the Fourteenth Amendment. The kind of burden that was thought possible in the *Hall* and *Morgan* cases, therefore, simply cannot exist here. It is, of course, possible that states could impose such onerous, harassing, and conflicting conditions on an interstate carrier's hiring of employees that the burden would hamper the carrier's satisfactory performance of its functions. But that is not this case. We hold that the Colorado statute as applied here to prevent discrimination in hiring on account of race does not impose a constitutionally prohibited burden upon interstate commerce.

Third. Continental argues that Federal law has so pervasively covered the field of protecting people in interstate commerce from racial discrimination that the states are barred from enacting legislation in this field. It is not contended, however, that the Colorado statute is in direct conflict with Federal law, (fn8) that it denies rights granted by Congress, (fn9) or that it stands as an obstacle to the full effectiveness of a Federal statute. (fn10) Rather Continental argues that: "When Congress has taken the particular subject-matter in hand coincidence is as ineffective as opposition, and a state law is not to be declared a help because it attempts to go farther than Congress has seen fit to go." (fn11)

But this Court has also said that the mere "fact of identity does not mean the automatic invalidity of state measures." (fn12) To hold that a State statute identical in purpose with a Federal statute is invalid under the supremacy clause, we must be able to conclude that the purpose of the Federal statute would to some extent be frustrated by the State statute. We can reach no such conclusion here.

Continental relies first on the Civil Aeronautics Act of 1938, (fn13) now the Federal Aviation Act of 1958, (fn14) and its broad general provisions forbidding air carriers to subject any particular person to "any unjust discrimination or any undue or unreasonable prejudice or disadvantage in any respect whatsoever" (fn15) and requiring "the promotion of adequate, economical, and efficient service by air carriers at reasonable charges, without unjust discriminations, undue preferences or advantages, or unfair or destructive competitive practices...." (fn16)

This is a familiar type of regulation, aimed primarily at rate discrimination injurious to shippers, competitors, and localities. (fn17) But we may assume, for present purposes, that these provisions prohibit racial discrimination against passengers and other customers (fn18) and that they protect job applicants or employees from discrimination on account of race. The Civil Aeronautics Board and the administrator of the Federal Aviation Agency have indeed broad authority over flight crews of air carriers, (fn19) much of which has been exercised by regulations. (fn20)

Notwithstanding this broad authority, we are satisfied that Congress in the Civil Aeronautics Act of 1938 and its successor had no express or implied intent to bar state legislation in this field and that the Colorado statute, at least so long as any power the Civil Aeronautics Board may have remains "dormant and unexercised," (fn21) will not frustrate any part of the purpose of the Federal legislation. (fn22)

There is even less reason to say that Congress, in passing the Railway Labor Act (fn23) and making certain of its provisions applicable to air carriers, intended to bar states from protecting employees against racial discrimination. No provision in the Act even mentions discrimination in hiring. It is true that in several cases we have held that the exclusive bargaining agents authorized by the act must not use their powers to discriminate against minority groups whom they are supposed to represent. (fn24) And we have held that employers too may be enjoined from carrying out provisions of a discriminatory bargaining agreement. (fn25)

But the duty the Act imposes is one of fair representation and it is imposed upon the union. The employer is merely prohibited from aiding the union in breaching its duty. Nothing in the Railway Labor Act or in our cases suggests that the Act places upon an air carrier a duty to engage only in fair nondiscriminatory hiring practices. The Act has never been used for that purpose, and we cannot hold it [that] bars Colorado's Anti Discrimination Act.

Finally, we reject the argument that Colorado's Anti-Discrimination Act cannot constitutionally be enforced because of executive orders requiring government contracting agencies to include in their contracts clauses by which contractors agree not to discriminate against employees or applicants because of their race, religion, color, or national origin. (fn26) The District Court purported to take judicial notice that "a certificated commercial carrier by air (such as respondent) is obligated to and in fact does transport United States mail under contract with the United States government."

The government answers that in fact it has no contract with Continental and that, while 49 U.S.C. Sec. 1375 requires air lines to carry mail, it does not forbid discrimination on account of race or compel the execution of a contract subject to executive orders. We do not rest on this ground alone, however, nor do we reach the question of whether an executive order can foreclose state legislation. It is impossible for us to believe that the executive intended for its orders to regulate air carrier discrimination among employees so pervasively as to preempt state legislation intended to accomplish the same purpose.

The judgment of the Supreme Court of Colorado is reversed and the cause is remanded for further proceedings not inconsistent with this opinion. It is so ordered.

---

fn1: Colo. Rev. Stat. Ann. (supp. 1960) Sec. 80-24-6.

fn2: The Commission also found that Continental was "guilty of a discriminatory and unfair employment practice in requiring on its application form, the racial identity of the applicant and the requirement of a photo to be attached to the application," contrary to the Commission's regulation.

fn3: 44 Stat. 577, as amended, 45 U.S.C. Secs. 151-188.

fn4: 52 Stat. 973, as amended, 49 U.S.C. (1952 ed.) Secs. 401-722, now Federal Aviation Act of 1958, 72 Stat. 731, 49 U.S.C. Secs. 1301 1542.

fn5: It is not claimed in this case that the Colorado act discriminated against interstate commerce, see, e.g., *Best & Co. v. Maxwell*, 311 u.s. 454 (1940), or that it places a substantial economic burden on Continental, see, e.g., *Bibb v. Navajo Freight Lines*, 359 U.S. 520 (1959).

fn6: See, e.g., *California v. Thompson*, 313 u.s. 109 (1941); *Erie R. Co. v. Williams*, 233 U.S. 685 (1914).

fn7: E.g., *Brown v. Board of Education*, 347 U.S. 483 (1954); *Bolling v. Bharpe*, 347 U.S. 497 (1954); *Bailey v. Patterson*, 369 U.S. 31 (1962).

fn8: See *McDermott v. Wisconsin*, 228 U.S. 115 (1913).

fn9: see, e.g., *United Mine Workers v. Arkansas Oak Flooring Co.*, 351 U.S. 62 (1956).

fn10: see, e.g., *Hill v. Florida*, 325 U.S. 538 (1945); *Hines v. Davidowitz*, 312 u.s. 52 (1941).

fn11: *Charleston & W.C.R. Co. v. Varnville Furniture Co.*, 237 U.S. 597, 604 (1915).

fn12: *California v. Zook*, 336 U.S. 725, 730 (1949).

fn13: 52 stat. 973, as amended, 49 U.S.C. (1952 ed.), secs. 401 722.

fn14: the Civil Aeronautics Act of 1938 was substantially reenacted by the Federal Aviation Act of 1958, 72 stat. 731, 49 U.S.C. secs. 1301 1542. Some of the powers and duties of the Civil Aeronautics Board were transferred to the administrator of the Federal Aviation Agency.

fn15: 49 U.S.C. (1952 ed.) sec. 484(b), now 49 U.S.C. sec. 1374(b).

fn16: 49 U.S.C. (1952 ed.) sec. 402(c), now 49 U.S.C. sec. 1302(c).

fn17: Compare Interstate Commerce Act sec. 3(1), 49 U.S.C. sec. 3(1).

fn18: See *Fitzgerald v. Pan American World Airways*, 229 f.2d 499 (c.a.2d cir. 1956); *United States v. City of Montgomery*, 201 f. supp. 590 (m.d. Ala. 1962); cf. *Henderson v. United States*, 339 U.S. 816 (1950); *Mitchell v. United States*, 313 U.S. 80 (1941).

fn19: See 49 U.S.C. (1952 ed.) secs. 552, 559, now 49 U.S. C. secs. 1422, 1429.

fn20: See, e.g., 14 cfr secs. 20.40, 20.42-20.45, 20.121, 21.1, 40.300.

fn21: *Bethlehem Steel Co. v. New York State Labor Rel. Bd.*, 330 U.S. 767, 775 (1947). See *Parker v. Brown*, 317 U.S. 341 (1943); *H.P. Welch Co. v. New Hampshire*, 306 U.S. 79 (1939).

fn22: If the Federal authorities seek to deal with discrimination in hiring practices and their power to do so is upheld, that would raise questions not presented here. Compare *California v. Thompson*, 313 U.S. 109 (1941), with *California v. Zook*, 336 U.S. 725 (1949).

fn23: 44 stat. 577, as amended, 45 U.S.C. secs. 151-188.

fn24: See, e.g., *Conley v. Gibson*, 355 U.S. 41 (1957); *Steele v. Louisiana & Nashville RR. Co.*, 323 U.S. 192 (1944).

fn25: See, e.g., *Brotherhood of RR Trainmen v. Howard*, 343 U.S. 768, 775 (1952).

fn26: Executive Order no. 10479, 18 Fed. reg. 4899 (Aug. 13, 1953), Executive order no. 10557, 19 Fed. reg. 5655 (Sept. 3, 1954), both revoked and superseded by Executive Order no. 10925, 26 Fed. reg. 1977 (Mar. 6, 1961).

APPENDIX B

The Life and Times of Marlon D. Green

June 6, 1929 — **Marlon DeWitt Green born in El Dorado, Arkansas, to McKinley and Lucy Green.**

Mar. 4, 1933 — Franklin D. Roosevelt becomes the 32nd president of the United States.

June 25, 1941 — President Roosevelt signs order banning racial discrimination in U.S. defense industries.

Sept. 1941 — Negro Air Corps formed at Tuskegee Institute, Alabama.

Dec. 8, 1941 — U.S. enters World War II, thus creating many jobs for Negroes in northern factories producing war materiel.

April 1943 — Race riots occur at Belle Island, Detroit, Michigan.

May 1943 — **Marlon D. Green graduates as valedictorian of Fairview Elementary School, El Dorado.**

1943-1946 — **Marlon D. Green attends Booker T. Washington High School in El Dorado.**

1944 — **Marlon D. Green and three siblings convert to Roman Catholicism.**

Apr. 12, 1945 — President Roosevelt dies in office; Harry S. Truman becomes the 33rd president, serves until 1953.

May 8, 1945 — Germany surrenders; Victory in Europe Day.

Aug. 15, 1945 — Japan surrenders; World War II ends.

Sept. 1946 — **Marlon D. Green attends Xavier Prep School in New Orleans, Louisiana, on a scholarship.**

Apr. 10, 1947 — Jackie Robinson becomes the first Negro major-league baseball player when he signs with the Brooklyn Dodgers.

May 1947 — **Marlon D. Green graduates as co-valedictorian from Xavier Prep School.**

Sept. 1947 — **Marlon D. Green enters Epiphany Apostolic College, New York.**

Dec. 1947	**Marlon D. Green expelled from Epiphany Apostolic College.**
Feb. 5, 1948	**Marlon D. Green enters active duty with U.S. Air Force, finishes basic training in May.**
June 5, 1948	**Marlon D. Green ships out to Wheeler Air Force Base, Oahu, Hawaii.**
July 26, 1948	President Harry S. Truman orders desegregation of the U.S. military.
Mar. 3, 1949	**Marlon D. Green transferred to Hickam Air Force Base, Hawaii.**
Mar. 1950	**Marlon D. Green transferred to Randolph Field, Texas, for pilot training.**
June 25, 1950	Communist North Korea invades South Korea, thus starting the Korean War.
Nov. 1950	**Marlon D. Green finishes basic pilot training, is assigned to Reese AFB, Texas, for multi-engine course.**
Mar. 24, 1951	**Marlon D. Green graduates from multi-engine course, is commissioned a second lieutenant. He is then transferred to Lake Charles Air Base, Louisiana. He begins dating Eleanor Gallagher.**
Spring 1951	**Marlon D. Green proposes to Eleanor Gallagher; she accepts.**
Dec. 29, 1951	**Marlon D. Green and Eleanor Gallagher wed in Los Angeles, California.**
Apr. 1952	**Marlon and Eleanor Green move to Columbus, Ohio; Marlon is assigned to an aerial refueling squadron based at Lockbourne Air Force Base.**
Jan. 20, 1953	Dwight D. Eisenhower sworn in as the 34th president of the United States.
Mar. 1953	**The Greens' first child, Joseph Benedict Green, is born in Ohio.**
June 1953	North Koreans and United Nations forces agree to a cease-fire and truce.
Nov. 1953	**Marlon D. Green is transferred to Mitchel Air Force Base, Long Island, New York.**
May 17, 1954	Landmark U.S. Supreme Court ruling in *Brown v. Topeka Board of Education*; "Separate but Equal" schools ruled unconstitutional.

June 1954   The Greens' second child, Maria Theresa Green, is born in New York.

Mar. 16, 1955   Marlon D. Green applies for test pilot training but is not chosen.

July 1955   Peter Vincent Green is born in New York.

Aug. 28, 1955   Chicago teenager Emmett Till is murdered in Mississippi.

Dec. 1, 1955   Rosa Parks refuses to give up her seat and move to the back of the bus in Montgomery, Alabama, thus touching off a year-long boycott of city buses, supported by the Reverend Martin Luther King, Jr., and resulting in the eventual desegregation of Montgomery's buses.

Feb. 1956   Autherine Lucy enrolls at the all-white University of Alabama, sparking anti-Negro demonstrations.

Summer 1956   Marlon D. Green attends amphibious aircraft (SA-16) training in Florida.

Aug. 1956   Marlon D. Green is transferred to Johnson Air Force Base, Japan.

Aug. 1956   Daughter Monica Helen Green is born in Japan.

April 1957   Marlon D. Green resigns his Air Force commission and the Greens return to the U.S., where he hopes to find a job as a commercial airline pilot. The family moves to Lansing, Michigan.

Apr.-June 1957 Marlon D. Green searches unsuccessfully for an airline pilot job.

June 24-25, 1957 Marlon D. Green is given a flight test at Continental Airlines' Denver headquarters. He is not hired, but other (white) pilots with lesser qualifications are.

July 1957   The Greens' fifth child, Paula Clare Green, is born in Michigan.

Aug. 13, 1957   Marlon D. Green files complaint against Continental with Colorado Anti-Discrimination Commission.

Aug. 28, 1957   Marlon D. Green hired as pilot for Michigan State Highway Department, but continues to apply for airline pilot jobs.

Sept. 10, 1957 Continental Airlines rejects the Colorado Anti-Discrimination Commission's demand that the carrier hire Marlon D. Green.

Sept. 23, 1957   Nine Negro students begin classes at all-white Central High School in Little Rock, Arkansas, which prompts civil unrest and the calling out of the Arkansas National Guard and federal troops to restore and maintain order.

May 7, 1958   **Colorado Anti-Discrimination Commission holds hearing on Continental's refusal to hire Green. Continental takes the position that, because it is engaged in interstate commerce, the Commission has no jurisdiction and cannot regulate its hiring practices.**

May 8, 1958   **Before returning to Michigan, Marlon D. Green meets with Denver priest, Monsignor George R. Evans, who refers him to attorney T. Raber Taylor.**

Sept. 20, 1958   Rev. Martin Luther King, Jr. is stabbed by deranged woman in Harlem.

Sept. 1958   **The Greens' sixth child, Philip Lawrence Green, is born in Michigan.**

Mar. 1959   **T. Raber Taylor, as the Greens' lawyer, prepares to take legal action against Continental.**

June 11, 1959   **Denver District Court hears Colorado Anti-Discrimination Commission lawsuit against Continental Airlines. Judge William A. Black sends Commission back to revise its complaint and sets date (June 26) for new trial.**

June 26, 1959   **Judge Black dismisses Commission's complaint. Taylor tells the Greens that he will appeal the case to the Colorado Supreme Court for a reduced fee.**

Feb. 2, 1960   The first "sit-in" takes place at segregated lunch counter in Greensboro, North Carolina; scores of sit-ins follow throughout the South.

Apr. 21, 1960   Congress passes the Civil Rights Bill of 1960.

June 6, 1960   **T. Raber Taylor argues the Green case before the Colorado Supreme Court.**

Aug. 15, 1960   **The Colorado Supreme Court announces its decision: the Court finds for Continental and rejects Green's claim of racial and job discrimination.**

Oct. 4, 1960   **Marlon D. Green resigns as pilot for the Michigan State Highway Department.**

Oct. 10, 1960	**Jobless, Marlon D. Green requests that his lawyer terminate his quest for justice, but Taylor decides to continue fighting.**
Oct. 25, 1960	**Denver District Court again hears Green's complaint again but rejects it.**
Jan. 20, 1961	John F. Kennedy sworn in as 35th president of the U.S.
Mar. 6, 1961	President Kennedy establishes the Commmittee on Equal Employment Opportunity.
May 5, 1961	"Freedom Rides" on buses begin in the South as a way of creating wider public awareness of racial oppression and inequality.
June 15, 1961	**U.S. Attorney General Robert F. Kennedy and U.S. Justice Department files a "friend of the court" brief with the U.S. Supreme Court on behalf of Marlon D. Green.**
Sept. 5, 1961	**Marlon D. Green meets with the Trappist monk Thomas Merton at Gethsemani Abbey in Kentucky.**
Mar. 28, 1963	**U.S. Supreme Court hears the *Colorado Anti-Discrimination Commission v. Continental Air Lines, Inc.* case.**
Apr. 22, 1963	**U.S. Supreme Court announces unanimous verdict in favor of Marlon D. Green.**
Apr. 1963	**Floyd E. Dominy, Commissioner of U.S. Bureau of Reclamation hires Green as Bureau pilot; Green family moves to Denver.**
May 8, 1963	**Continental Airlines offers pilot's job to Marlon D. Green; Taylor and Green study clauses and provisions of offer.**
Aug. 28, 1963	Marlon D. Green and over 200,000 attend Rev. Dr. Martin Luther King, Jr.'s "I Have a Dream" speech at Lincoln Memorial in Washington, D.C.
Sept. 15, 1963	Sixteenth Street Baptist Church in Birmingham, Alabama, bombed by segregationists.
Nov. 22, 1963	President John F. Kennedy assassinated in Dallas, Texas, by Lee Harvey Oswald; Lyndon B. Johnson becomes 36th president.
July 2, 1964	Civil Rights Act of 1964 passed by Congress.
July 15, 1964	**Denver District Court rules that Continental Airlines must end its delaying tactics and hire Marlon D. Green.**

July 18, 1964   The first in a series of race riots that will continue across the country off and on for over a decade begins in New York City.

Aug. 4, 1964   Three civil rights workers found murdered in Mississippi.

Sept. 1964   Green family buys a home in Denver.

Nov. 3, 1964   Continental makes amended job offer to Marlon D. Green.

Dec. 2, 1964   Marlon D. Green accepts Continental's offer, resigns from Bureau of Reclamation.

Jan. 25, 1965   Marlon D. Green attends Continental training class.

Feb. 21, 1965   Black leader Malcolm X assassinated in New York City.

Mar. 1965   Marlon D. Green makes first flight for Continental.

Mar. 21-25, 1965 Rev. King leads 54-mile march from Selma to Montgomery, Alabama, to call attention to plight of Negroes in the South.

Aug. 6, 1965   Voting Rights Act of 1965 signed into law by President Johnson. Literacy and other voter tests are outlawed.

Apr. 4, 1968   Rev. King assassinated in Memphis, Tennessee, by James Earl Ray; rioting breaks out across U.S.

June 5, 1968   Presidential candidate Robert F. Kennedy assassinated in Los Angeles, California, by Sirhan Sirhan.

Aug. 1968   Riots occur during Democratic National Convention in Chicago.

Autumn 1968   Marlon D. Green leaves family.

Jan. 20, 1969   Richard M. Nixon sworn in as 37th president of the United States.

1969   Marlon D. Green moves to Los Angeles.

Jan. 1970   Marlon and Eleanor Green are divorced.

1972   Marlon D. Green marries Dolores Taylor in Los Angeles.

Feb. 1974   Son Victor born to Marlon and Dolores Green.

Aug. 9, 1974   President Nixon resigns; Vice-President Gerald R. Ford becomes 38th president.

1975   Marlon and Dolores Green are divorced.

1976	Organization of Black Airline Pilots (OBAP) formed.
Jan. 20, 1977	James E. "Jimmy" Carter, Jr. sworn in as 39th president of the United States.
1977	**Marlon D. Green marries Sylvia Johnson in Hawaii.**
Aug. 6, 1978	**Marlon D. Green retires from Continental Airlines.**
1979	**Marlon and Sylvia Green are divorced. Marlon moves to the Seychelles Islands for a year.**
Jan. 20, 1981	Ronald W. Reagan sworn in as 40th president of the United States.
Sept. 1981	**Marlon D. Green marries Colleen Wiltshire in New Zealand.**
1982	**Marlon and Colleen are divorced.**
1983	**Marlon D. Green returns to U.S.**
Jan. 20, 1989	George H. W. Bush sworn in as 41st president of the United States.
Jan. 20, 1993	William J. "Bill" Clinton sworn in as 42nd president of the United States.
Jan. 20, 2001	George W. Bush sworn in as 43rd president of the United States. Gen. Colin L. Powell, former Chairman of the Joint Chiefs of Staff, is named U.S. Secretary of State—the first African-American to hold that position.
Jan. 26, 2005	Dr. Condoleezza Rice becomes the 66th U.S. Secretary of State and the first African American female to serve in the position.
Apr. 5, 2005	**Marlon D. Green suffers stroke in Miami, is hospitalized.**
Nov. 10, 2005	**Marlon D. Green inducted into Arkansas Aviation Historical Society Hall of Fame.**
Feb. 29, 2008	**Marlon D. Green returns to Denver, moves into a senior living community.**
Nov. 4, 2008	Barack H. Obama is elected 44th president of the United States.

ACKNOWLEDGMENTS

THIS BOOK COULD not have been completed—or even begun—without the generous and unstinting assistance of a great many people.

First in line to be garlanded with thanks are Marlon and Eleanor Green, who gave unselfishly of their time over a period of years while this project grew in breadth and depth. Their intense interest in seeing their story told, no matter how painful, was inspirational and never ending.

Of equal importance is their daughter, Paula Green, who has spent years sorting through boxes and albums of memorabilia and putting it into more than a semblance of order. She also previously conducted numerous interviews with her father ("Marlon Green Questionnaire") which proved invaluable to my research. I also thank Marlon and Eleanor's other children, Joseph, Maria/Marie, Monica, and Philip for their assistance, contributions, and encouragement.

I was fortunate to have the distinct honor of meeting with the Green's attorney, T. Raber Taylor, and his wife Josephine ("Jo"), just a few weeks before his death in 2004. I also wish to thank all the Taylor daughters—Anne, Carol, Joanne, Kay, Peggy, Rae, and especially Mary Taylor Hassouna, another extremely valuable team member of the project, who has maintained in perfect order all of her father's legal records and correspondence relating to the Marlon Green case and made them available to me. Without these timeless documents, the writing of this book would have been impossible.

Other Green family members who were instrumental in helping me understand the family dynamics and the tenor of the times in El Dorado were James Green and his former wife Thelma, and Allen and Mae Green.

Green family friends deserving of thanks for their help on this project include Cleo Moran, Norbert ("Nobby") Wiley, George Reid, Ed and Ruby Kammerer, Richard J. Brake, Carol Miyagishima, Bill and Lillian Hopson, and former Continental flight attendant Carolyn Shelton for her unequivocating views on racism in the airline industry. I also owe thanks to former Continental pilot David Price, who gave me additional insights into the workings of the company in the 1970s.

Others who were interviewed played a significant role in Marlon's life and also contributed invaluable material to the book. These include former U.S. Bureau of Reclamation Commissioner Floyd Dominy and former New York State Assistant Attorney General Shirley Adelson Siegel. I also greatly appreciate the interview granted by journalist John Seigenthaler, Sr., who was close to Robert Kennedy and deeply committed to the cause of equality.

Thanks are also due to Rebecca "Becca" Baird, and Abigail "Abby" Hoverstock, who, as graduate students in Library and Information Management at Emporia State University, spent seventy hours at Eleanor's home sorting, archiving, and cataloguing the Green family archives in anticipation of a future donation of the collection to a college or university. Their Herculean efforts greatly simplified my search for documents and other relevant material. Appreciation must also go to their volunteer advisor, Allaina Howard Wallace.

Dr. Morton Gitelman's Master of Laws thesis, "The Green Case: A Study in Constitutional Litigation," was also of great help in understanding many of the legal complexities.

Others who read the progression of drafts of the manuscript and offered their insights and helpful suggestions were Dr. Vincent Harding of the Iliff School of Theology in Denver, Von Hardesty of the Smithsonian Air and Space Museum in Washington, D.C., my agent Sandra Bond, my editor/publisher Nan Wisherd, and my wife, Dr. Mary Ann Watson.

To everyone involved in this project I offer my heartiest and humblest gratitude. That being said, any errors of omission or commission are mine alone.

SOURCES

CHAPTER 1: SOUTHERN LIVING

1. James Green interview by author, Nov. 12, 2005.
2. www.IUPUI.edu/ ~ aao/kkk.
3. www.boomtown.org.; www.arkansastravel.com.
4. Marlon Green interview by author, Mar. 20, 2004.
5. James Green interview by author, Nov. 12, 2005.
6. Marlon Green interview by author, Mar. 20, 2004.
7. James Green interview by author, Nov. 12, 2005.
8. Marlon Green interview by author, Mar. 20, 2004.
9. James Green interview by author, Nov. 12, 2005.
10. Marlon Green interview by author, Mar. 20, 2004; and James Green interview by author, Nov. 12, 2005.
11. James Green interview by author, Nov. 12, 2005.
12. afroamhistory.about.com/cs/aphiliprandolph.
13. Letters to the Editor, *LIFE*, Sept. 21, 1942.
14. Marlon Green interview by author, Mar. 20, 2004.
15. James Green interview by author, Nov. 12, 2005.
16. Marlon Green interview by author, Mar. 20, 2004.
17. James Green interview by author, Nov. 12, 2005.
18. Marlon Green interview by author, Mar. 20, 2004.
19. info.detnews.com/history.
20. Marlon Green interview by author, Mar. 20, 2004, and James Green interview by author, Nov. 12, 2005.
21. Marlon Green interview by author, Mar. 20, 2004.
22. James Green interview by author, Nov. 12, 2005.
23. Marlon Green interview by author, Mar. 20, 2004.

CHAPTER 2: MARCHING TOWARD EQUALITY

1. James Green interview by author, Nov. 12, 2005.
2. Marlon Green autobiography, n.d., Green family archives.
3. Marlon Green questionnaire, n.d., Green family archives.
4. Marlon Green interview by author, Mar. 20, 2004.
5. *Ebony*, Dec. 1957 ("Catholics Lead in School Desegregation in Many Sectors").
6. *U.S. News and World Report*, Jan. 11, 1999 ("Saint-in-Waiting: Katherine Drexel Could Be Next," Gary Cohen).
7. Marlon Green interview by author, Mar. 20, 2004.
8. *Denver Post*, April 3, 2005 ("Trials Urged in '46 Racial Killings"); www.essays.cc.
9. Marlon Green interview, Mar. 20, 2004.
10. Marlon Green autobiography, n.d., Green family archives.
11. Binkin, Martin; Mark J. Eitelberg; Alvin J. Schexnider; and Marvin M. Smith, *Blacks and the Military*, (Washington, D.C., 1982), 13-14.
12. www.ipoaa.com/blackfacts.
13. Binkin, et al, 11-20.

14. Ibid, 20.
15. Dwight D. Eisenhower, *Crusade in Europe*, (Garden City, NY, 1948), 58-59.
16. Binkin, et al, 20-23.
17. Ibid, 23-24.
18. www.afa.org/magazine/July1998/0798integrate.
19. www.blackwings.com;www.africanamericans.com/99thPursuitSquadron.
20. www.nasaui.ited.uidaho.edu; www.fatherryan.org; www.wpafb.af.mil; www.acepilots.com.
21. www.toptags.com/aama/events/fmutiny.
22. Gropman, Alan L. *The Air Force Integrates: 1945-1964* (Second Edition), (Washington, D.C., 1998), 1, 11-21; www.toptags.com/aama/events/fmutiny; www.afa.org/magazine/July1998/0798integrate.
23. National Park Service brochure, "Port Chicago Naval Magazine," n.d.
24. www.hartford-hwp.com/archives/45a.
25. Binkin, et al, 26.
26. Marlon Green interview by author, Mar. 20, 2004.

CHAPTER 3: THE KNACK

1. Marlon Green autobiography, n.d., Green family archives.
2. Marlon Green interview by author, Mar. 20, 2004.
3. Eleanor Green interview by author, May 17, 2004.
4. Marlon Green interview by author, Mar. 20, 2004.
5. Airman Promotion Efficiency Report, Jan. 25, 1950, Green family archives.
6. Marlon Green interview by author, Mar. 20, 2004.
7. www.boeing.com/history/bna/t6.
8. Marlon Green interview by author, Mar. 20, 2004.

CHAPTER 4: ELEANOR

1. Eleanor Green interview by author, May 17, 2004.
2. en.wikipedia.org/wiki/Anti-Irish_racism; www.yale.edu/ynhti/curriculum/units/1990/5/90.05.07.x.
3. Eleanor Green interview by author, May 17, 2004.
4. R. Bentley Anderson, *Black, White, and Catholic: New Orleans Interracialism, 1947-1956* (Nashville, 2005), xiii.
5. Ibid, 15, 143-145, 174, 178.
6. Letter, Cleo Moran to Eleanor Green, March 2005.
7. Eleanor Green interview by author, May 17, 2004.
8. Eleanor Green e-mail to author, Jan. 15, 2008.
9. Eleanor Green interview by author, May 17, 2004.
10. Marlon Green interview by author, Mar. 20, 2004.
11. Eleanor Green interview by author, May 17, 2004.
12. Marlon Green interview by author, Mar. 20, 2004.
13. Eleanor Green interview by author, May 17, 2004.
12. Cleo Moran interview by author, August 27, 2006.

CHAPTER 5: REFUSING TO CONFORM

1. Eleanor Green interview by author, May 17, 2004.
2. Marlon Green interview by author, Mar. 20, 2004.
3. James Green interview by author, Nov. 12, 2005.
4. Eleanor Green interview by author, May 17, 2004.
5. Marlon Green interview by author, Mar. 20, 2004; and Eleanor Green interview by author, May 17, 2004.
6. Letter, Fichter to William & Anna Gallagher, May 16, 1951, Green family archives.
7. Marlon Green interview by author, Mar. 20, 2004.
8. Letter, Fichter to Eleanor Green, Dec. 6, 1951, Green family archives.
9. Letter, Fichter to Eleanor Green, Dec. 21, 1951, Green family archives.
10. www.fmuiv.edu/urbanaffairs/jem; www.spartacus.schoolnet.co.uk/USAmoore.
11. Marlon Green interview by author, Mar. 20, 2004; and Eleanor Green interview by author, May 17, 2004.
12. Marlon Green interview by author, Mar. 20, 2004; Letter, request for transfer, M. Green to U.S. Air Force, April 3, 1952, Green family archives.
13. Eleanor Green interview by author, May 17, 2004.
14. Letter, Marlon to Eleanor, Oct. 29, 1952, Green family archives.
15. Marlon Green interview by author, Mar. 20, 2004.
16. Unknown newspaper clipping, Nov. 12, 1952, Green family archives.
17. Marlon Green interview by author, Mar. 20, 2004.
18. www.strategic-air-command.com.
19. Marlon Green interview by author, Mar. 20, 2004.
20. Marlon Green interview by author, Mar. 20, 2004; and Eleanor Green interview, May 17, 2004.
21. Marlon Green interview by author, Mar. 20, 2004; and Eleanor Green interview, May 17, 2004.
22. en.wikipedia.org/wiki/Hempstead_Plains.
23. Marlon Green interview by author, Mar. 20, 2004.
24. Letter, Ralph L. Knapp to Commander, Ninth Air Force, April 6, 1955, Green family archives.
25. Letter, Headquarters, Air Force Flight Test Center, to Tactical Air Command, June 28, 1955, Green family archvies.
26. Eleanor Green interview by author, May 17, 2004.
27. *New York Times*, Jan. 8, 1955 ("Marian Anderson Wins Ovation in First Opera Role at the 'Met,'" by Howard Taubman).
28. Paul Hendrickson, *Sons of Mississippi* (New York, 2003), 6.
29. Marlon Green interview by author, Mar. 20, 2004.
30. Eleanor Green interview by author, May 17, 2004.

CHAPTER 6: ESCAPADE IN JAPAN

1. Marlon Green interview by author, Mar. 20, 2004; and Eleanor Green interview by author, May 17, 2004.
2. Marlon Green interview by author, Mar. 20, 2004.
3. Eleanor Green interview by author, May 17, 2004.
4. www.city.iruma.saitama.jp/i-society.

5. Marlon Green interview by author, Mar. 20, 2004; and Eleanor Green interview by author, May 17, 2004.
6. Eleanor Green interview by author, May 17, 2004.
7. Marlon Green interview by author, Mar. 20, 2004.
8. *Stars and Stripes* (Pacific Edition), Dec. 24, 1956 ("Yule Drop Aids 5 on Icy Peak").
9. Marlon Green interview by author, Mar. 20, 2004.
10. *New York Times*, Oct. 2, 1956 ("Airlines Proclaim a Joint Policy to Clear Way for Negro Pilots").
11. *Time*, Oct. 15, 1956 ("Big Step").
12. Marlon Green interview by author, Mar. 20, 2004.

CHAPTER 7: ROCKS IN HIS JAWS

1. www.centennialofflight.gov; www.BessieColeman.com.
2. www.fact-index.com/hubert_julian.
3. avstop.com/History/BlackAirlines; *Airways*, Feb. 2000 ("Green, Martin and Young—Three Pioneers," Stan Solomon).
4. *New York Times*, Nov. 19, 1998 ("Perry H. Young Jr., 79, Pioneering Pilot, Dies").
5. Marlon Green interview by author, Mar. 20, 2004.
6. Eleanor Green interview by author, May 17, 2004.
7. Findings of investigator, Nov. 29, 1957, Green family archives.
8. Marlon Green interview by author, Mar. 20, 2004.
9. Eleanor Green interview by author, May 17, 2004.
10. Letter, Marlon Green to Rogers and Durfee, Apr. 1, 1959, T. Raber Taylor archives.
11. Eleanor Green interview by author, May 17, 2004.
12. Marlon Green interview by author, Mar. 20, 2004.
13. Eleanor Green interview by author, May 17, 2004.
14. Marlon Green interview by author, Mar. 20, 2004.
15. Letter, Marlon Green to Rogers and Durfee, Apr. 1, 1959, T. Raber Taylor archives.
16. Marlon Green interview by author, Mar. 20, 2004.
17. Motion to Strike, T. Raber Taylor to Denver District Court, June 25, 1959, T. Raber Taylor archives.
18. Marlon Green interview by author, Mar. 20, 2004.
19. Robert J. Serling, *Maverick: The Story of Robert Six and Continental Airlines* (Garden City, NY, 1974), 321.
20. www.randomhouse.com/knopf/authors/lawrence.
21. Serling, 15-107; *Denver Post*, June 25, 1950 ("Continental Air Chief Bob Six Has Devoted Career to Aviation").
22. Marlon Green interview by author, Mar. 20, 2004.

CHAPTER 8: A VICTIM OF HAPPENSTANCE

1. Marlon Green interview by author, Mar. 20, 2004.
2. Letter, Chapman to Taylor, Mar. 26, 1959, T. Raber Taylor archives.
3. Caroline M. Fannin; Betty K. Gubert; Miriam Sawyer, *Distinguished African-Americans in Aviation and Space Science* (Westport, CT, 2002), 138-140.
4. T. Raber Taylor archives.
5. Eleanor Green interview by author, May 17, 2004.

6. *New York Times*, Sept. 1, 1957 ("Little Rock Sets Integration Date," by Benjamin Fine).

7. *Montgomery Advertiser and Alabama Journal*, quoted in *New York Times*, Sept. 8, 1957).

8. *New York Times*, Sept. 1, 1957 ("Little Rock Sets Integration Date," by Benjamin Fine); Sept. 3, 1957 ("Militia Sent To Little Rock; School Integration Put Off," by Benjamin Fine); Sept. 4, 1957 ("Little Rock Told To Integrate Now Despite Militia," by Benjamin Fine); Sept. 5, 1957 ("Arkansas Troops Bar Negro Pupils; Governor Defiant," by Benjamin Fine); Sept. 6, 1957 ("Little Rock Board Seeks Stay In School Integration," by Benjamin Fine, "President Warns Governor Faubus He'll Uphold Law," by W. H. Lawrence); Sept. 7, 1957 ("Little Rock Faces Showdown Today Over Integration," by Benjamin Fine); Sept. 8, 1957 ("U.S. Court Denies Integration Stay For Little Rock," by Benjamin Fine, "President Weighs Integration Move," by Anthony Lewis); Sept. 9, 1957 ("Faubus Bids U.S. Recede On Order For Integration," by Benjamin Fine, "Eisenhower Firm On Enforcing Law," by W. H. Lawrence); Sept. 10, 1957 ("U.S. To Seek Writ To Force Faubus and Guard To Permit Integration; Extended Court Battle Expected," by Benjamin Fine); Sept. 11, 1957 ("N.A.A.C.P. Submits Little Rock Plea; Court Sits Today," by Anthony Lewis); Sept. 12, 1957 ("High Court Hears Little Rock Plea; May Rule Today," by Anthony Lewis); Sept. 13, 1957 ("Court Bars Little Rock Delay; President Calls For Support; Faubus Orders 4 Schools Shut," by Anthony Lewis and Claude Sitton); Sept. 14, 1957 ("Faubus Says U.S. Court Can't Bar Closing," by Claude Sitton); Sept. 15, 1957 ("Little Rock Suit To Open Schools Expected Today," by Claude Sitton); Sept. 16, 1957 ("4 Little Rock Schools Stay Shut; Board Presses Faubus On Plan," by Claude Sitton).

9. Michael Korda. *Ike: An American Hero* (New York, 2007), 697-699.

10. Marlon Green interview by author, Mar. 20, 2004.

11. Letter, Taylor to Marlon Green, Oct. 30, 1959, T. Raber Taylor archives.

12. Letter, Seidenberg to Chapman, Nov. 25, 1957 (mentioned in letter, Chapman to Taylor, Mar, 26, 1959), T. Raber Taylor archives.

13. Letter, Chapman to Taylor, Mar. 26, 1959, T. Raber Taylor archives; Marlon Green interview by author, Mar. 20, 2004.

14. *Lansing State Journal*, Nov. 8, 1957 (headline missing).

15. Marlon Green interview by author, Mar. 20, 2004.

16. Decision of the Colorado Anti-Discrimination Commission, June 22, 1959, T. Raber Taylor archives.

17. Marlon Green questionnaire, n.d., Green family archives.

18. *Rocky Mountain News*, Nov. 23, 1999 ("When the Klan Ruled Colorado," by Manny Gonzales).

19. Morley Collection, Colorado State Archives.

20. Marlon Green questionnaire, n.d., Green family archives.

21. www.hollandhart.com.

22. *Denver City Directory*. Denver: The Gazeteer Company, 1957, passim.

23. *Denver Post*, Apr. 22, 1963 ("U.S. Backs Negro Pilot Seeking Job on Airline").

24. Decision of the Colorado Anti-Discrimination Commission, June 22, 1959, T. Raber Taylor archives.

25. Marlon Green interview by author, Mar. 20, 2004.

CHAPTER 9: THE FASTEST GUN IN DENVER

1. Marlon Green interview by author, Mar. 20, 2004.
2. *Lansing State Journal*, Aug. 13, 1958 ("Negro Pilot Criticizes FEPC").
3. *New York Times*, Sept. 20, 1958 ("Dr. King, Negro Leader, Stabbed By Woman In A Store In Harlem").
4. Ibid ("President Scored Over Integration").
5. *Rocky Mountain News*, Oct. 27, 1958 ("Bob Six Slings Fastest Gun in Denver," by Pasquale Marranzino).
6. Marlon Green interview by author, Mar. 20, 2004.
7. Eleanor Green interview by author, May 17, 2004.
8. "Answer" to Denver District Court, March 1959, T. Raber Taylor archives.
9. Letter, Eleanor Green to Charles A. Lindbergh, Nov. 2, 1958, Green family archives.
10. Letter, Brake to Taylor, Mar. 16, 1959, T. Raber Taylor archives.
11. Letter, Taylor to Brake, Mar. 28, 1959; Letter, Marlon Green to Taylor, Mar. 27, 1959, T. Raber Taylor archives.
12. Letter, Marlon Green to Taylor, Mar. 27, 1959, T. Raber Taylor archives.
13. Letter, Chachere to Taylor, Mar. 31, 1959, T. Raber Taylor archives.
14. Letter, Reids to Taylor, Apr. 1, 1959.
15. Norb Wiley interview by author, Mar. 8, 2006.
16. Letter, Wileys to Taylor, Mar. 31, 1959.
17. Letter, Marlon Green to Smith, Mar. 9, 1959, Green family archives.
18. Letter, Brown to Smith, Mar. 23, 1959, Green family archives.

CHAPTER 10: MOST UNSOUND

1. *Denver Post*, June 11, 1959 ("Conair Case Delayed: Amplification Asked In Negro Pilot Case").
2. www.jimcrowhistory.org.
3. Letter, Taylor to Marlon Green, June 19, 1959.
4. *Denver Post*, June 11, 1959 ("Conair Case Delayed: Amplification Asked In Negro Pilot Case").
5. Marlon Green interview by author, Mar. 20, 2004.
6. en.wikipedia.org/wiki/Walter_Paepcke.
7. Marlon Green interview by author, Mar. 20, 2004; Letter, Marlon Green to Taylor, June 14, 1959, Green family archives.
8. Eleanor Green interview by author, May 17, 2004.
9. Letter, Poindexter to Eleanor Green, June 17, 1959, Green family archives.
10. Letters, Poindexter to Eleanor Green, undated, Green family archives.
11. Letter, Taylor to Marlon Green, June 15, 1959, T. Raber Taylor archives.
12. Letter, Taylor to Marlon Green, June 19, 1959, T. Raber Taylor archives.
13. Mort Gitelman, Masters of Law Thesis, University of Illinois, 1965, 28.
14. Letter, Taylor to Marlon Green, June 25, 1959, T. Raber Taylor archives.
15. *Denver Post*, June 25, 1959 ("Judge Voids Order Requiring Continental to Hire Negro Pilot").
16. Ibid.
17. Letter, Taylor to Marlon Green, June 25, 1959, T. Raber Taylor archives.

18. Taylor biography, courtesy of Mary Taylor Hassouna.
19. Letter, Taylor to Marlon Green, July 17, 1959, T. Raber Taylor archives.
20. Letter, Marlon Green to Taylor, July 20, 1959, T. Raber Taylor archives.
21. Marlon Green interview by author, Mar. 20, 2004.
22. Letter, Thomas to Chapman, Taylor, and Nagel, July 24, 1959, T. Raber Taylor archives.
23. Letter, Taylor to Marlon Green, Aug. 15, 1959, T. Raber Taylor archives.

CHAPTER 11: GUIDED BY DIVINE PROVIDENCE

1. Letter, Marlon Green to Taylor, Aug. 19, 1959, T. Raber Taylor archives.
2. www.infoplease.com/year/1959.
3. www.stanford.edu/group/King/about_king/king-struggle/1957-1959.
4. www.uwsp.edu/equity/civilrightssymposium; Encarta.MSN.com; afroamhistory.about.com/library/blgriffin_v_princeedward.
5. *U.S. News and World Report*, Jan. 9, 1959 ("A Judge Finds New York Schools Separate and Unequal").
6. Timothy B. Tyson, *Radio Free Dixie: Robert F. Williams and the Roots of Black Power* (Chapel Hill, NC, 1999), passim.
7. Letter, Marlon Green to Taylor, Sept. 23, 1959, T. Raber Taylor archives.
8. Eleanor Green interview by author, May 17, 2004.
9. *Ebony*, Feb. 1958 ("Speaking of People: Michigan Highway Pilot").
10. Marlon Green interview by author, Mar. 20, 2004.
11. Reid interview by author, Mar. 10, 2006.
12. Marlon Green interview by author, Mar. 20, 2004.
13. E-mail, Kate Emmons to Paula Green, Feb. 23, 2005.
14. www.africanamericans.com; www.stanford.edu/group/King.
15. www.san.beck.org.
16. *New York Times*, Feb. 9, 1960 ("Negroes' Sitdown Hits 2 More Cities"); Feb. 18, 1960 ("500 Are Dispersed at Racial Dispute"); Feb. 28, 1960 ("South is Warned of Time of Change").
17. *New York Times*, Mar. 2, 1960 ("Tuskegee Boycott by Students;" "Students Boycott Stores").
18. *New York Times*, Mar. 16, 1960 ("350 Negro Student Demonstrators Held in South Carolina Stockade"); Mar. 31, 1960 ("Fire Hoses Disperse Texas Negro Crowd").
19. *Time*, May 2, 1960 ("The South: A Universal Effort").
20. www.africanamericans.com/CivilRightsActof1960.
21. *New York Times*, Apr. 25, 1960 ("N.A.A.C.P. Denies Biloxi Riot Role"); *Time*, May 16, 1960 ("Races on the Beach").
22. www.infoplease.com/year/1960.
23. Marlon Green interview by author, Mar. 20, 2004.
24. Letter, Marlon Green to Hill, Oct. 4, 1960, Green family archives.
25. Letter, Marlon Green to Taylor, June 1, 1960, T. Raber Taylor archives.
26. Letter, Taylor to Marlon Green, June 6, 1960, T. Raber Taylor archives.
27. *Denver Post*, Aug. 15, 1960 ("Negro Pilot's Charge Ordered Heard Again"); Marlon Green interview by author, Mar. 20, 2004.
28. Eleanor Green interview by author, May 17, 2004.
29. Letter, Taylor to Marlon Green, Aug. 24, 1960, T. Raber Taylor archives.
30. Letter, Marlon Green to Taylor, Sept. 5, 1960, T. Raber Taylor archives.

31. Letter, Taylor to Marlon Green, Sept. 20, 1960, T. Raber Taylor archives.
32. Marlon Green interview by author, Mar. 20, 2004.
33. Norbert Wiley interview by author, Mar. 8, 2006.
34. Norbert Wiley e-mail to Paula Green, Mar. 14, 2006.
35. Letter, Marlon Green to Taylor, Oct. 10, 1960, T. Raber Taylor archives.
36. Letter, Taylor to Marlon Green, Oct. 11, 1960, T. Raber Taylor archives.

CHAPTER 12: A KNIFE IN HIS HEART

1. Letter, Taylor to Marlon Green, Oct. 26, 1960, T. Raber Taylor archives.
2. Letter, Marlon Green to Taylor, Nov. 1, 1960, T. Raber Taylor archives.
3. Letter, Marlon Green to Taylor, Jan. 3, 1961, T. Raber Taylor archives.
4. *Denver Post*, Jan. 8, 1961 ("Negro Pilot Loses Conair Suit").
5. Letter, Taylor to Marlon Green, Jan. 9, 1961, T. Raber Taylor archives.
6. *Denver Post*, Jan. 8, 1961 ("Agency Held Lacking in Power Over Airline").
7. Letter, Eleanor Green to Hoyt, Jan. 12, 1961.
8. Letter, Eleanor Green to Taylor, Jan. 12, 1961, T. Raber Taylor archives.
9. Letter, Taylor to Marlon Green, Jan. 12, 1961, T. Raber Taylor archives.
10. Letter, Taylor to White, undated, T. Raber Taylor archives.
11. Letter, Taylor to Kennedy, Feb. 16, 1961, T. Raber Taylor archives.
12. Letter, Kennedy to Taylor, Feb. 23, 1961, T. Raber Taylor archives.
13. *Denver Post*, Jan. 24, 1961 (Editorial: "National Handicap Exposed").
14. www.ferris.edu/news.
15. Letter, Eleanor Green to Taylor, Aug. 28, 1961; Eleanor Green interview by author, May 17, 2004.
16. Letter, Marlon Green to Taylor, Feb. 20, 1961, T. Raber Taylor archives.; Eleanor Green interview by author, May 17, 2004.
17. Letter, Taylor to Crowley, Apr. 6, 1961; letter, Taylor to Marlon Green, Apr. 7, 1961, both in T. Raber Taylor archives.
18. Letter, Marlon Green to Taylor, Apr. 14, 1961, T. Raber Taylor archives.
19. Letter, Marlon Green to Gewirtz, June 8, 1961, Green family archives.
20. Letter, Marlon Green to Taylor, Apr. 14, 1961, T. Raber Taylor archives.
21. www.africanamericans.com/FreedomRiots.
22. www.iwfr.org/civilhistory.asp.
23. Seigenthaler interview by author, June 1, 2006.
24. www.africanamericans.com/FreedomRiots.
25. www.iwfr.org/civilhistory.asp; www.africanamericans.com/FreedomRiots.
26. Seigenthaler interview by author, June 1, 2006; www.africanamericans.com/FreedomRiots.
27. Seigenthaler interview by author, June 1, 2006.
28. www.firstamandmentcenter.org; www.wikipedia.org/wiki/John_Seigenthaler,-Sr.
29. Seigenthaler interview by author, June 1, 2006.
30. www.majorcox.com/columns/mann; www.africanamericans.com/FreedomRiots.
31. Seigenthaler interview by author, June 1, 2006.
32. *The Papers of John F. Kennedy, Vol. 1*, 3 vols, (Washington, D.C. 1962), 391.
33. Seigenthaler interview by author, June 1, 2006; www.africanamericans.com/FreedomRiots.
34. Letter, Marlon Green to Albers, July 2, 1961, Green family archives.
35. Letter, Taylor to Marshall, May 16, 1961, T. Raber Taylor archives.

36. Letter, Marlon Green to Halaby, May 31, 1961, Green family archives.
37. Letter, Marlon Green to Gewirtz, June 8, 1961, Green family archives.
38. Letter, Eleanor Green to Taylor, Aug. 6, 1961, Green family archives.
39. Letter, Marlon Green to Rahman, June 8, 1961, Green family archives.
40. *Denver Post*, June 14, 1961 (Editorial: "Anti-Bias Law Has Friends in Court"); June 15, 1961 ("Justice Dept. Seeks to Aid Negro Pilot").
41. Marlon Green interview by author, Mar. 20, 2004.
42. Eleanor Green interview by author, May 17, 2004.
43. Marlon Green interview by author, Mar. 20, 2004.
44. Letter, Marlon Green to Taylor, Aug. 1, 1961, T. Raber Taylor archives.
45. Letter, Taylor to Marlon Green, Aug. 7, 1961, T. Raber Taylor archives.
46. Letter, Eleanor Green to Taylor, Aug. 6, 1961, T. Raber Taylor archives.

CHAPTER 13: OFFICIALLY A PAUPER

1. Serling, 179-209.
2. Letter, Taylor to Marlon and Eleanor Green, Aug. 14, 1961, T. Raber Taylor archives.
3. Thomas Merton, *Thoughts in Solitude* (New York, 1958), 81.
4. Letter, Merton to Marlon Green, Aug. 23, 1961, Green family archives.
5. Marlon Green interview by author, Mar. 20, 2004.
6. *Denver Post*, Aug. 25, 1961 ("Robert F. Six Weds TV Actress Meadows").
7. Letter, Marlon Green to Taylor, Aug. 15, 1961, T. Raber Taylor archives.
8. Merton, *Raids on the Unspeakable* (New York, 1966), 60-61, quoted in letter, Marlon Green to Taylor, Aug. 15, 1961, T. Raber Taylor archives.
9. Marlon Green interview by author, Aug. 1, 2005.
10. Merton, *Turning Toward the World: The Pivotal Years* (San Francisco, 1996), 158.
11. Letter, Marlon Green to Continental Southern Lines, Inc., Sept. 5, 1961, Green family archives.
12. Marlon Green interview by author, Aug. 1, 2005.
13. Letter, Eleanor Green to Taylor, Aug. 28, 1961, T. Raber Taylor archives; Eleanor Green interview by author, May 17, 2004.
14. Letter, Taylor to Marlon Green, Oct. 23, 1961, T. Raber Taylor archives.
15. Letter, Marlon Green to Taylor, Oct. 30, 1961, T. Raber Taylor archives.
16. *New York Times*, Nov. 30, 1961 ("5 Negroes Beaten by Mississippi Mob," by Claude Sitton).
17. Eleanor Green interview by author, May 17, 2004.
18. *Denver Post*, Feb. 13, 1962 ("High Court Rules Airline Needn't Hire Negro Pilot").
19. Letter, Eleanor Green to Taylor, Feb. 25, 1962, T. Raber Taylor archives.
20. *Denver Post*, Mar. 5, 1962 ("Race Unit to Appeal Job Hearing," by Jim Ritchie).
21. Letter, Taylor to Marlon Green, Mar. 6, 1962, T. Raber Taylor archives.
22. Letters, Marlon Green to Taylor, Mar. 10 and 26, and May 28, 1962, T. Raber Taylor archives.
23. Marlon Green interview by author, Mar. 20, 2004.
24. Marie Green Stocks interview by author, Aug. 20, 2006.
25. Marlon Green interview by author, Mar. 20, 2004.
26. Letter, Taylor to Marlon Green, Mar. 22, 1962, T. Raber Taylor archives.
27. Letter, Marlon Green to Taylor, Mar. 26, 1962, T. Raber Taylor archives.

28. Letter, Taylor to Powell, May 14, 1962, T. Raber Taylor archives.
29. William L. O'Neill, *A Democracy at War: America's Fight at Home and Abroad in World War II* (New York, 1993), 240.
30. Letter, Taylor to Buckley, May 8, 1962, T. Raber Taylor archives.
31. Letter, Taylor to Griswold, May 11, 1962, T. Raber Taylor archives.
32. Letter, Terrones to Taylor, May 29, 1962, T. Raber Taylor archives.
33. Letter, Taylor to Marlon Green, June 1, 1962, T. Raber Taylor archives.
34. Letter, Taylor to Marlon Green, June 15, 1962, T. Raber Taylor archives.
35. Letter, Mosk to Dunbar, June 15, 1962, T. Raber Taylor archives.
36. Notification Form, U.S. Supreme Court to Taylor, Dunbar, Westfeldt, June 18, 1962, T. Raber Taylor archives.
37. Memo, Rabkin and Leskes, to Taylor, July 5, 1962, T. Raber Taylor archives.
38. Letter, Marlon Green to Cox, July 9, 1962, T. Raber Taylor archives.
40. Letter, Marlon Green to Taylor, July 23, 1962, T. Raber Taylor archives.
40. *New York Times*, Oct. 1, 1962 ("Negro at Mississippi U. as Barnett Yields; 3 Dead in Campus Riot, 6 Marshals Shot," by Claude Sitton); Oct. 3, 1962 ("Barnette Contempt Case Put Off, Court Clears University's Aides; Campus Calm, 3,500 Troops Leave," by Foster Hailey); Oct. 4, 1962 ("Meredith Plans to Leave Campus," by Claude Sitton); Oct. 5, 1962 ("U.S. Order Shifts Mississippi Game," by Claude Sitton).
41. Letter, Taylor to Marlon Green, Oct. 9, 1962, T. Raber Taylor archives.
42. *Lansing State Journal*, Oct. 9, 1962 ("Bias Case to be Aired").
43. John Polmar and John D. Gresham, *Defcon-2: Standing on the Brink of War during the Cuban Missile Crisis* (New York, 2006), passim.
44. Letter, Marlon Green to Taylor, Oct. 30, 1962, T. Raber Taylor archives.
45. Letter, Taylor to Marlon Green, Nov. 2, 1962, T. Raber Taylor archives.
46. Polmar and Gresham, 277.
47. Letter, Marlon Green to Taylor, Dec. 17, 1962, T. Raber Taylor archives.
48. Eleanor Green interview by author, May 17, 2004.
50. Letter, Cullinan to Taylor, Jan. 23, 1963, T. Raber Taylor archives.
51. Letter, Carr to Eleanor Green, Jan. 29, 1963, Green family archives.

CHAPTER 14: NINE WHITE MEN IN BLACK ROBES

1. Memo, Mar. 29, 1963, T. Raber Taylor archives.
2. Letter, Marlon Green to Taylor, Mar. 8, 1963, T. Raber Taylor archives.
3. Marlon Green interview by author, Mar. 20, 2004.
4. www.cr.nps.gov.
5. Maria Green notebook entry, Mar. 29, 1963, Green family archives.
6. Peter Green notebook entry, Mar. 29, 1963, Green family archives.
7. Marlon Green interview by author, Mar. 20, 2004.
8. www.mnc.net/norway/warren.
9. Transcript of Supreme Court hearing, Mar. 28, 1963, Green family archives.
10. Marlon Green interview by author, Mar. 20, 2004.
11. Siegel interview by author, Dec. 15, 2005.
12. Transcript of Supreme Court hearing, Mar. 28, 1963, Green family archives.
13. Marlon Green interview by author, Mar. 20, 2004.
14. Transcript of Supreme Court hearing, Mar. 28, 1963, Green family archives.

CHAPTER 15: HOPEFUL

1. Transcript of Supreme Court hearing, Mar. 28, 1963, Green family archives.
2. Marlon Green interview by author, Mar. 20, 2004.
3. Transcript of Supreme Court hearing, Mar. 28, 1963, Green family archives.
4. Joseph Green comment, Green questionnaire, n.d., Green family archives.
5. *New York Times*, Mar. 29, 1963 ("Police Loose a Dog on Negroes' Group; Minister is Bitten," by Claude Sitton).
6. Marlon Green interview by author, Mar. 20, 2004.
7. Eleanor Green interview by author, May 17, 2004.
8. Marlon Green interview by author, Mar. 20, 2004.
9. *San Francisco Chronicle*, Apr. 24, 1963 (Editorial: "Color Line on the Air Lanes").
10. Eleanor Green interview by author, May 17, 2004.
11. Letter, James to Marlon Green, Apr. 25, 1963, Green family archives.
12. Letter, Merton to Marlon Green, May 8, 1963, Green family archives.
13. Wiley e-mail to Paula Green, Aug. 28, 2007.
14. Marlon Green interview by author, Mar. 20, 2004.
15. Eleanor Green e-mail to author, Jan. 15, 2008.

CHAPTER 16: A BLACK THUMB

1. Marc Reisner, *Cadillac Desert: The American West and Its Disappearing Water* (New York, 1987), 214-225.
2. Ibid, 236.
3. Ibid, 251-252.
4. *Counterpunch*, Nov. 7, 2000.
5. John McPhee, *Encounters with the Archdruid* (New York, 1971), 163.
6. Ibid., 168.
7. *Radio High Country News*, Aug. 28, 2000.
8. Dominy interview by author, Aug. 2, 2004.
9. *New York Times*, Apr. 30, 1963 ("U.S. Employs Negro Rejected by Airline").
10. *Denver Post*, May 8, 1963 ("Conair Job Weighed by Green").
11. Marlon Green interview by author, Mar. 20, 2004.
12. *Time*, Letters to the Editor, May 17, 1963.
13. Miscellaneous documents in Green family archives.
14. Marlon Green interview, Mar. 20, 2004.
15. Eleanor Green interview by author, May 17, 2004.
16. *Colorado Heritage*, Autumn 2005 ("From Five Points to Struggle Hill: The Race Line and Segregation in Denver," by Holly L. Wasinger).
17. Dominy interview by author, Aug. 2, 2004.
18. Marlon Green interview by author, Mar. 20, 2004.
19. *New York Times*, May 3, 1963 ("500 Are Arrested in Negro Protest at Birmingham"); May 4, 1963 ("Dogs and Hoses Repulse Negroes at Birmingham").
20. www.stanford.edu/group/King.
21. Ibid.
22. afroamhistory.about.com.
23. Marlon Green interview by author, Mar. 20, 2004.
24. Candace Fleming, *Our Eleanor: A Scrapbook Look at Eleanor Roosevelt's Remarkable Life* (New York, Atheneum Books, 2005), 50.

25. www.trumanlibrary.org/hstpaper/civilrights ("Truman Speech to NAACP").
26. www.usconstitution.net/dream.
27. Marlon Green interview by author, Mar. 20, 2004.

CHAPTER 17: THE LONG, HOT SUMMER

1. *New York Times*, Sept. 16, 1963 ("Birmingham Bomb Kills 4 Negro Girls in Church; Riots Flare; 2 Boys Slain"); www.ferris.edu/news.
2. *The Papers of John F. Kennedy, Vol. 3, 1963.* Washington: U.S. Government Printing Office, 1964, 681.
3. www.stanford.edu/group/King.
4. *The Papers of John F. Kennedy, Vol. 3,* 1963, 692-693.
5. *New York Times*, Oct. 16, 1963 ("Martin Luther King Wins the Nobel Peace Prize").
6. Ibid.
7. Marlon Green interview by author, Mar. 20, 2004.
8. *Washington Post*, June 5, 1964 ("Johnson Speaks At Howard U. Commencement").
9. Marlon Green interview by author, Mar. 20, 2004.
10. *Rocky Mountain News*, July 15, 1964 ("Judge Rules Continental Airlines Must Hire Negro Pilot").
11. *New York Times*, July 19, 1964 ("Thousands Riot In Harlem; Scores Are Hurt," by Paul L. Montgomery and Francis X. Clines, "Johnson Decries Racial Disorders"); July 20, 1964 ("Violence Flares Again in Harlem; Restraint Urged"); July 21, 1963 ("Violence Erupts for Third Night").
12. *New York Times*, July 26, 1964 ("Rochester Police Battle Race Riot").
13. *New York Times*, Aug. 3, 1964 ("Negroes and Police Clash in Jersey City; 30 Reported Injured").
14. www.ipoaa.com.
15. *New York Times*, Aug. 13, 1964 ("Paterson, Elizabeth, Hit By Violence," by Fred Powledge).
16. *Chicago Tribune*, Aug. 17, 1964 ("Stolen Gin Bottle Sparks Riot").
17. *New York Times*, Aug. 29, 1964 ("300 Negroes Riot in Philadelphia").
18. Paula Green comment, Marlon Green questionnaire, n.d., Green family archives.
19. Eleanor Green interview by author, May 17, 2004.
20. Marlon Green questionnaire, n.d., Green family archives.
21. *Denver Post*, Feb. 12, 1965 ("Continental Airlines Training Negro Pilot").
22. *New York Times*, Nov. 19, 1964 ("Hoover and King Discuss Dispute," by Anthony Lewis).
23. Dominy interview by author, Aug. 2, 2004.
24. *Minot Daily News*, Dec. 2, 1964 ("Minot Visitor Wins Anti-Discrimination Airline Pilot Case").
25. Gubert, 152-153.
26. Dominy interview by author, Aug. 2, 2004.
27. Marlon Green questionnaire, n.d., Green family archives.
28. Marlon Green interview by author, Mar. 20, 2004.
29. Dominy interview by author, Aug. 2, 2004.

CHAPTER 18: I PRESUME YOU'RE GREEN

1. Marlon Green interview by author, Mar. 20, 2004.
2. Letter, McCloskey to Marlon Green, n.d.
3. Marlon Green interview by author, Mar. 20, 2004; Green family archives.
4. *New York Times*, Feb. 22, 1965 ("Malcolm X Shot to Death at Rally Here").
5. FBI memo, Mar. 25, 1965; www.stanford.edu/group/King; www.alabamamoments.state.al.us; www.emergingpictures.com; www.paperlessarchives.com.
6. www.stanford.edu/group/King.
7. Memo, Bell to Continental employees, Aug. 6, 1965, Green family archives.
8. www.africanamericans.com/WattsRiots.
9. *New York Times*, Jan. 11, 1966 ("Civil Rights Worker Killed in Mississippi").
10. Siegel interview by author, Dec. 15, 2005.
11. *New York Times*, June 7, 1966 ("Meredith is Shot in Back on Walk in Mississippi," by Roy Reed).
12. *New York Times*, June 27, 1966 ("12,000 End Rights March to Jackson; Meredith Hailed at Mississippi's Capitol," by Gene Roberts).
13. Marlon Green interview by author, Mar. 20, 2004; Eleanor Green interview by author, Dec, 16, 2005.
14. *Rocky Mountain News*, July 15, 1967 ("10 Are Killed as Rioting Continues in Newark, NJ"); www.67riots.rutgers.edu.
15. www.67riots.rutgers.edu.
16. www.sc.edu/library/socar/mpc/exhiit/mcnair/civrights.
17. www.ipoaa.com.

CHAPTER 19: TURBULENCE AFTER TAKEOFF

1. Marlon Green interview by author, Mar. 20, 2004.
2. Cleo Moran interview by author, Aug. 27, 2006.
3. Eleanor Green e-mail to author, Jan. 15, 2008.
4. Eleanor Green interview by author, Dec, 16, 2005.
5. *Flying*, Sept. 2005 ("When Airplanes Feel Fatigued," by Peter Garrison).
6. Marlon Green interview by author, Mar. 20, 2004.
7. Eleanor Green interview by author, Dec, 16, 2005.
8. Marlon Green interview by author, Mar. 20, 2004.
9. Eleanor Green interview by author, Dec, 16, 2005.
10. history1900s.about.com/cs/martinlutherking.
11. Ching, Juliet, *The Assasination of Robert F. Kennedy* (New York, 2002), passim.
12. www.cgi.cnn.com.
13. Serling, 244.
14. Marlon Green interview by author, Mar. 20, 2004.
15. Eleanor Green interview by author, Dec, 16, 2005.
16. *Denver Post*, Feb. 7, 1970 ("School Buses Bombed").
17. *Time*, Mar. 16, 1970 ("Rebellion at Lamar").
18. www.may41970.com.
19. www.ferris.edu/news; www.detnews.com.

20. Hugh D. Graham, *The Civil Rights Era: Origins and Development of National Policy, 1960-1972* (New York, 1990), 454-456; Aldon D. Morris, *The Origins of the Civil Rights Movement: Black Communities Organizing for Change* (New York, 1984), passim; www.stanford.edu/group/blackpanthers.
21. Marlon Green questionnaire, n.d., Green family archives.
22. Marlon Green interview by author, Aug. 1, 2005.
23. Marlon Green questionnaire, n.d., Green family archives.
24. Marlon Green interview by author, Mar. 20, 2004; Eleanor Green interview by author, May 17, 2004.
25. *New York Times*, Aug. 25, 1972 ("H.E.W. Will Study Syphilis Project").
26. Marlon Green interview by author, Mar. 20, 2004.
27. Eleanor Green interview by author, Dec, 16, 2005.
28. Marlon Green questionnaire, n.d., Green family archives.
29. www.infoplease.com/year/1974.
30. Shelton interview by author, Nov. 11, 2005.
31. Price interview by author, June 15, 2007.
32. Marlon Green interview by author, Mar. 20, 2004.

CHAPTER 20: TAILSPIN

1. www.watson.org/~lisa/blackhistory/school-integration/boston/phase1.
2. J. Anthony Lucas, *Common Ground: A Turbulent Decade in the Lives of Three American Families* (New York, 1985), 241.
3. Lucas, passim.
4. www.blackflix.com/blaxploitation.
5. www.museum.tv/archives.
6. www.obap.org.
7. *Ebony*, Feb. 1986 ("Spreading Their Wings: Black Pilots, Totaling 175, Want to Pave the Way for More" by Frank White III).
8. Marlon Green interview by author, Mar. 20, 2004.
9. Martha Derthick and Paul J. Quirk, *The Politics of Deregulation* (Washington, D.C., 1985), passim.
10. T.A. Heppenheimer, *Turbulent Skies: The History of Commercial Aviation* (New York, 1995), 325-339.
11. Marlon Green interview by author, Mar. 20, 2004.
12. Heppenheimer, 339.
13. Marlon Green interview by author, Mar. 20, 2004.
14. Marlon Green questionnaire, n.d., Green family archives.

CHAPTER 21: NEW BATTLES

1. Eleanor Green interview by author, Dec, 16, 2005.
2. Marlon Green interview by author, Mar. 20, 2004; e-mail from Paula Green, Apr. 25, 2005.
3. E-mail from Paula Green, Apr. 25, 2005.

EPILOGUE: AUTHOR'S REFLECTIONS

1. Author's observations.
2. Marlon Green interview by author, Aug. 1, 2005.
3. Paula Green, note to author, Dec. 6, 2007.
4. Author's observations.
5. *Denver Post*, June 14, 1981 ("The New Insensitivity," by Jacqueline Trescott, reprinted from the *Washington Post*).
6. Harold Field e-mail, Feb. 5, 2006.
7. Gunnar Myrdal, *An American Dilemma: The Negro Problem & Modern Democracy* (New York, 1944, reprinted 1972), 1022.
8. Marlon Green interview by author, Nov. 5, 2008.
9. *Denver Post*, Nov. 5, 2008 ("Obama Wins").

BIBLIOGRAPHY

INTERVIEWS:

Dominy, Floyd, interviewed by author, Aug. 2, 2004.
Green, Eleanor, multiple interviews by author, Feb. 17, 2004; May 17, 2004;
   Dec. 16, 2005; Aug. 17, 2006.
Green, James Z., interviewed by author, Nov. 12, 2005.
Green, Marlon D., multiple interviews by author, Mar. 20-21, 2004; Sept. 12,
   2004; Aug. 1, 2005; Dec. 12, 2005; Aug. 28, 2008; Nov. 5, 2008.
Green, Paula, interviewed by author, Dec. 16, 2005.
Moran, Cleo, interviewed by author, Aug. 27, 2006.
Price, David, interviewed by author, June 15, 2007.
Reid, George, interviewed by author, Mar. 12, 2006.
Seigenthaler, John, Sr., interviewed by author, June 1, 2006.
Shelton, Caroline, interviewed by author, Nov. 11, 2005.
Siegel, Shirley A., interviewed by author, Dec. 15, 2005.
Stocks, Marie Green, interviewed by author, Dec. 16, 2005.
Wiley, Norbert, interviewed by author, Mar. 8, 2006.

CORRESPONDENCE:

Green family archives:

Brake, Richard J. Letter to Marlon Green, Dec. 28, 2007.

Brown, Prentiss M., Jr. Letter to Cyrus R. Smith, Mar. 23, 1959.

Carr, Fr. John F. Letter to Eleanor Green, Jan. 29, 1963.

Chachere, Joan Stanley. Letter to T. Raber Taylor, Mar. 31, 1959.

Emmons, Kate. E-mail to Eleanor Green, Feb. 23, 2005.

Fichter, Fr. Joseph. Letters to Eleanor Green, Dec. 6, 1951; Dec. 21, 1951;
William and Anna Gallagher, May 16, 1951.

Green, Eleanor. Letter to Palmer Hoyt, Jan. 12, 1961; letter to Charles
Lindbergh, Nov. 2, 1958; letters to T. Raber Taylor, Jan. 12, 1961; May 24,
1961; Aug. 6, 1961; Aug. 28, 1961; Feb. 13, 1962; Feb. 25, 1962; note to
author, Dec. 6, 2007.

Green, Marlon D. Letters to Joseph H. Albers, July 2, 1961; Louis Buckley, May 8, 1962; Continental Southern Lines, Inc., Sept. 5, 1961; Archibald Cox, July 9, 1962; Stanley Gewirtz, June 8, 1961; Erwin Griswold, May 11, 1962; Letter to Najeeb Halaby, head of FAA, May 31, 1961; Howard E. Hill, Oct. 4, 1960; Nov. 1, 1960; Jan. 3, 1961; Ralph L. Knapp, April 6, 1955; Adam Clayton Powell, May 14, 1962; Tengku Abdul Rahman, June 8, 1961; Cyrus R. Smith, Mar. 9, 1959; T. Raber Taylor: Mar. 27, 1959; June 14, 1959; July 25, 1959; Aug. 19, 1959; Sept. 23, 1959; June 1, 1960; Sept. 5, 1960; Oct. 10, 1960; Apr. 14, 1961; Aug. 1, 1961; Aug. 15, 1961; Feb. 27, 1962; Mar. 6, 1962; Mar. 10, 1962; Mar. 22, 1962; Mar. 26, 1962; May 28, 1962; July 23, 1962; Oct. 30, 1962; Dec. 17, 1962; Jan. 29, 1963; Mar. 8, 1963.

Fr. M. James. Letter to the Greens, Apr. 25, 1963.

McCloskey, L. D. "Mac." Letter to Marlon Green, undated (probably early 1965).

Merton, Thomas. Letter to Marlon Green, Aug. 23, 1961; Apr. 25, 1963.

Moran, Cleo. Letter to Eleanor Green, March 2005

Poindexter, Barbara. Letters to Eleanor Green, n.d. (1959?)

Reid, George and Dorothy. Letter to T. Raber Taylor, Apr. 1, 1959.

Roosevelt, Eleanor. Letter to Barbara Poindexter, Jan. 2, 1959.

Thomas, Charles S. Letters to T. Raber Taylor, Roy Chapman, and Robert Nagel, July 24, 1959.

Wiley, Norbert and Sheila. Letter to T. Raber Taylor, Apr. 1, 1959.

Wiley, Norbert. E-mail to Paula Green, Mar. 14, 2006; Aug. 28, 2007.

T. Raber Taylor archives:

"Answer" to Denver District Court, March 1959, T. Raber Taylor archives.

Taylor, T. Raber. Letter to Richard J. Brake, Mar. 28, 1959.

Taylor, T. Raber. Letter to Louis Buckley, Regional Director, U.S. Department of Labor, May 8, 1962.

Taylor, T. Raber. Letter to Patrick J. Crowley, Apr. 6, 1961.

Taylor, T. Raber. Letters to Marlon Green, Mar. 27, 1959; Apr. 7, 1959; June 15, 1959; June 19, 1959; June 25, 1959; July 17, 1959; Aug. 15, 1959; June 6, 1960; Aug. 24, 1960; Sept. 20, 1960; Oct. 11, 1960; Oct. 26, 1960; Jan. 9, 1961; Jan. 12, 1961; Apr. 7, 1961; Aug. 1, 1961; Aug. 2, 1961; Aug. 7, 1961; Aug. 14, 1961; Mar. 6, 1962; Mar. 22, 1962; June 1, 1962; June 15, 1962; Oct. 9, 1962; Nov. 2, 1962; letter to the Greens, Aug. 14, 1961; letters to Robert F. Kennedy, Feb. 16, 1961; Mar. 3, 1961; letters to Burke Marshall, Mar. 14, 1961; Mar. 25, 1961; May 16, 1961; Byron White, undated.

Brake, Richard J. Letter to T. Raber Taylor, March 16, 1959.

Chachere (née Stanley), Joan. Letter to T. Raber Taylor, Mar. 31, 1959.

Cullinan, E. P. Letter to T. Raber Taylor, Jan. 23, 1963.

Kennedy, Robert F. Letter to T. Raber Taylor, Feb. 23, 1961.

Marshall, Burke. Letter to T. Raber Taylor, June 28, 1961.

Marshall, Daniel G. Letter to T. Raber Taylor, Nov. 5, 1962.

Mosk, Stanley. Letter to Duke Dunbar, June 15, 1962.

Rabkin, Sol. Letter to Louis J. Lefkowitz, Apr. 2, 1963; memo to T. Raber Taylor, July 5, 1962.

Reid, Dorothy. Letter to John A. Hannah, June 20, 1961.

Robison, Joseph B. Letter to T. Raber Taylor, Oct. 15, 1962.

Steinhauser, Sheldon. Letter to T. Raber Taylor, Oct. 22, 1962.

Terrones, Edward. Letters to T. Raber Taylor, Feb. 16, 1962; May 29, 1962.

U.S. Supreme Court. Letter to T. Raber Taylor, Mosk, Dunbar, June 18, 1962.

BOOKS:

Anderson, R. Bentley. *Black, White, and Catholic: New Orleans Interracialism, 1947-1956*. Nashville: Vanderbilt University Press, 2005.

Binkin, Martin; Mark J. Eitelberg; Alvin J. Schexnider; and Marvin M. Smith, *Blacks and the Military*. Washington, D.C.: The Brookings Institution, 1982.

Carson, Clayborne; Susan Carson; Adrienne Clay; Virginia Shadron; and Kieran Taylor, editors. *The Papers of Martin Luther King, Jr.: Symbol of the Movement, January 1957-December 1958*, Vol. 4. Berkeley and Los Angeles: University of California Press, 2000.

Cashin, Sheryll. *The Failures of Integration: How Race and Class are Undermining the American Dream*. New York: Public Affairs, 2004.

Ching, Juliet. *The Assassination of Robert F. Kennedy*. New York: Rosen Publishing, 2002.

Derthick, Martha, and Paul J. Quirk. *The Politics of Deregulation*. Washington, D.C.: Brookings Institution, 1985.

Eisenhower, Dwight D. *Crusade in Europe*. Garden City, NY: Doubleday, 1948.

Fannin, Caroline M.; Betty K. Gubert, and Miriam Sawyer. *Distinguished African-Americans in Aviation and Space Science*. Westport, CT: Oryx Press, 2002.

Farber, David, and Beth Bailey. *The Columbia Guide to America in the 1960s*. New York: Columbia University Press, 2001.

Fleming, Candace. *Our Eleanor: A Scrapbook Look at Eleanor Roosevelt's Remarkable Life*. New York: Atheneum Books, 2005.

Graham, Hugh D. *The Civil Rights Era: Origins and Development of National Policy, 1960-1972*. New York: Oxford University Press, 1990.

Gropman, Alan L. *The Air Force Integrates: 1945-1964* (Second Edition). Washington, D.C.: Smithsonian Institution Press, 1998.

Hardesty, Von; and Dominick Pisano. *Black Wings: The American Black in Aviation*. Washington, D.C.: Smithsonian, 1984.

Hendrickson, Paul. *Sons of Mississippi*. New York: Knopf, 2003.

Heppenheimer, T. A. *Turbulent Skies: The History of Commercial Aviation*. New York: John Wiley & Sons, 1995.

Katz, Ephraim. *The Film Encyclopedia*. New York: Putnam/Perigee, 1979.

Korda, Michael. *Ike: An American Hero*. New York: HarperCollins, 2007.

Lucas, J. Anthony. *Common Ground: A Turbulent Decade in the Lives of Three American Families*. New York: Knopf, 1985.

McFarland, Keith D., and David L. Roll. *Louis Johnson and the Arming of America*. Bloomington: Indiana University Press, 2005.

McPhee, John. *Encounters with the Archdruid*. New York: Noonday/Farrar, Straus and Giroux, 1971.

Merton, Thomas. *Raids on the Unspeakable*. New York: New Directions, 1966.

_____. *Thoughts in Solitude*. New York: Farrar, Strauss, Giroux, 1958.

_____. *Turning Toward the World: The Pivotal Years*. San Francisco: Harper, 1996.

Morris, Aldon D. *The Origins of the Civil Rights Movement: Black Communities Organizing for Change*. New York: Free Press, 1984.

Myrdal, Gunnar. *An American Dilemma: The Negro Problem & Modern Democracy*, Vols. 1 and 2. New York: Harper & Row, 1944, reprinted 1972.

O'Neill, William L. *A Democracy at War: America's Fight at Home and Abroad in World War II*. New York: Free Press, 1993.

The Papers of John F. Kennedy, 3 vols, Vol. 1, 1962; Vol. 3, 1963. Washington: U.S. Government Printing Office, 1962, 1964.

Polmar, John, and John D. Gresham. *Defcon-2: Standing on the Brink of War during the Cuban Missile Crisis*. New York: John Wiley and Sons, 2006.

Reisner, Marc. *Cadillac Desert: The American West and Its Disappearing Water*. New York: Penguin, 1987.

Serling, Robert J. *Maverick: The Story of Robert Six and Continental Airlines.* Garden City, NY: Doubleday, 1974.

Smith, Jessie C. *Black Firsts: 4,000 Ground-Breaking and Pioneering Historical Firsts* (Second Edition). Canton, MI: Visible Ink Press, 2006.

Tygiel, Jules. *Baseball's Great Experiment: Jackie Robinson and His Legacy.* New York: Oxford University Press, 1983.

Tyson, Timothy B. *Radio Free Dixie: Robert F. Williams and the Roots of Black Power.* Chapel Hill, NC: University of North Carolina Press, 1999.

Zinn, Howard. *Postwar America, 1945-1971.* New York: MacMillan, 1973.

NEWSPAPERS:

Chicago Tribune: Aug. 17, 1964 ("Stolen Gin Bottle Sparks Riot").

Denver Post: Feb. 19, 1925 ("Blind Grand Junction Man Meets Helen Keller"); June 25, 1950 ("Continental Air Chief Bob Six Has Devoted Career to Aviation," by George McWilliams); June 8, 1953 ("Cherry Hills Board Agrees to Let Six Buy Home There"); June 11, 1959 ("Conair Case Delayed: Amplification Asked In Negro Pilot Case"); June 25, 1959 ("Judge Voids Order Requiring Continental to Hire Negro Pilot"); Aug. 15, 1960 ("Negro Pilot's Charge Ordered Heard Again," by Jim Ritchey); Sept. 19, 1960 ("Negro Pilot Rehearing Denied"); Jan. 8, 1961 ("Negro Pilot Loses Conair Suit," "Agency Held Lacking in Power Over Airline"); Jan. 24, 1961 (Editorial: "National Handicap Exposed"); Mar. 31, 1961 ("U.S. Considers Negro Pilot Case"); June 12, 1961 ("U.S. Asks Right to Intervene in Dispute of Negro, Airline"); June 14, 1961 (Editorial: "Anti-Bias Law Has Friends in Court"); June 15, 1961 ("Justice Dept. Seeks to Aid Negro Pilot"); July 25, 1961 ("Sen. Carroll Praises Colorado for Anti-Discrimination Record"); Aug. 25, 1961 ("Robert F. Six Weds TV Actress Meadows"); Feb. 13, 1962 ("High Court Rules Airline Needn't Hire Negro Pilot"); Feb. 16, 1962 (Editorial: "Bias Ruling Should Be Appealed"); Mar. 5, 1962 ("Race Unit to Appeal Job Hearing," by Jim Ritchie); Apr. 22, 1963 ("U.S. Backs Negro Pilot Seeking Job on Airline," by Bob Whearley); May 8, 1963 ("Conair Job Weighed by Green"); Feb. 12, 1965 ("Continental Airlines Training Negro Pilot"); Feb. 7, 1970 ("School Buses Bombed," by David Jenkins); ("Ex-Klan Leader Behind '66 Death of Rights Activist"); Apr. 3, 2005 ("Trials Urged in '46 Racial Killings," by Eliot McLaughlin). Nov. 6, 2006.

Detroit Free Press: Apr. 30, 1963 ("Negro Flier Wins U.S. Pilot Job").

Jet: May 12, 1997.

Kansas City Star: Jan. 30, 1963 ("8 Killed in Airliner Crash Here").

Lansing (MI) *State Journal*: Aug. 4, 1957 ("Job As Airline Pilot Eludes Lansing Negro," by Frank Hand); Aug. 13, 1958 ("Negro Pilot Criticizes FEPC"); Dec. 21, 1958 ("Complaint Held Valid"); Oct. 9, 1962 ("Bias Case to be Aired"); Mar. 29, 1963 ("U.S. Court Hears Marlon Green," by Robert N. Branson); May 1, 1963 ("Negro Pilot Takes U.S. Flying Job").

Minot (SD) *Daily News*: Dec. 2, 1964 ("Minot Visitor Wins Anti-Discrimination Airline Pilot Case," by Carl Flagstad).

New York Times: Jan. 8, 1955 ("Marian Anderson Wins Ovation In First Opera Role At The 'Met," by Howard Taubman); Oct. 2, 1956 ("Airlines Proclaim A Joint Policy To Clear Way For Negro Pilots," by Richard Witkin); Sept. 1, 1957 ("Little Rock Sets Integration Date," by Benjamin Fine); Sept. 3, 1957 ("Militia Sent To Little Rock; School Integration Put Off," by Benjamin Fine); Sept. 4, 1957 ("Little Rock Told To Integrate Now Despite Militia," by Benjamin Fine); Sept. 5, 1957 ("Arkansas Troops Bar Negro Pupils; Governor Defiant," by Benjamin Fine); Sept. 6, 1957 ("Little Rock Board Seeks Stay In School Integration," by Benjamin Fine, "President Warns Governor Faubus He'll Uphold Law," by W. H. Lawrence); Sept. 7, 1957 ("Little Rock Faces Showdown Today Over Integration," by Benjamin Fine); Sept. 8, 1957 ("U.S. Court Denies Integration Stay For Little Rock," by Benjamin Fine, "President Weighs Integration Move," by Anthony Lewis); Sept. 9, 1957 (Faubus Bids U.S. Recede On Order For Integration," by Benjamin Fine, "Eisenhower Firm On Enforcing Law," by W. H. Lawrence); Sept. 10, 1957 ("U.S. To Seek Writ To Force Faubus and Guard To Permit Integration; Extended Court Battle Expected," by Benjamin Fine); Sept. 11, 1957 ("N.A.A.C.P. Submits Little Rock Plea; Court Sits Today," by Anthony Lewis); Sept. 12, 1957 ("High Court Hears Little Rock Plea; May Rule Today," by Anthony Lewis); Sept. 13, 1957 ("Court Bars Little Rock Delay; President Calls For Support; Faubus Orders 4 Schools Shut," by Anthony Lewis and Claude Sitton); Sept. 14, 1957 ("Faubus Says U.S. Court Can't Bar Closing," by Claude Sitton); Sept. 15, 1957 ("Little Rock Suit To Open Schools Expected Today," by Claude Sitton); Sept. 16, 1957 ("4 Little Rock Schools Stay Shut; Board Presses Faubus On Plan," by Claude Sitton); Sept. 20, 1958 ("Dr. King, Negro Leader, Stabbed By Woman In A Store In Harlem", "President Scored Over Integration"); Feb. 9, 1960 ("Negroes' Sitdown Hits 2 More Cities"); Feb. 18, 1960 ("500 Are Dispersed At Racial Dispute"); Feb. 28, 1960 ("Nashville Seizes 76 In Race Clash," "South Is Warned of Time of Change"); Mar. 2, 1960 ("Tuskegee Boycott By Students," "Students Boycott Stores"); Mar. 16, 1960 ("350 Negro Student Demonstrators Held In South Carolina Stockade"); Mar. 31, 1960 ("Fire Hoses Disperse Texas

Negro Crowd"); Apr. 25, 1960 ("N.A.A.C.P. Denies Biloxi Riot Role"); Nov. 30, 1961 ("5 Negroes Beaten By Mississippi Mob," by Claude Sitton); Feb. 13, 1962 ("Negro Loses College Plea"); Feb. 14, 1962 ("33 Negroes Seized By Georgia Police"); Oct. 1, 1962 ("Negro at Mississippi U. as Barnett Yields; 3 Dead In Campus Riot, 6 Marshals Shot," by Claude Sitton); Oct. 3, 1962 ("Barnett Contempt Case Put Off, Court Clears University's Aides; Campus Calm, 3,500 Troops Leave," by Foster Hailey); Oct. 4, 1962 ("Meredith Plans To Leave Campus," by Claude Sitton); Oct. 5, 1962 ("U.S. Order Shifts Mississippi Game," by Claude Sitton); Mar. 29, 1963 ("Police Loose A Dog On Negroes' Group; Minister Is Bitten," by Claude Sitton); Mar. 29, 1963 ("High Court Hears Negro Pilot Case," by Anthony Lewis); Apr. 23, 1963 ("High Court Gives Negro Pilot Right To Job On Airline," by Anthony Lewis); Apr. 29, 1963 ("High Court Hears Negro Pilot Case"); Apr. 30, 1963 ("U.S. Employs Negro Rejected By Airline"); May 3, 1963 ("500 Are Arrested In Negro Protest At Birmingham," by Foster Hailey); May 4, 1963 ("Dogs And Hoses Repulse Negroes At Birmingham," by Foster Hailey); Aug. 30, 1963 ("Leaders Of March Pledge Widening Of Rights Drive," by Hedrick Smith); Sept. 16, 1963 ("Birmingham Bomb Kills 4 Negro Girls In Church; Riots Flare; 2 Boys Slain," by Claude Sitton); Oct. 16, 1963 ("Integration Wins Church's Backing", "Sit-In Case Issues Trouble Justices", "Negro School Boycott Ends"); July 19, 1964 ("Thousands Riot In Harlem; Scores Are Hurt," by Paul L. Montgomery and Francis X. Clines", "Johnson Decries Racial Disorders"); July 20, 1964 ("Violence Flares Again In Harlem; Restraint Urged"); July 26, 1964 ("Rochester Police Battle Race Riot"); Aug. 3, 1964 ("Negroes And Police Clash In Jersey City; 30 Reported Injured"); Aug. 12, 1964 ("Atlanta Restaurant Defies High Court, Again Bars Negroes"); Aug. 13, 1964 ("Paterson, Elizabeth, Hit By New Violence," by Fred Powledge); Aug. 21, 1964 ("Jackson Schools End Segregation," by Donald Janson); Aug. 23, 1964 ("Joblessness Rate Of Negro Youths Increases to 25%," by Edwin L. Dale, Jr.); Aug. 29, 1964 ("300 Negroes Riot In Philadelphia"); Oct. 15, 1964 ("Martin Luther King Wins The Nobel Peace Prize"); Oct. 20, 1964 ("Hoover Draws Angry Response For Comment On Central Park," by John Sibley); Oct. 21, 1964 ("8 Men Are Indicted In Racial Bombings"); Nov. 19, 1964 ("Restaurants Desegregated Quietly In McComb, Miss."), Dec. 2, 1964 ("Hoover And King Discuss Dispute," by Anthony Lewis); Feb. 22, 1965 ("Malcolm X Shot To Death At Rally Here," by Peter Kihss); Jan. 11, 1966 ("Georgia House Bars War Critic," by Roy Reed); June 7, 1966 ("Meredith Is Shot In Back On Walk In Mississippi," by Roy Reed); June 27, 1966 ("12,000 End Rights March To Jackson; Meredith Hailed At Mississippi's Capitol," by Gene Roberts); Aug. 25, 1972 ("H.E.W. Will Study Syphilis Project"); Nov. 19, 1998 ("Perry H. Young Jr., 79, Pioneering Pilot, Dies").

Poughkeepsie (NY) *Journal*: Feb. 10, 1964 ("City Man Found Shot to Death in Kansas City").

Rocky Mountain News: Oct. 27, 1958 ("Bob Six Slings Fastest Gun in Denver," by Pasquale Marranzino); Apr. 1, 1959 ("Negro Asks Court to Help Get Pilot Job"); June 26, 1959 ("Negro Pilot Loses Decision"); June 14, 1961 ("U.S. to Back Anti-Bias Unit in Continental Airlines Case"); July 19, 1961 ("Conair Files Brief in Negro Case"); July 15, 1964 ("Judge Rules Continental Airlines Must Hire Negro Pilot"); July 15, 1967 ("10 Are Killed as Rioting Continues in Newark, NJ"); Nov. 23, 1999 ("When the Klan Ruled Colorado," by Manny Gonzales).

San Francisco Chronicle: Apr. 24, 1963 (Editorial: "Color Line on the Air Lines").

Seattle Times: Aug. 16, 2003 ("Pilot Who Stood Up to Racism Opened Cockpit Door for Many," by Dominic Gates).

Stars and Stripes (Pacific Edition); Dec. 24, 1956 ("Yule Drop Aids 5 on Icy Peak").

Washington Post: June 5, 1964 ("Johnson Speaks At Howard U. Commencement"); Aug. 5, 2003 ("The 21st Century's Answer to the Wright Brothers: Father and Daughter Team Up in 737 Cockpit").

PERIODICALS:

"Big Step." *Time*, October 15, 1956.

"Black Pilots: Only Handful Now Hold Flying Posts with Scheduled Passenger Airlines." *Ebony*, January 1978.

"Blacks in Aviation History: Flying Heroes and Heroines Soared Despite the Odds." *Ebony*, February 1994.

"Breakthrough on the Airlines." *Ebony*, Nov. 1965.

"Catholics Lead in School Desegregation in Many Sectors." *Ebony*, Dec. 1957.

Clotfelter, Charles T. "An Imperfect Desegregation." *The Chronicle of Higher Education*, Apr. 2, 2004.

Cohen, Gary. "Saint-in-Waiting: Katherine Drexel Could Be Next." *U.S. News and World Report*, Jan. 11, 1999.

Cottrol, Robert J.; Raymond T. Diamond; and Leland B. Ware, *"Brown v. Board of Education:* A Contested Legacy—A New View of the Role of the Courts." *The Chronicle of Higher Education*, Apr. 2, 2004.

_____. "The Decline of the Idea of Caste: Setting the Stage for Brown v. Board." *American Educator*, Summer 2004.

_____. "NAACP v. Jim Crow: The Legal Strategy that Brought Down 'Separate But Equal' by Toppling School Segregation." *American Educator*, Summer 2004.

Garrison, Peter. "When Airplanes Feel Fatigued." *Flying*, Sept. 2005.

"The History of Brown v. Board of Education." *American Educator*, Summer 2004.

Hill, Tony. "Where Do We Go From Here? The Politics of Black Education, 1780–1980." *Boston Review*, October 1981.

Hornblower, Margot. "The Still-Unfriendly Skies." *Time*, August 28, 1995.

Irons, Peter. "Jim Crow's Schools." *American Educator*, Summer 2004.

"A Judge Finds New York Schools Separate and Unequal." *U.S. News and World Report*, January 9, 1959.

Letters to the Editor. *Life*, Sept. 21, 1942.

Letters to the Editor. *Time*, May 3, 1963; May 17, 1963; March 16, 1970.

Ogletree, Charles J., Jr. "The Flawed Compromise of 'All Deliberate Speed.'" *The Chronicle of Higher Education*, April 2, 2004.

"Philip Hart, '30 - Famous Alumnus." (Obituary) *West Catholic Alumni Emissary*, Winter 2004-2005.

"Profiles of Success: William C. McClearn." *The Colorado Lawyer*, December 2004.

"Race Riots of the Past: A Worry for the Future." *U.S. News and World Report*, July 15, 1962.

"Races on the Beach." *Time*, May 16, 1960.

"Rebellion at Lamar." *Time*, Mar. 16, 1970.

Reich, David. "Eyes on the Skies: Even as a Boy, Neal Loving Knew He Wanted to Fly." *Wayne State Magazine*, Spring 1998.

Romero, Tom I., II. "Turbulence a Mile High: Equal Employment Opportunity in the Colorado Sky." *The Colorado Lawyer*, Vol. 32., No. 9. September 2003.

Solomon, Stan. "Green, Martin and Young—Three Pioneers." *Airways*, Feb. 2000.

"The South: A Universal Effort." *Time*, May 2, 1960.

"Speaking of People: Michigan Highway Pilot." *Ebony*, February 1958.

"The Supreme Court: Opening the Cockpit Doors." *Time*, May 3, 1963.

"T. Raber Taylor: A Man for Others." *The Oznam News*, Fall 2004.

Tatum, Beverly D. "Building a Road to a Diverse Society." *The Chronicle of Higher Education*, Apr. 2, 2004.

Wasinger, Holly. "From Five Points to Struggle Hill." *Colorado Heritage*, Autumn 2005.

White, Frank, III. "Spreading Their Wings: Black Pilots, Totaling 175, Want to Pave the Way for More." *Ebony*, February 1986.

WEB SITES:

afroamhistory.about.com ("A. Philip Randolph")
detnews.com ("Pontiac race riots")
encarta.msn.com
en.wikipedia.org/wiki/Anti-Irish_racism ("Discrimination against Irish in America")
en.wikipedia.org/wiki/Charles_Coughlin ("Father Coughlin")
en.wikipedia.org/wiki/Civil_Rights_Act_of_1960
en.wikipedia.org/wiki/Civil_Rights_Act_of_1964
en.wikipedia.org/wiki/Hempstead_Plains ("History of Hempstead Plains")
en.wikipedia.org/wiki/Julian_Bond ("Julian Bond")
en.wikipedia.org/wiki/Little_Rock_Nine ("Integration of Little Rock Central High School")
en.wikipedia.org/wiki/Walter_Paepcke ("Walter Paepcke")
history1900s.about.com/cs/martinlutherking

history.nasa.gov/apollo204/grissom
homepages.tcp.co.uk ("Robert Kennedy assassination")
users.evl.net
www.achievement.org ("Rosa Parks")
www.africanamericans.com/WattsRiots ("Watts Riot")
www.africanamericans.com/FreedomRiots ("Freedom Rides")
www.alabamamoments.state.al.us
www.arkansastravel.com ("El Dorado, Arkansas")
www.avstop.com/History/BlackAirlines/AugustMartin ("August Martin")
www.BessieColeman.com ("Bessie Coleman")
www.blackflix.com/blaxploitation ("Blaxploitation films")
www.boomtown.org. ("El Dorado, Arkansas")
www.caselaw.lp.findlaw.com ("U.S. Supreme Court: Colorado Anti-
    Discrimination Commission v. Contintental, 372 U.S. 714 - 1963")
www.centralhigh57.org ("Little Rock Central High 40th Anniversary")
www.cgi.cnn.com ("1968 Democratic National Convention")
www.chicagodocfestival.org/murderemmitt ("Murder of Emmett Till")
www.city.iruma.saitama.jp/i-society ("Irumagawa, Japan")
www.college.hmco.com/history ("Earl Warren")
www.crimelibrary.com/terrorists_spies/terrorists/birmingham_church
www.cr.nps.gov. ("U.S. Supreme Court")
www.ecapc.org ("Diane Nash")
www.edwards.af.mil
www.emergingpictures.com
www.fact-index.com/hubert_julian ("Herbert Julian")
www.fmuiv.edu/urbanaffairs/jem ("Harry T. Moore")
www.geocities.com/lemaycurtis ("Curits LeMay")
www.history.navy.mil/faqs/faq57-4.htm ("Doris Miller")
www.hollandhart.com/peopleprofile.cfm ("Patrick M. Westfeldt")
www.imbd.com ("Stepin Fetchit")
www.infoplease.com/year/1959
www.infoplease.com/year/1960
www.infoplease.com/year/1974
www.ipoaa.com ("New York Draft Riots")
www.ipoaa.com ("Freedom Summer deaths")
www.IUPUI.edu/ ~ aao/kkk.html ("History of KKK")
www.iwfr.org/civilhistory.asp ("Immigrant Workers Freedom Ride Coalition")
www.jimcrowhistory.org ("History of 'Jim Crow'")
www.jsc.nasa.gov/bios ("Virgil Grissom")
www.law.umkc.edu/faculty/projects/ftrials/price&bowers/Killen
www.majorcox.com/columns/mann ("Floyd Mann")
www.may41970.com ("Jackson State College shootings")
www.merton.org ("Thomas Merton")
www.midcoast.com ("Amos and Andy")

www.mnc.net/norway/warren ("Earl Warren")

www.museum.tv/archives ("Black TV Shows")

www.npr.org/programs/morning/features/2002/jul/tuskegee ("Tuskegee Syphilis Experiment")

www.obap.org ("Organization of Black Airline Pilots")

www.oyez.org/oyez/tour ("Supreme Court Building")

www.paperlessarchives.com ("Viola Liuzzo")

www.randolph.af.mil ("History of Randolph AFB")

www.san.beck.org ("Sit-ins")

www.sc.edu/library/socar/mpc/exhiit/mcnair/civrights ("The Challenge of Civil Rights")

www.sierraclub.org ("David Browder")

www.67riots.rutgers.edu ("Newark Riots," "Detroit Riots")

www.spartacus.schoolnet.co.uk/USAmoore ("Harry T. Moore")

www.stanford.edu/group/King ("Authorine Lucy," "Freedom Summer Deaths," "J. Edgar Hoover")

www.stanford.edu/group/blackpanthers ("Black Panthers")

www.strategic-air-command.com/people/LeMay ("Curtis LeMay")

www.supremecourthisotry/org ("Earl Warren")

www.thedailycamera.com ("Byron 'Whizzer' White")

www.trumanlibrary.org/hstpaper/civilrights("Truman Speech to NAACP")

www.watson.org/ ~ lisa/blackhistory-integration/lilrock ("School Integration in Little Rock")

www.watson.org/-lisa/blackhistory/post-civilwar/plessy

www.watson.org/ ~ lisa/blackhistory/schoolintegration/boston/phase1 ("Boston Under the Phase I Plan")

www.wpafb.af.mil ("Curtis LeMay")

www.yale.edu ("Warren Court")

www.yale.edu/ynhti/curriculum/units/1990/5/90.05.07.x ("Discrimination against Irish in America")

MISCELLANEOUS:

Bell, Harrold W. Memo to Continental employees, Aug. 6, 1965 (Green family archives).

"Brown v. Board of Education." National Park Service pamphlet. Washington, D.C.: GPO, 2000.

Carlson, Susan. "Marlon Green Story," monograph, University of Colorado Archives, n.d. (1964?).

Denver City Directory, 1957. Denver: The Gazeteer Company, 1957.

Gitelman, Morton. "The Green Case: A Study in Constitutional Litigation." Master of Laws thesis, University of Illinois, 1965.

Green, Marlon D. Two-page autobiographical sketch, Oct. 24, 1952.

"Little Rock Central High School." National Park Service pamphlet. Washington, D.C.: GPO, n.d.

"Martin Luther King, Jr." National Park Service pamphlet.Washington, D.C.: GPO, 2003.

"Port Chicago Naval Magazine," National Park Service pamphlet. Washington, D.C.: GPO, n.d.

Tavis Smiley Show. National Public Radio. "African-American Aviators," August 15, 2003.

T. Raber Taylor biography, Mary Taylor Hassouna collection.

Various private papers of T. Raber Taylor re: *Marlon D. Green v. Continental Airlines* (loaned through the courtesy of Mary Taylor Hassouna).

Various private papers of the Green family (loaned through the courtesy of Eleanor Green).

Warren Commission Report, passim.

INDEX

(Italics = photograph)

ABOUT THE AUTHOR

FLINT WHITLOCK is a critically acclaimed, award-winning author and military historian with nine books and dozens of magazine articles to his credit.

His first book, *Soldiers On Skis*, a history of the 10th Mountain Division in World War II, was published in 1992 and was nominated for a Pulitzer Prize. Two of his books, *Given Up For Dead*, the story of American prisoners-of-war sent to a Nazi slave-labor camp, and *Capt. Jepp and the Little Black Book*, a biography of Elrey B. Jeppesen, the man who invented aerial navigation, were both finalists in the Colorado Book Awards competition, sponsored by the Colorado Endowment for the Humanities.

Another work, *Distant Bugles, Distant Drums*, about Colorado's role in the Civil War, won the 2007 Southwest Book Award. Two more books (*The Rock of Anzio* and *The Depths of Courage*) have been featured selections of the Military Book Club.

Additionally, Flint has appeared on the History Channel, the Fox News Channel's "War Stories with Oliver North," and is seen in a new documentary about the 10th Mountain Division, *The Last Ridge*.

Flint lives in Denver, Colorado, with his wife, Dr. Mary Ann Watson. They have three grown children.

Other books by Flint Whitlock:

Soldiers On Skis:
A Pictorial Memoir of the 10th Mountain Division
(with Bob Bishop)

The Rock of Anzio:
From Sicily to Dachau — A History of the
45th Infantry Division

The Fighting First:
The Untold Story of the Big Red One on D-Day

Given Up For Dead:
American POWs in the Nazi Concentration Camp at Berga

Distant Bugles, Distant Drums:
The Union Response to the Confederate
Invasion of New Mexico

*Capt. Jepp and the Little Black Book:
How Ex-Barnstormer and Aviation Pioneer
Elrey B. Jeppesen Made the Skies Safer for Everyone
(with Terry L. Barnhart)

The Depths of Courage:
American Submariners at War with Japan, 1941-1945
(with Ron Smith)

*Internal Conflicts
(a novel)

*Available at *www.cablepublishing.com*

The Organization of Black Airline Pilots (OBAP)

Captain Marlon Green and Captain August Martin (America's first African-American commercial cargo pilot) pursued their goals, daring to dream at different times and in different places. They both wanted not to achieve greatness, but to use their skills and abilities for gainful employment. In 2009, as we turn another significant page in our nation's history, we acknowledge the extraordinary milestone achieved with the rendering of Captain Green's unanimous U.S. Supreme Court ruling in April 1963; we do so, standing on the shoulders of Captains Green and Martin. We hope to pursue our goals with the same dignity, tenacity, and dedication so that many others now and in the future may benefit from our pursuits.

—Cheryl Chew
Executive Director of OBAP

Founded in 1976, the Organization of Black Airline Pilots (OBAP) is a 501(c)(3) membership organization based in Silver Spring, Maryland. OBAP's mission is to enhance, advance and promote educational opportunities in aviation and to develop and sustain a process for the ongoing mentoring of our youth.

OBAP's Programs

Project Aerospace is the title given to the umbrella approach to OBAP's "Cradle to Career" education and professional development strategy. It aligns youth outreach, mentoring, scholarship and career development programs in a focused effort to develop the next generation of aviation professionals.

- **Aerospace Professionals in Schools** - This program brings pilots into elementary, middle and high schools to talk with students, planting the idea of aviation or aerospace as potential career tracks. Currently, OBAP reaches approximately 75,000 students annually.

- **Aviation Career Education (ACE) Camps** - Co-sponsored by the FAA and the National Black Coalition of Federal Aviation Employees (NBCFAE), ACE camps offer middle and high school students a first-level exposure to the aviation industry through aviation career exploration experiences. Serves thousands of students nationwide. In 2009, OBAP plans to expand its collaboration with the National Hispanic Coalition of Federal Aviation Employees (NHCFAE).
- **Solo Flight Academies** - Currently, OBAP teams up with Delta Air Lines and Delaware State University to offer this academy each summer. Two weeks of full submersion in aviation training leads participants through the thrill of his or her first solo flight. Hundreds of students have been able to solo through our academies.
- **Private Pilot Flight Academy (PPFA)** - In this program OBAP pays for certain costs (ground school, flight training, etc.) related to obtaining a private pilot license. Successful students are expected to graduate from the PPFA with their FAA private pilot license.
- **Aerospace Professional Development Program (PPDP)** - This program helps aviators and others in OBAP's membership make the decisions needed to "go professional." It includes mentorship, job placement and scholarship programs. To date, OBAP has been able to award — through the generous donations of our corporate and private sponsors — over $1 million in scholarships.

Our Vision

OBAP is working to make a national difference in a worldwide industry. We continue to monitor the overall economic climate, as well as changes within aviation and aerospace, and we will adapt to these realities as our programs evolve and grow.

The future for OBAP is bright. We want OBAP to be known as the stellar organization that enables our qualified youth and young professionals to enter the careers they desire.

OBAP National Office
8630 Fenton Street, Suite 126
Silver Spring, MD 20910
Telephone: 800-JET-OBAP (800-538-6227)
E-mail: nationaloffice@obap.org   Web Site: www.obap.org